TIGER & BUNNY

ART BY **MIZUKI SAKAKIBARA**

PLANNING / ORIGINAL STORY **SUNRISE**

ORIGINAL SCRIPT **Masafumi Nishida**

ORIGINAL CHARACTER AND HERO DESIGN **Masakazu Katsura**

5

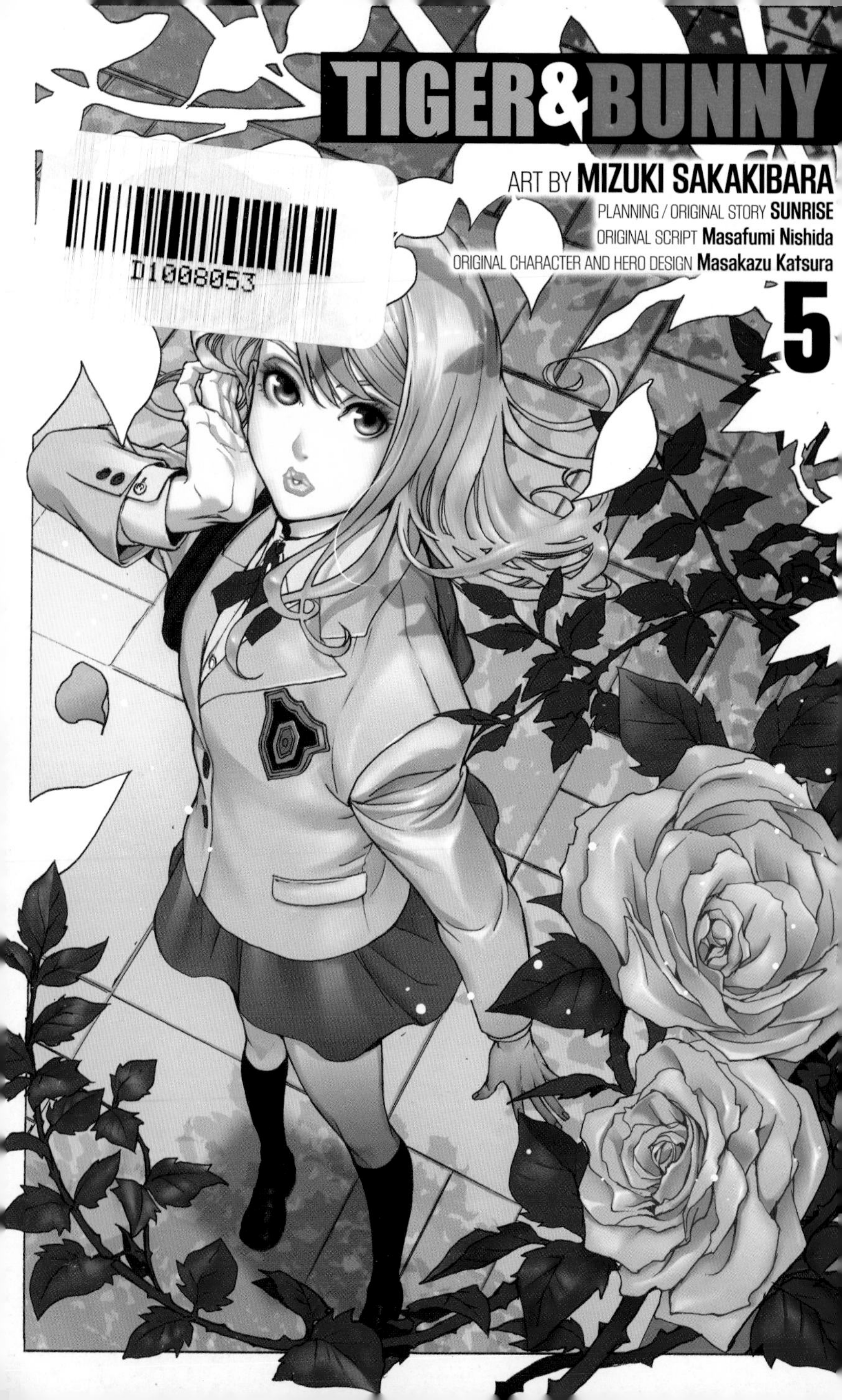

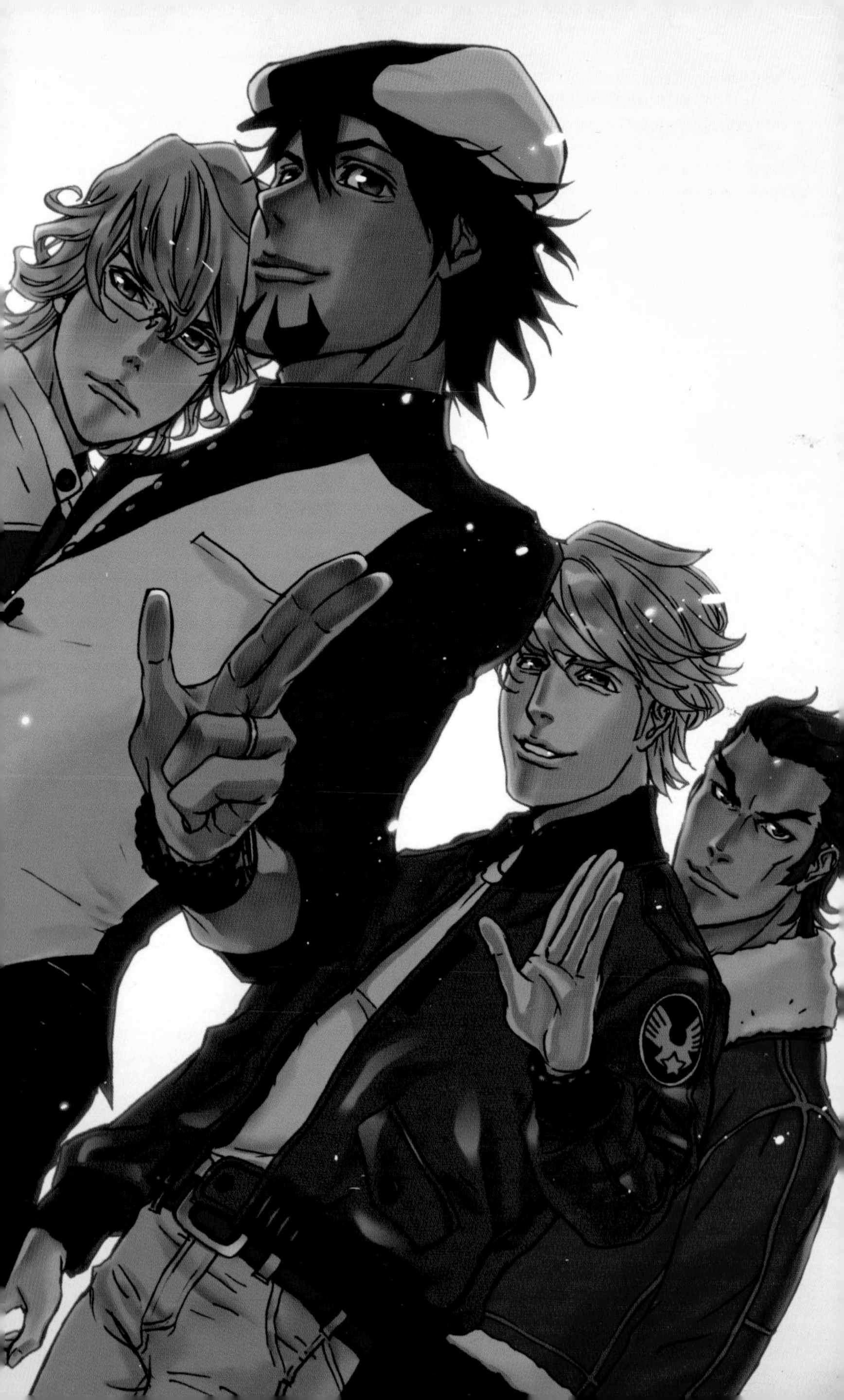

CONTENTS

#18   Spare the Rod and Spoil the Child, Part 2 ———— 005

#19   Spare the Rod and Spoil the Child, Part 3 ———— 039

#20   The Die Is Cast ———— 079

#21   Take Heed of the Snake in the Grass ———— 119

TIGER & BUNNY

MIZUKI SAKAKIBARA

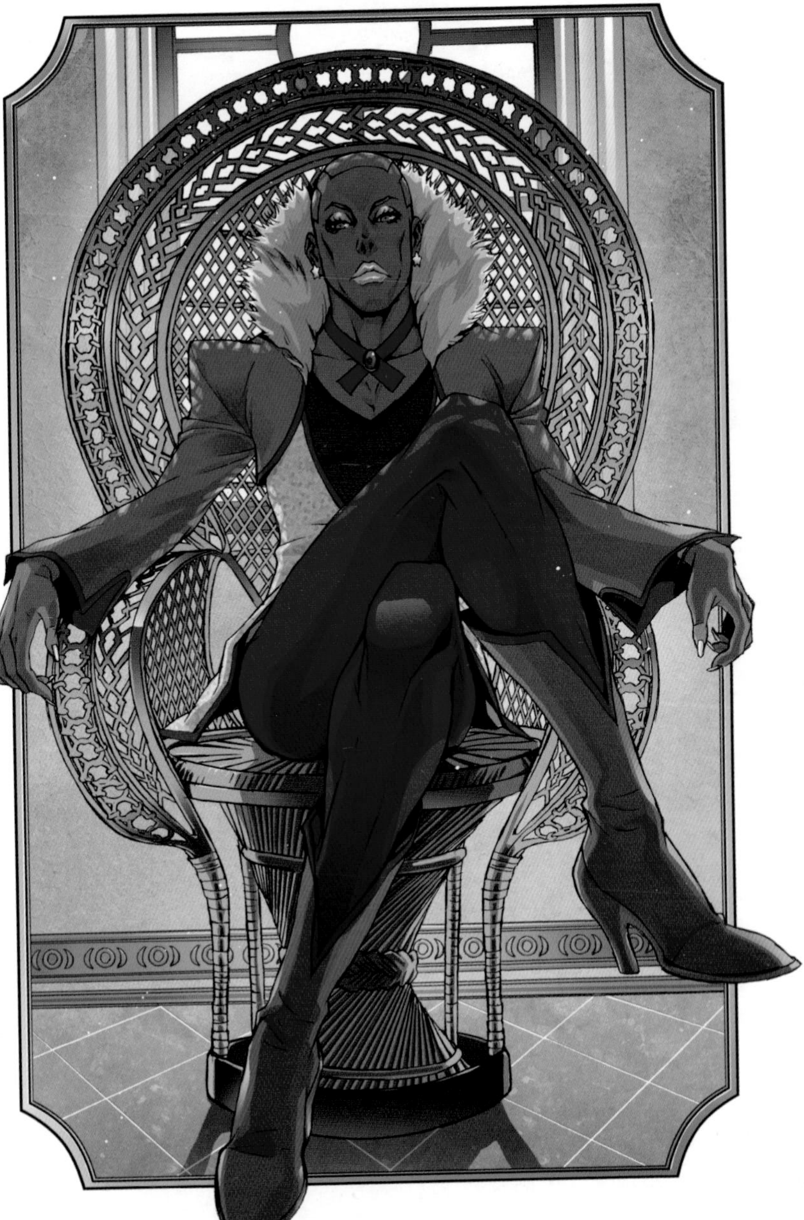

#18 Spare the Rod and Spoil the Child, Part 2

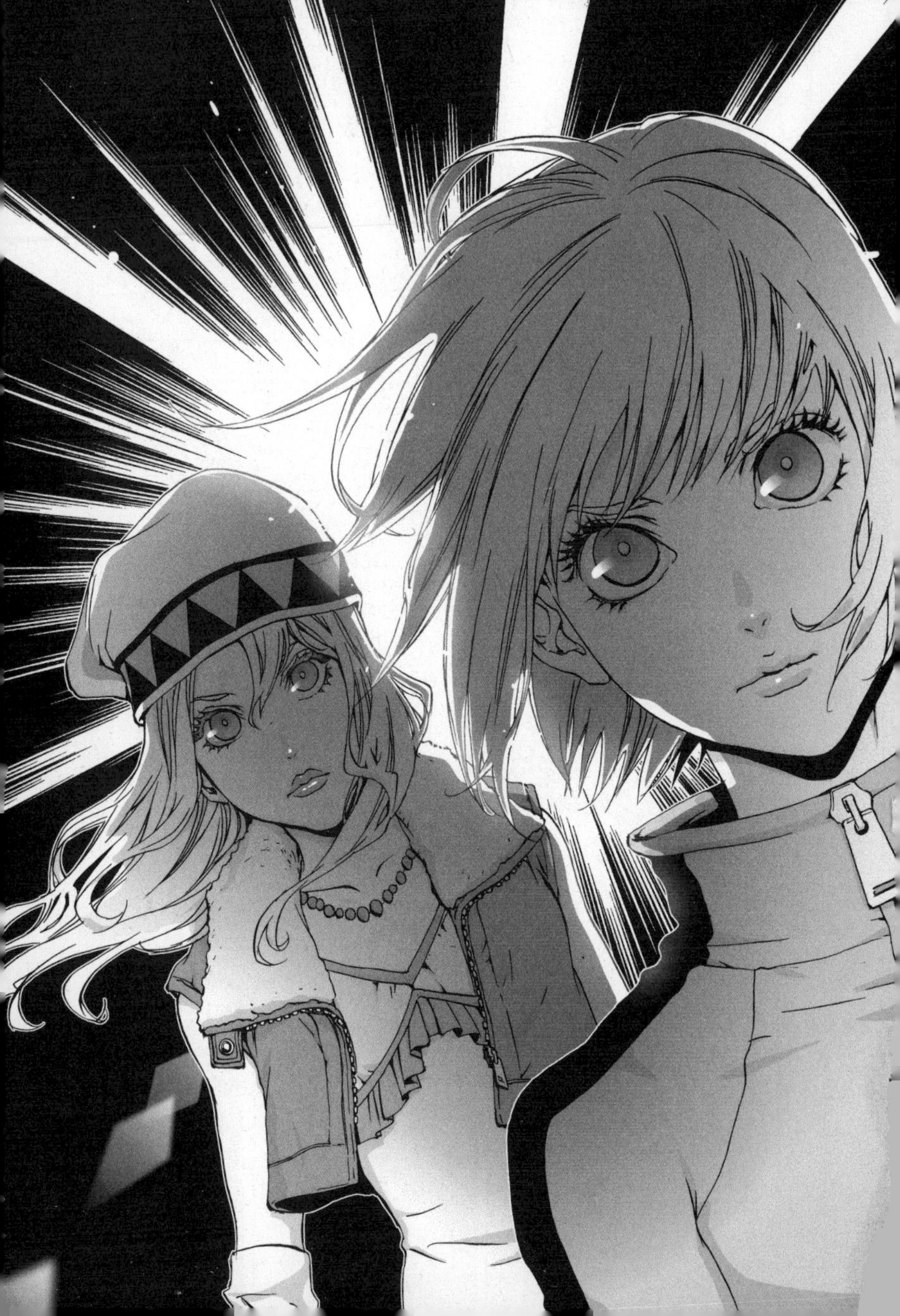

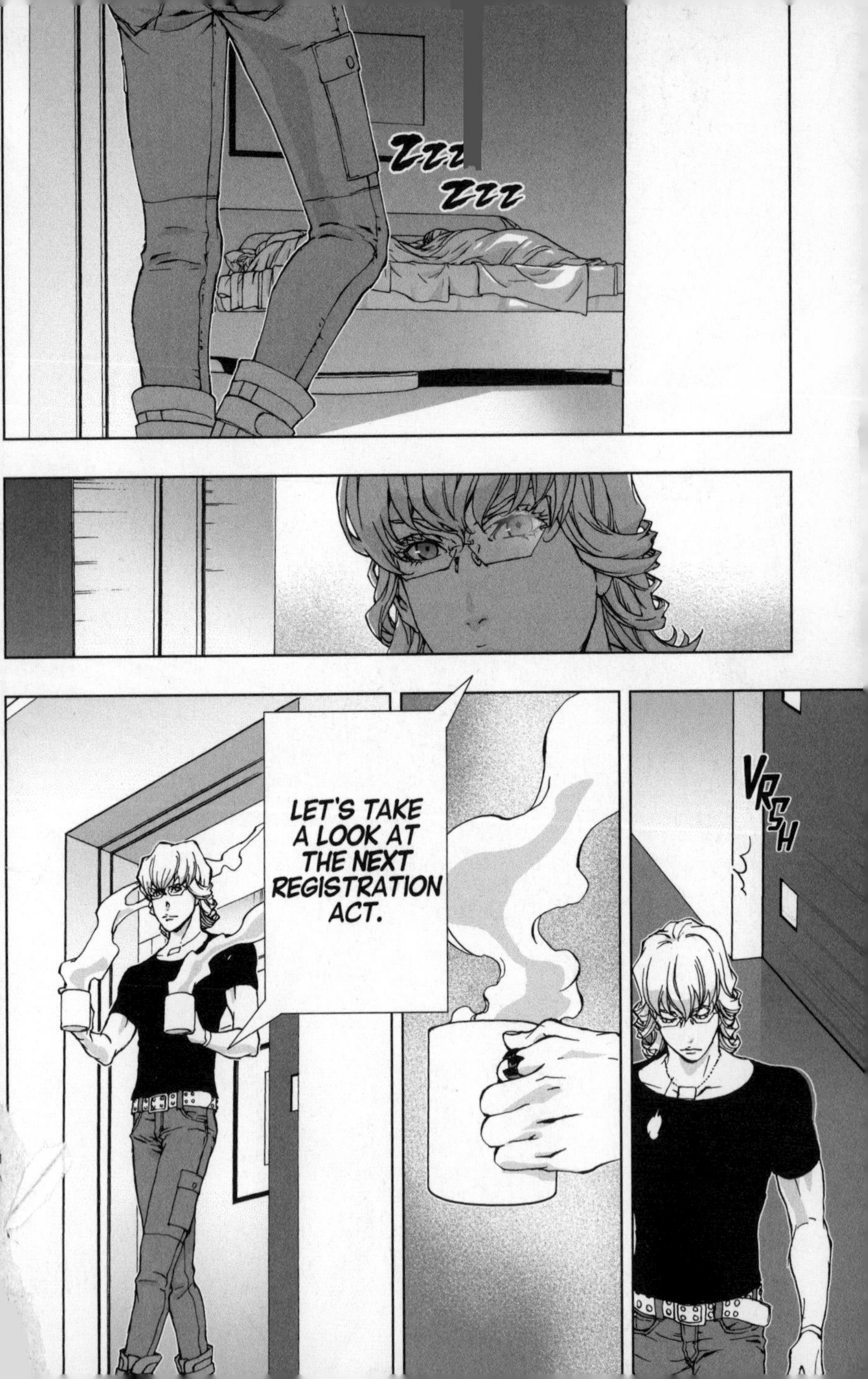
ZZZZ
ZZZ
VRSH
LET'S TAKE A LOOK AT THE NEXT REGISTRATION ACT.

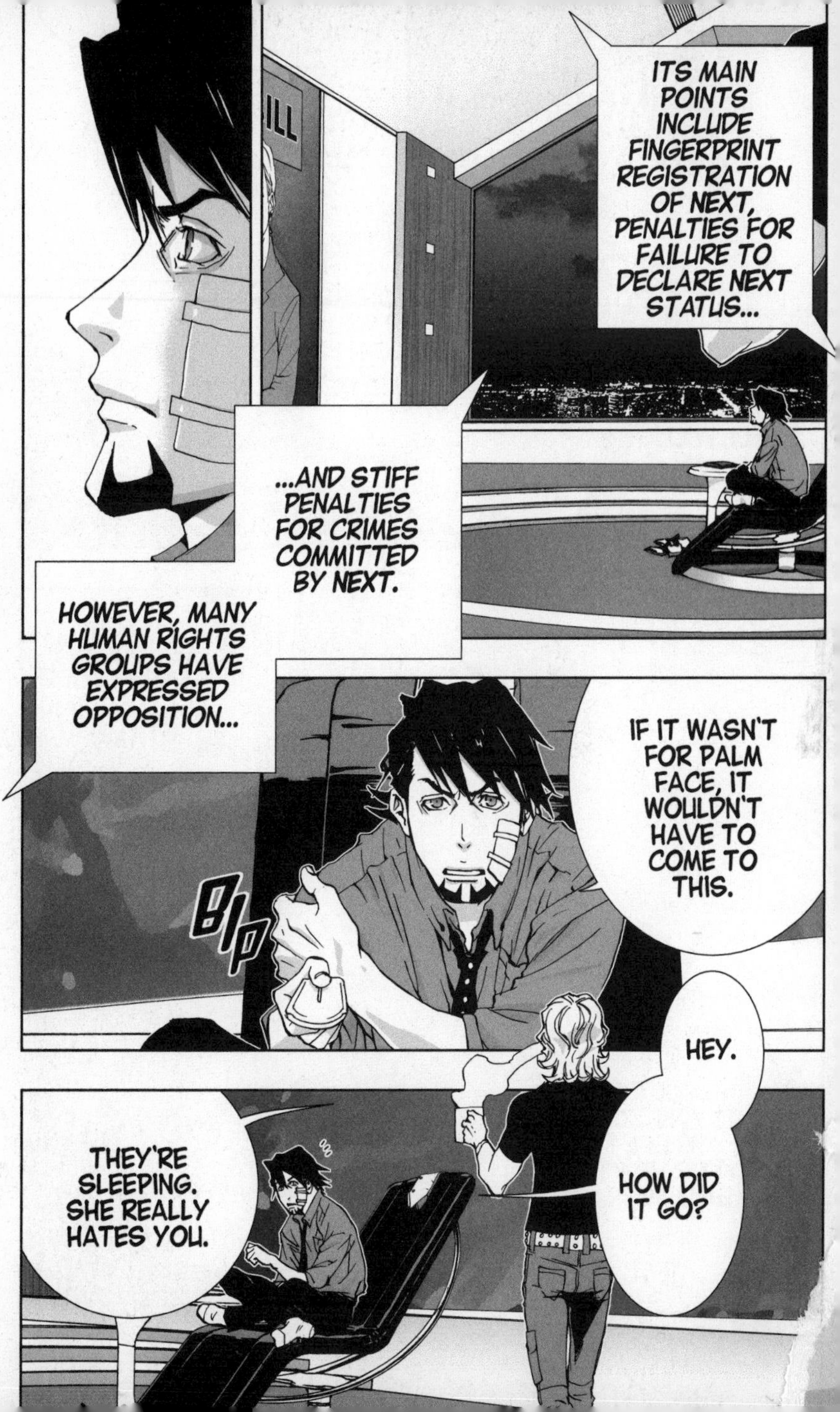
ITS MAIN POINTS INCLUDE FINGERPRINT REGISTRATION OF NEXT, PENALTIES FOR FAILURE TO DECLARE NEXT STATUS...
...AND STIFF PENALTIES FOR CRIMES COMMITTED BY NEXT.
HOWEVER, MANY HUMAN RIGHTS GROUPS HAVE EXPRESSED OPPOSITION...
IF IT WASN'T FOR PALM FACE, IT WOULDN'T HAVE TO COME TO THIS.
BIP
HEY.
HOW DID IT GO?
THEY'RE SLEEPING. SHE REALLY HATES YOU.

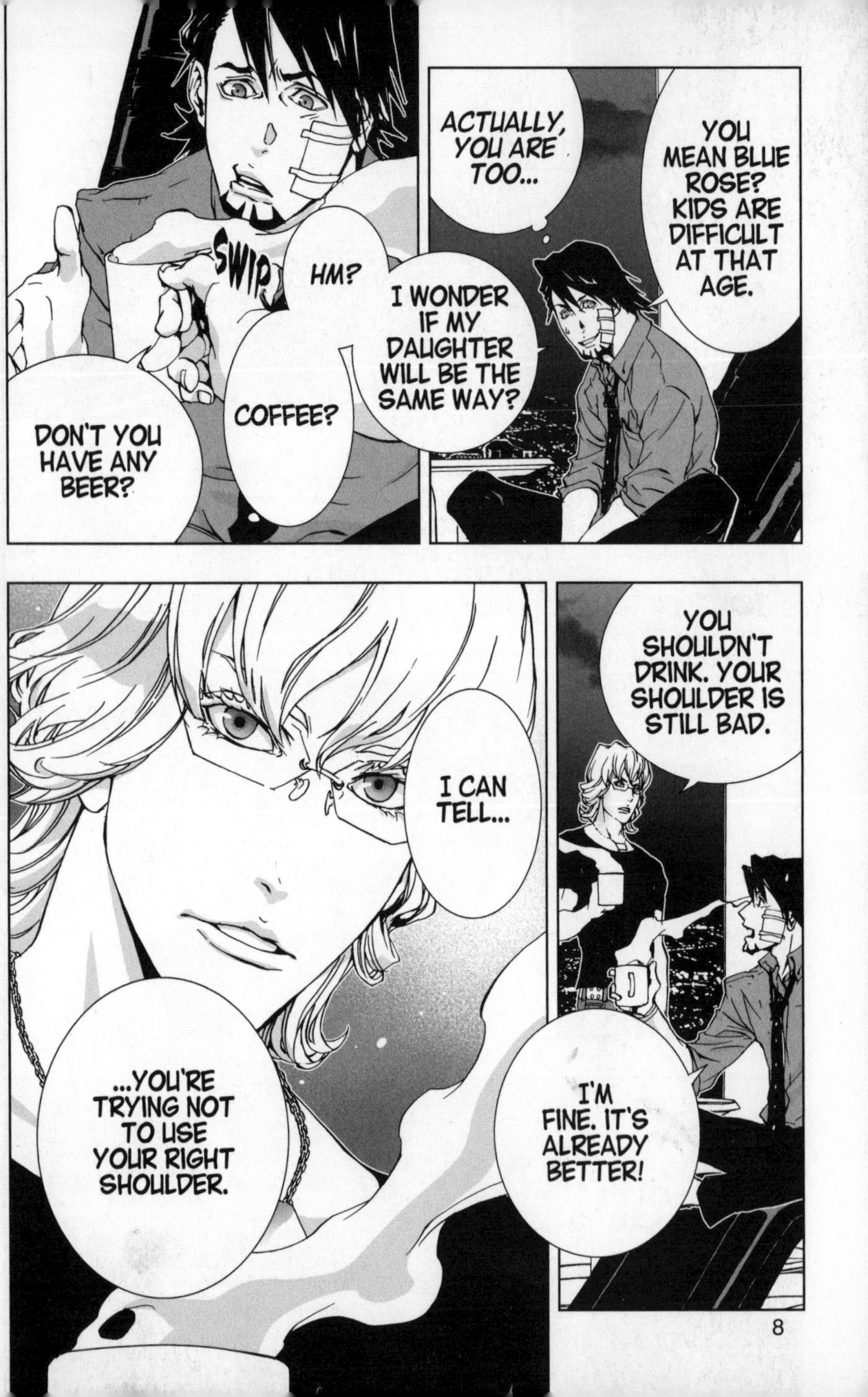
YOU MEAN BLUE ROSE? KIDS ARE DIFFICULT AT THAT AGE.
ACTUALLY, YOU ARE TOO...
I WONDER IF MY DAUGHTER WILL BE THE SAME WAY?
SWIP
HM?
COFFEE?
DON'T YOU HAVE ANY BEER?
YOU SHOULDN'T DRINK. YOUR SHOULDER IS STILL BAD.
I'M FINE. IT'S ALREADY BETTER!
I CAN TELL...
...YOU'RE TRYING NOT TO USE YOUR RIGHT SHOULDER.

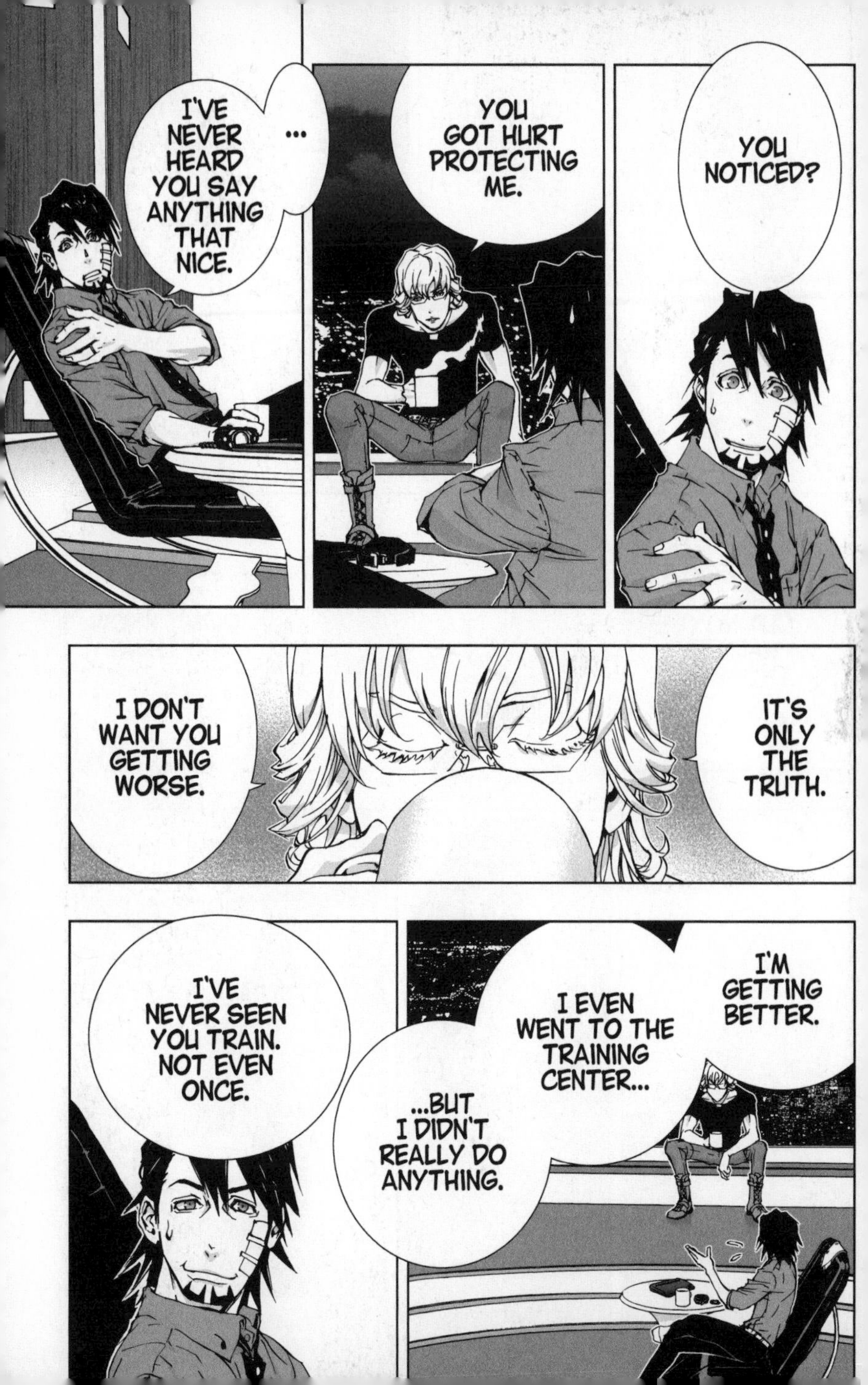
YOU NOTICED?
YOU GOT HURT PROTECTING ME.
...
I'VE NEVER HEARD YOU SAY ANYTHING THAT NICE.
IT'S ONLY THE TRUTH.
I DON'T WANT YOU GETTING WORSE.
I'M GETTING BETTER.
I EVEN WENT TO THE TRAINING CENTER...
...BUT I DIDN'T REALLY DO ANYTHING.
I'VE NEVER SEEN YOU TRAIN. NOT EVEN ONCE.

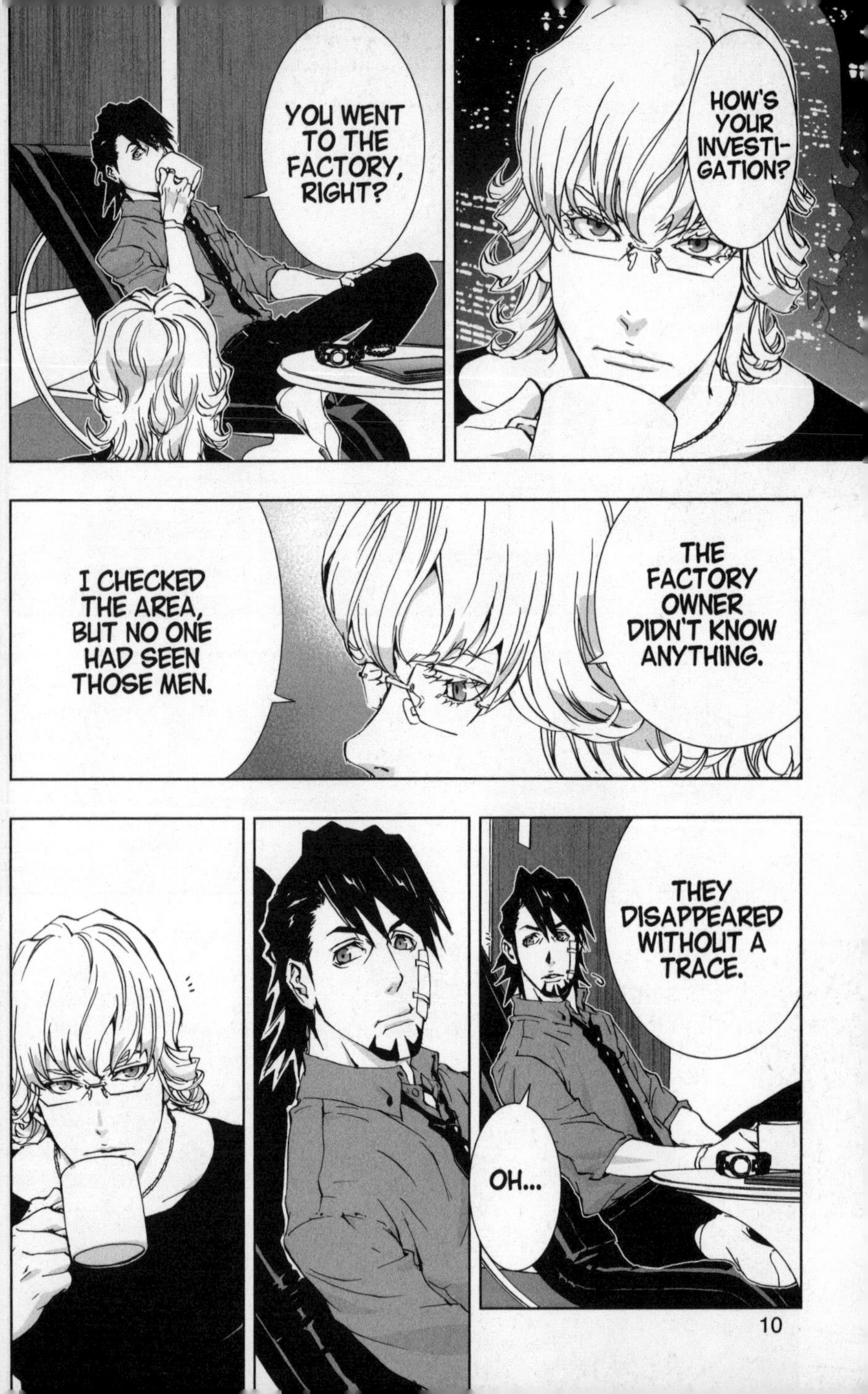
HOW'S YOUR INVESTIGATION?
YOU WENT TO THE FACTORY, RIGHT?
THE FACTORY OWNER DIDN'T KNOW ANYTHING.
I CHECKED THE AREA, BUT NO ONE HAD SEEN THOSE MEN.
THEY DISAPPEARED WITHOUT A TRACE.
OH...

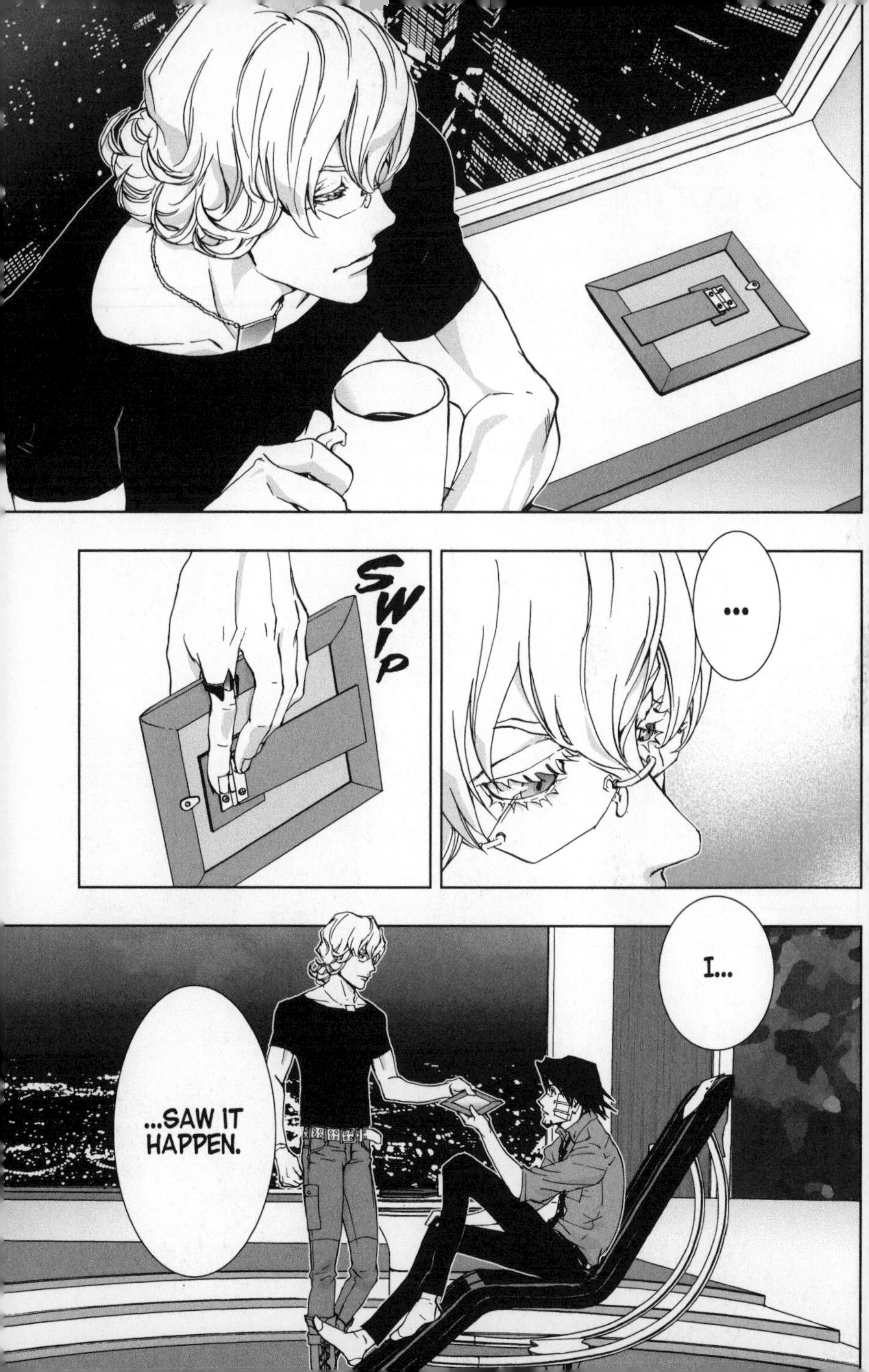
...
SWIP
I...
...SAW IT HAPPEN.

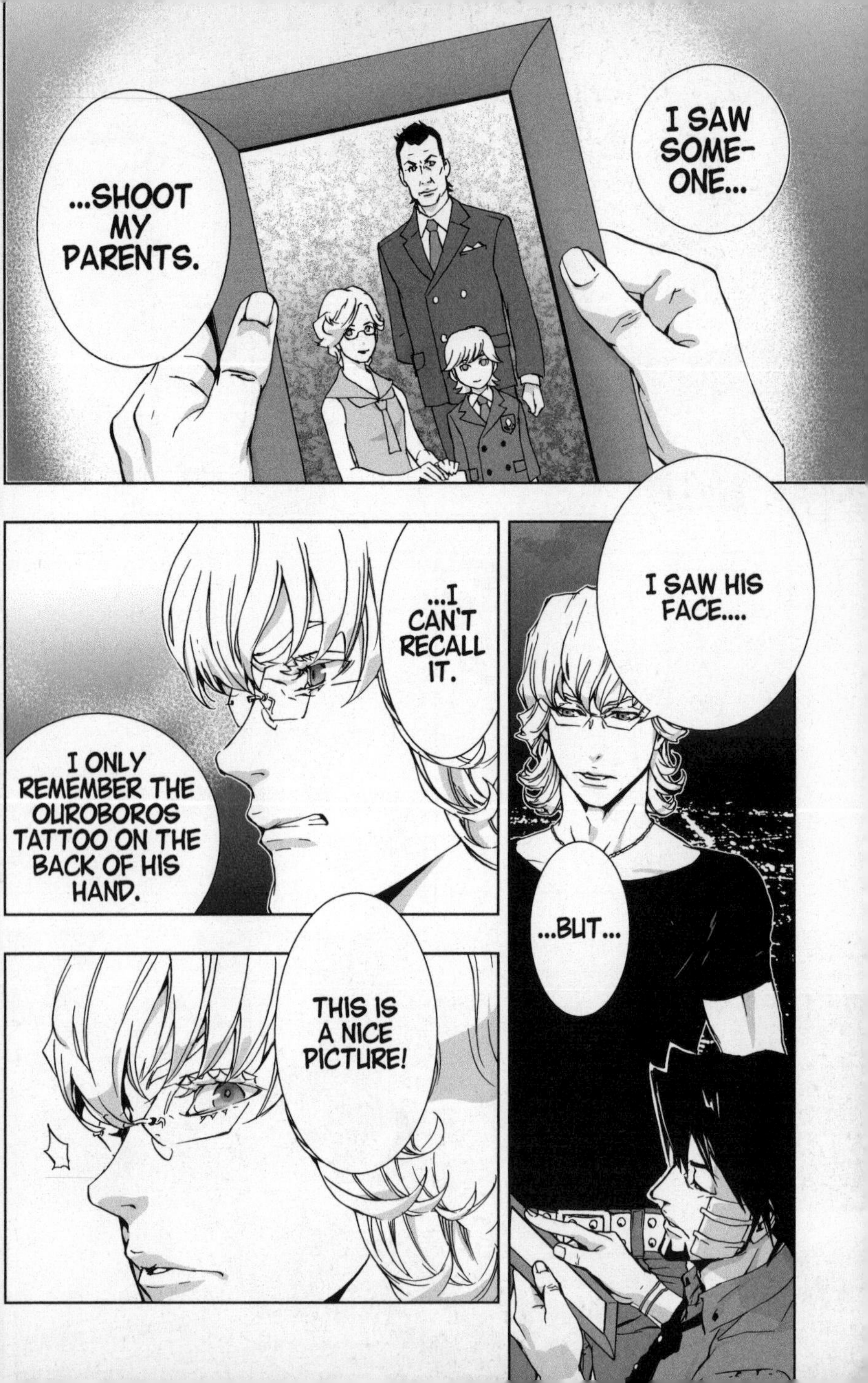
I SAW SOME-ONE...
...SHOOT MY PARENTS.
I SAW HIS FACE....
...BUT...
...I CAN'T RECALL IT.
I ONLY REMEMBER THE OUROBOROS TATTOO ON THE BACK OF HIS HAND.
THIS IS A NICE PICTURE!

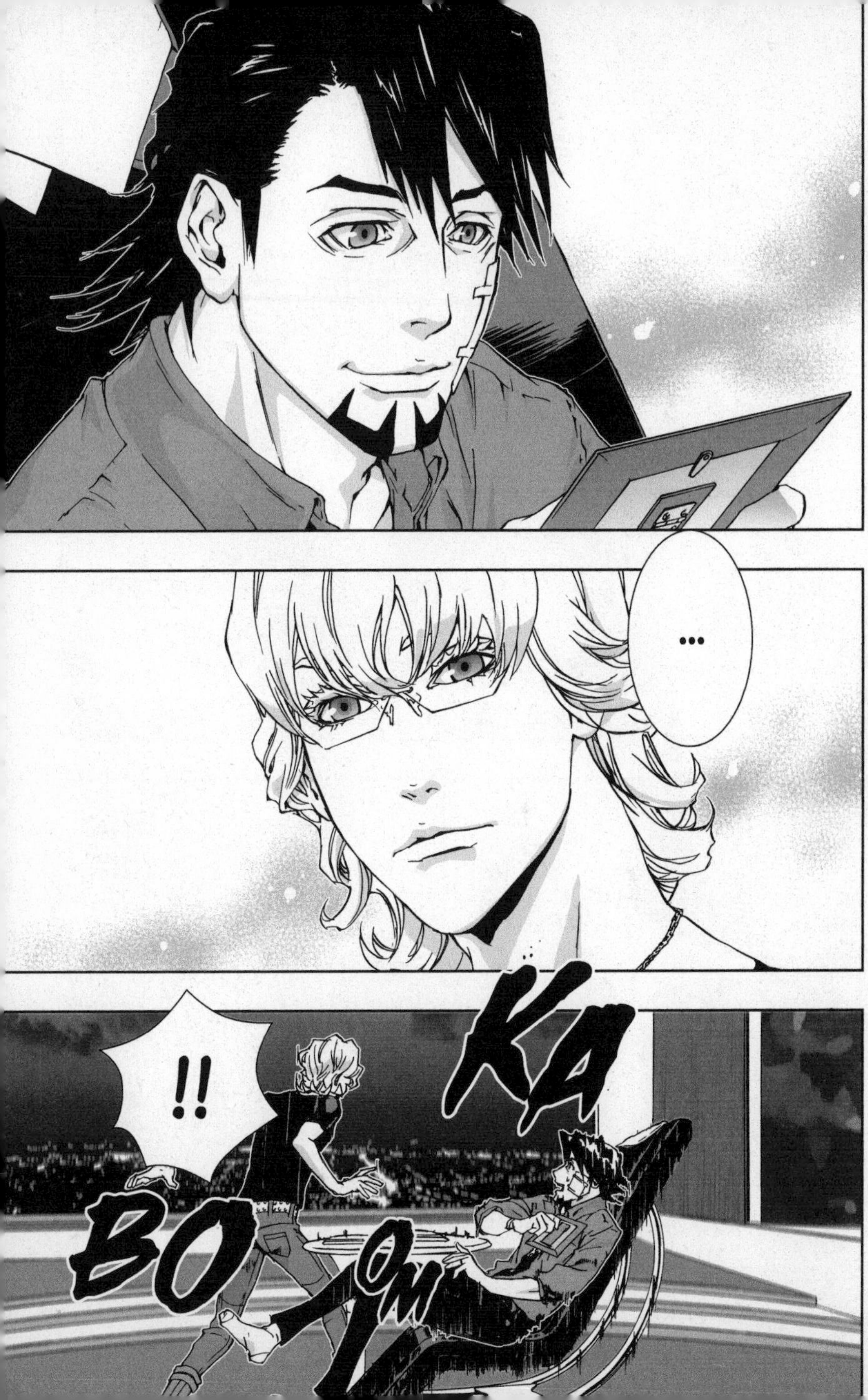
...
!!
KA
BOOM

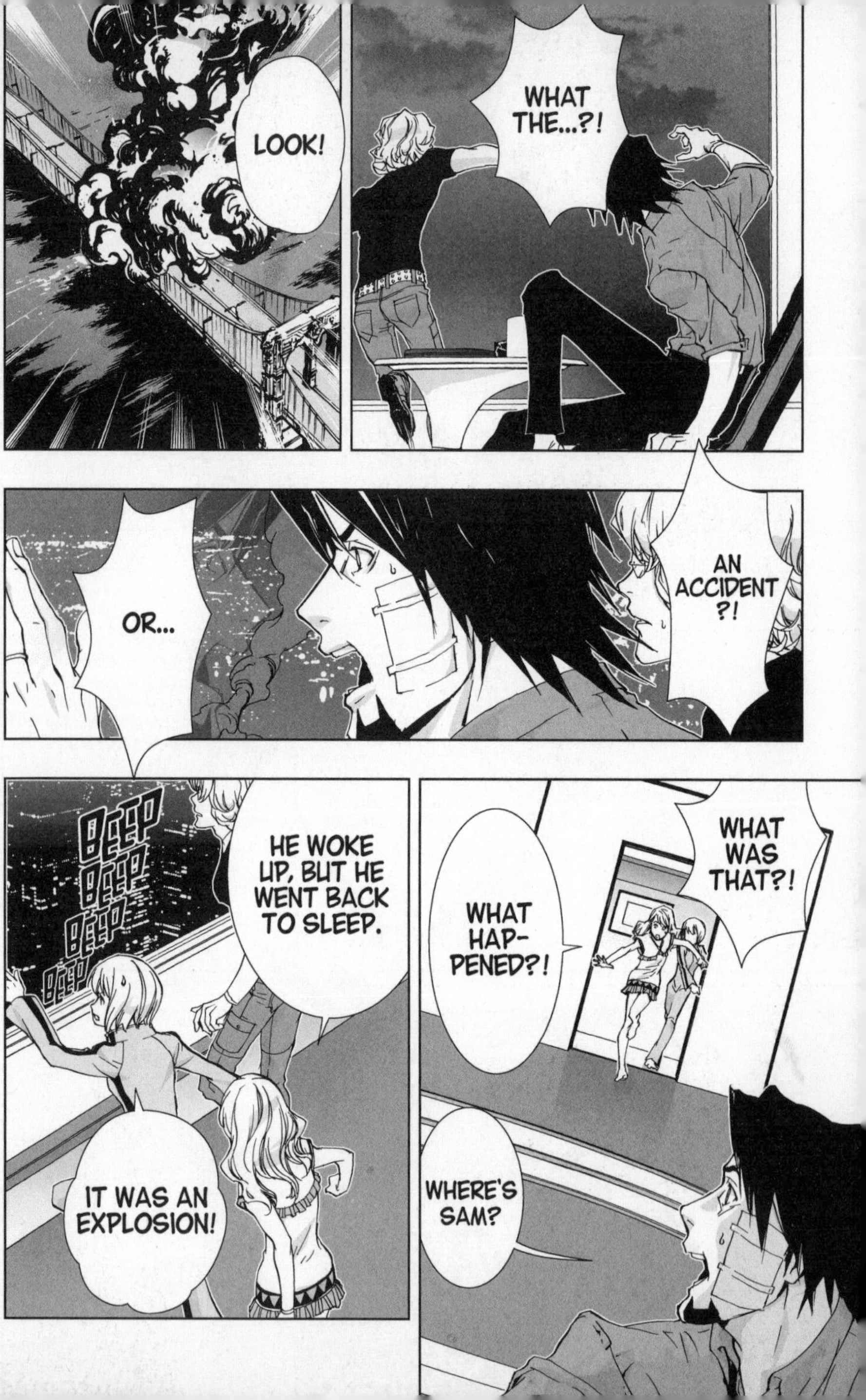
WHAT THE...?!
LOOK!
AN ACCIDENT ?!
OR...
WHAT WAS THAT?!
WHAT HAP-PENED?!
WHERE'S SAM?
HE WOKE UP, BUT HE WENT BACK TO SLEEP.
BEEP
BEEP
BEEP
BEEP
IT WAS AN EXPLOSION!

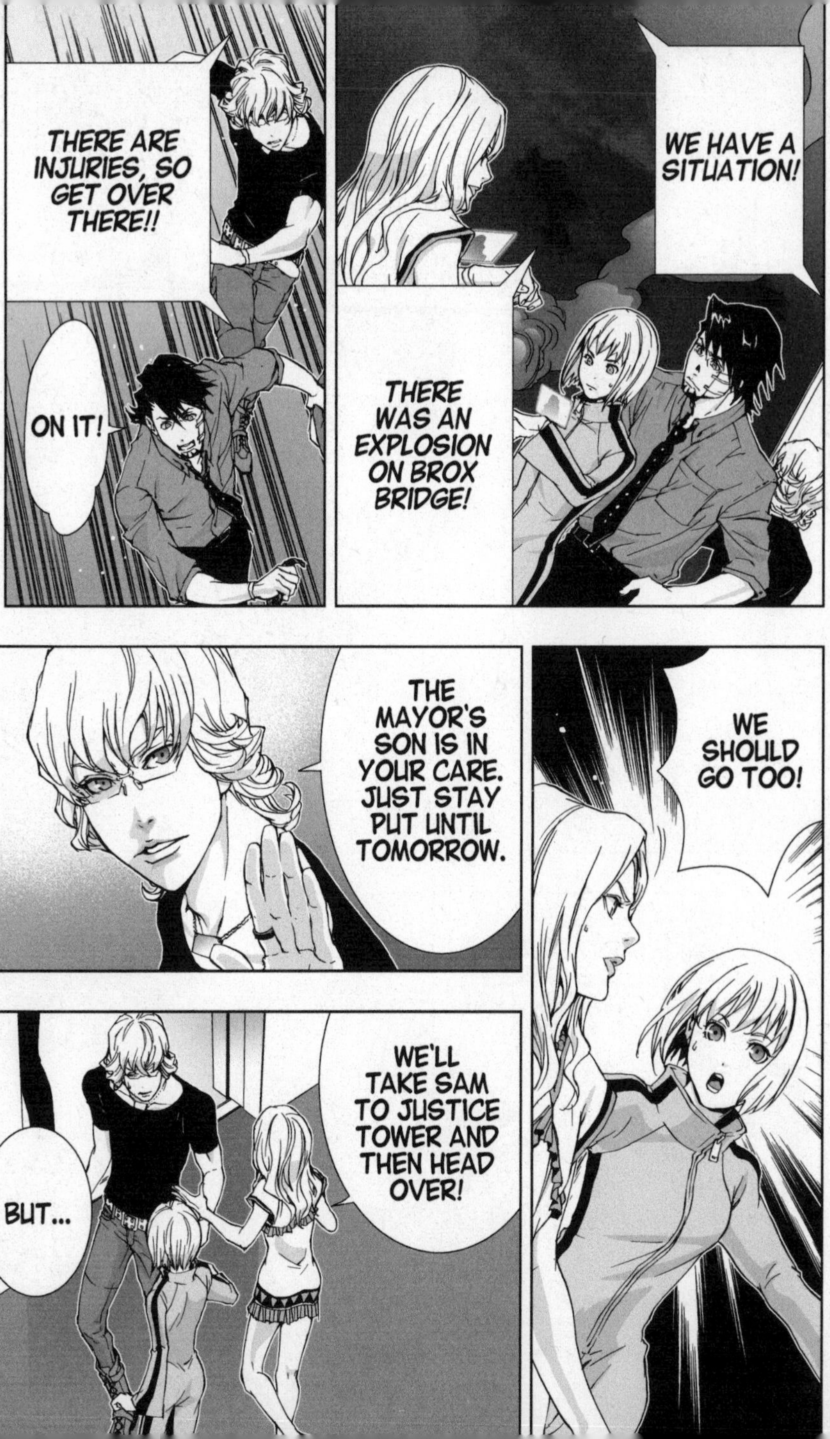
WE HAVE A SITUATION!
THERE WAS AN EXPLOSION ON BROX BRIDGE!
THERE ARE INJURIES, SO GET OVER THERE!!
ON IT!
WE SHOULD GO TOO!
THE MAYOR'S SON IS IN YOUR CARE. JUST STAY PUT UNTIL TOMORROW.
WE'LL TAKE SAM TO JUSTICE TOWER AND THEN HEAD OVER!
BUT...

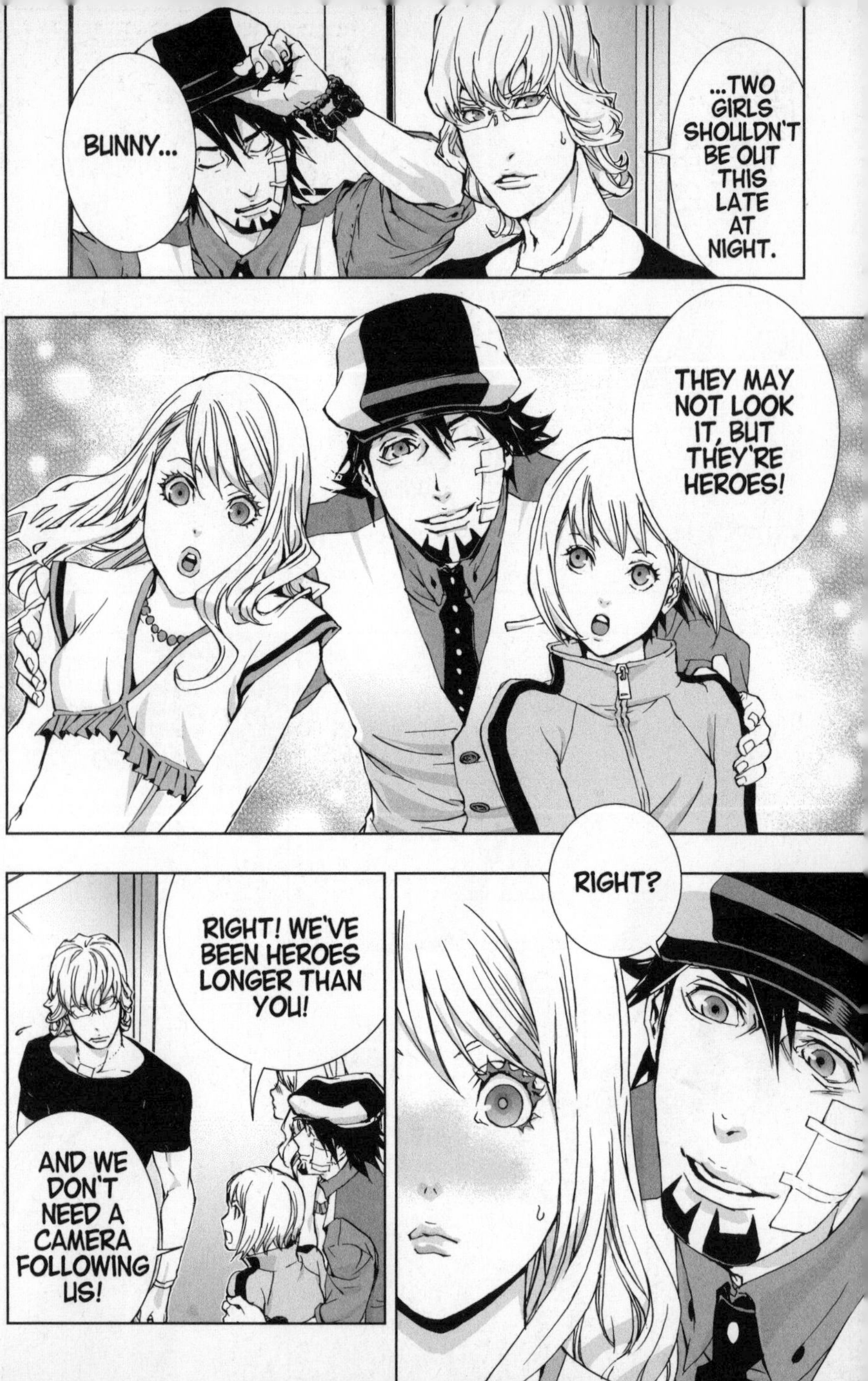
...TWO GIRLS SHOULDN'T BE OUT THIS LATE AT NIGHT.
BUNNY...
THEY MAY NOT LOOK IT, BUT THEY'RE HEROES!
RIGHT?
RIGHT! WE'VE BEEN HEROES LONGER THAN YOU!
AND WE DON'T NEED A CAMERA FOLLOWING US!

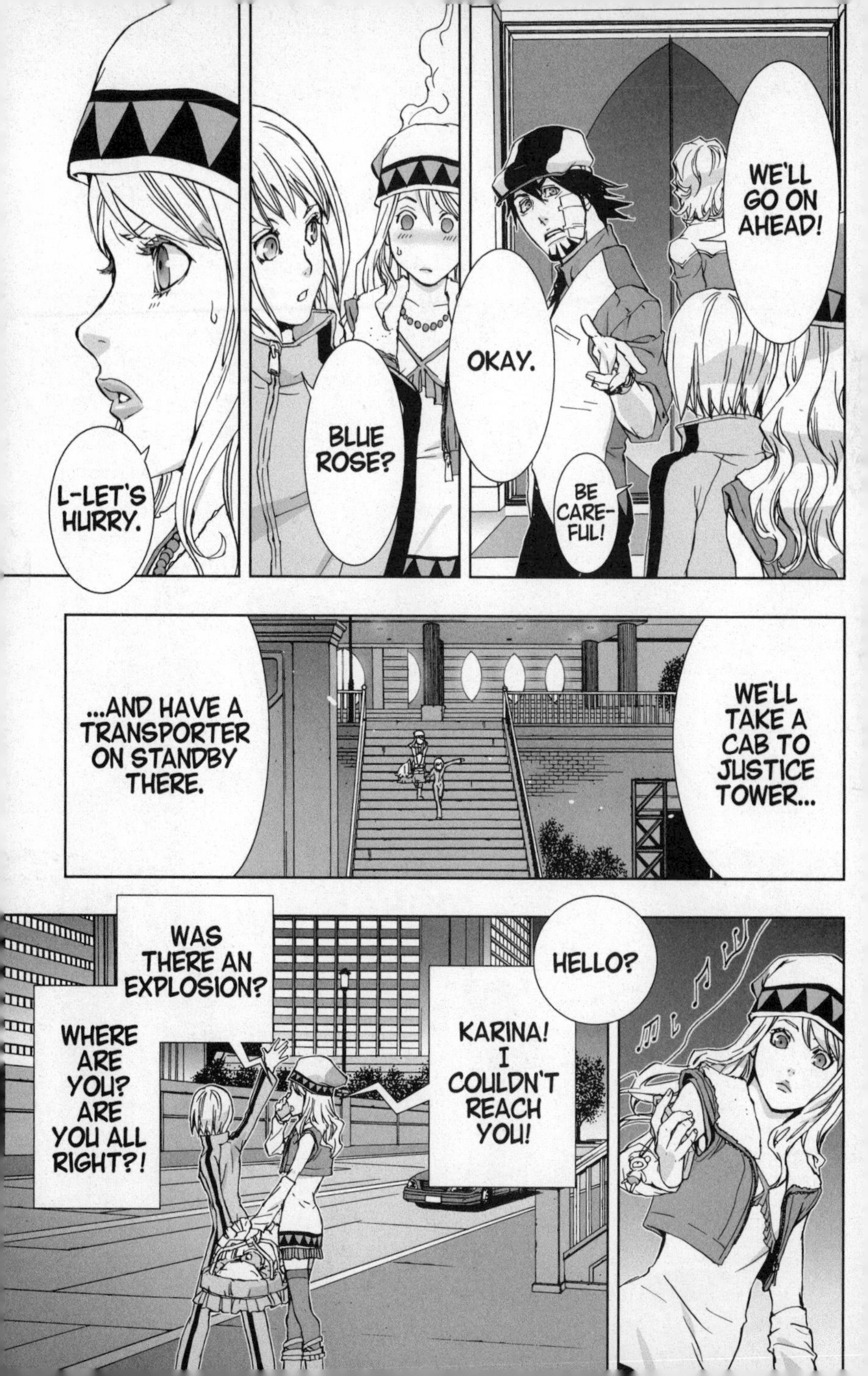

WE'LL GO ON AHEAD!
OKAY.
BE CARE-FUL!
BLUE ROSE?
L-LET'S HURRY.
WE'LL TAKE A CAB TO JUSTICE TOWER...
...AND HAVE A TRANSPORTER ON STANDBY THERE.
HELLO?
KARINA! I COULDN'T REACH YOU!
WAS THERE AN EXPLOSION?
WHERE ARE YOU? ARE YOU ALL RIGHT?!

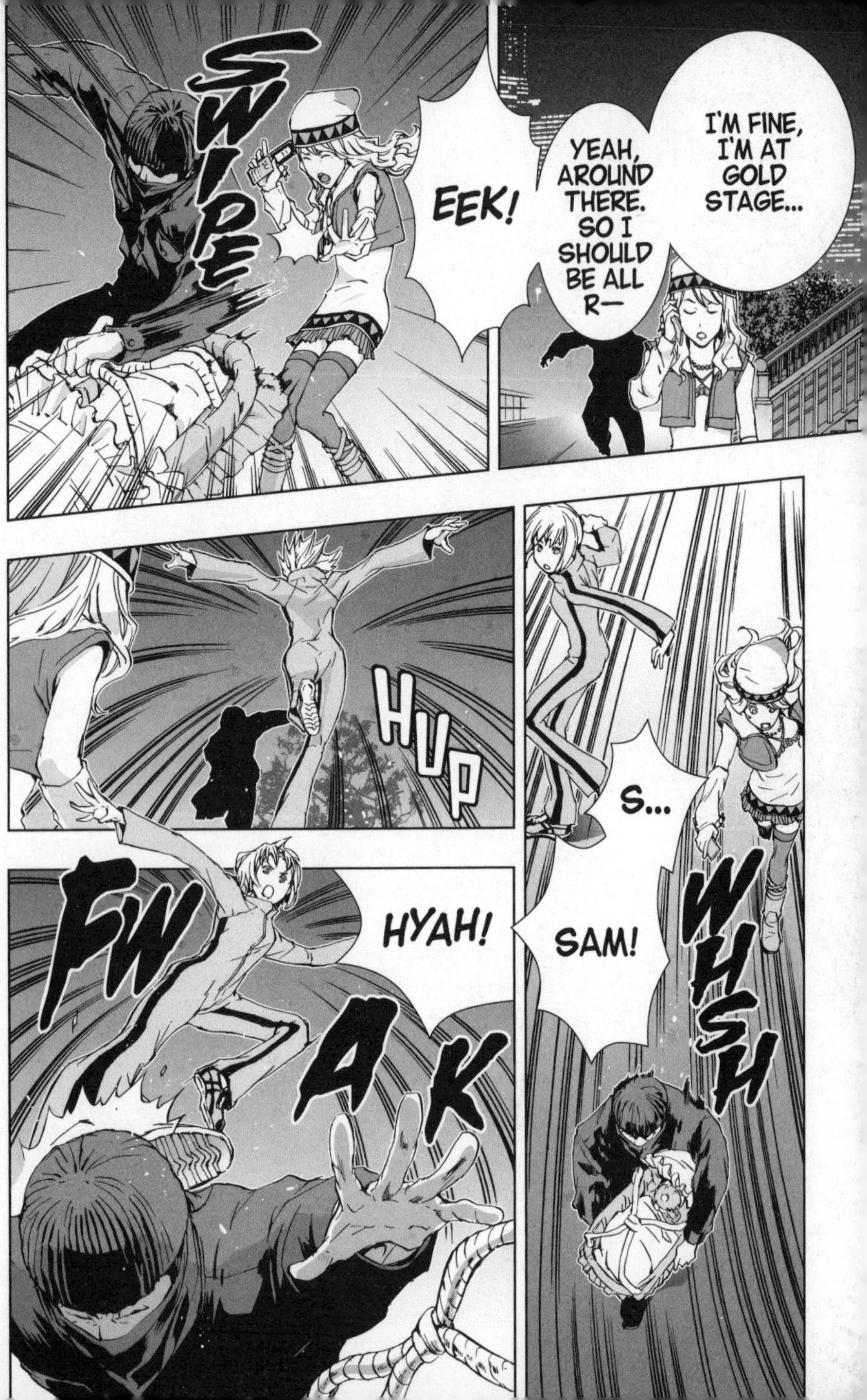
I'M FINE, I'M AT GOLD STAGE...
YEAH, AROUND THERE. SO I SHOULD BE ALL R—
EEK!
SWIPE
S...
WHSH
SAM!
HUP
HYAH!
FWAK

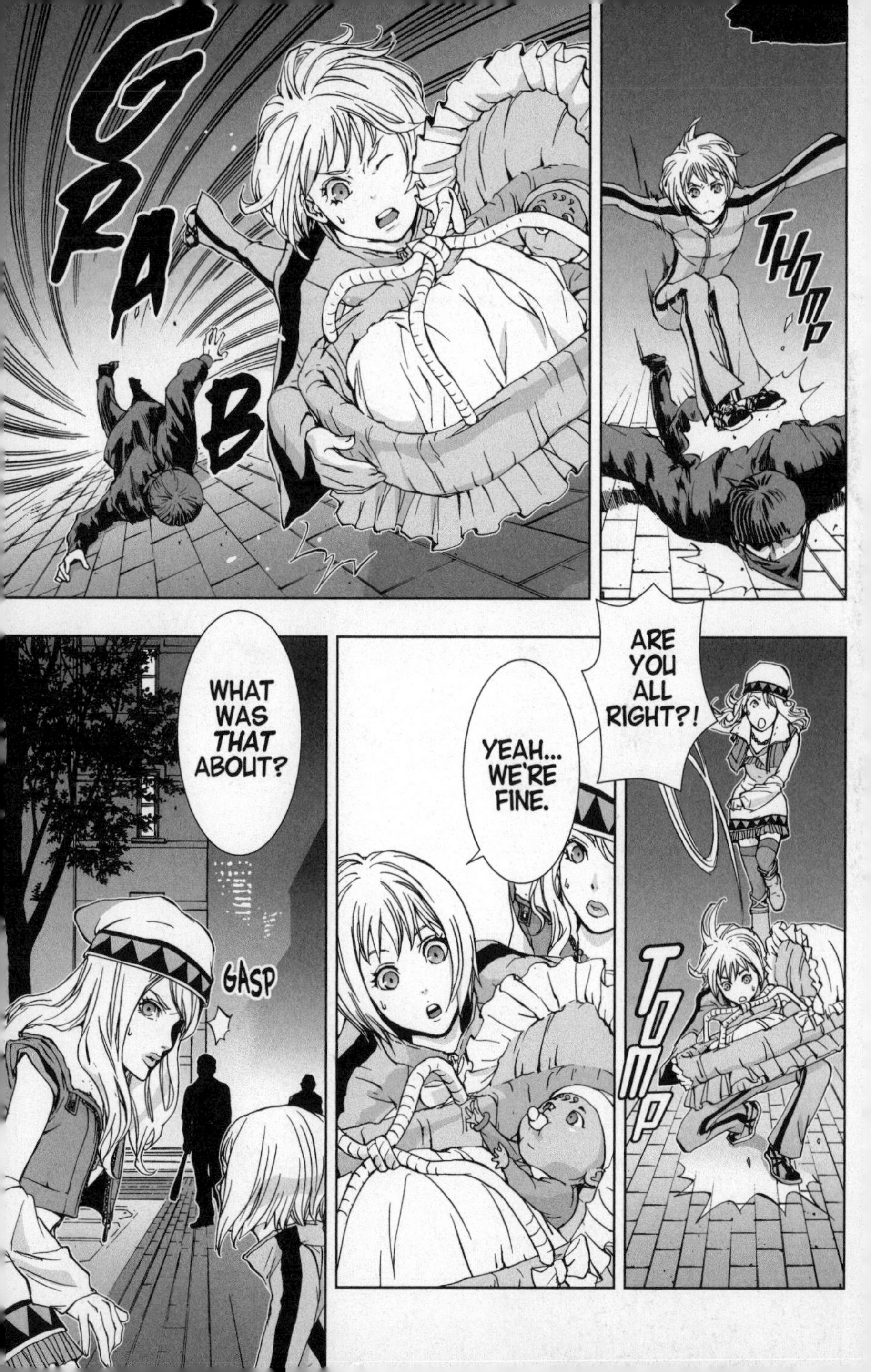
THOMP
GRAB
ARE YOU ALL RIGHT?!
TOMP
YEAH... WE'RE FINE.
WHAT WAS THAT ABOUT?
GASP

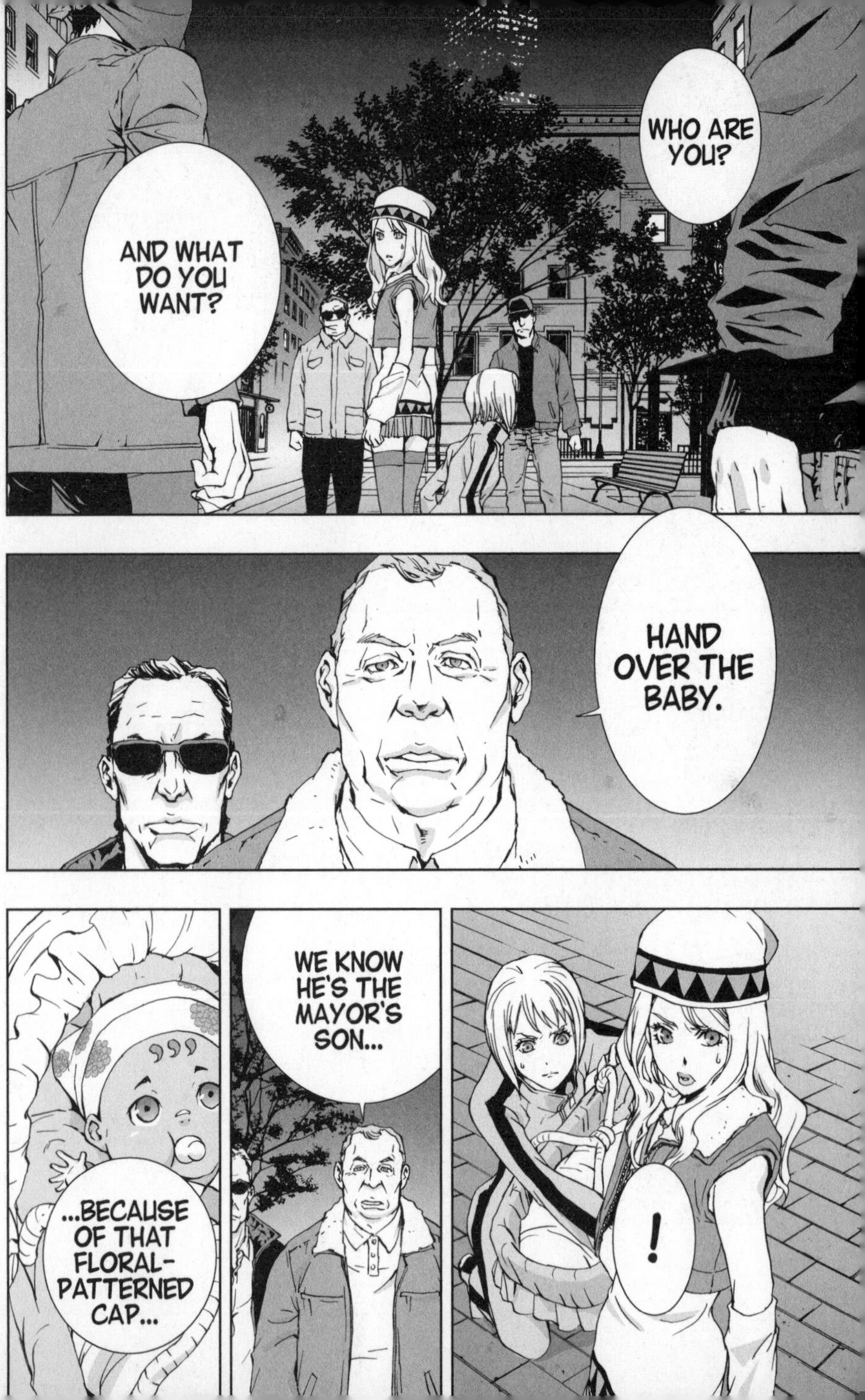
WHO ARE YOU?
AND WHAT DO YOU WANT?
HAND OVER THE BABY.
!
WE KNOW HE'S THE MAYOR'S SON...
...BECAUSE OF THAT FLORAL-PATTERNED CAP...

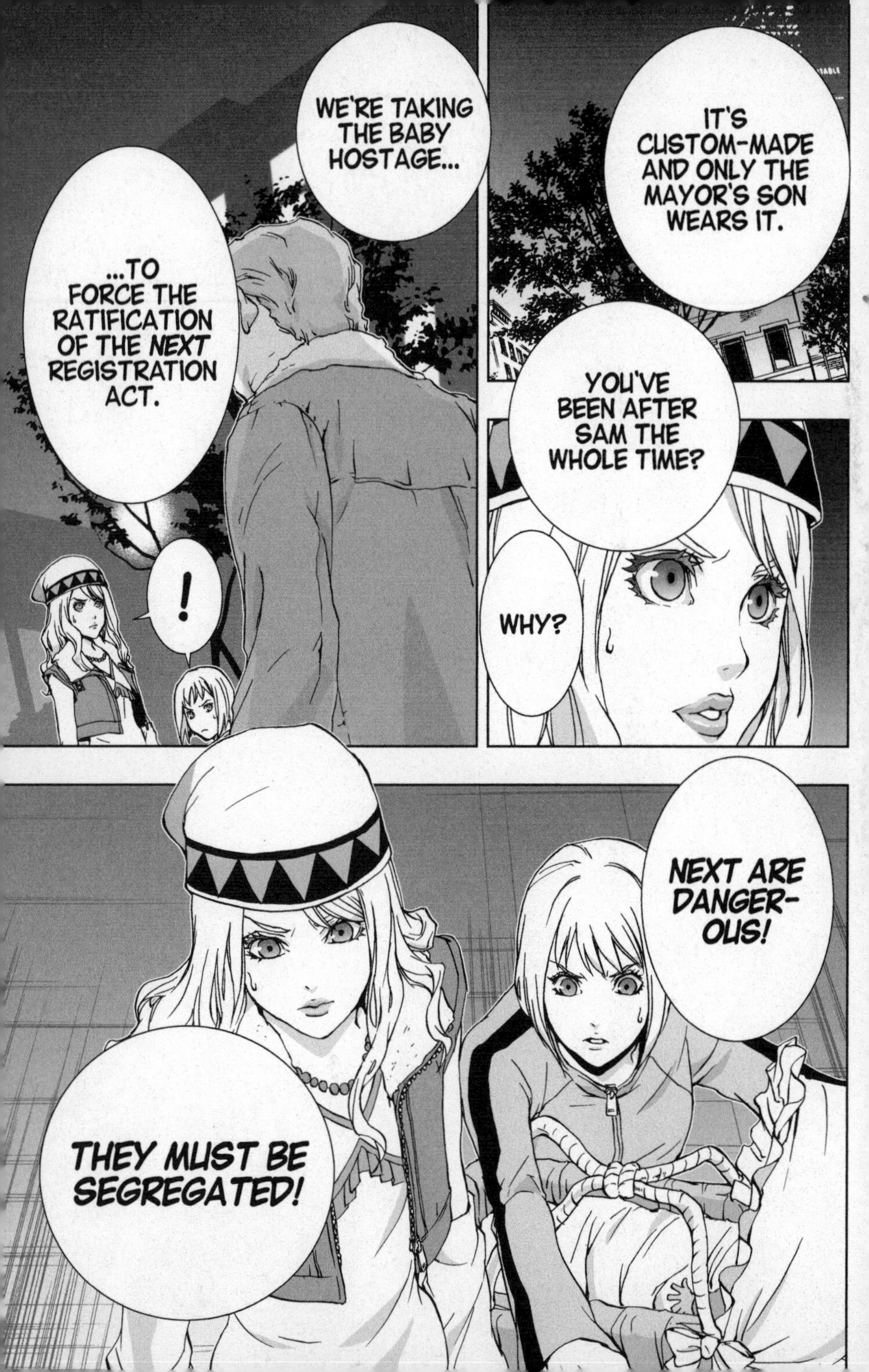
IT'S CUSTOM-MADE AND ONLY THE MAYOR'S SON WEARS IT.
YOU'VE BEEN AFTER SAM THE WHOLE TIME?
WHY?
WE'RE TAKING THE BABY HOSTAGE...
...TO FORCE THE RATIFICATION OF THE *NEXT* REGISTRATION ACT.
!
NEXT ARE DANGER-OUS!
THEY MUST BE SEGREGATED!

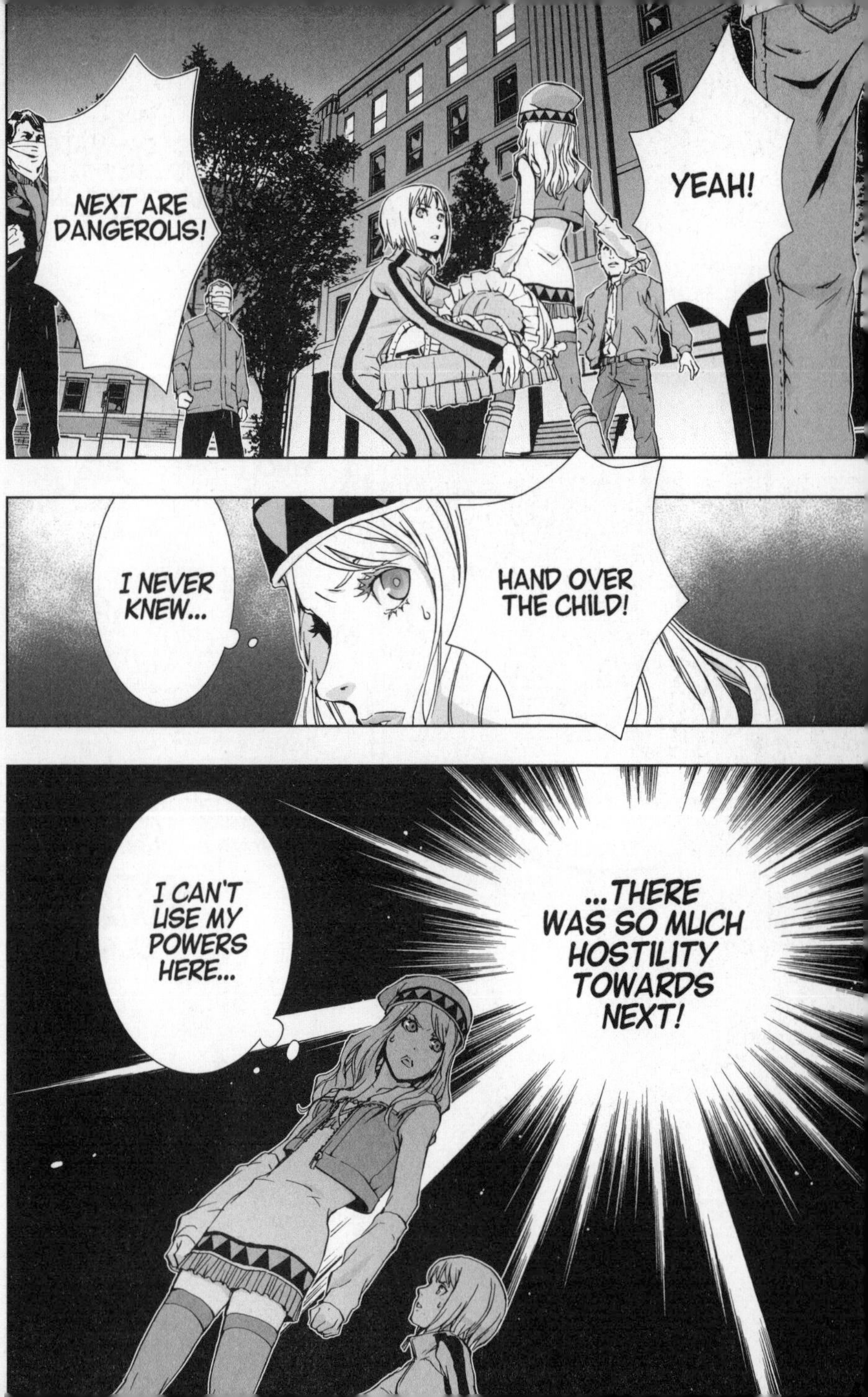
YEAH!
NEXT ARE DANGEROUS!
HAND OVER THE CHILD!
I NEVER KNEW...
...THERE WAS SO MUCH HOSTILITY TOWARDS NEXT!
I CAN'T USE MY POWERS HERE...

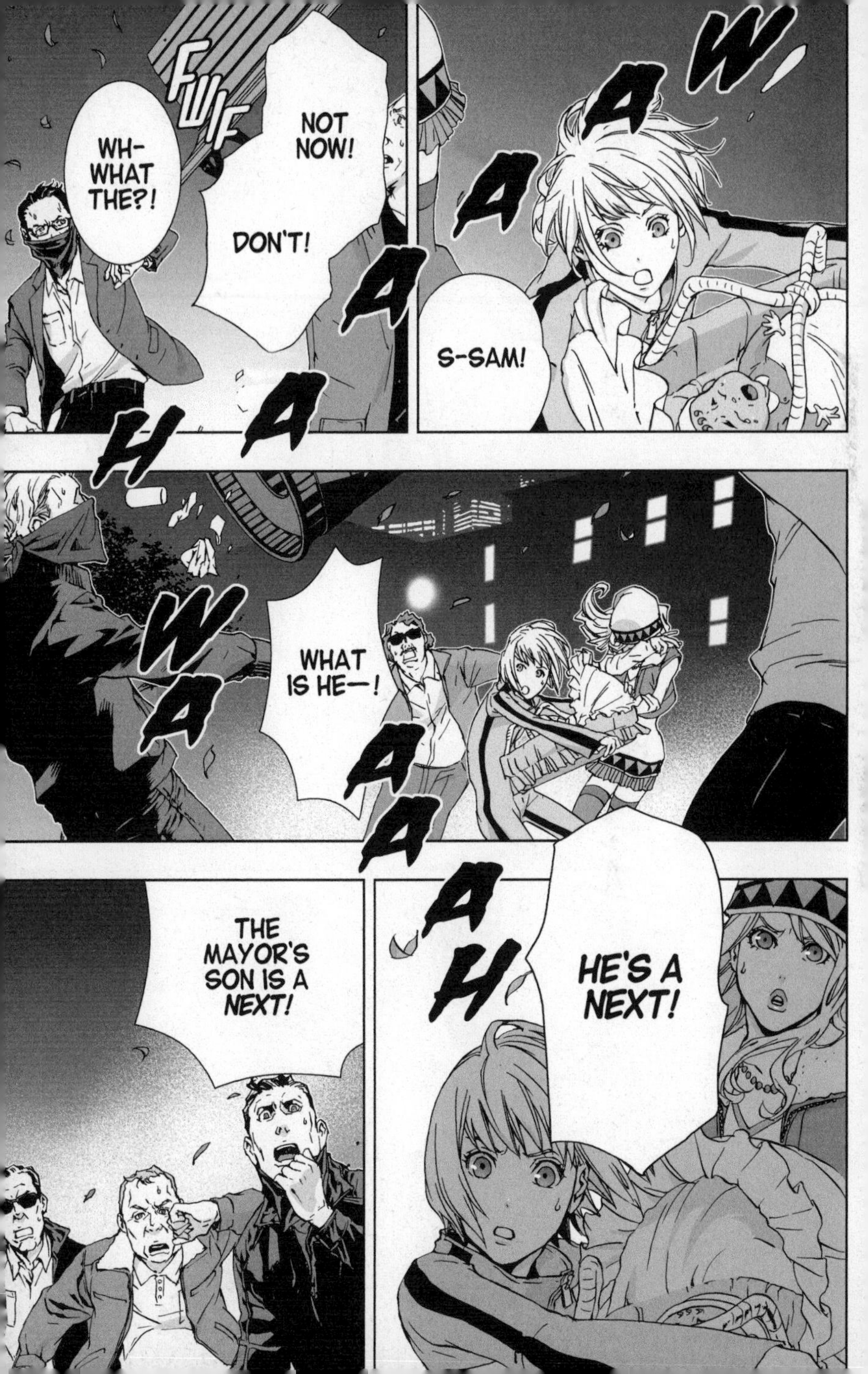

S-SAM!
HAAAAW!
NOT NOW!
DON'T!
FWIF
WH-WHAT THE?!
WHAT IS HE—!
WAAAAH
HE'S A NEXT!
THE MAYOR'S SON IS A NEXT!

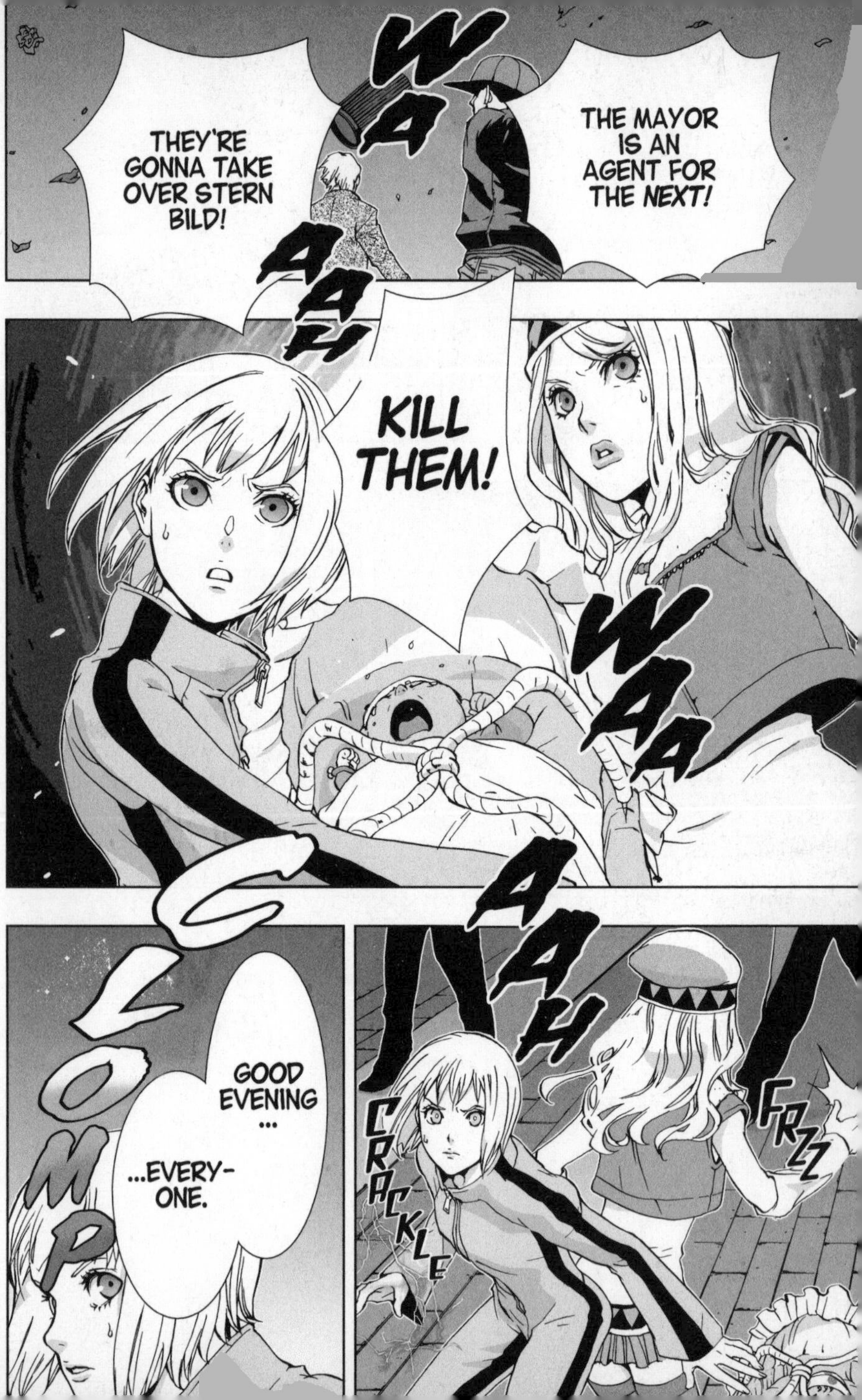
THE MAYOR IS AN AGENT FOR THE NEXT!
WAAAH
THEY'RE GONNA TAKE OVER STERN BILD!
KILL THEM!
WAAAAH
FRZZ
CRACKLE
CLOMP
GOOD EVENING ...
...EVERY-ONE.

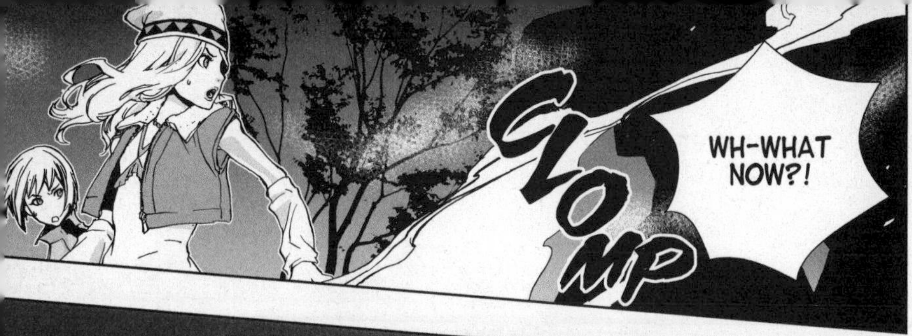
WH-WHAT NOW?!
GLOMP
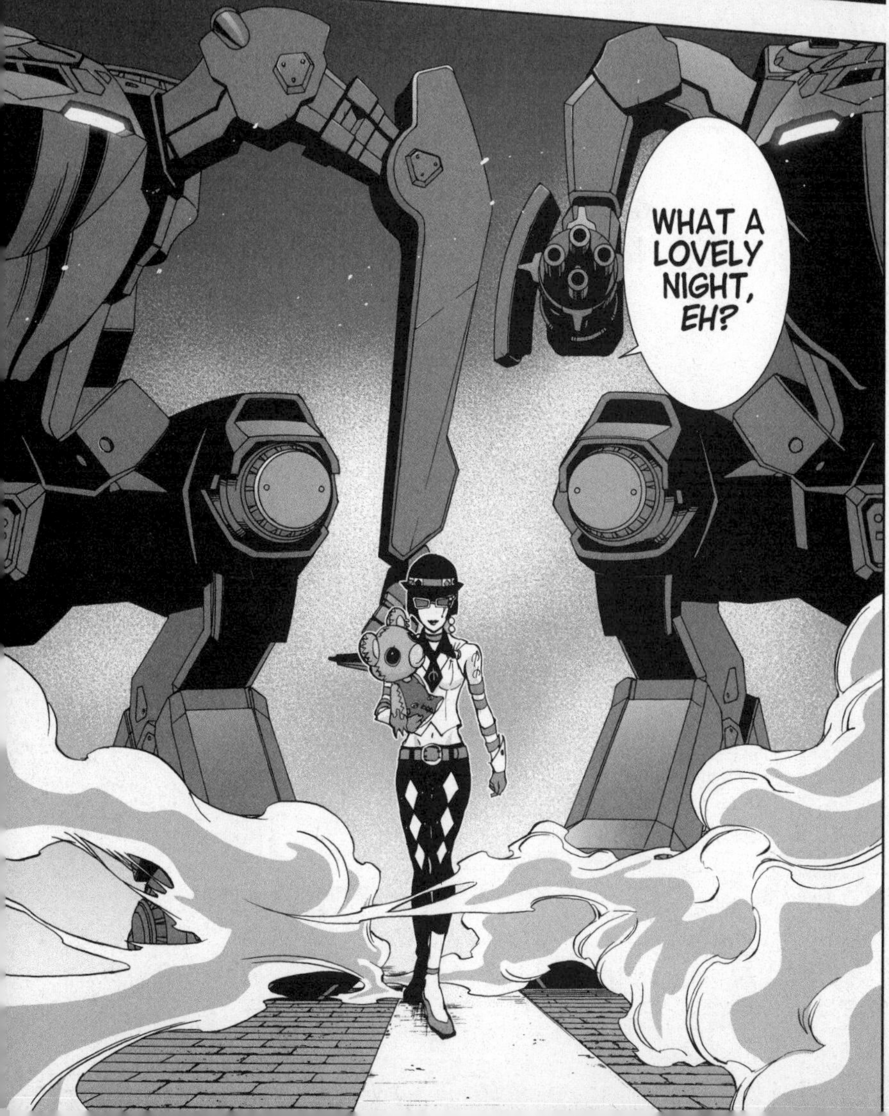
WHAT A LOVELY NIGHT, EH?

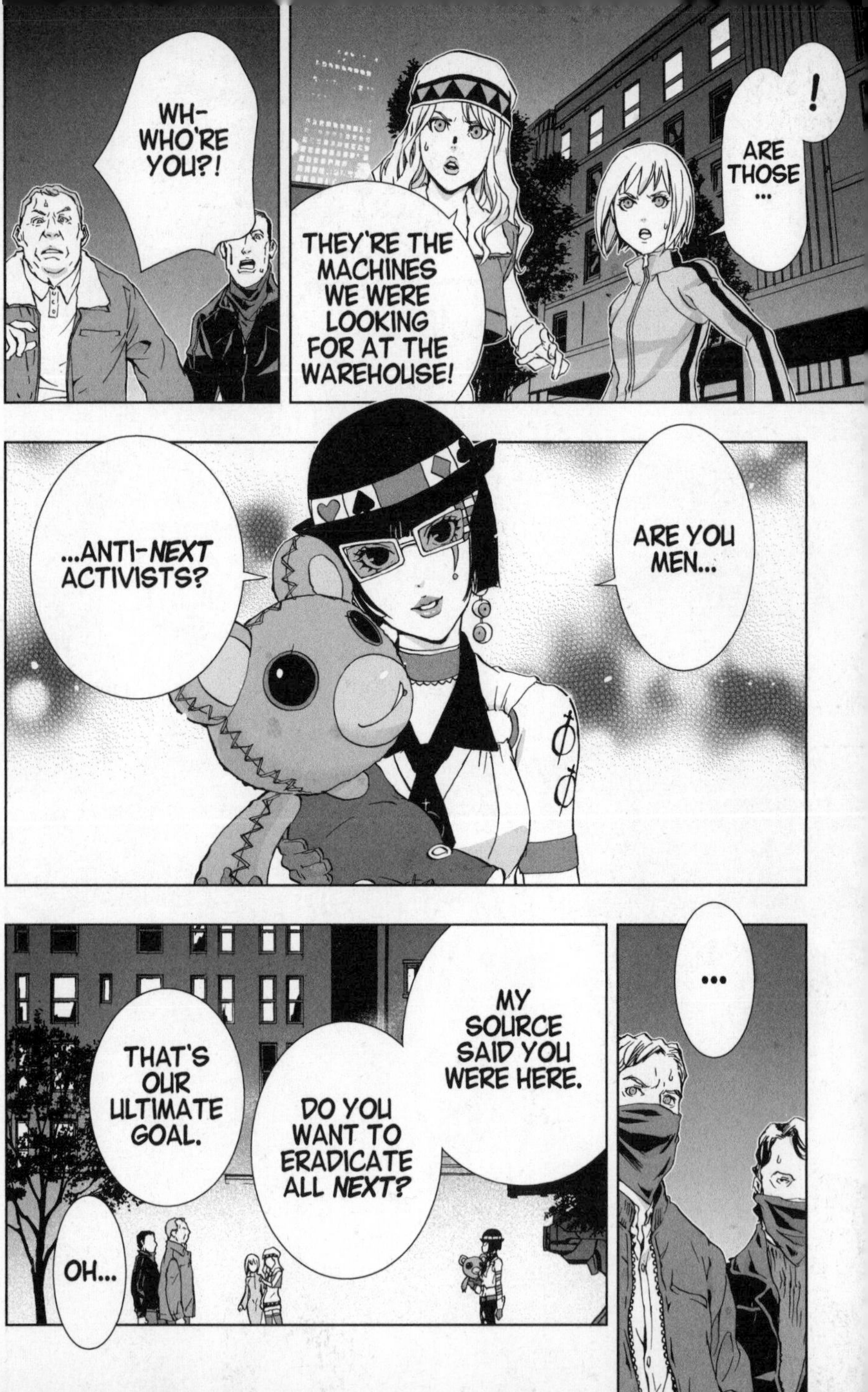
!
ARE THOSE ...
THEY'RE THE MACHINES WE WERE LOOKING FOR AT THE WAREHOUSE!
WH- WHO'RE YOU?!
ARE YOU MEN...
...ANTI-*NEXT* ACTIVISTS?
...
MY SOURCE SAID YOU WERE HERE.
DO YOU WANT TO ERADICATE ALL *NEXT*?
THAT'S OUR ULTIMATE GOAL.
OH...

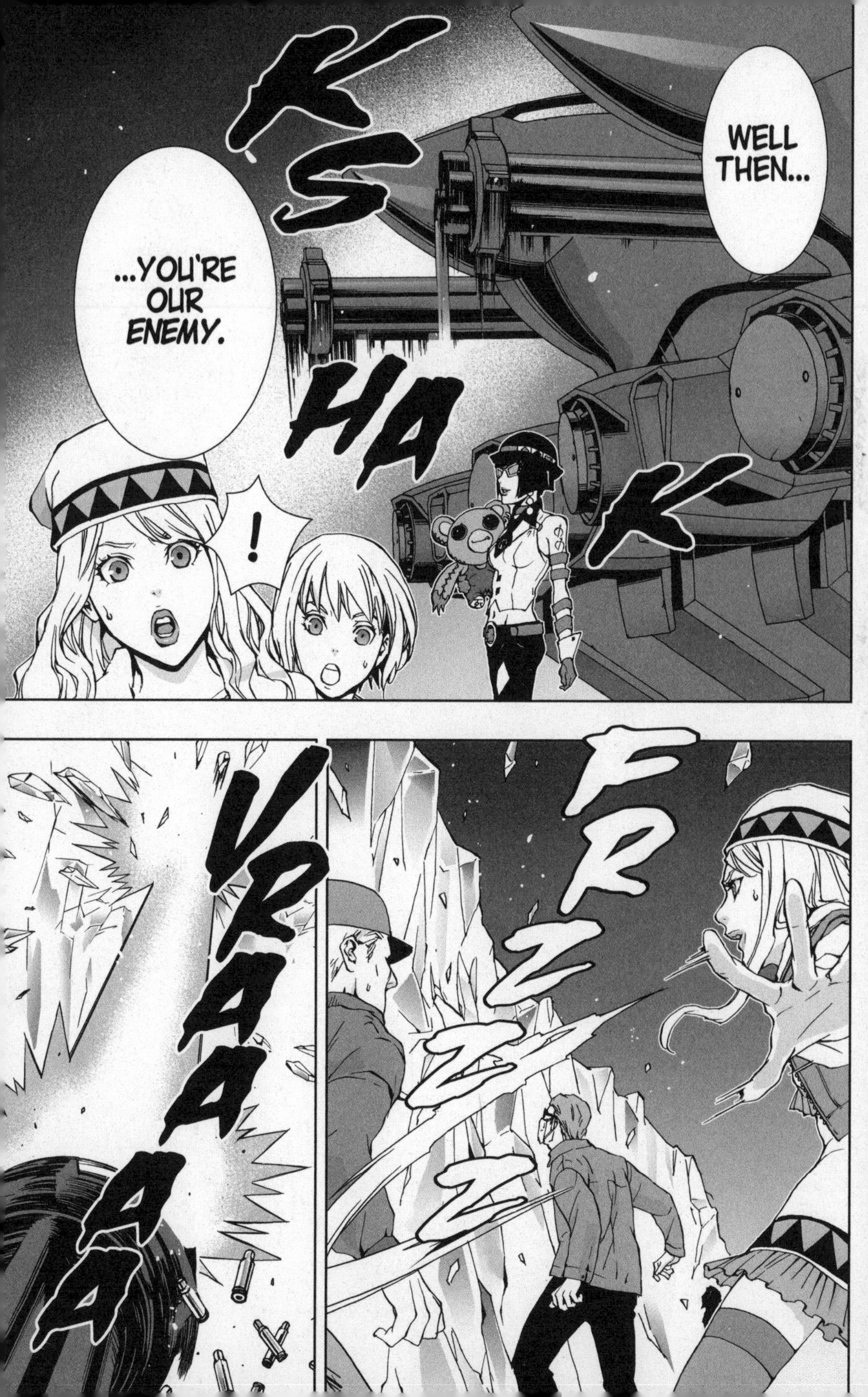
WELL THEN...
KSHAKK
...YOU'RE OUR ENEMY.
!
FRZZZZ
VRAAAAA

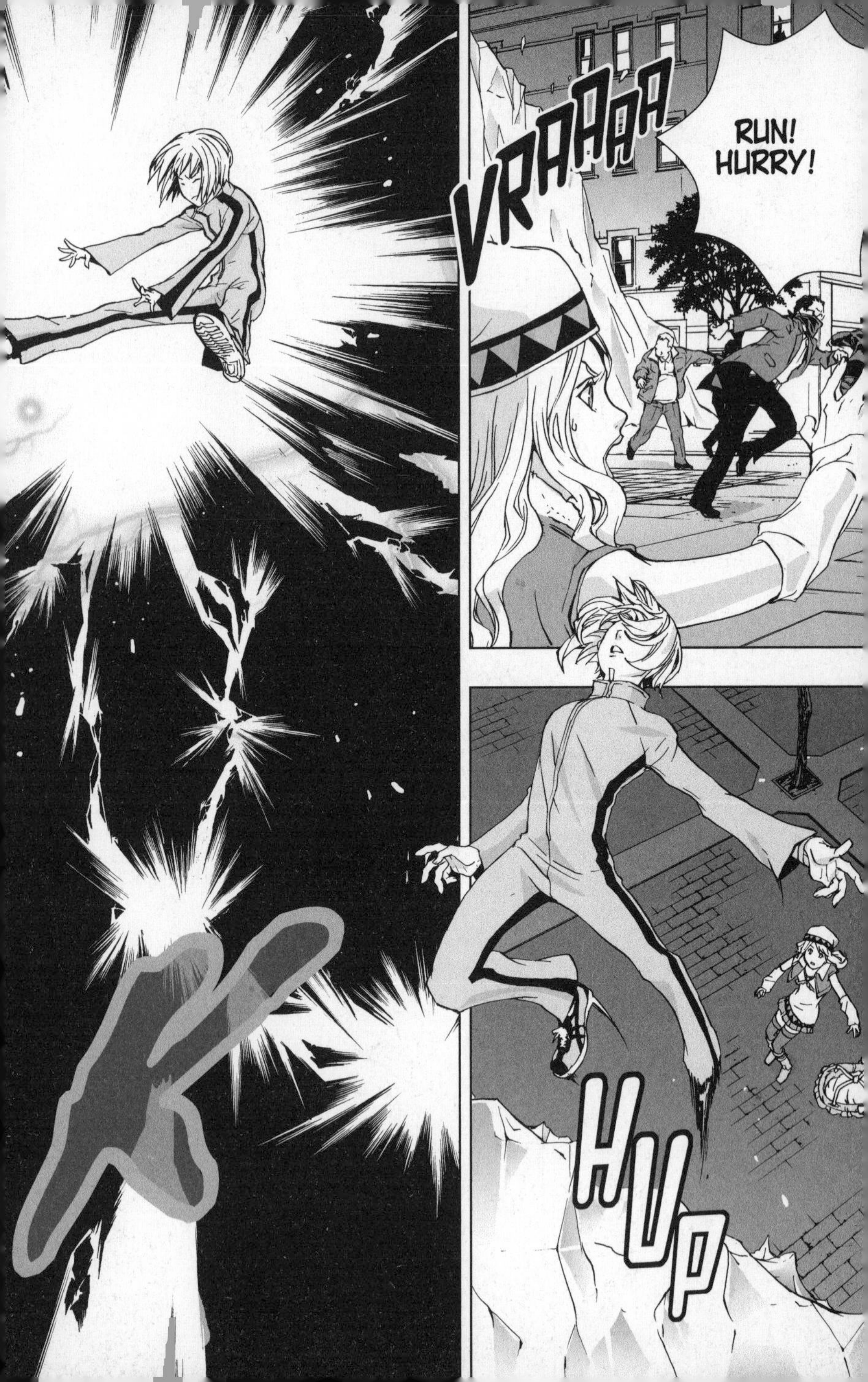
RUN! HURRY!
VRAAAA
HUP

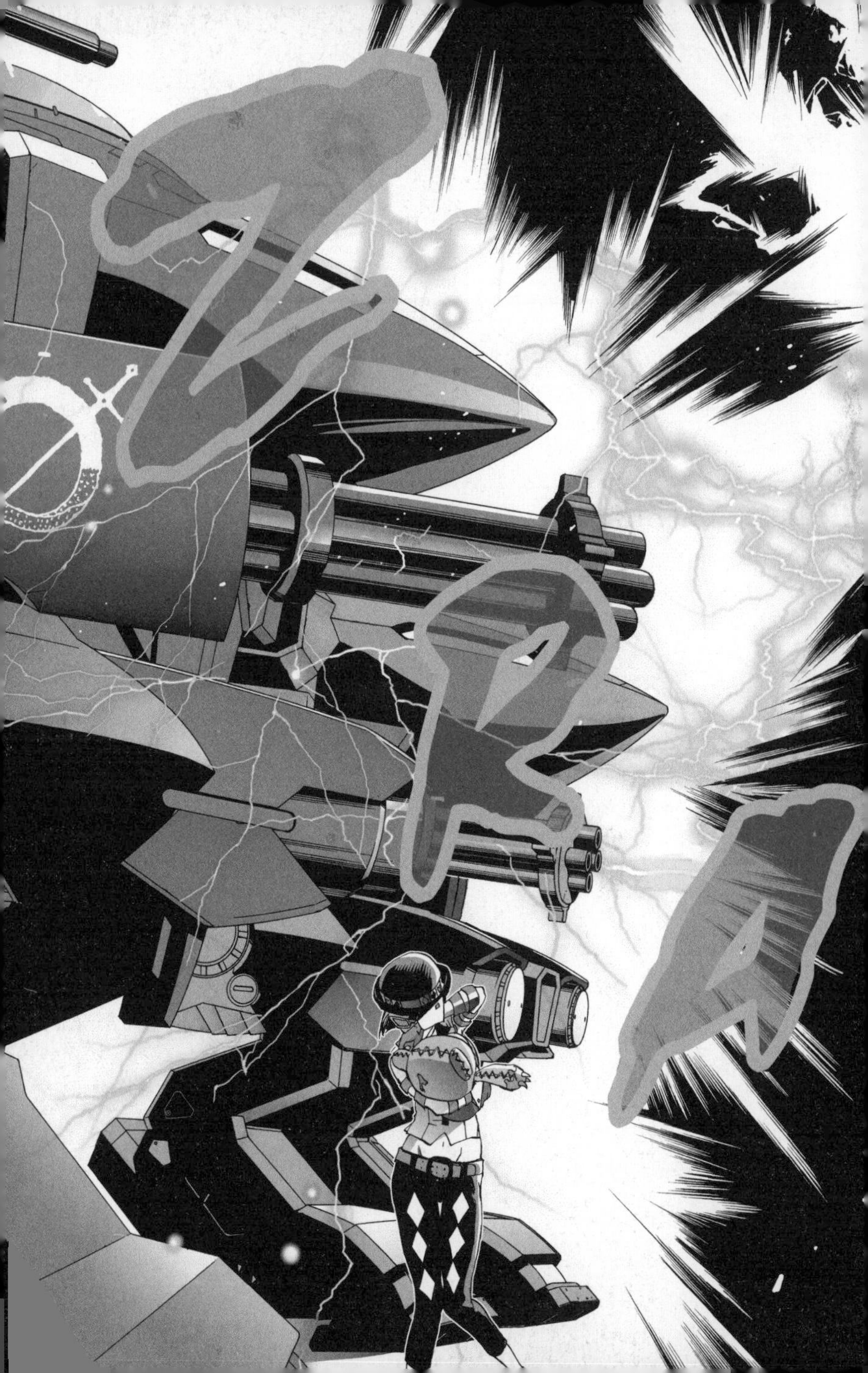

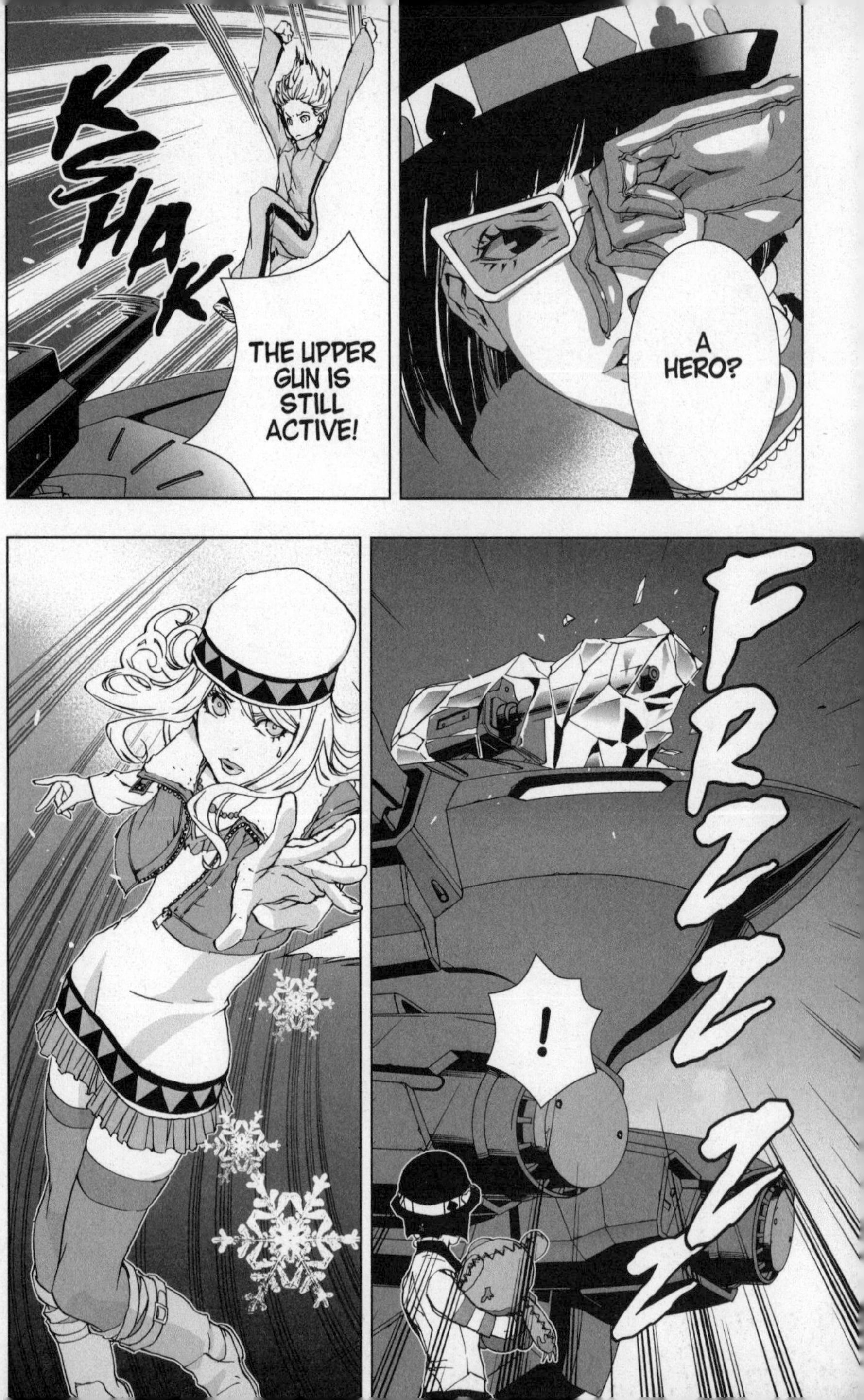
A HERO?
KSHAK
THE UPPER GUN IS STILL ACTIVE!
FRZZZZ
!

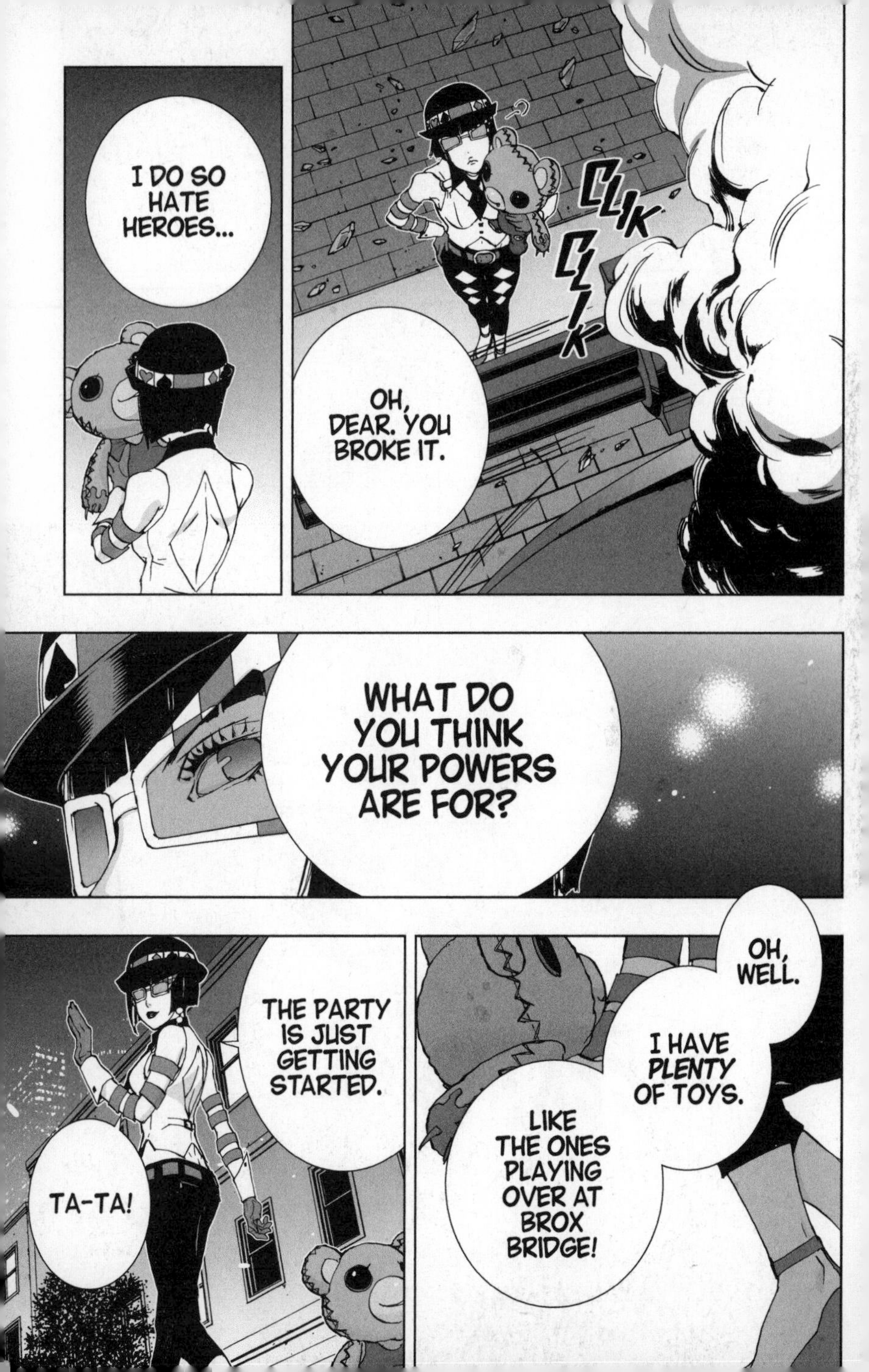
CLIK CLIK
OH, DEAR. YOU BROKE IT.
I DO SO HATE HEROES...
WHAT DO YOU THINK YOUR POWERS ARE FOR?
OH, WELL.
I HAVE PLENTY OF TOYS.
LIKE THE ONES PLAYING OVER AT BROX BRIDGE!
THE PARTY IS JUST GETTING STARTED.
TA-TA!

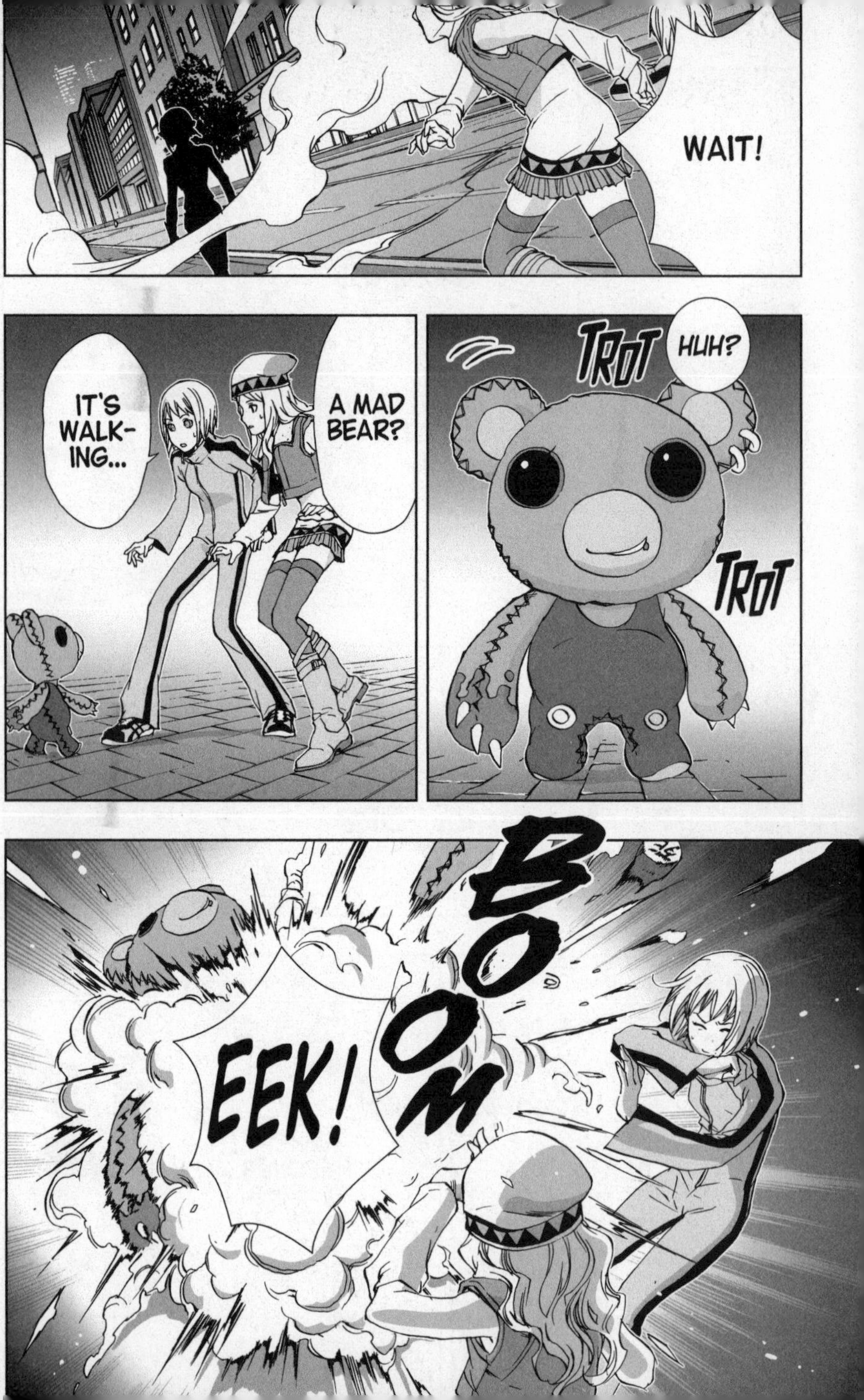
WAIT!
HUH?
TROT
TROT
A MAD BEAR?
IT'S WALKING...
BOOM
EEK!

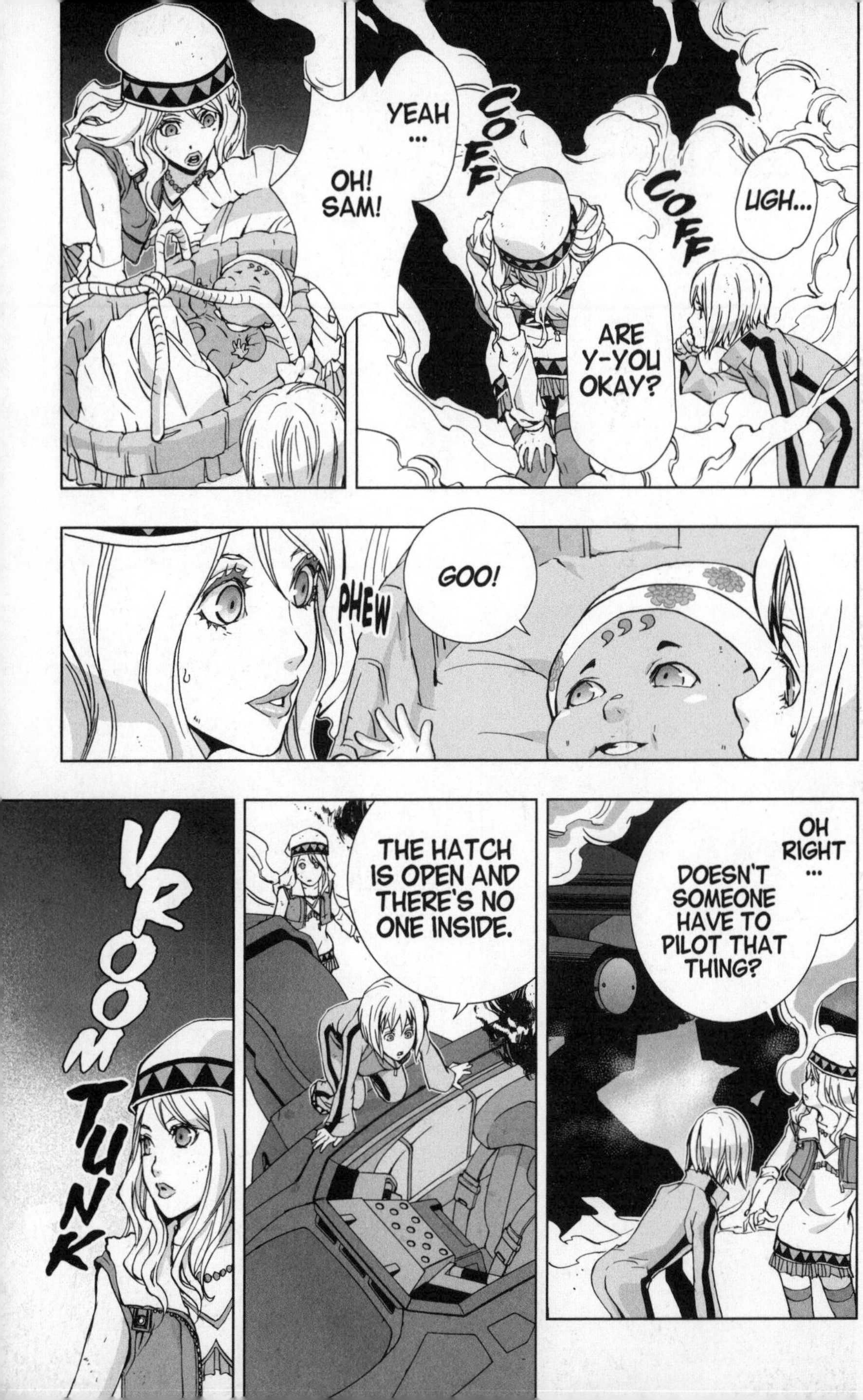
UGH...
COFF
COFF
ARE Y-YOU OKAY?
YEAH ...
OH! SAM!
GOO!
PHEW
OH RIGHT ...
DOESN'T SOMEONE HAVE TO PILOT THAT THING?
THE HATCH IS OPEN AND THERE'S NO ONE INSIDE.
VROOM
TUNK

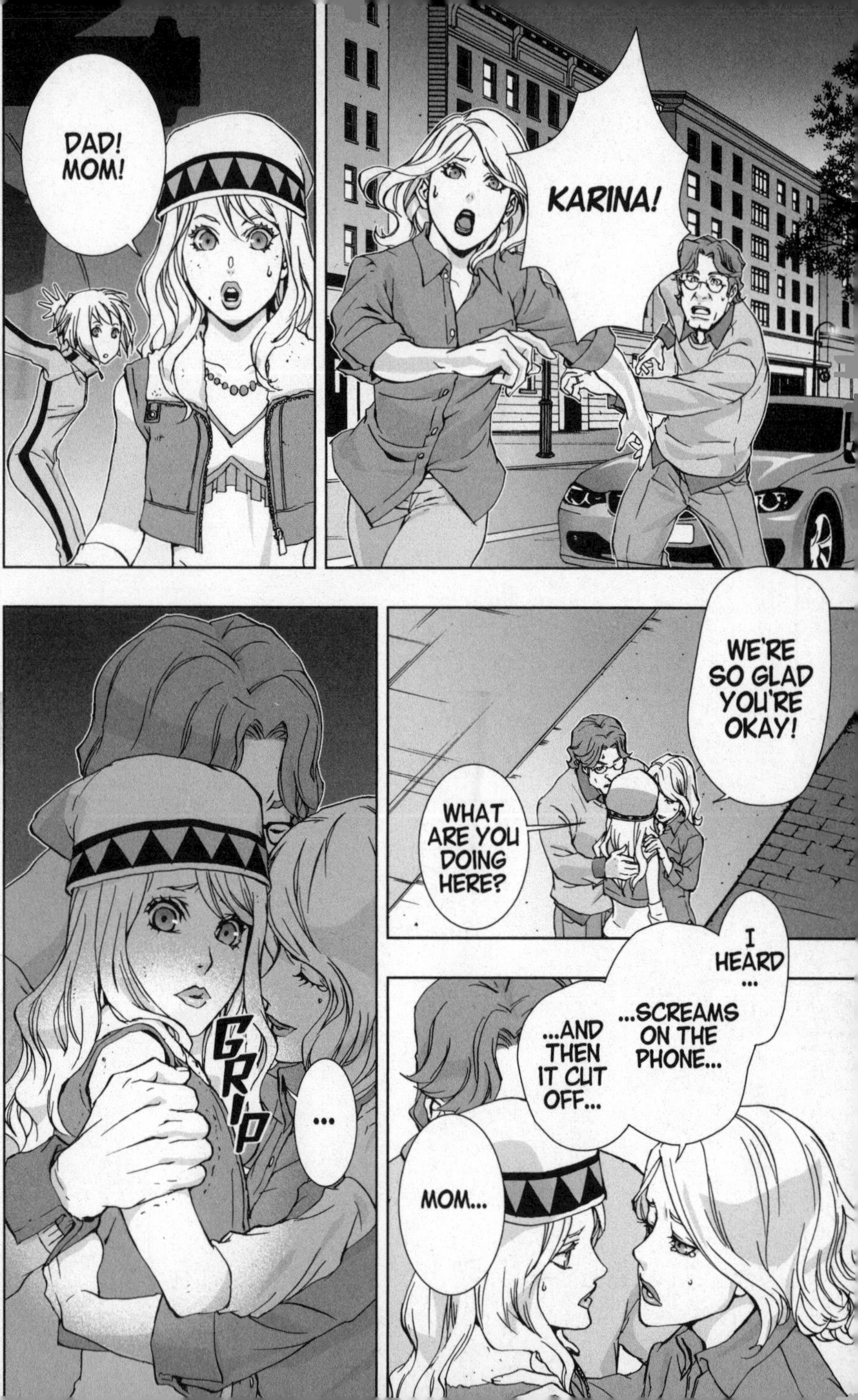
KARINA!
DAD! MOM!
WE'RE SO GLAD YOU'RE OKAY!
WHAT ARE YOU DOING HERE?
I HEARD...
...SCREAMS ON THE PHONE...
...AND THEN IT CUT OFF...
MOM...
GRIP
...

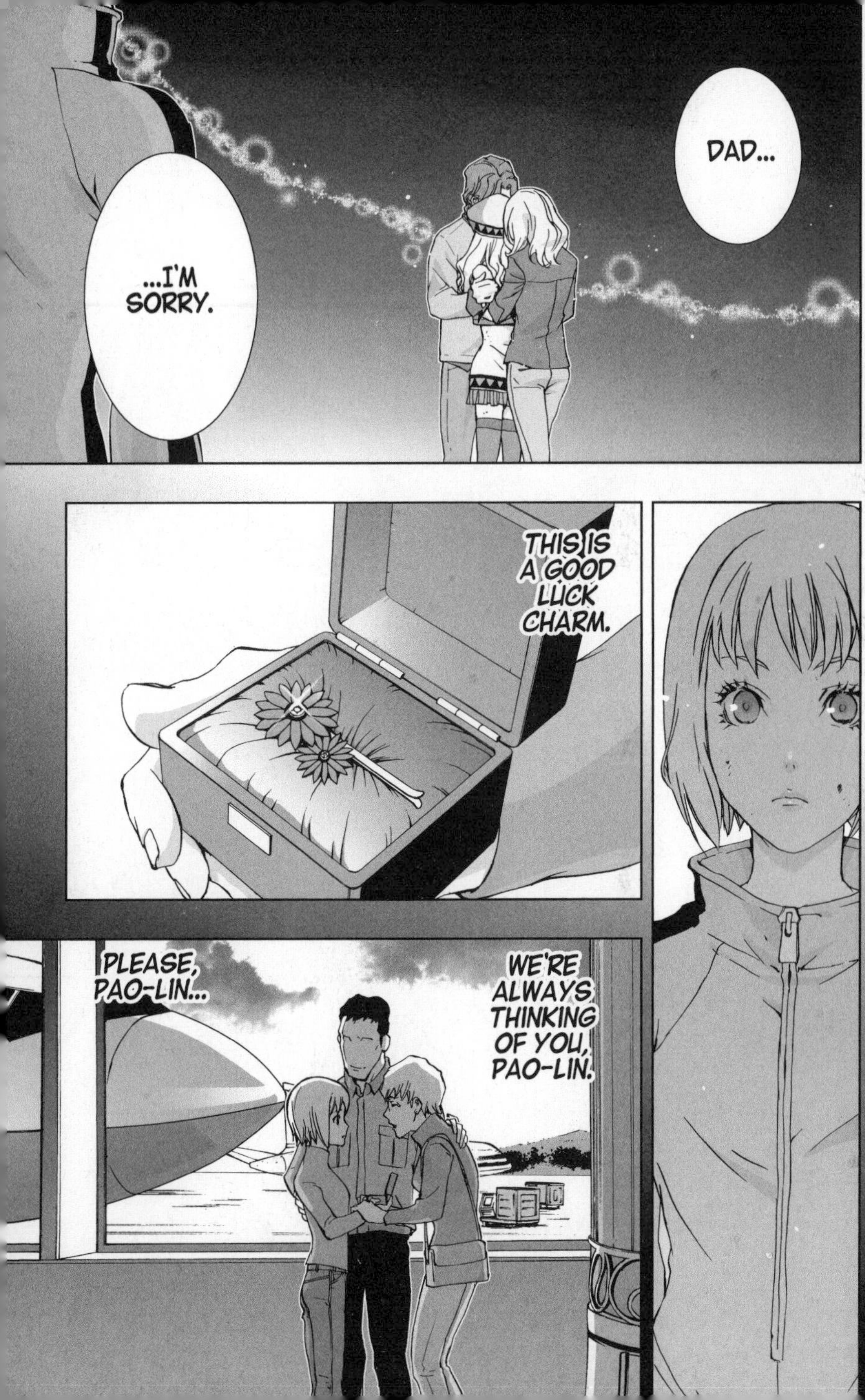
DAD...
...I'M SORRY.
THIS IS A GOOD LUCK CHARM.
WE'RE ALWAYS THINKING OF YOU, PAO-LIN.
PLEASE, PAO-LIN...

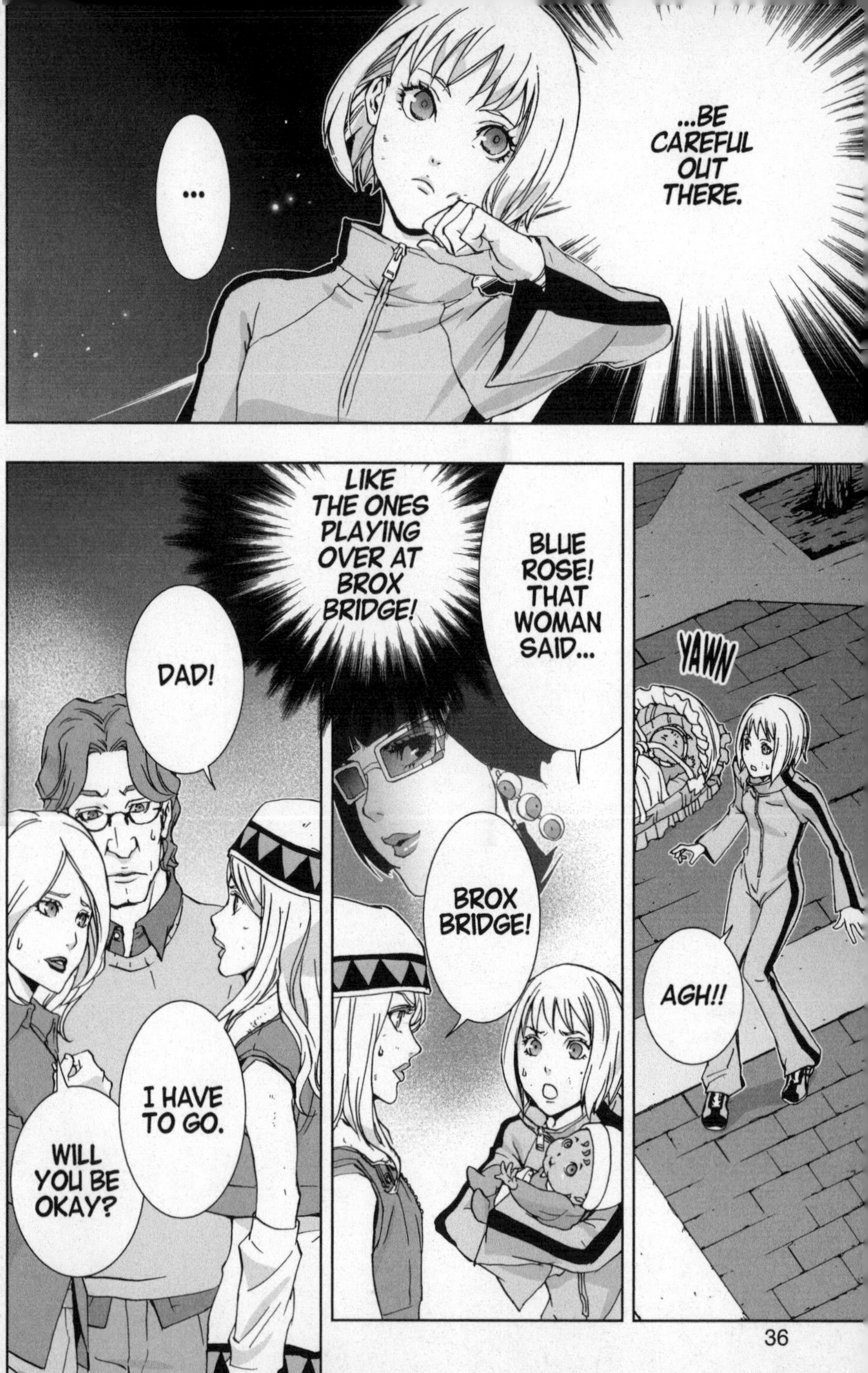
...BE CAREFUL OUT THERE.
...
YAWN
AGH!!
BLUE ROSE! THAT WOMAN SAID...
LIKE THE ONES PLAYING OVER AT BROX BRIDGE!
BROX BRIDGE!
DAD!
I HAVE TO GO.
WILL YOU BE OKAY?

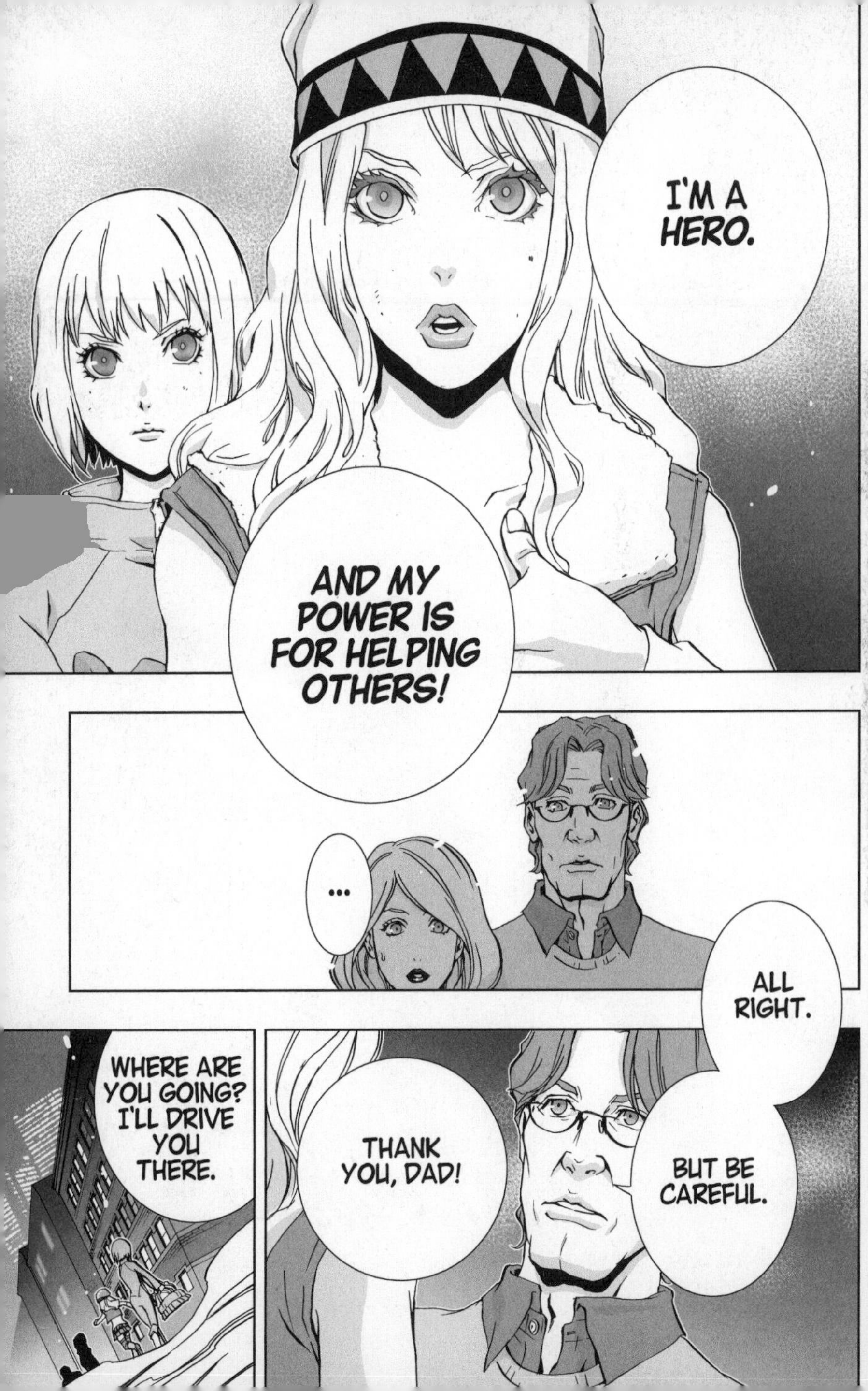
I'M A HERO.
AND MY POWER IS FOR HELPING OTHERS!
...
ALL RIGHT.
BUT BE CAREFUL.
THANK YOU, DAD!
WHERE ARE YOU GOING? I'LL DRIVE YOU THERE.

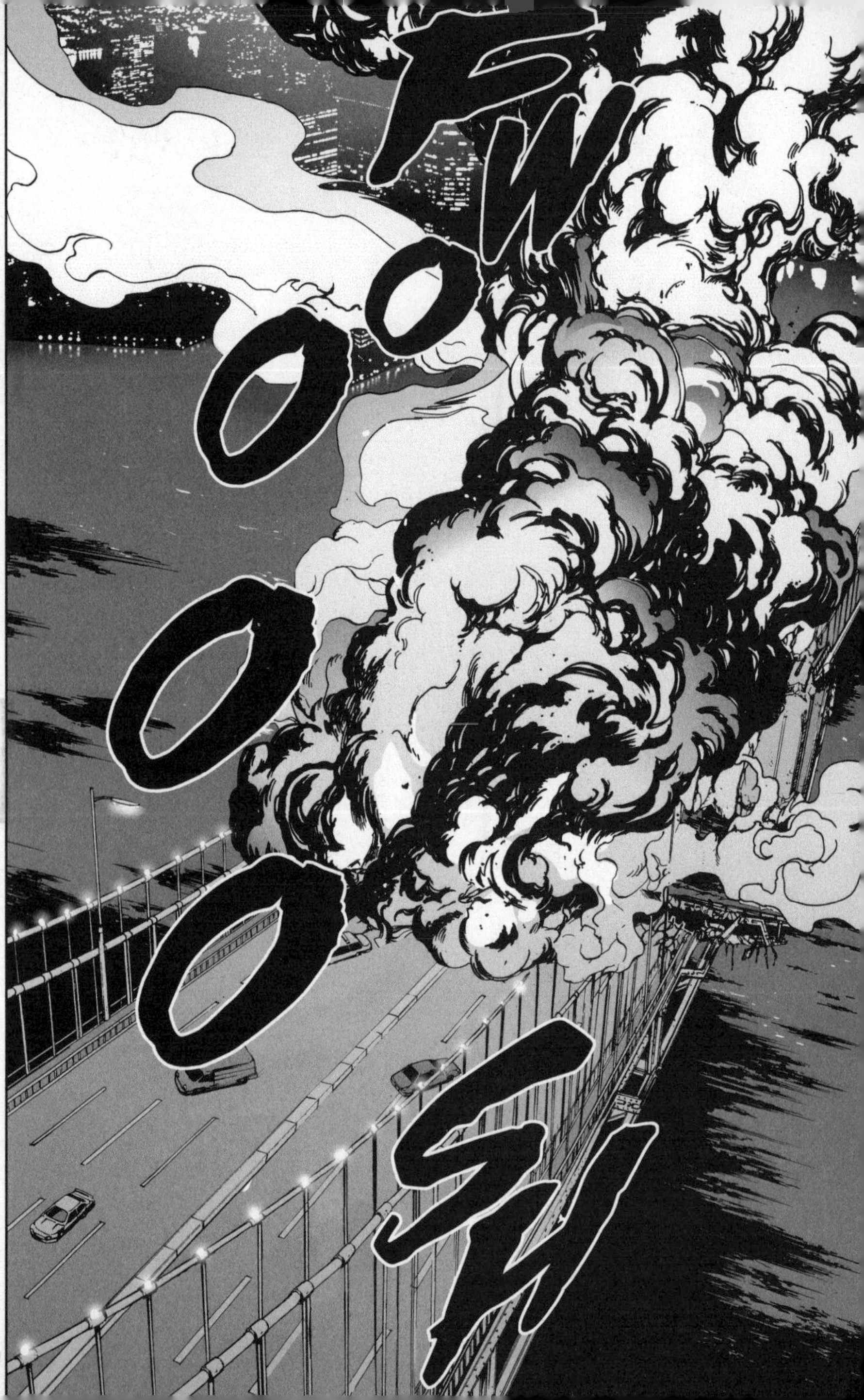
FWOOOOSH

#19 Spare the Rod and Spoil the Child, Part 3

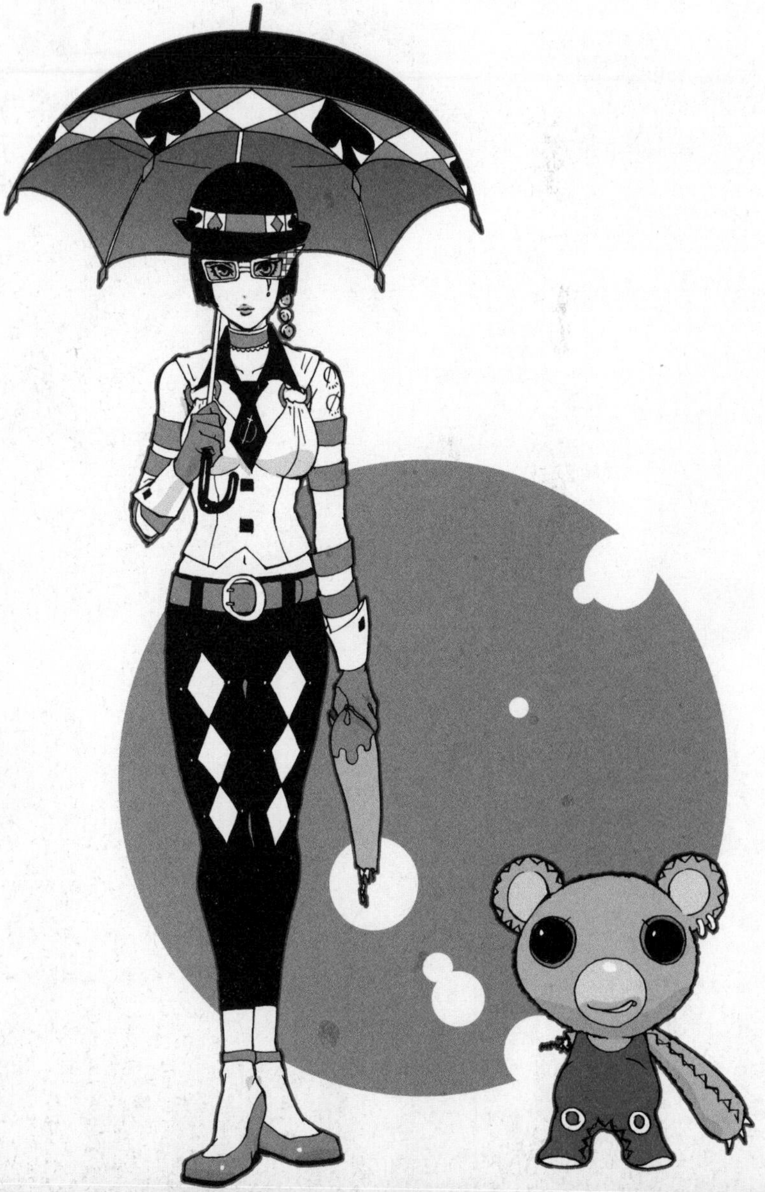

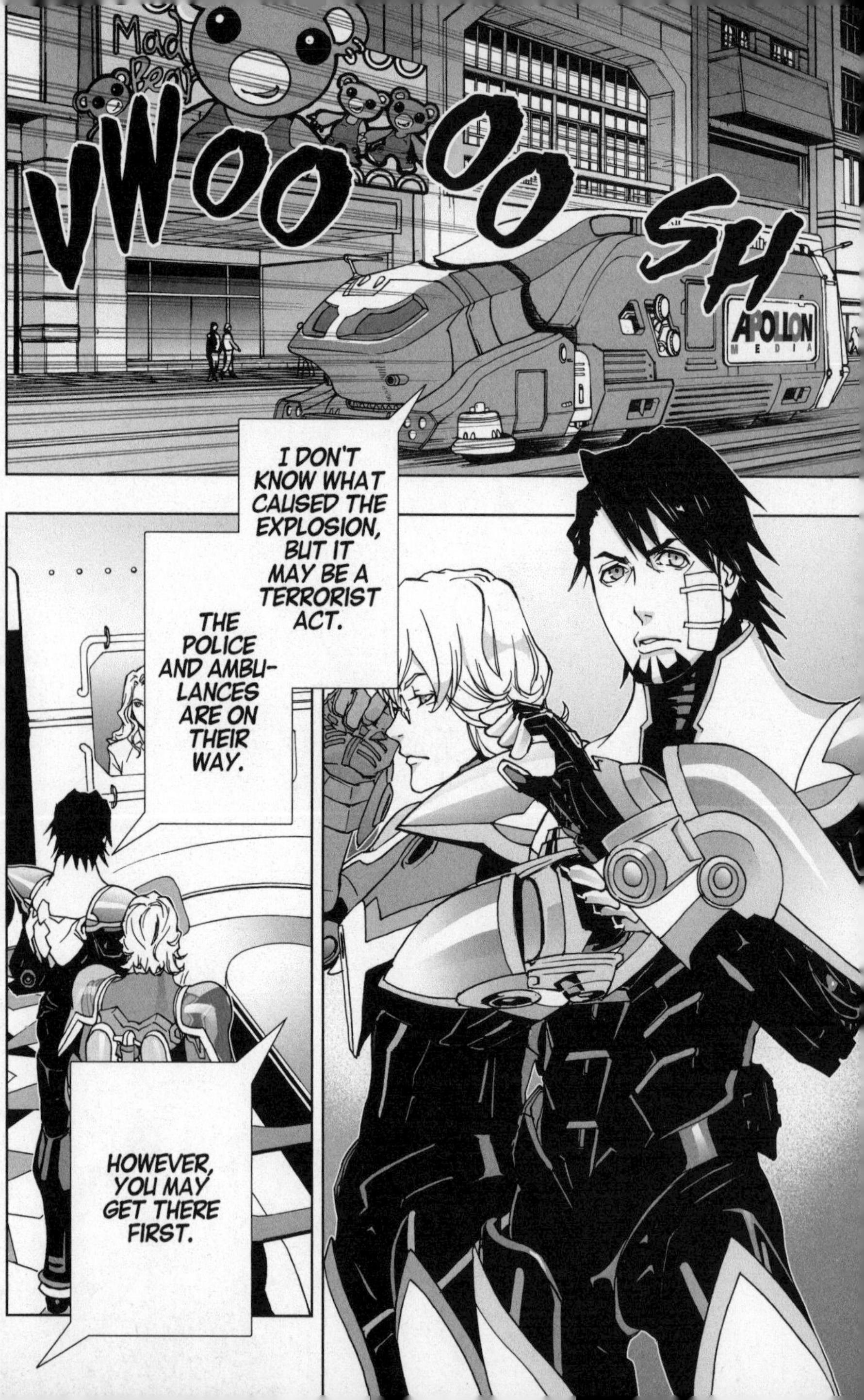
VWOOOOSH
APOLLON MEDIA
I DON'T KNOW WHAT CAUSED THE EXPLOSION, BUT IT MAY BE A TERRORIST ACT.
THE POLICE AND AMBU-LANCES ARE ON THEIR WAY.
HOWEVER, YOU MAY GET THERE FIRST.

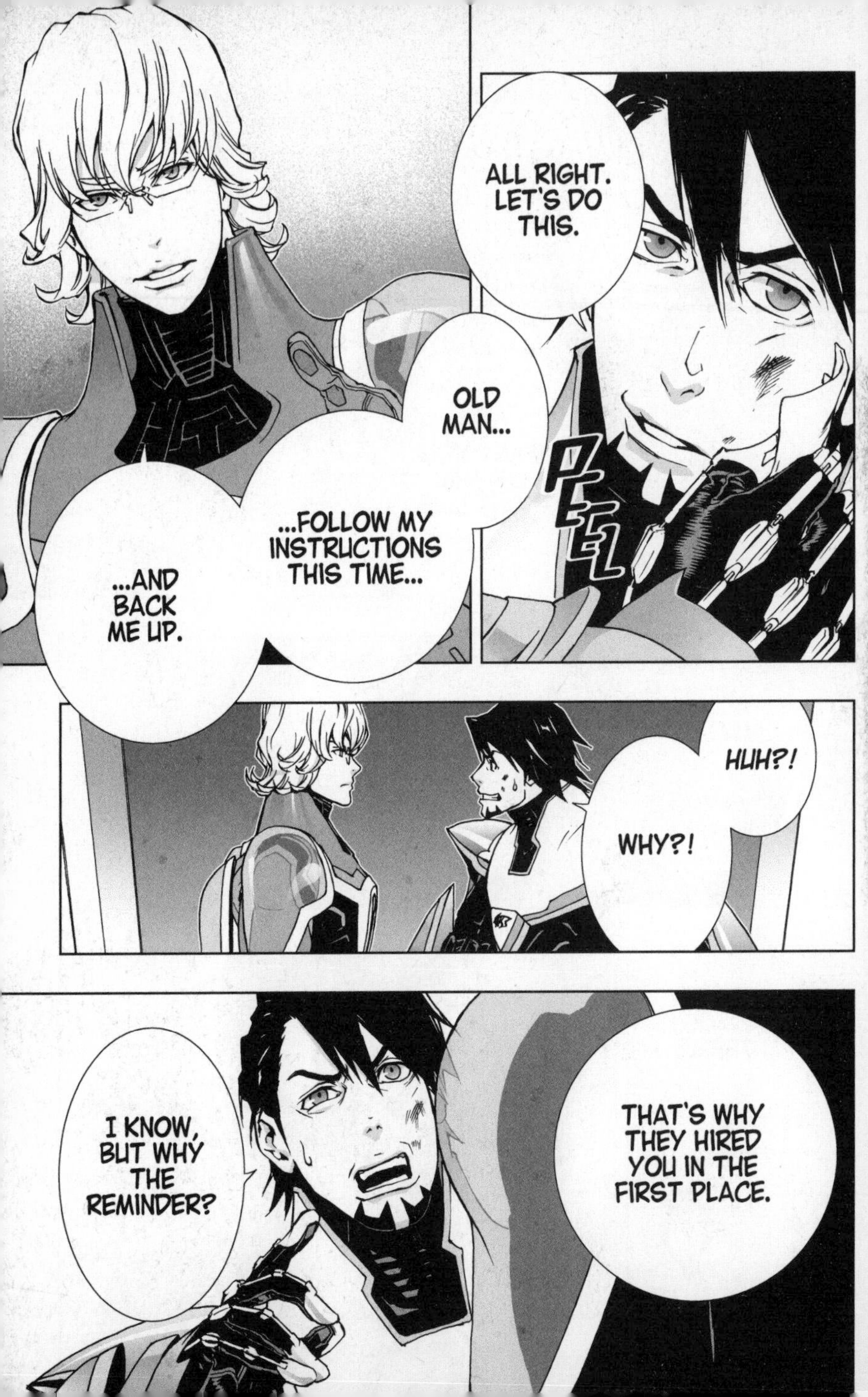
ALL RIGHT. LET'S DO THIS.
PEEL
OLD MAN...
...FOLLOW MY INSTRUCTIONS THIS TIME...
...AND BACK ME UP.
HUH?!
WHY?!
THAT'S WHY THEY HIRED YOU IN THE FIRST PLACE.
I KNOW, BUT WHY THE REMINDER?

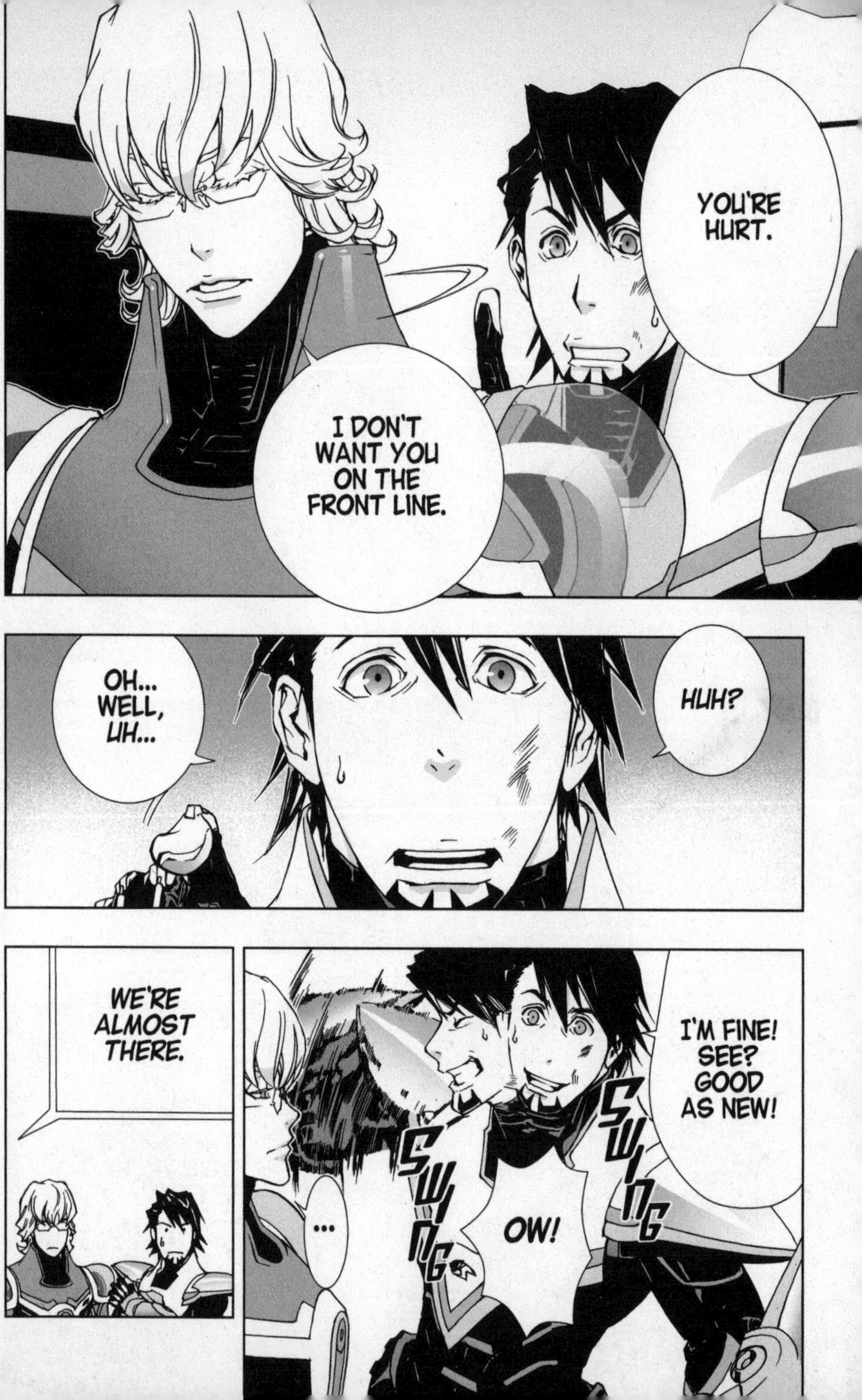
YOU'RE HURT.
I DON'T WANT YOU ON THE FRONT LINE.
HUH?
OH... WELL, UH...
I'M FINE! SEE? GOOD AS NEW!
SWING
SWING
OW!
...
WE'RE ALMOST THERE.

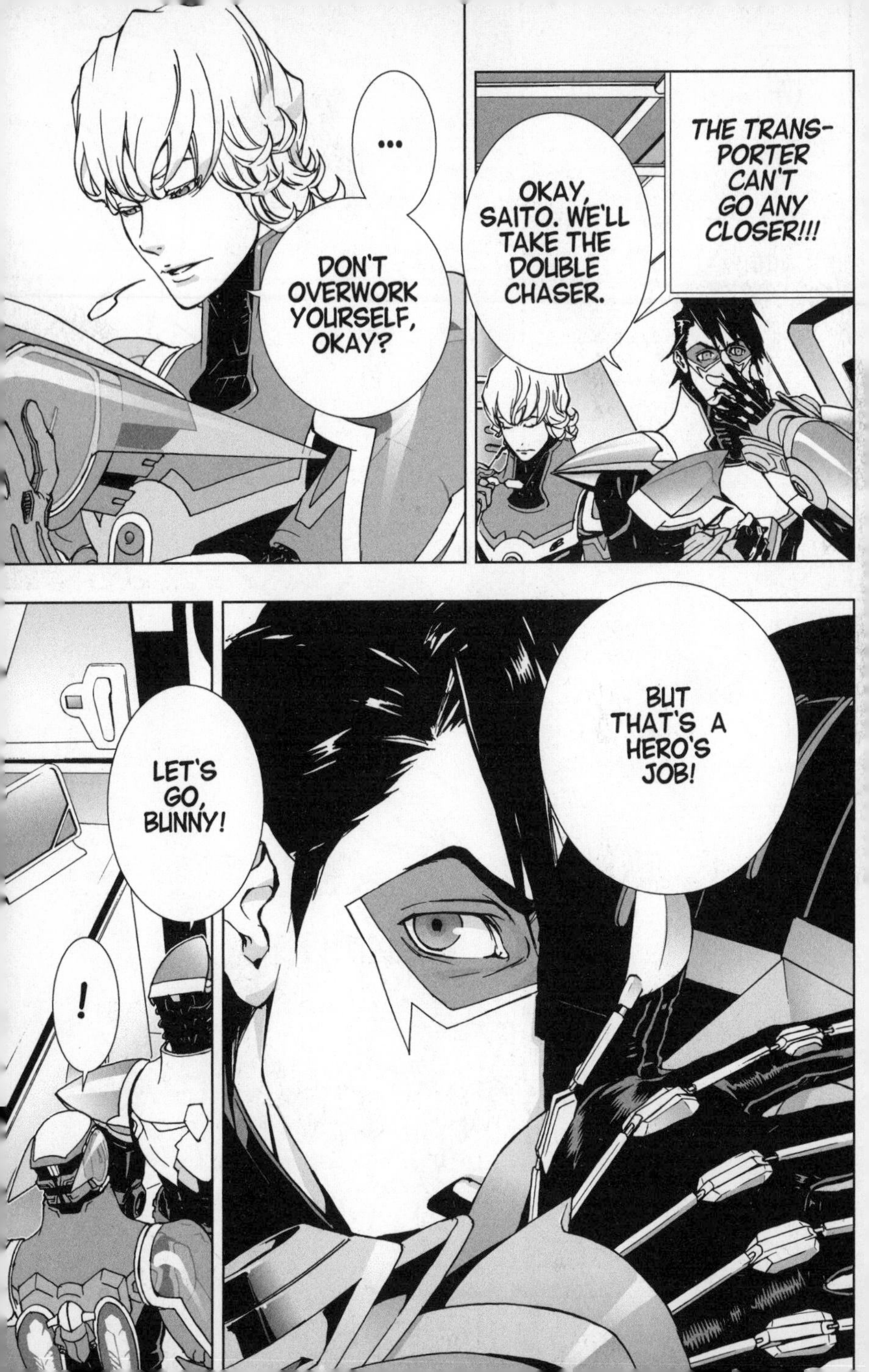
THE TRANS-PORTER CAN'T GO ANY CLOSER!!!
OKAY, SAITO. WE'LL TAKE THE DOUBLE CHASER.
...
DON'T OVERWORK YOURSELF, OKAY?
BUT THAT'S A HERO'S JOB!
LET'S GO, BUNNY!
!

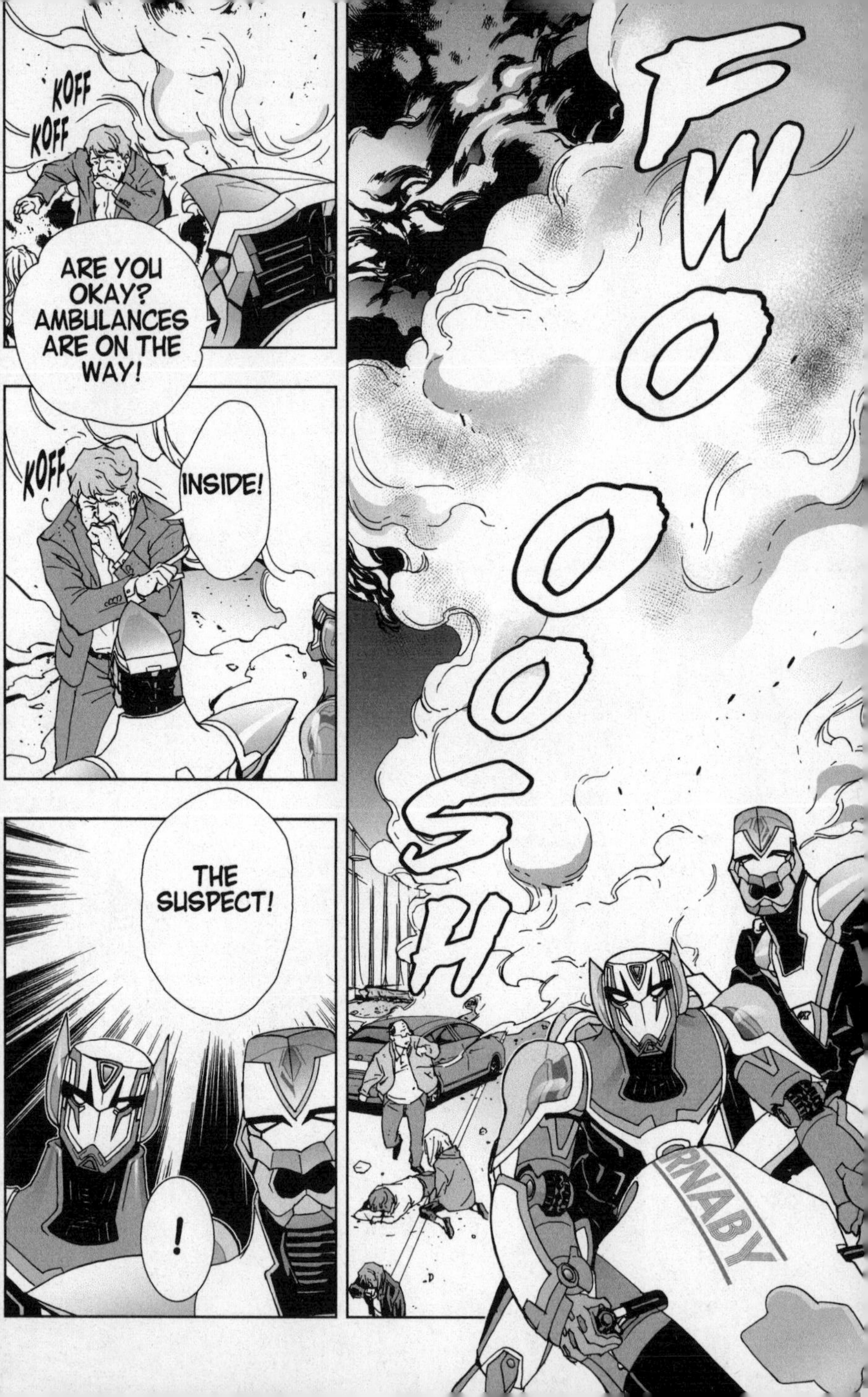
FWOOOOSH
RNABY
KOFF KOFF
ARE YOU OKAY? AMBULANCES ARE ON THE WAY!
KOFF
INSIDE!
THE SUSPECT!
!

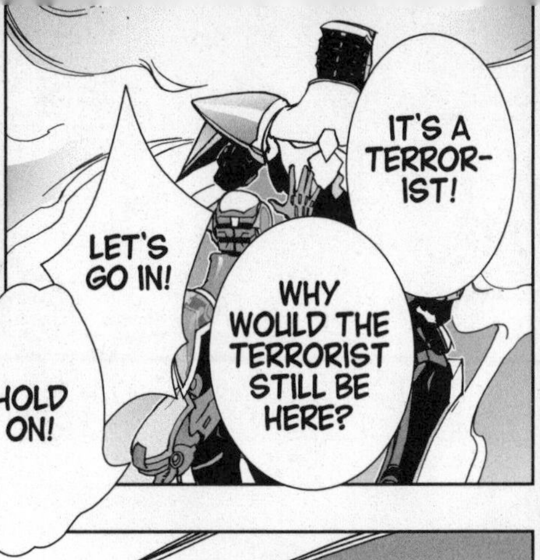
IT'S A TERROR-IST!
WHY WOULD THE TERRORIST STILL BE HERE?
LET'S GO IN!
HOLD ON!
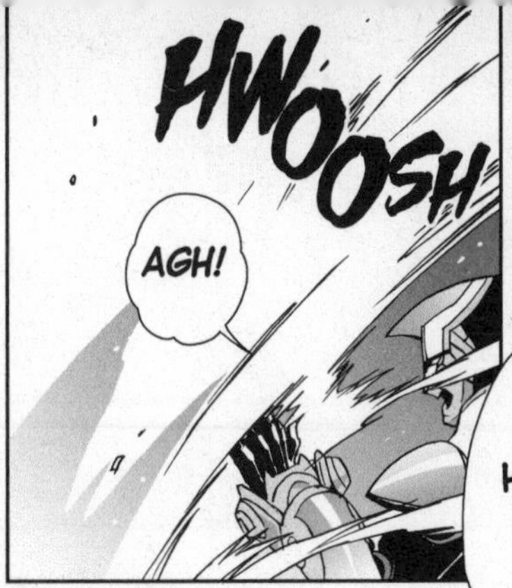
HWOOSH
AGH!
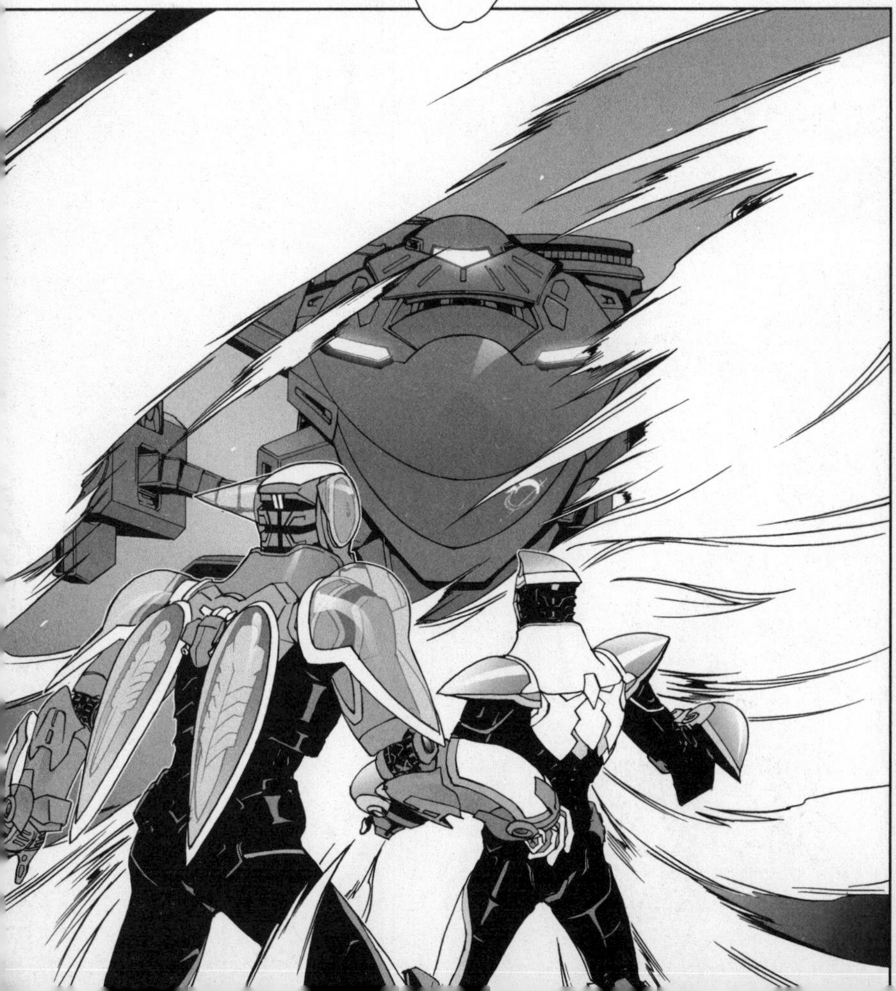

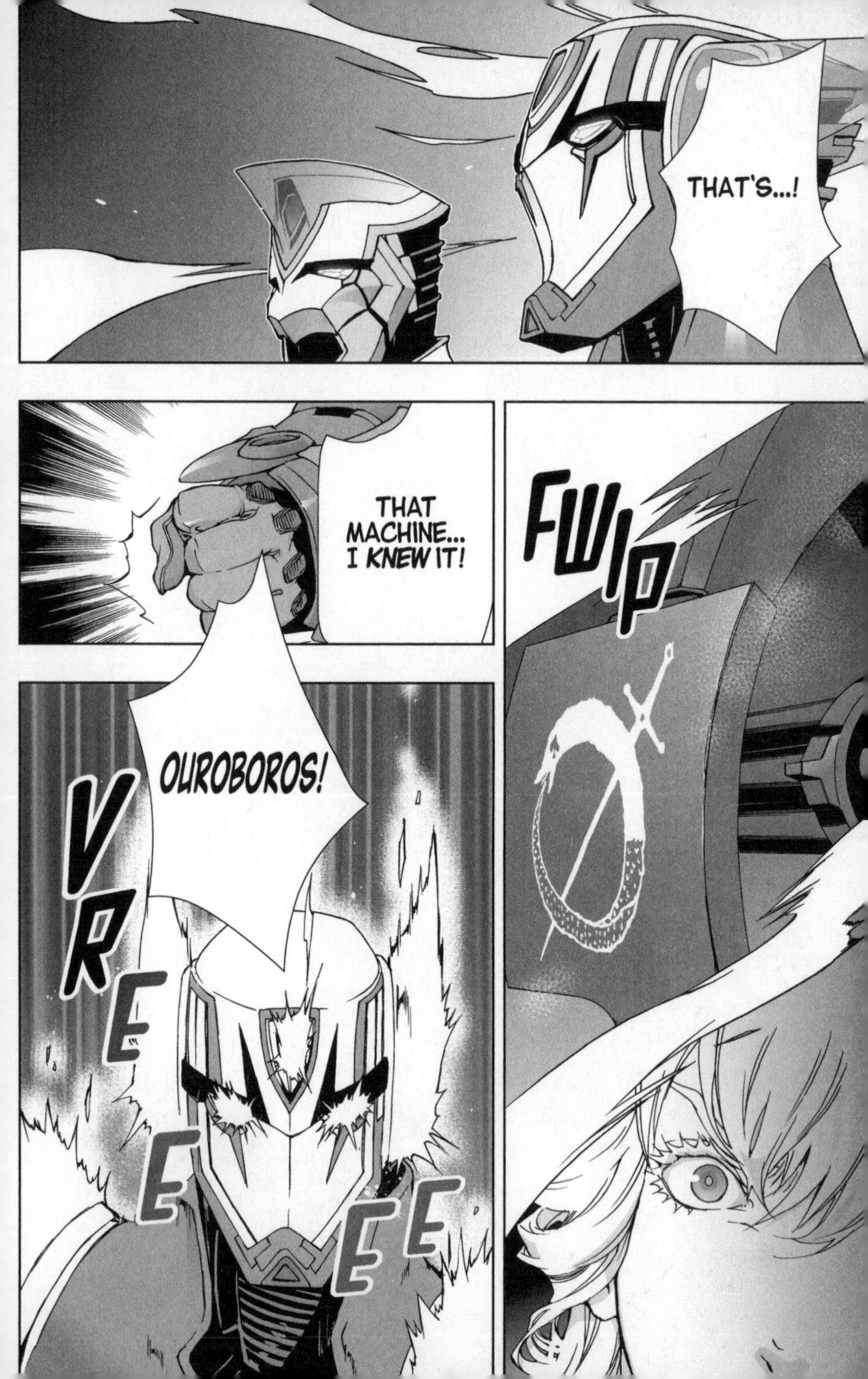
THAT'S...!
FWIP
THAT MACHINE... I KNEW IT!
OUROBOROS!
VREEEEE

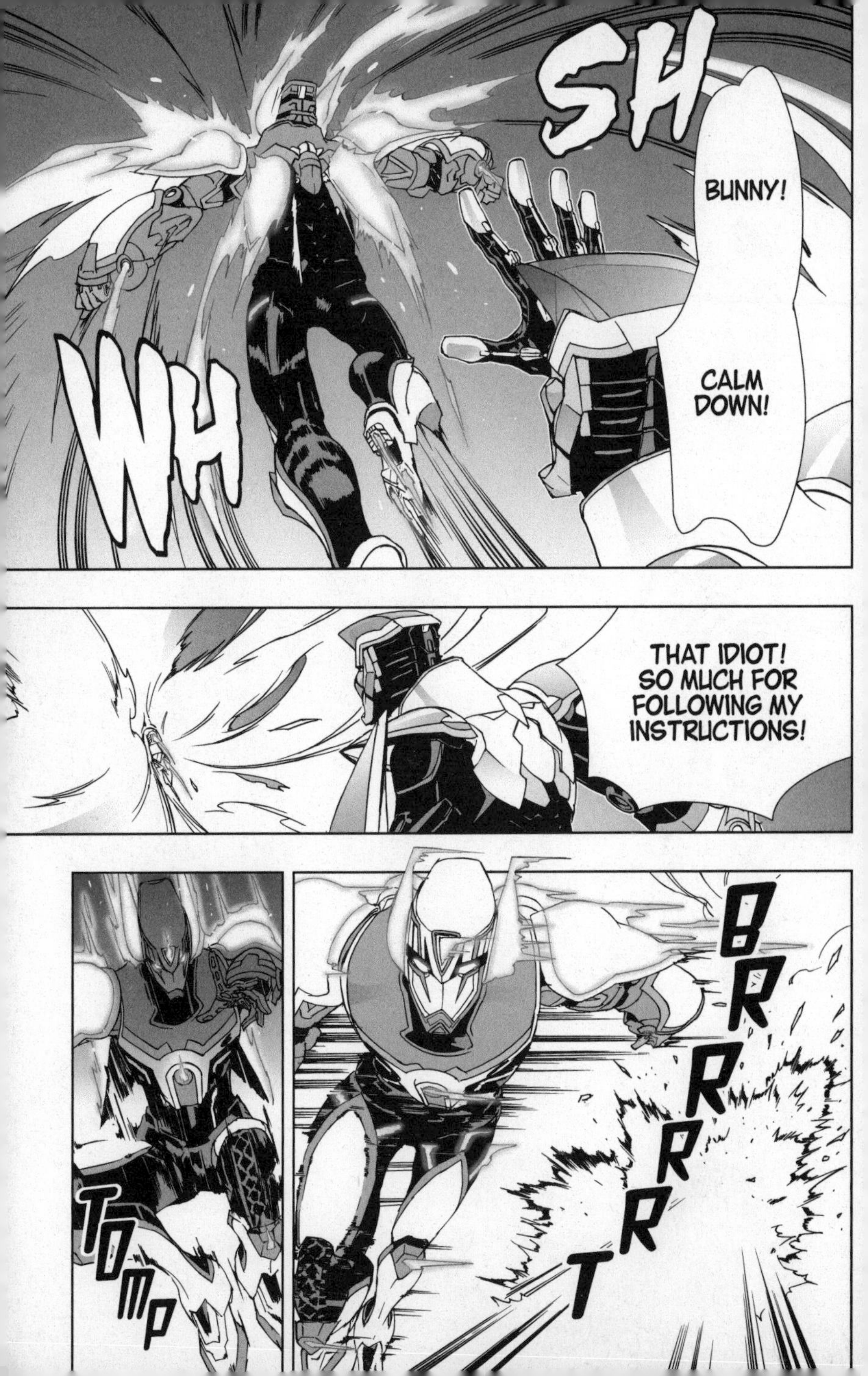
BUNNY! CALM DOWN!
SH
WH
THAT IDIOT! SO MUCH FOR FOLLOWING MY INSTRUCTIONS!
BRRRRRT
TOMP

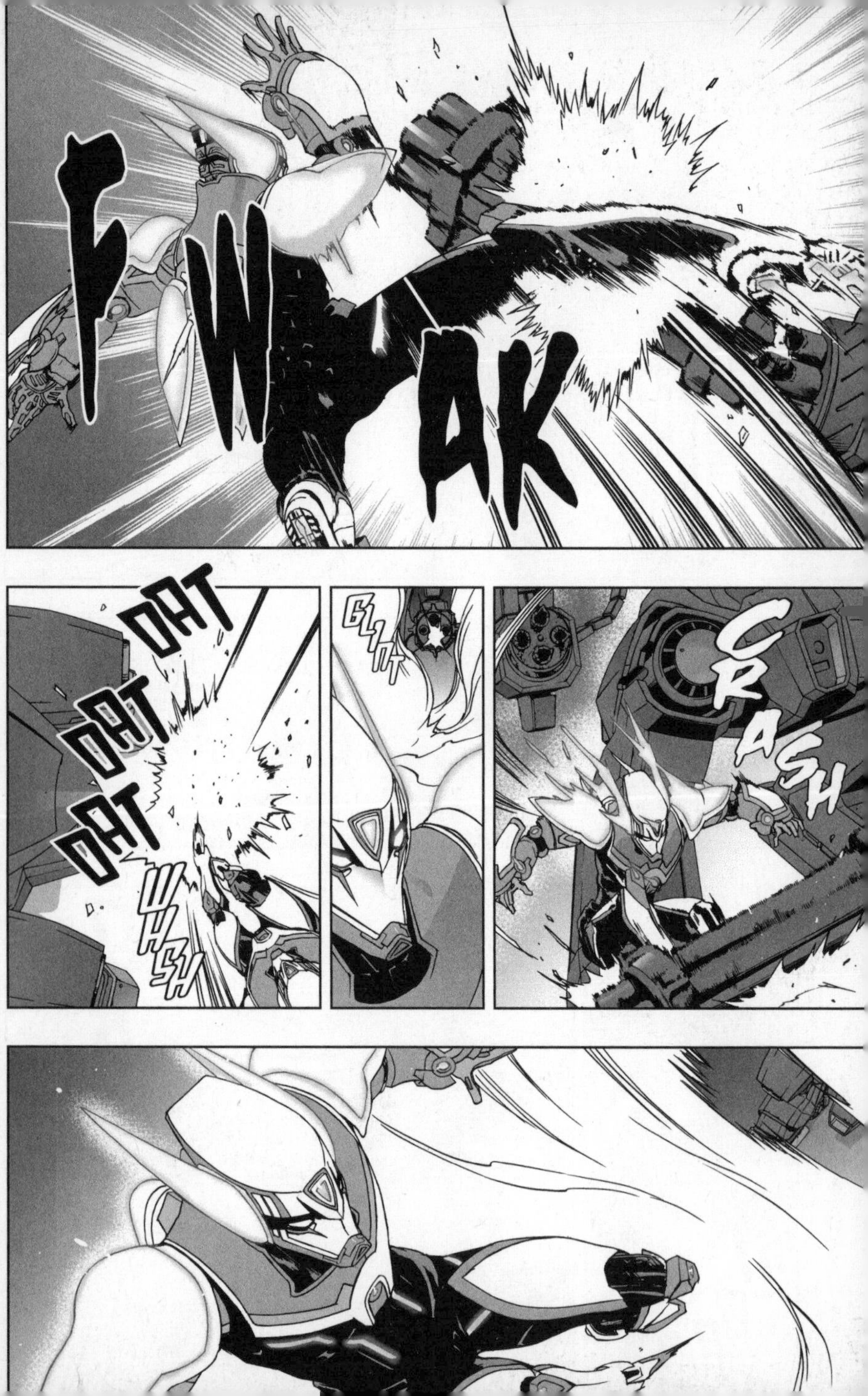
FWAK
CRASH
GLINT
DAT DAT DAT DAT
SHSH

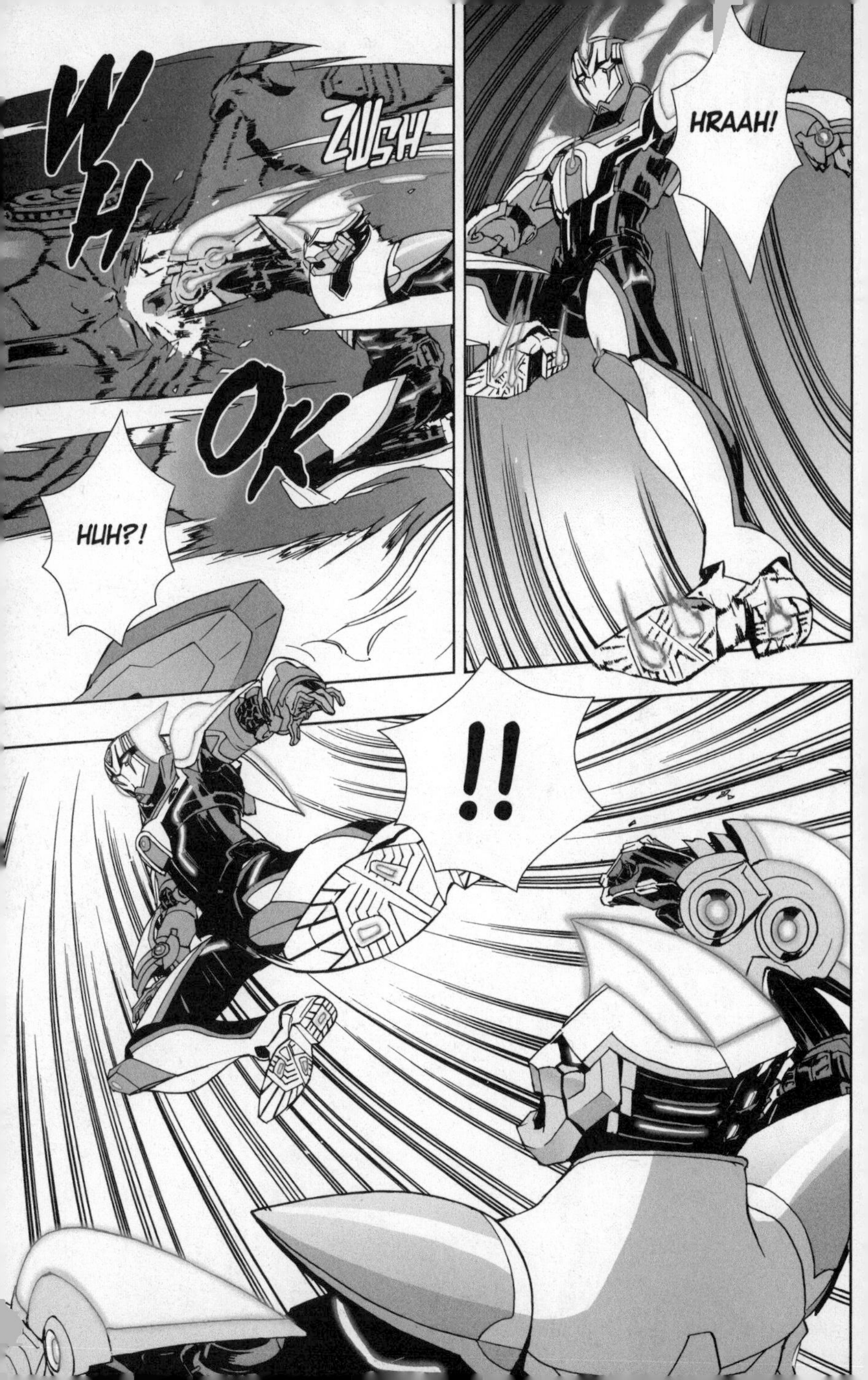
HRAAH!
ZUSH
WHOK
HUH?!
!!

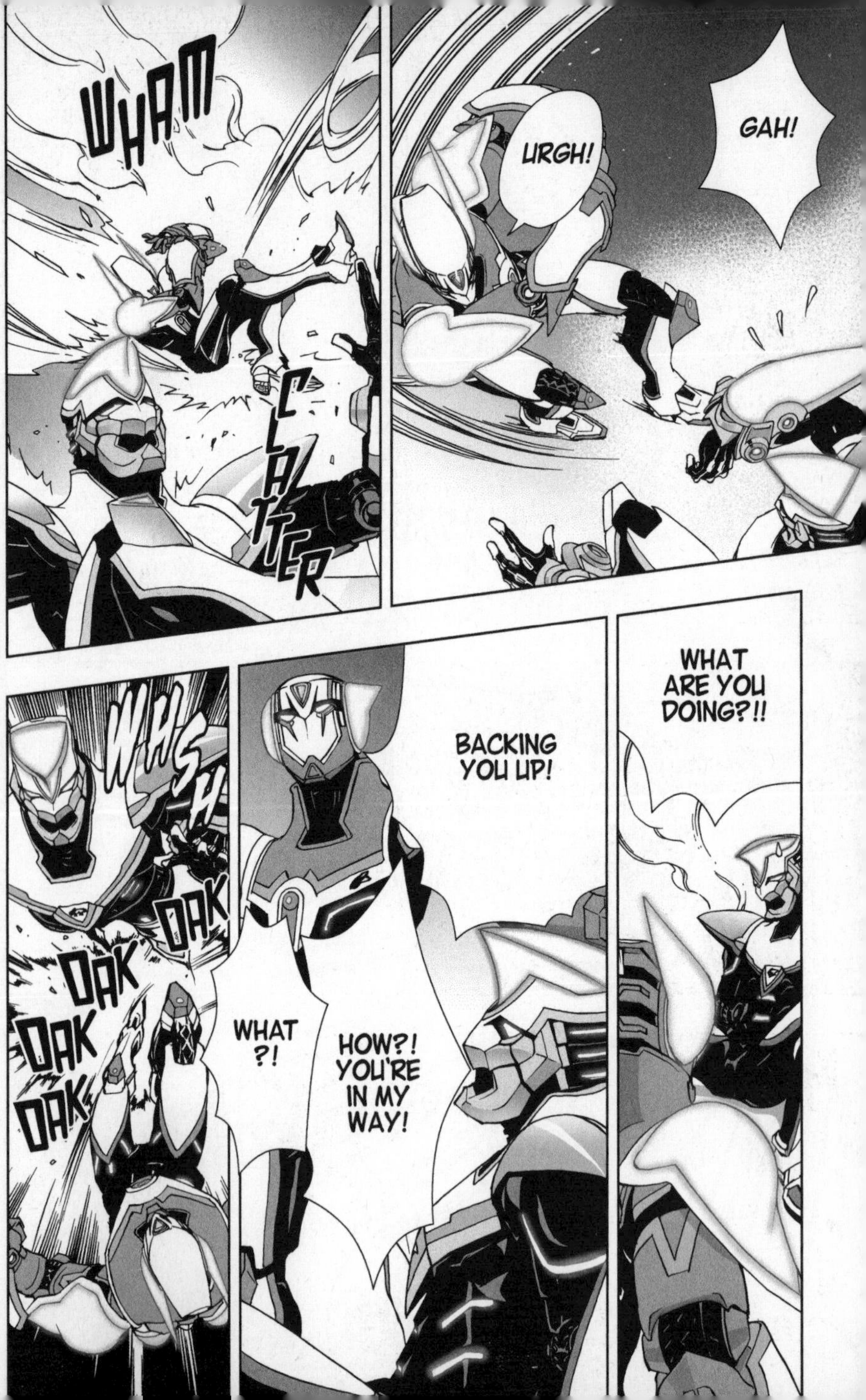
GAH!
URGH!
WHAM
CLATTER
WHAT ARE YOU DOING?!!
BACKING YOU UP!
WHAT ?! HOW?! YOU'RE IN MY WAY!
WHASH
DAK
DAK
DAK
DAK

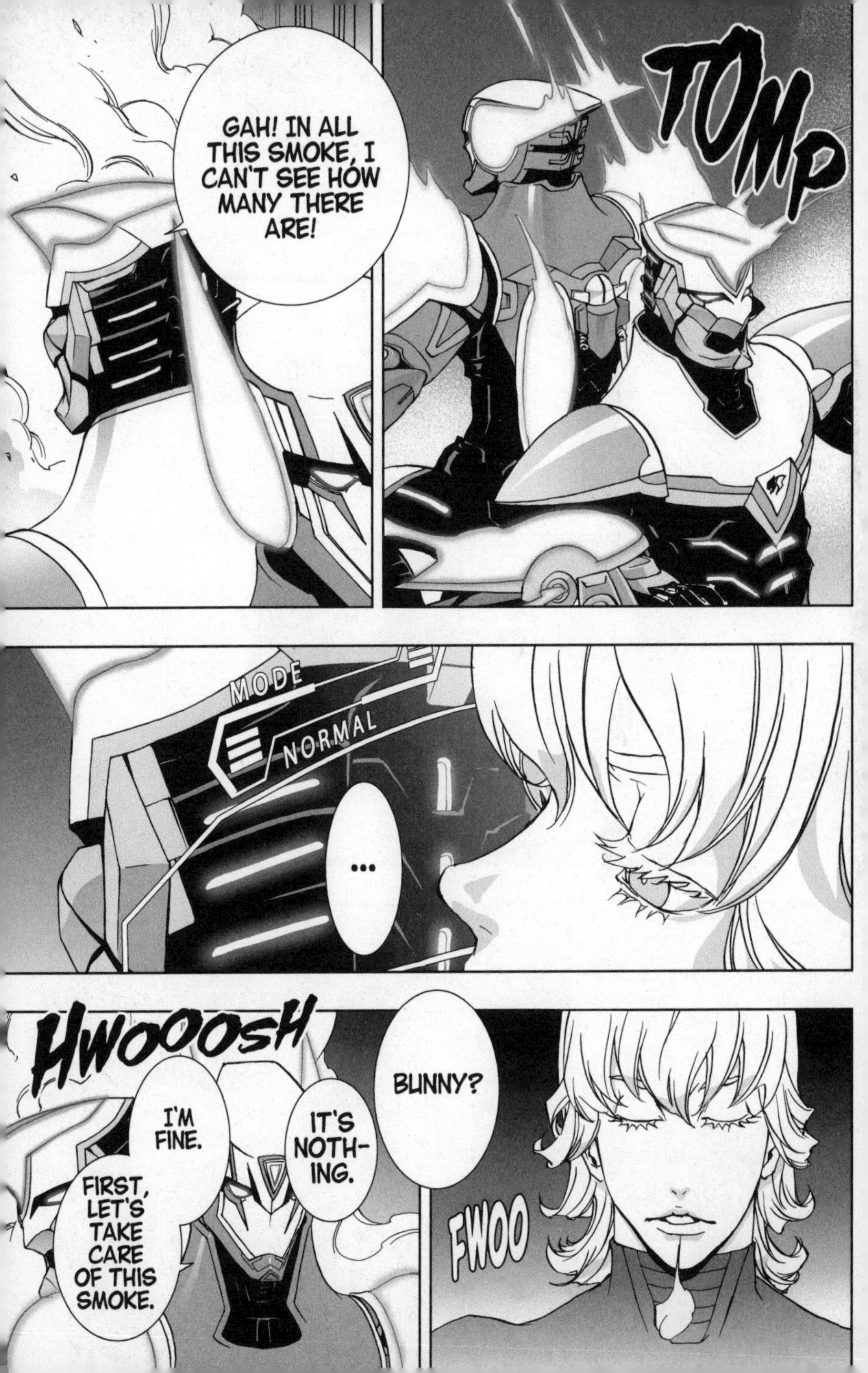
TOMP
GAH! IN ALL THIS SMOKE, I CAN'T SEE HOW MANY THERE ARE!
MODE
NORMAL
...
FWOO
HWOOOSH
BUNNY?
IT'S NOTHING.
I'M FINE.
FIRST, LET'S TAKE CARE OF THIS SMOKE.

SKY HIGH! YOU CAME AT THE PERFECT TIME!

OOOS!

HWA

SKY HIGH!

YOU GOT IT!

AGNES! GET SKY HIGH TO BLOW AWAY THE SMOKE!

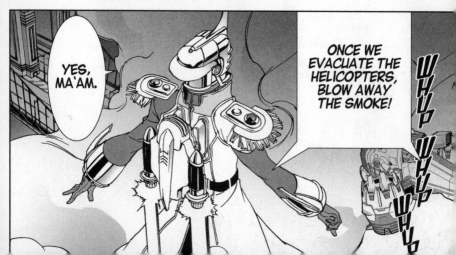

YES, MA'AM.

ONCE WE EVACUATE THE HELICOPTERS, BLOW AWAY THE SMOKE!

WHUP WHUP WHUP

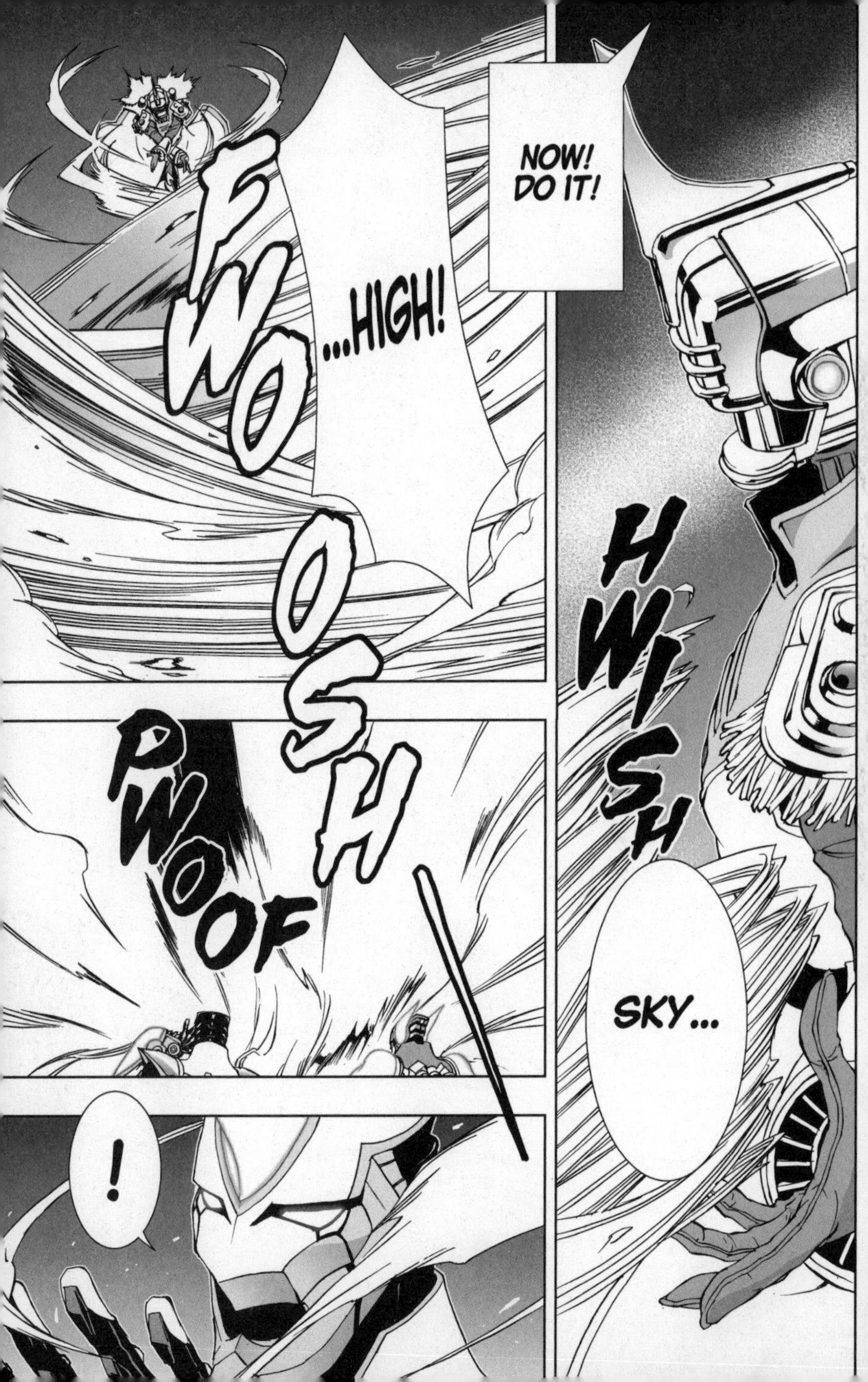
NOW! DO IT!
HWISH
SKY...
FWOOOSH
...HIGH!
PWOOF
!

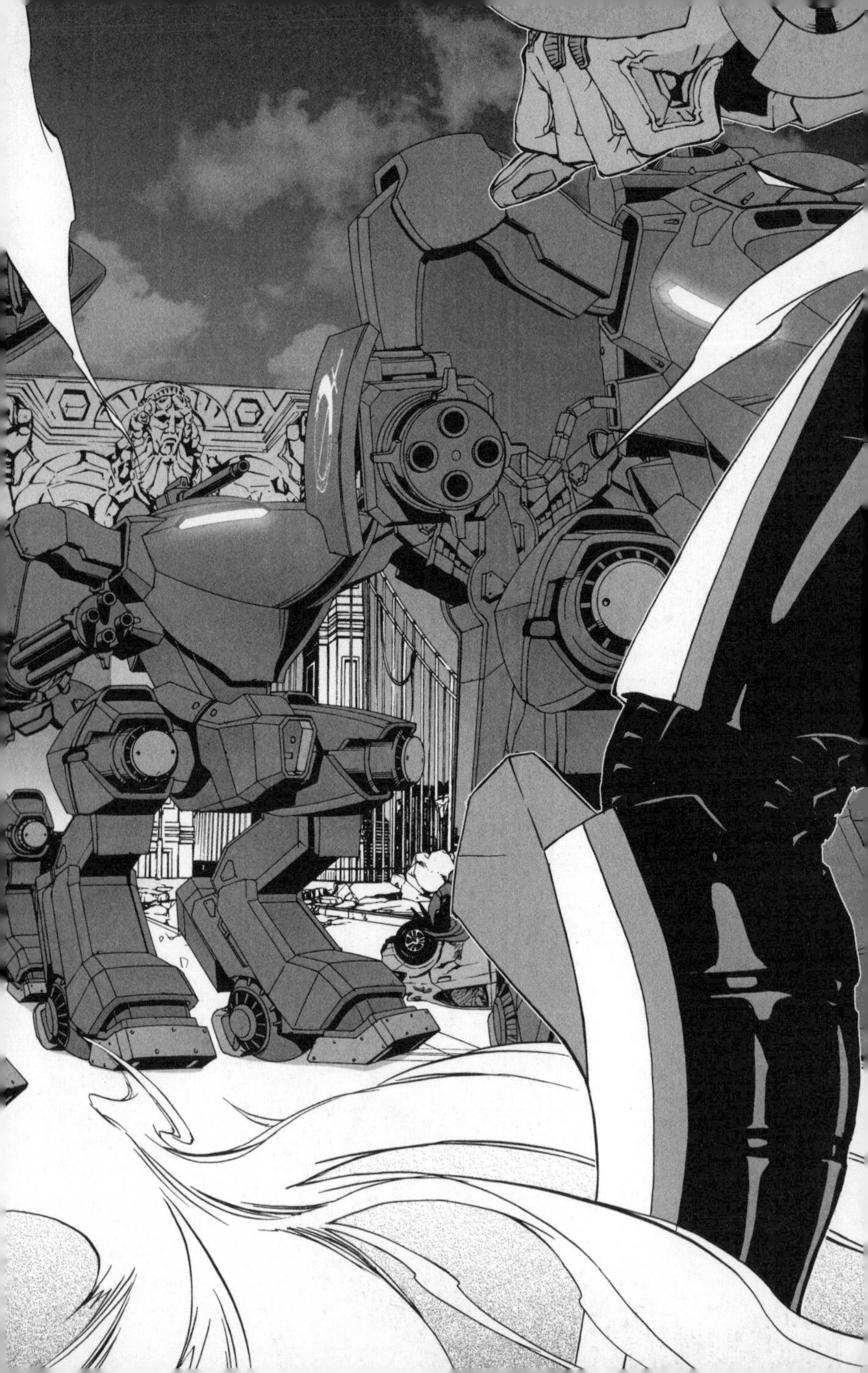

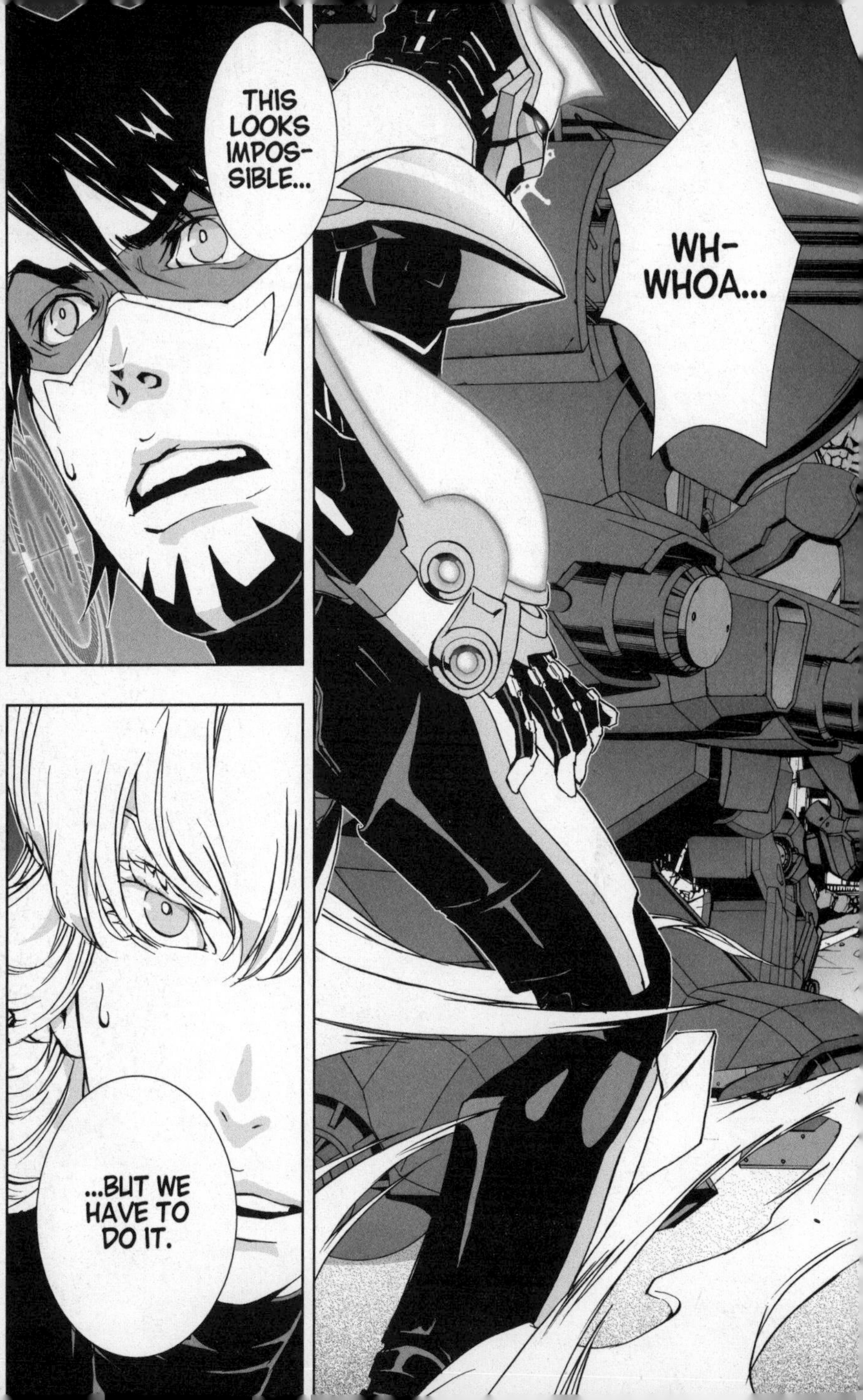
WH-WHOA...
THIS LOOKS IMPOSSIBLE...
...BUT WE HAVE TO DO IT.

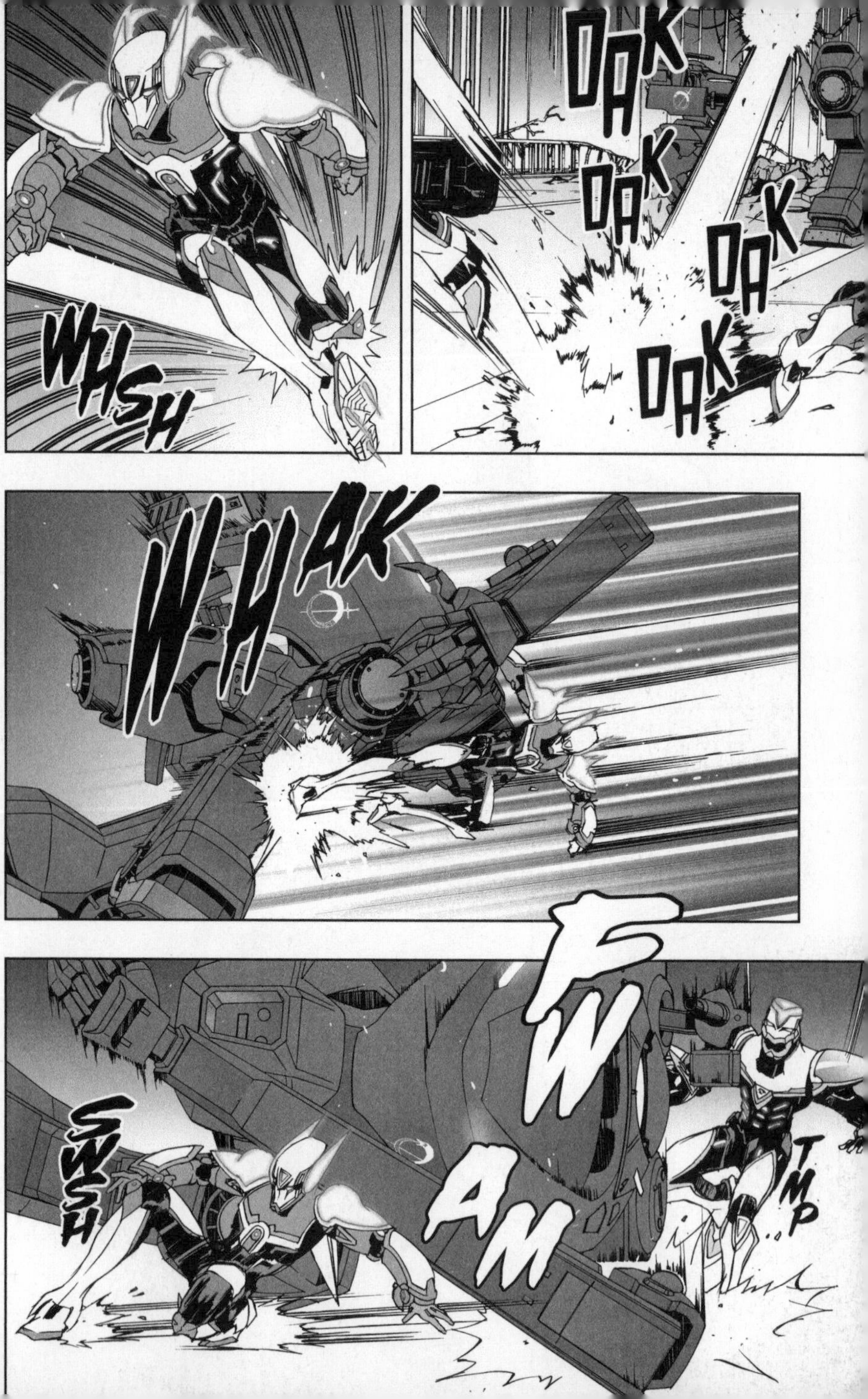
DAK
DAK
DAK
DAK
WHSH
WHAK
FWAM
TMP
SWSH

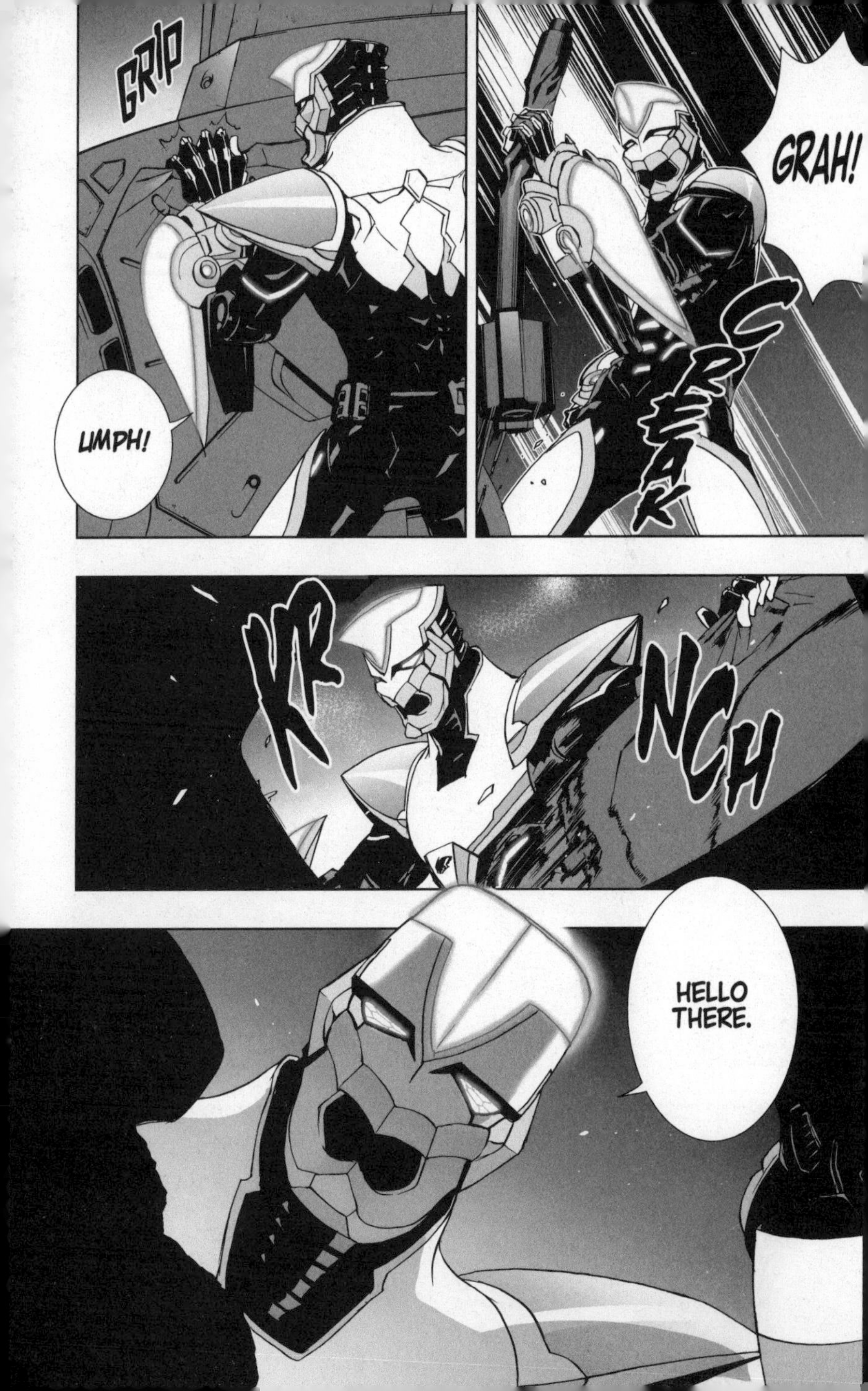
GRAH!
CREAK
GRIP
UMPH!
KR
NCH
HELLO THERE.

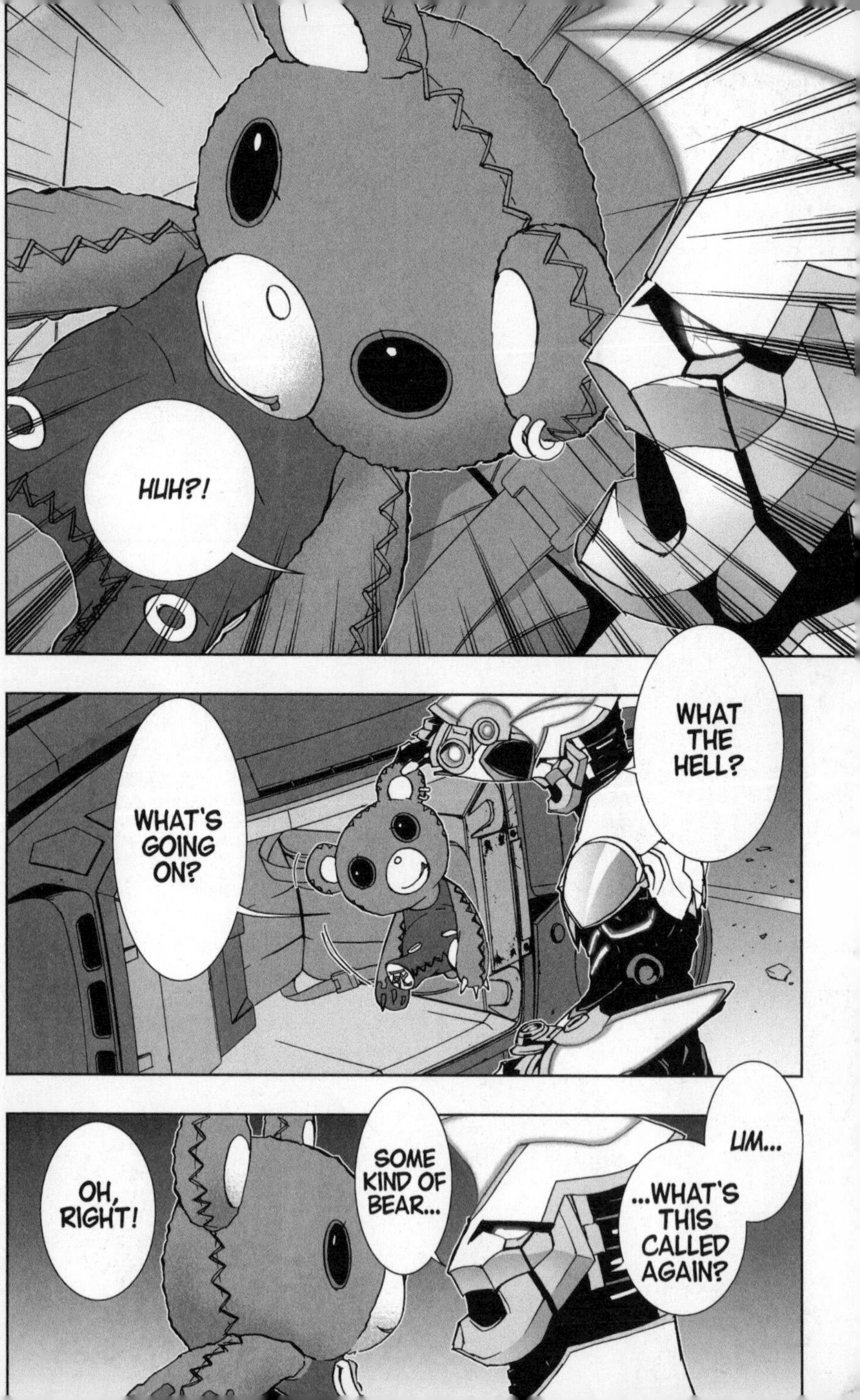
HUH?!
WHAT THE HELL?
WHAT'S GOING ON?
UM...
...WHAT'S THIS CALLED AGAIN?
SOME KIND OF BEAR...
OH, RIGHT!

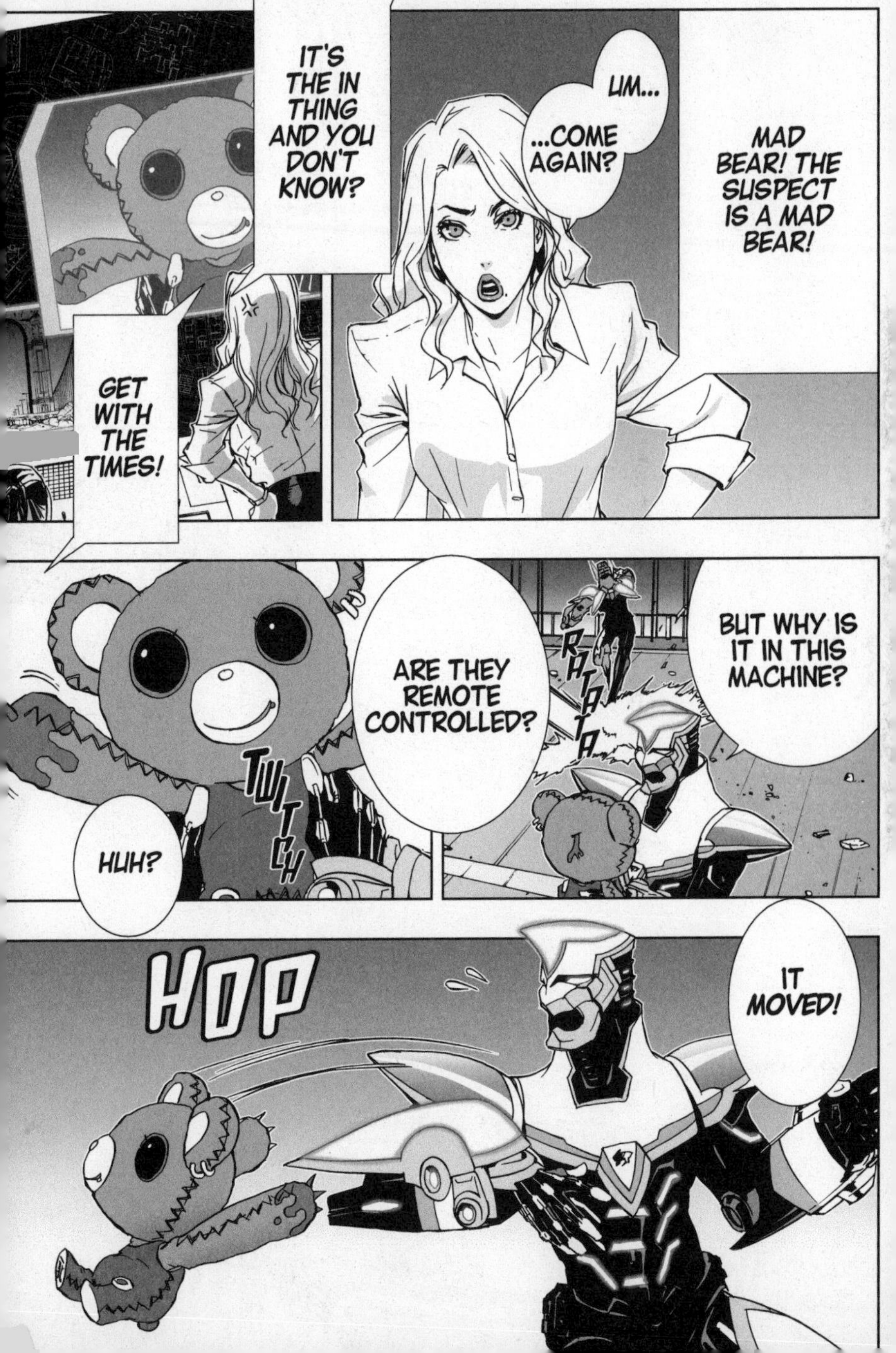
MAD BEAR! THE SUSPECT IS A MAD BEAR!
UM...
...COME AGAIN?
IT'S THE IN THING AND YOU DON'T KNOW?
GET WITH THE TIMES!
BUT WHY IS IT IN THIS MACHINE?
RATATA
ARE THEY REMOTE CONTROLLED?
TWITCH
HUH?
IT MOVED!
HOP

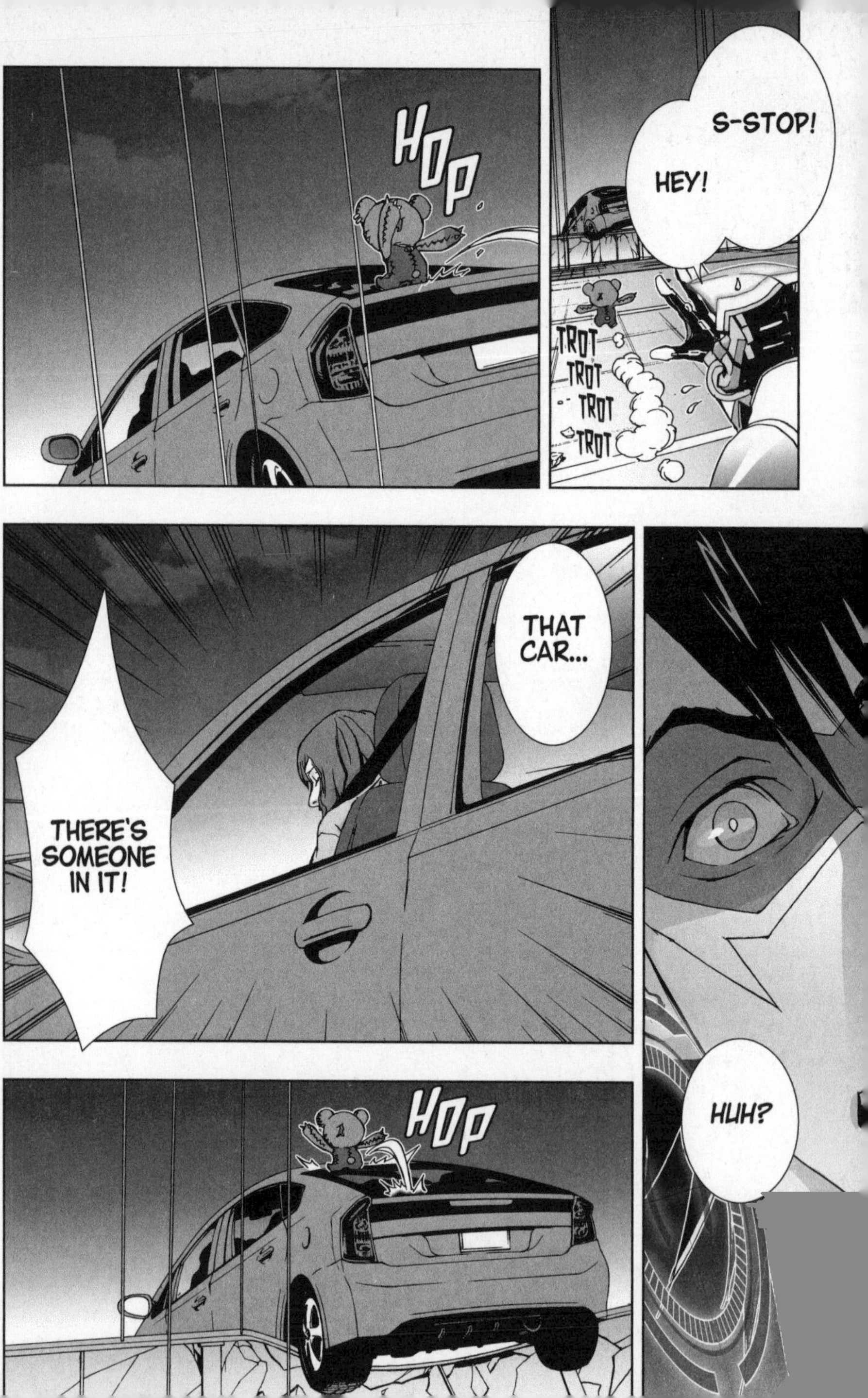
S-STOP!
HEY!
TROT
TROT
TROT
TROT
HOP.
HUH?
THAT CAR...
THERE'S SOMEONE IN IT!
HOP

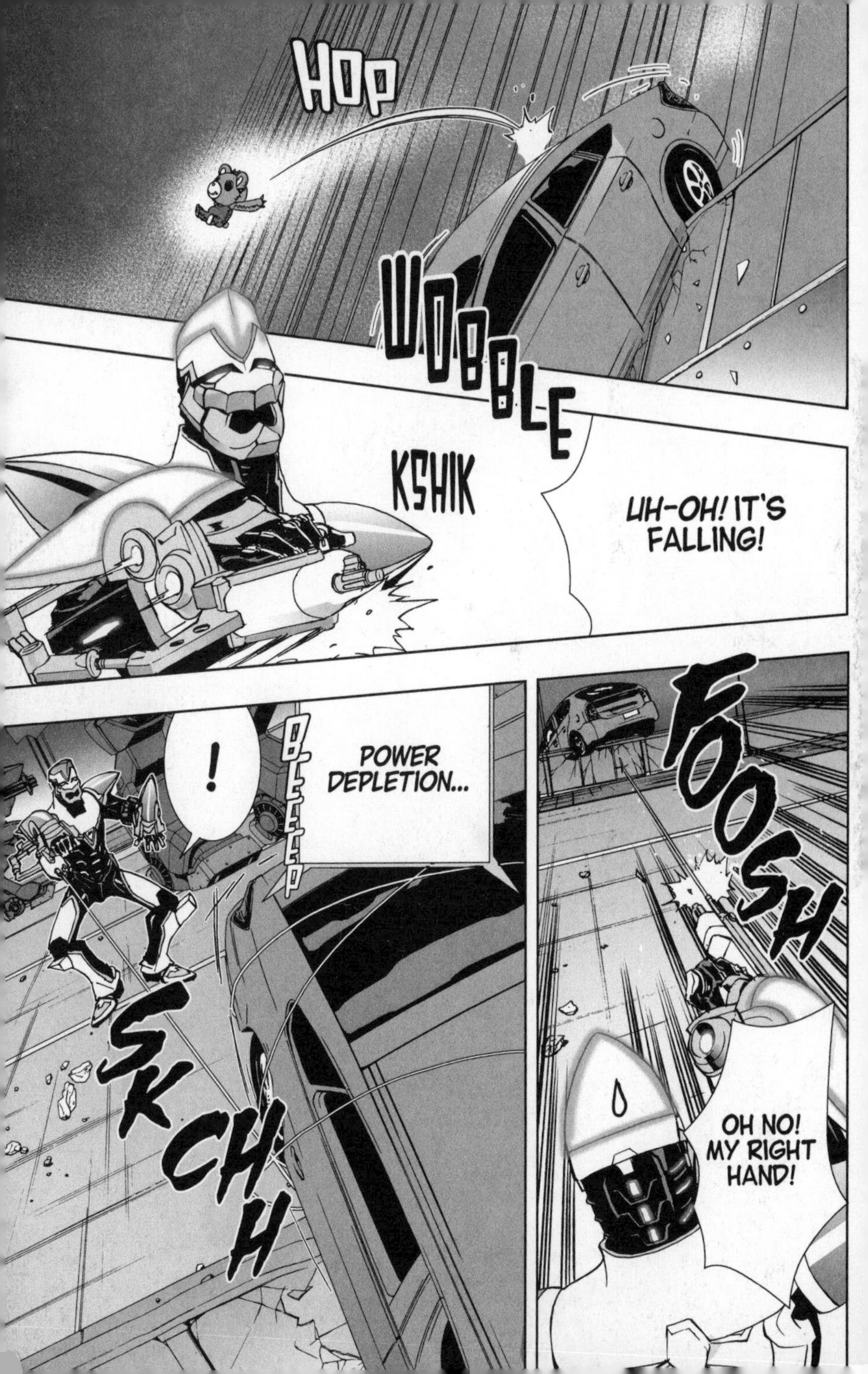
HOP
WOBBLE
UH-OH! IT'S FALLING!
KSHIK
FOOSH
OH NO! MY RIGHT HAND!
POWER DEPLETION...
BLEEEP
!
SKCHH

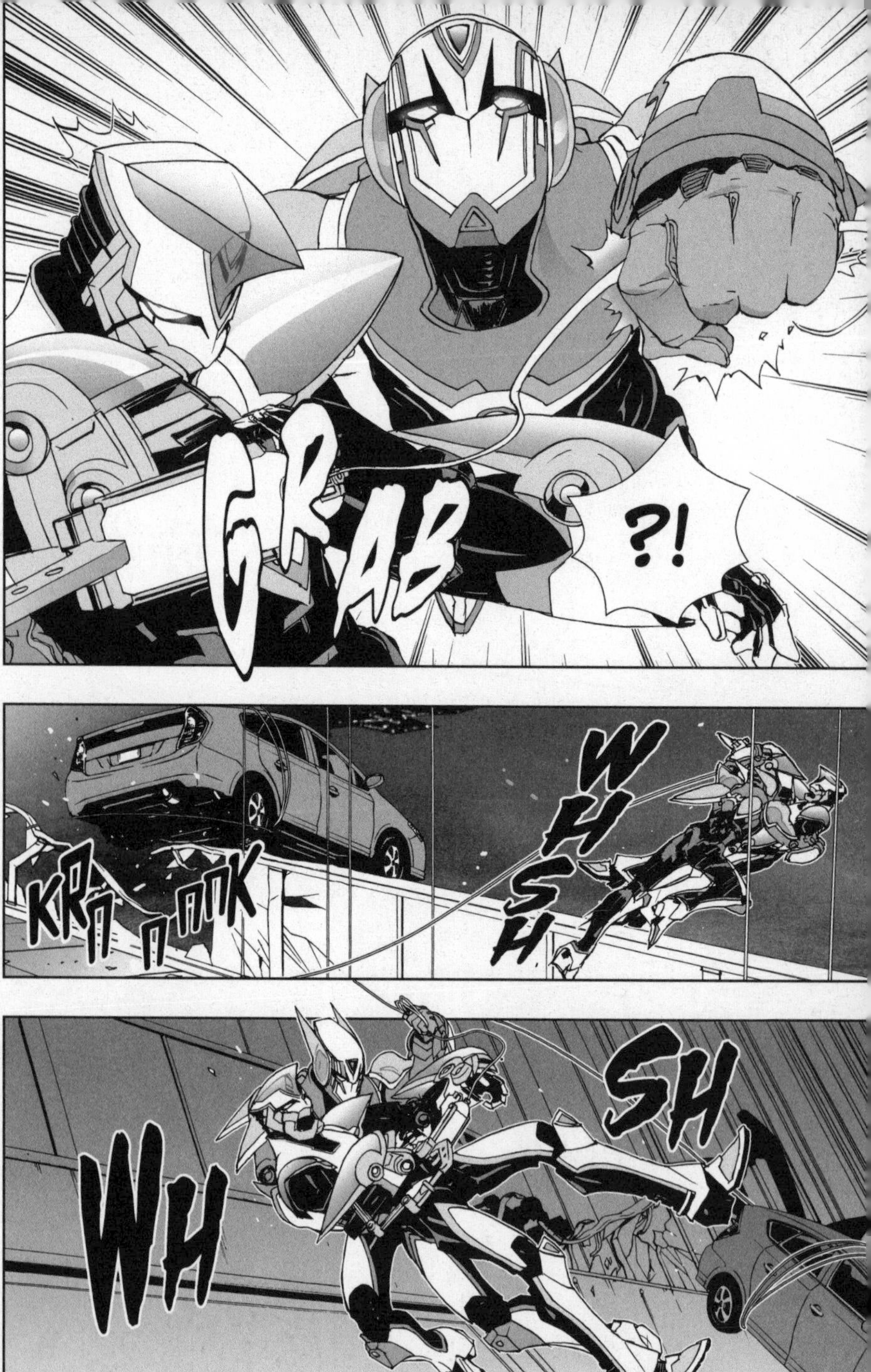
?!
GRAB
WHSH
KRAAANK
SH
WH

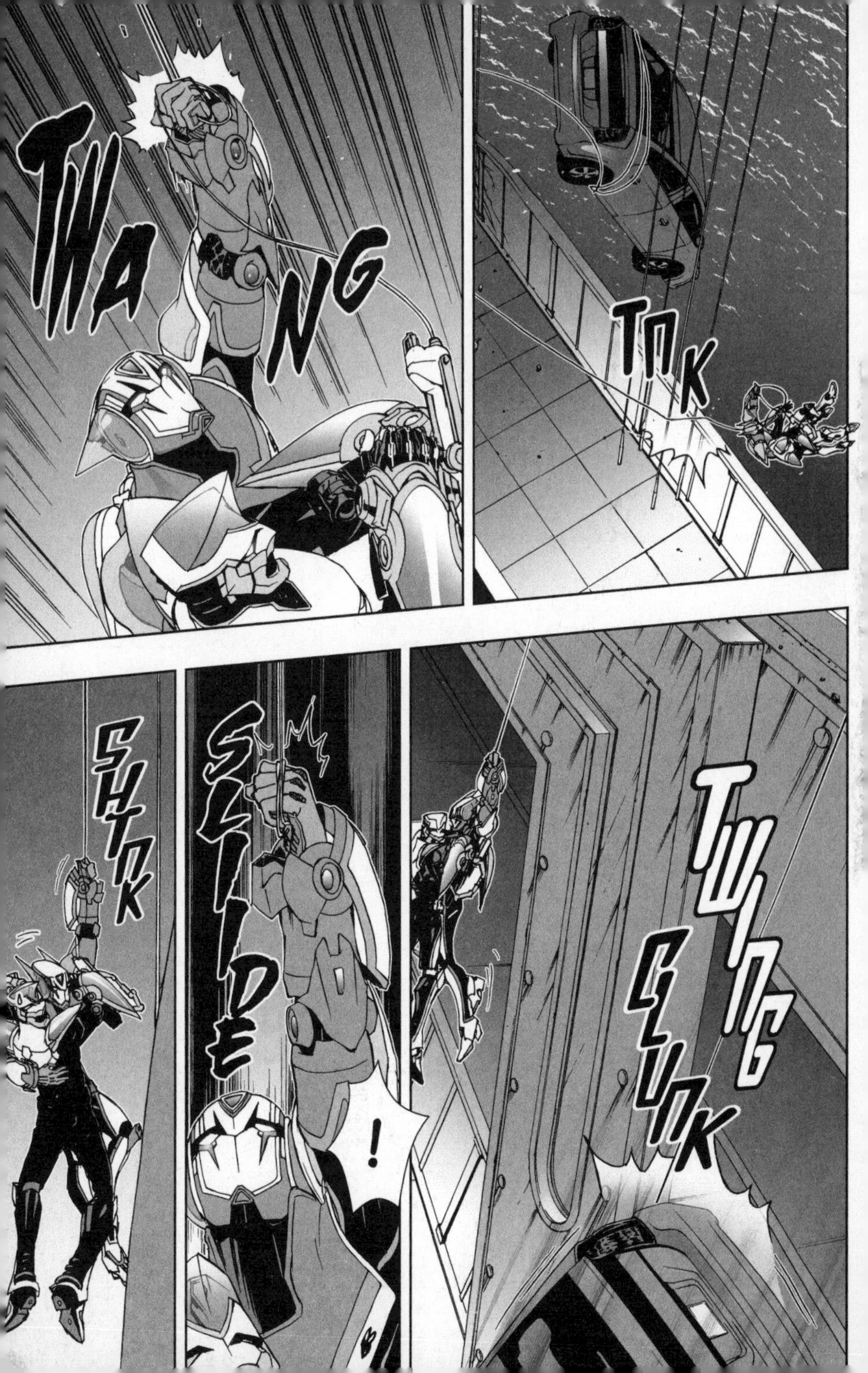
TNK
THWANG
TWING
CLUNK
SLIIDE
!
SHTNK

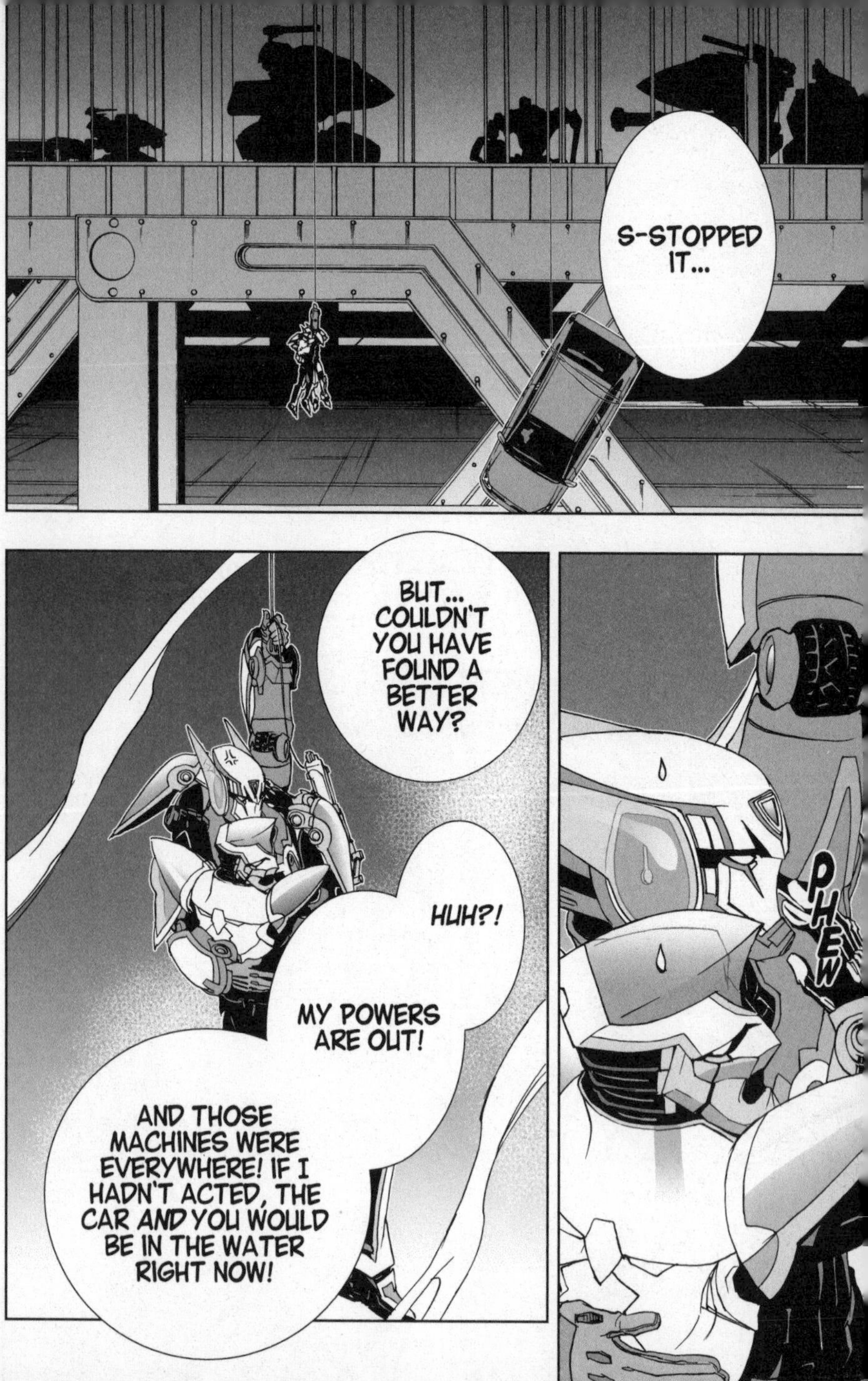
S-STOPPED IT...
PHEW
BUT... COULDN'T YOU HAVE FOUND A BETTER WAY?
HUH?!
MY POWERS ARE OUT!
AND THOSE MACHINES WERE EVERYWHERE! IF I HADN'T ACTED, THE CAR AND YOU WOULD BE IN THE WATER RIGHT NOW!

BESIDES, YOU SHOULDN'T BE SO QUICK TO USE YOUR WIRES, OLD MAN!

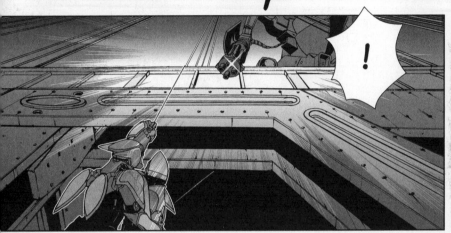

!

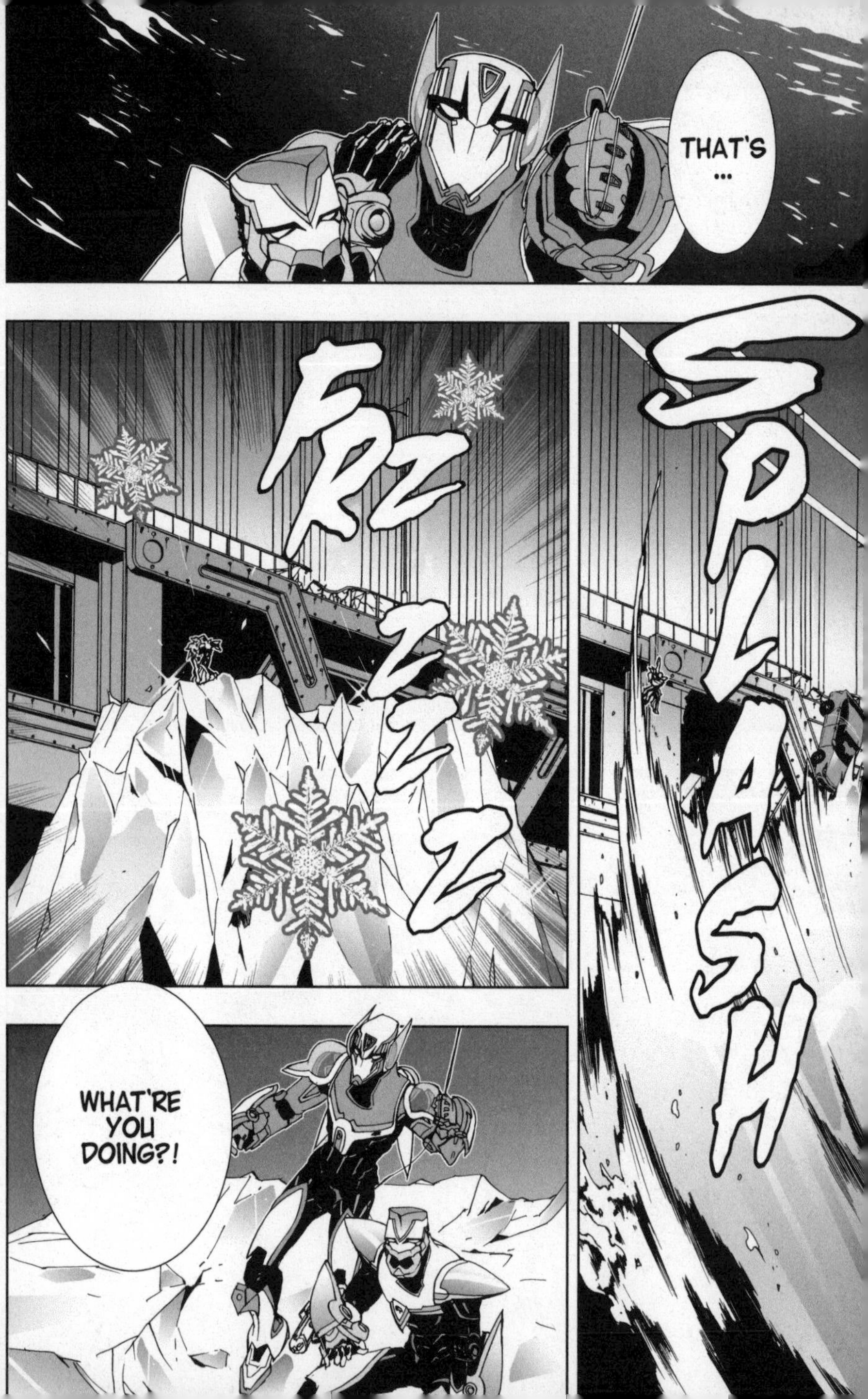
THAT'S ...
SPLASH
FRZZZZ
WHAT'RE YOU DOING?!

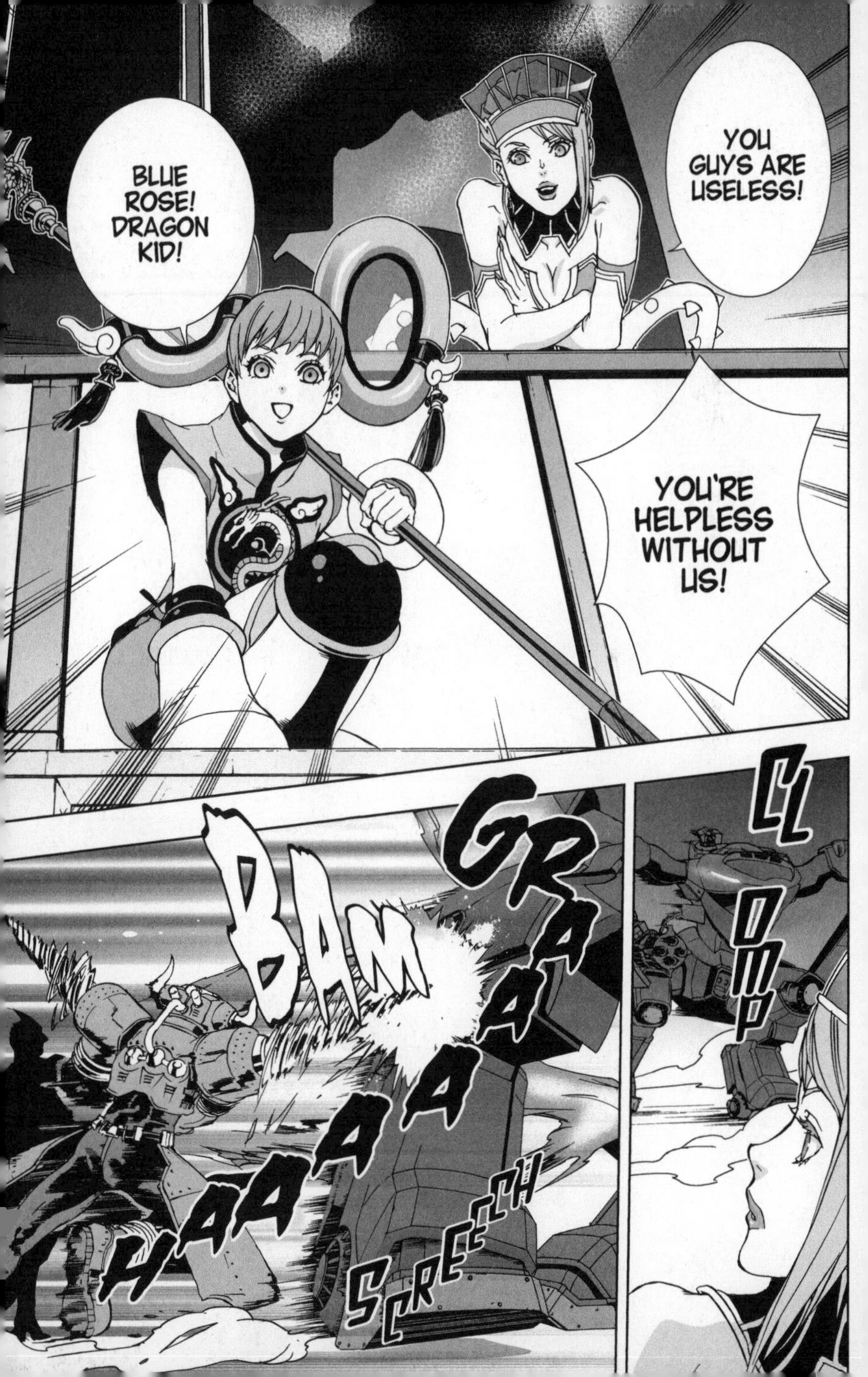
YOU GUYS ARE USELESS!
BLUE ROSE! DRAGON KID!
YOU'RE HELPLESS WITHOUT US!
CLOMP
GRAAAA
BAM
HAAAAA
SCREEECH

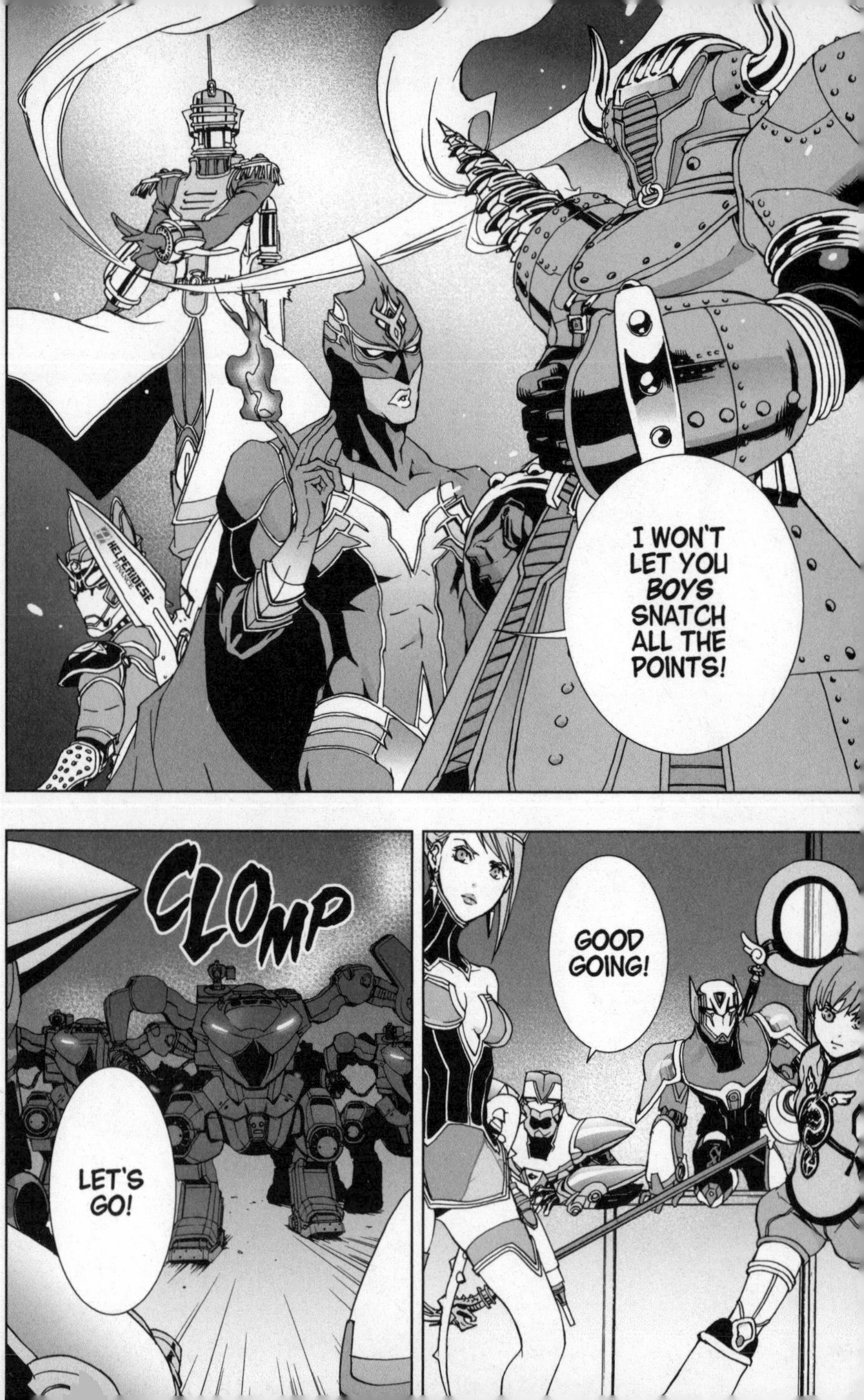

I WON'T LET YOU BOYS SNATCH ALL THE POINTS!
GOOD GOING!
CLOMP
LET'S GO!

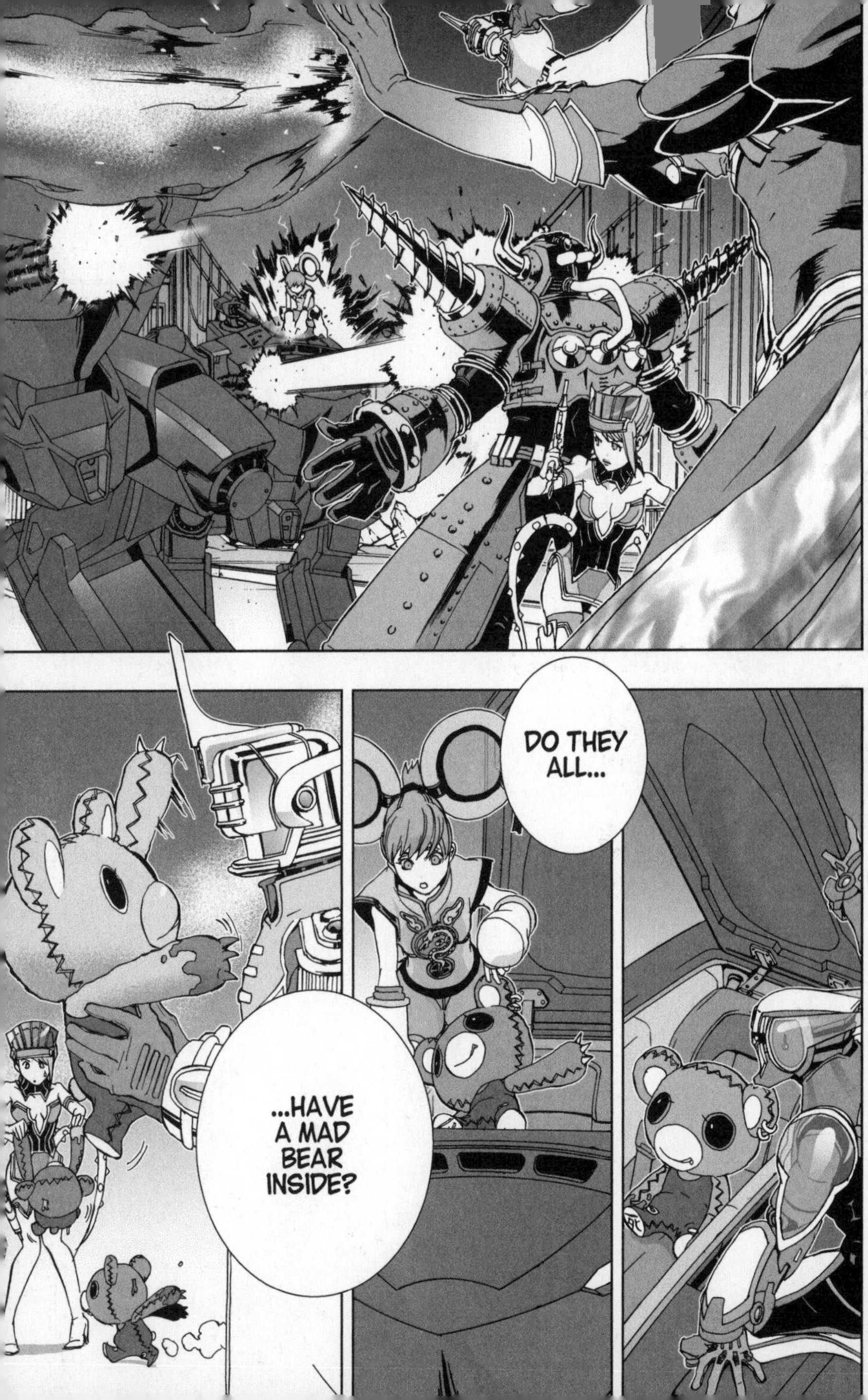
DO THEY ALL...
...HAVE A MAD BEAR INSIDE?

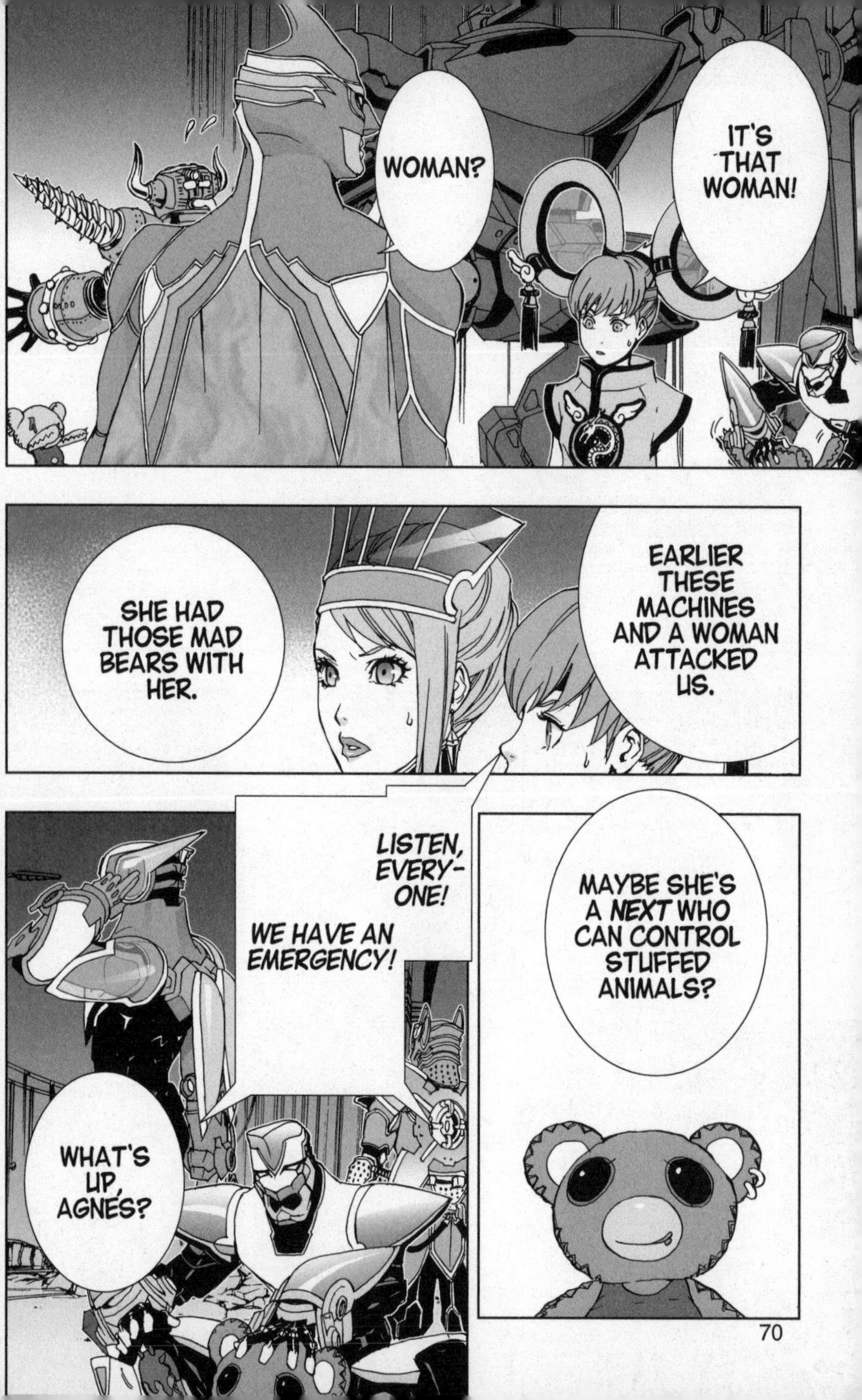
IT'S THAT WOMAN!
WOMAN?
EARLIER THESE MACHINES AND A WOMAN ATTACKED US.
SHE HAD THOSE MAD BEARS WITH HER.
MAYBE SHE'S A *NEXT* WHO CAN CONTROL STUFFED ANIMALS?
LISTEN, EVERY-ONE!
WE HAVE AN EMERGENCY!
WHAT'S UP, AGNES?

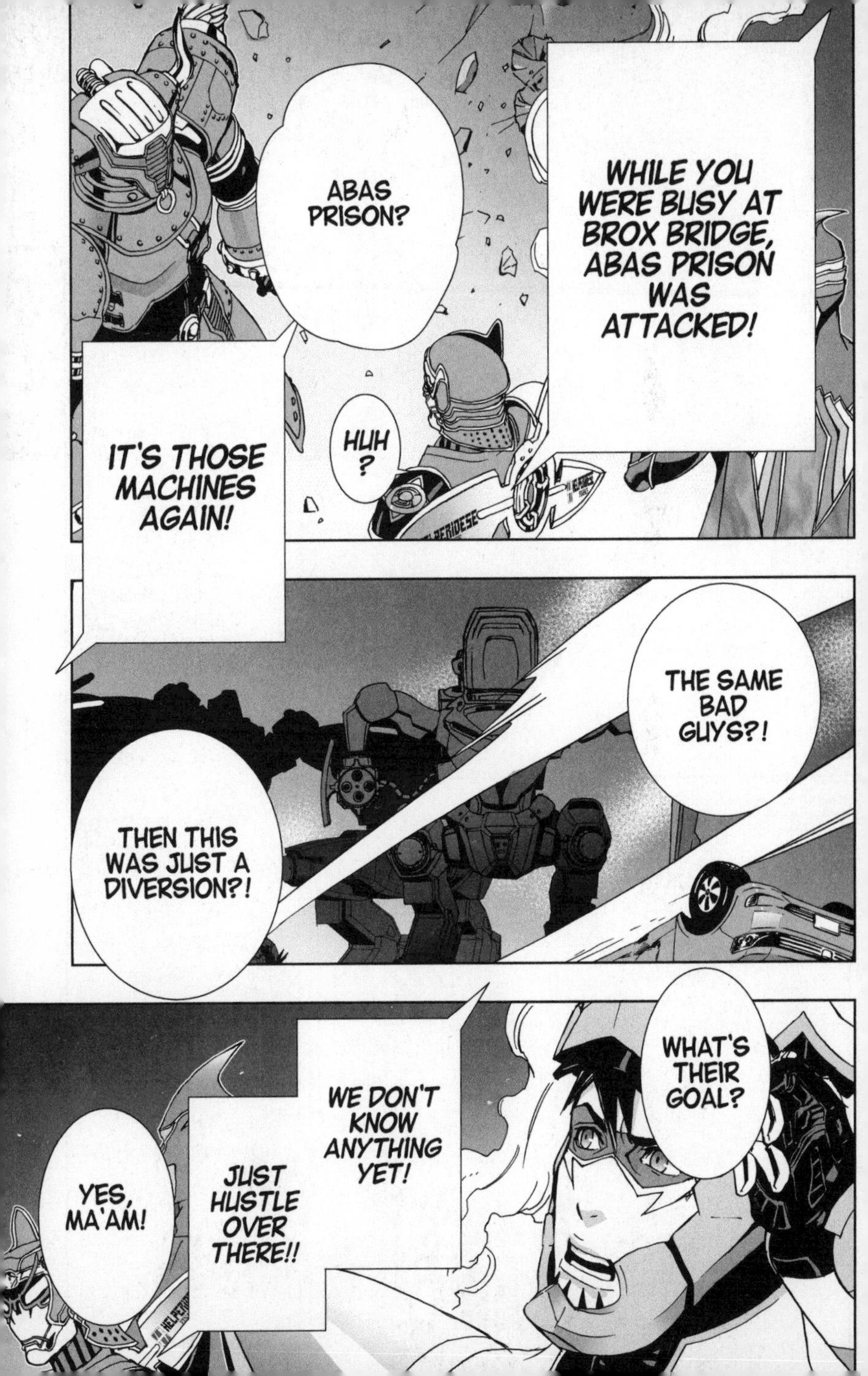
WHILE YOU WERE BUSY AT BROX BRIDGE, ABAS PRISON WAS ATTACKED!
ABAS PRISON?
HUH?
IT'S THOSE MACHINES AGAIN!
THE SAME BAD GUYS?!
THEN THIS WAS JUST A DIVERSION?!
WHAT'S THEIR GOAL?
WE DON'T KNOW ANYTHING YET!
JUST HUSTLE OVER THERE!!
YES, MA'AM!

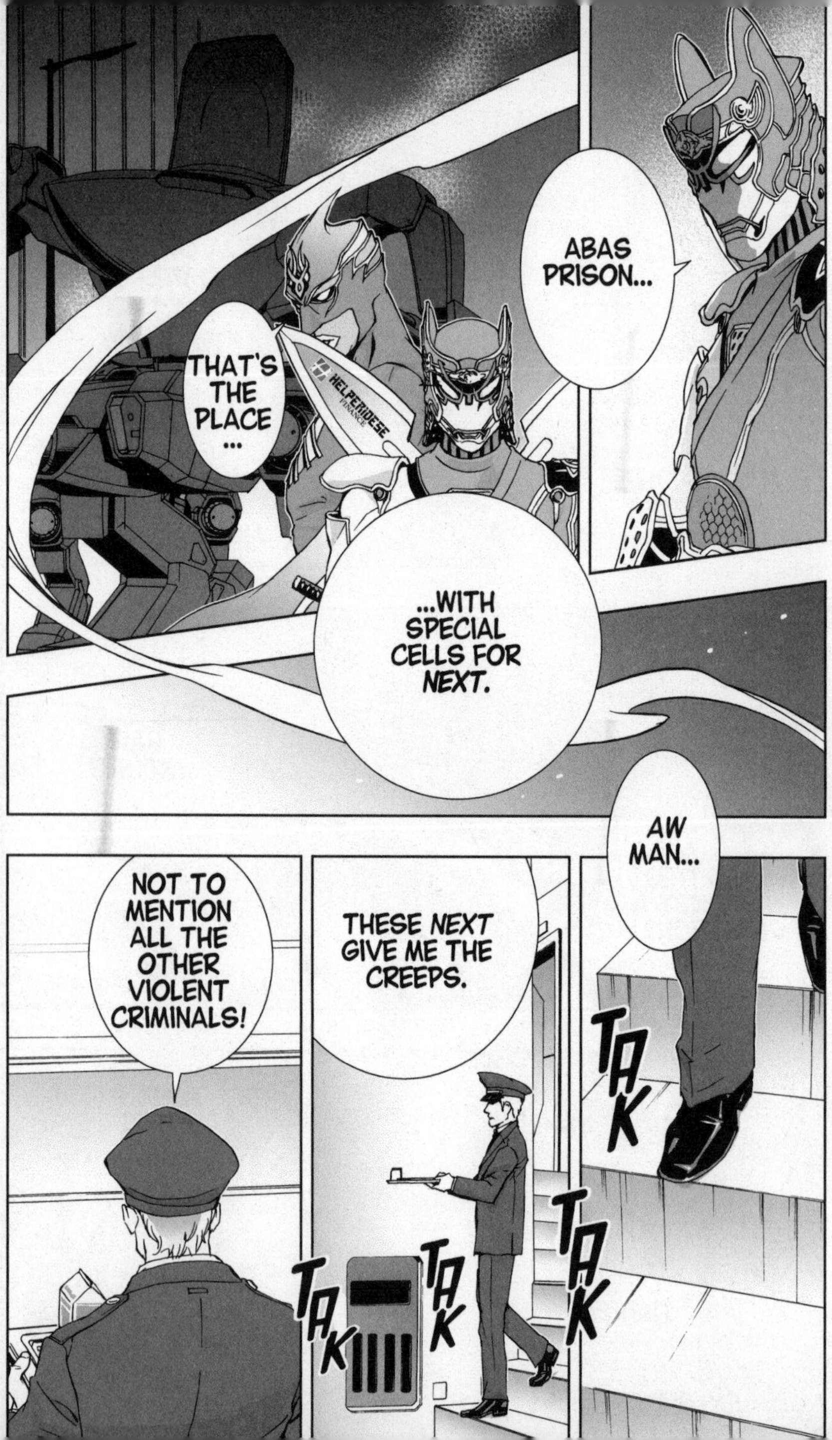
ABAS PRISON...
THAT'S THE PLACE ...
HELPERIDESE FINANCE
...WITH SPECIAL CELLS FOR NEXT.
AW MAN...
TAK TAK
TAK TAK
THESE NEXT GIVE ME THE CREEPS.
TAK TAK
TAK TAK
NOT TO MENTION ALL THE OTHER VIOLENT CRIMINALS!

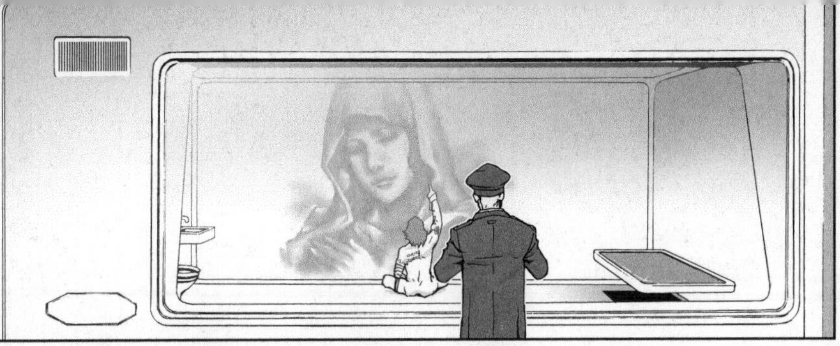

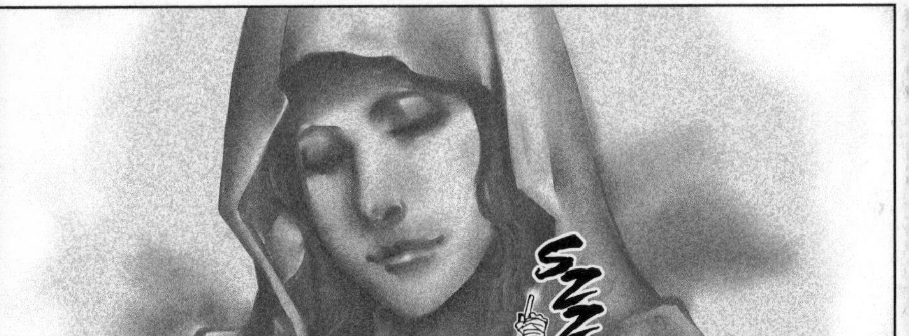
SZZZZ

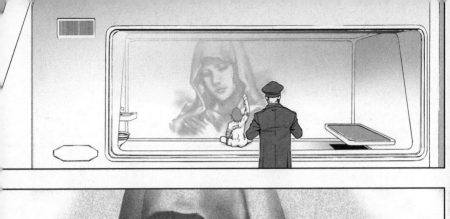

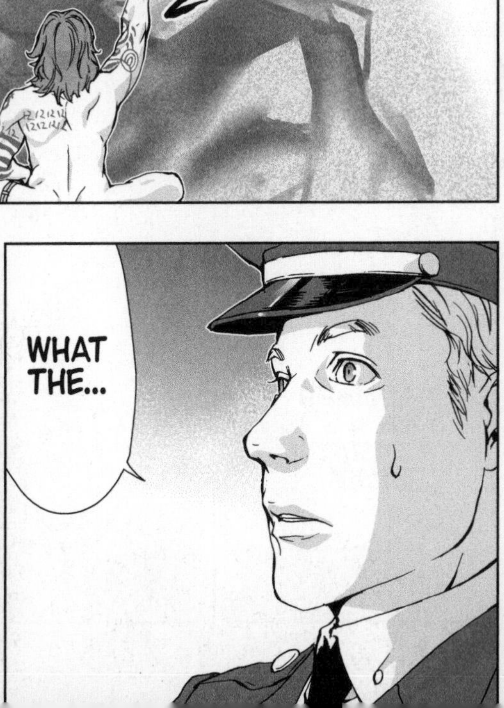
WHAT THE...

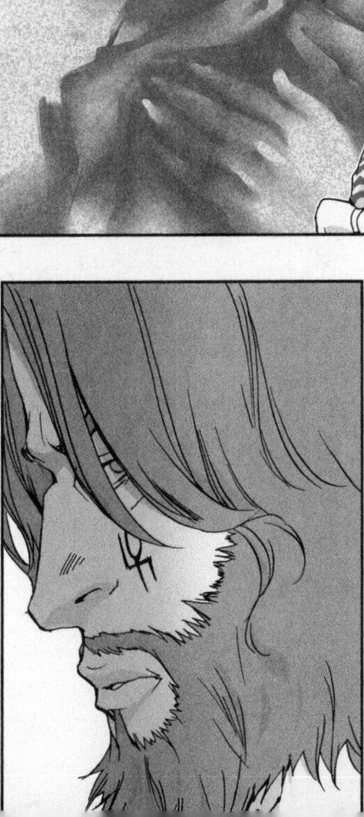

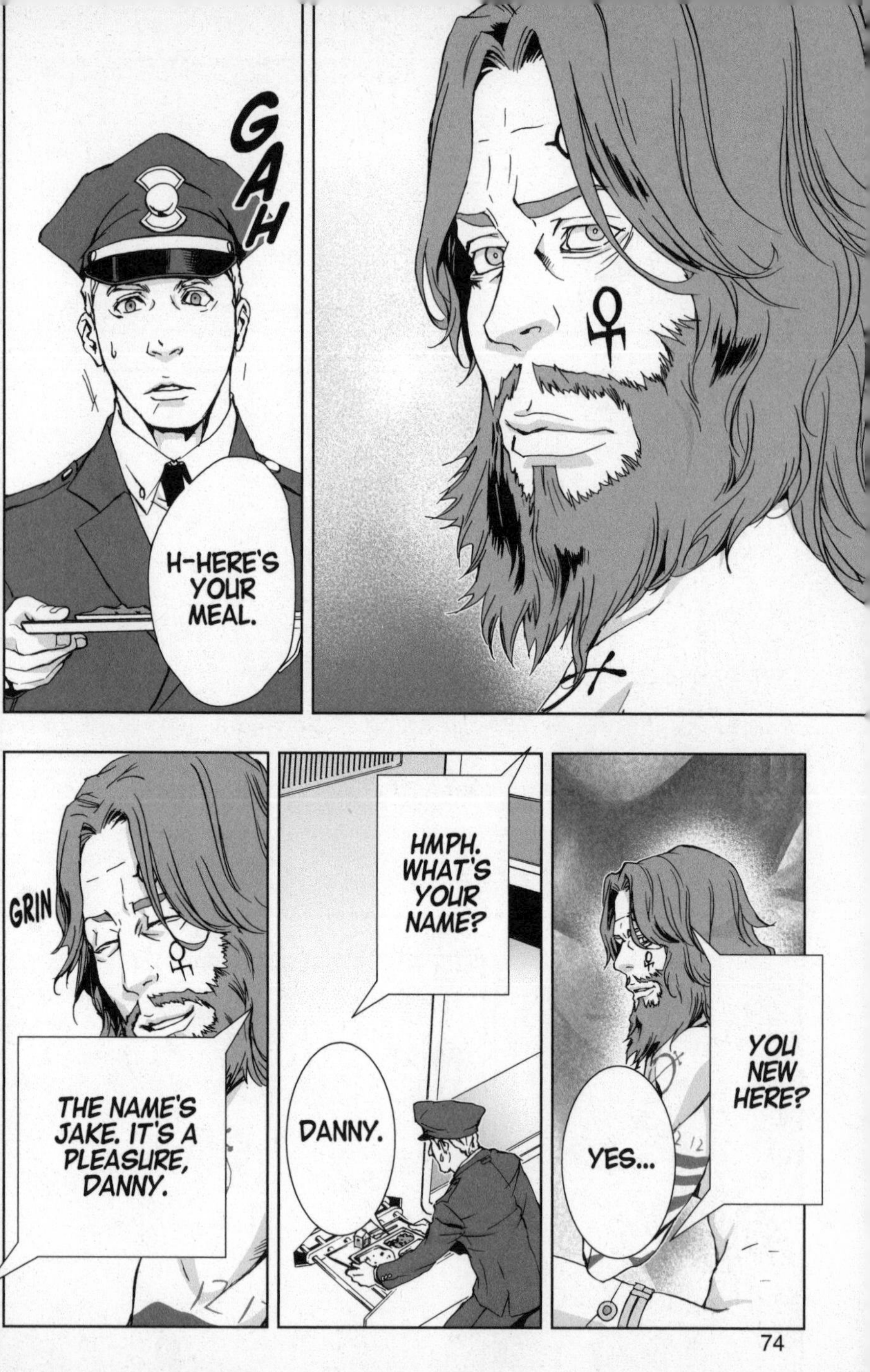
GAH
H-HERE'S YOUR MEAL.
YOU NEW HERE?
YES...
HMPH. WHAT'S YOUR NAME?
DANNY.
GRIN
THE NAME'S JAKE. IT'S A PLEASURE, DANNY.

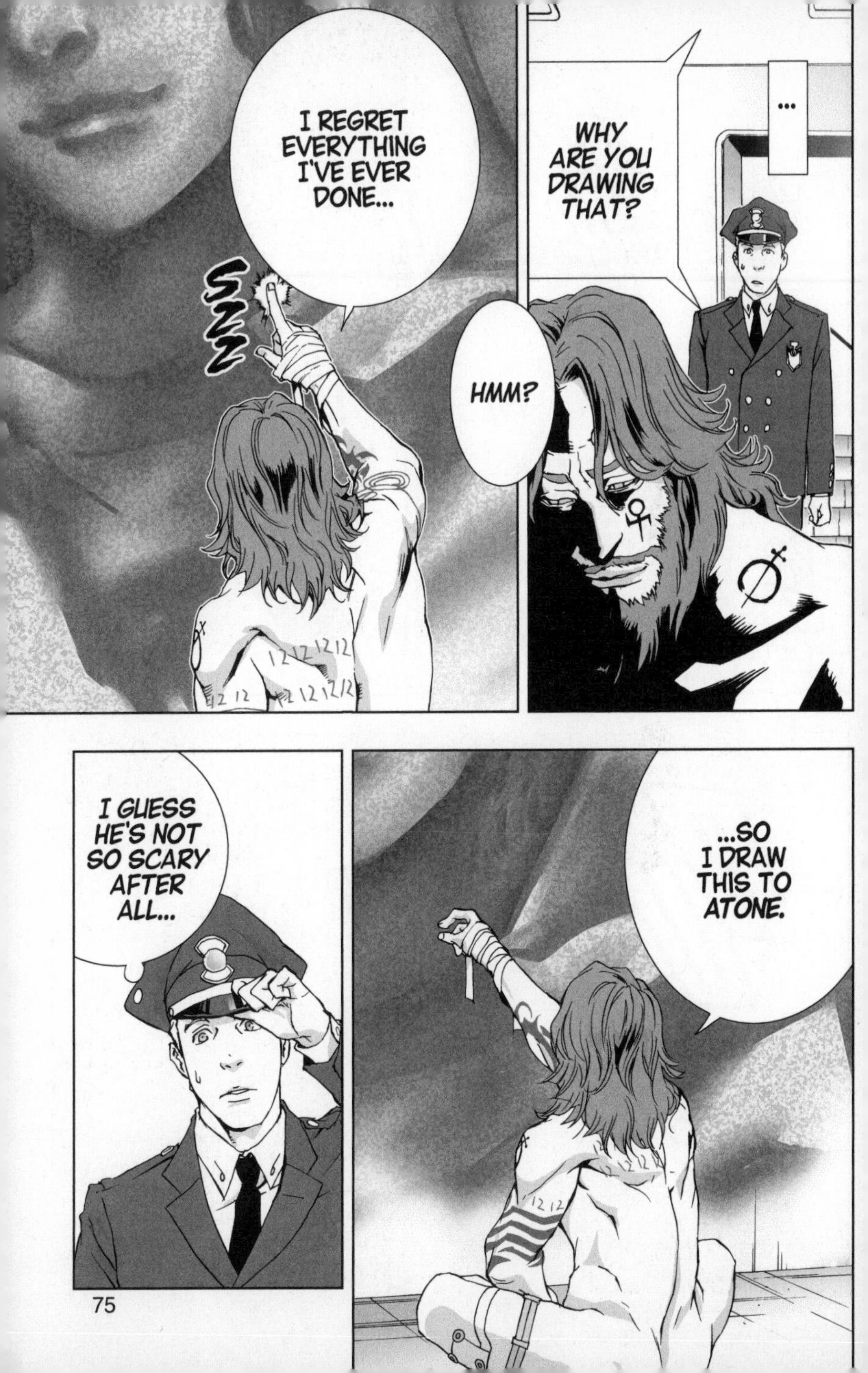
...
WHY ARE YOU DRAWING THAT?
HMM?
I REGRET EVERYTHING I'VE EVER DONE...
SZZZ
...SO I DRAW THIS TO ATONE.
I GUESS HE'S NOT SO SCARY AFTER ALL...

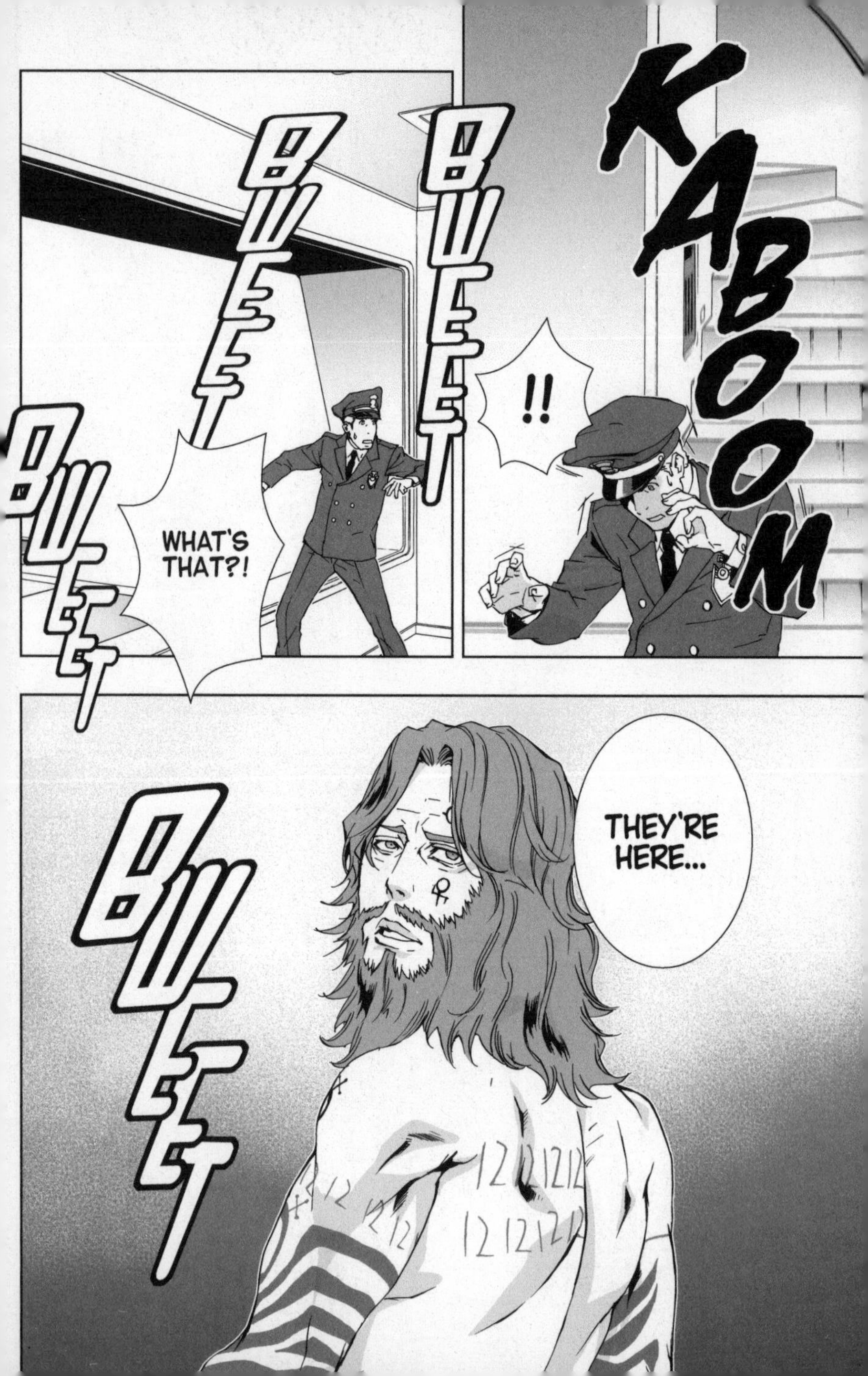
KABOOM
!!
BWEEET
BWEEET
WHAT'S THAT?!
BWEEET
THEY'RE HERE...
BWEEET

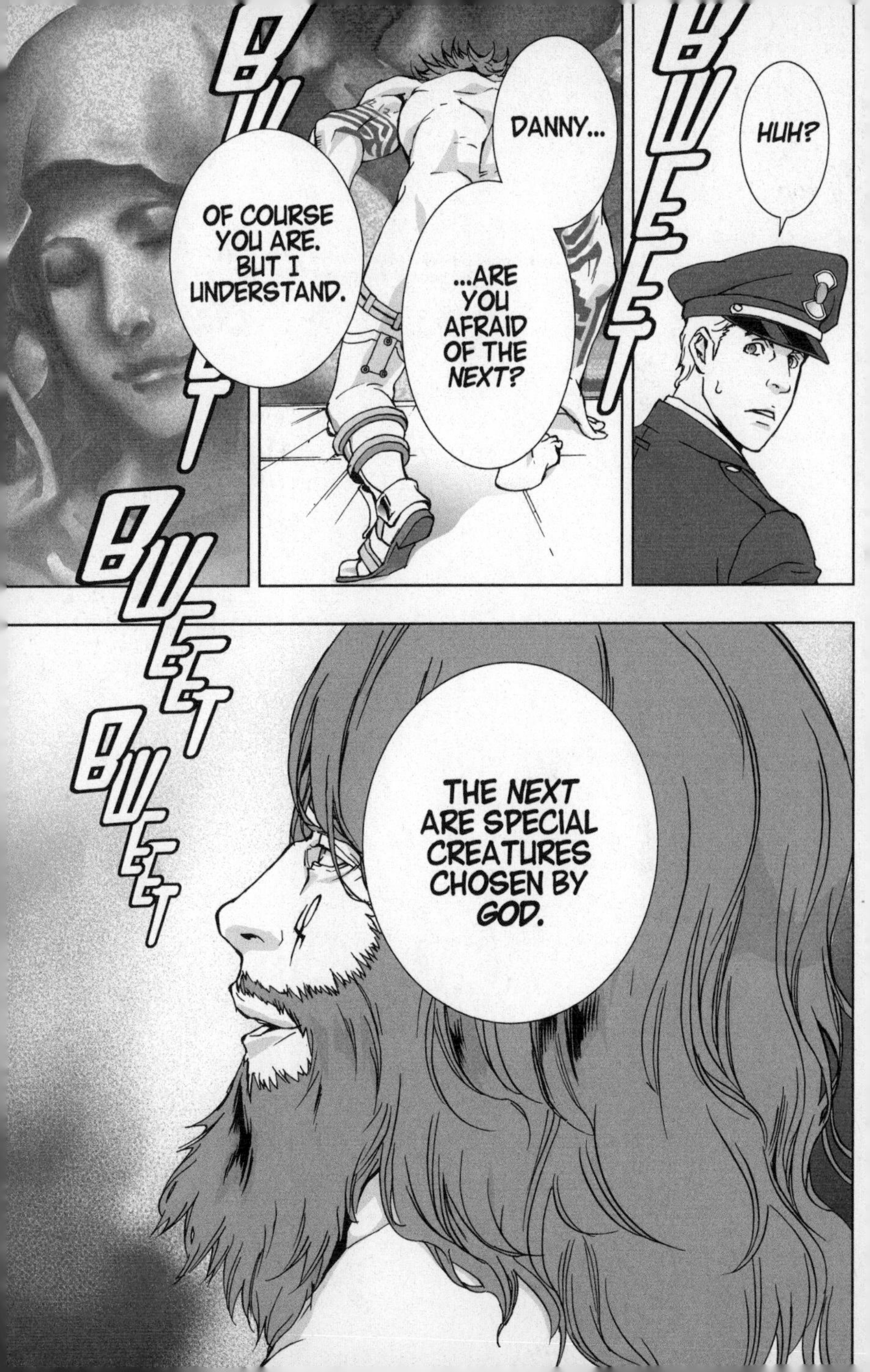
BWEEEET
HUH?
DANNY...
...ARE YOU AFRAID OF THE *NEXT*?
OF COURSE YOU ARE. BUT I UNDERSTAND.
BWEEET
BWEEET
THE *NEXT* ARE SPECIAL CREATURES CHOSEN BY *GOD*.

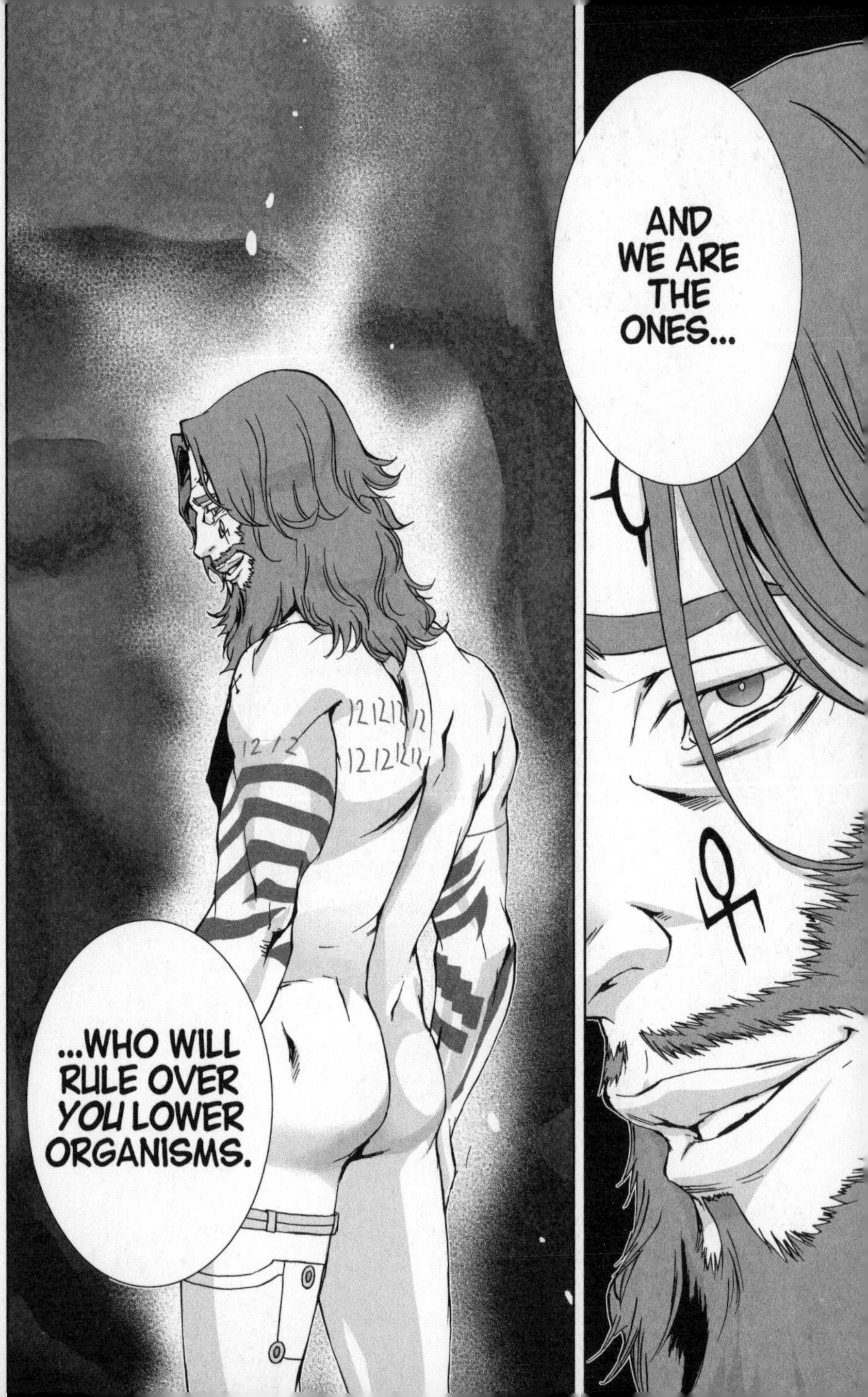
AND WE ARE THE ONES...
...WHO WILL RULE OVER *YOU* LOWER ORGANISMS.

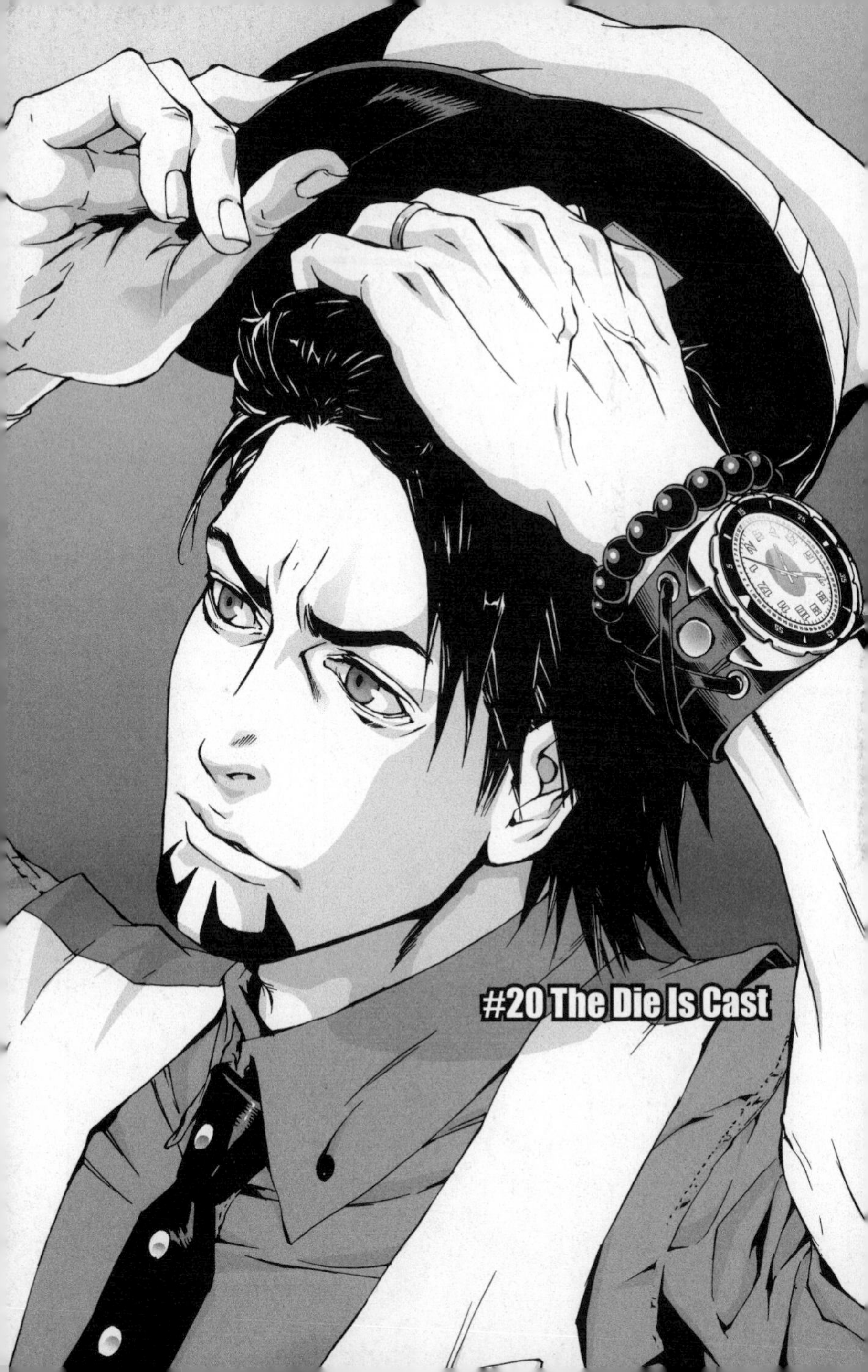
#20 The Die Is Cast

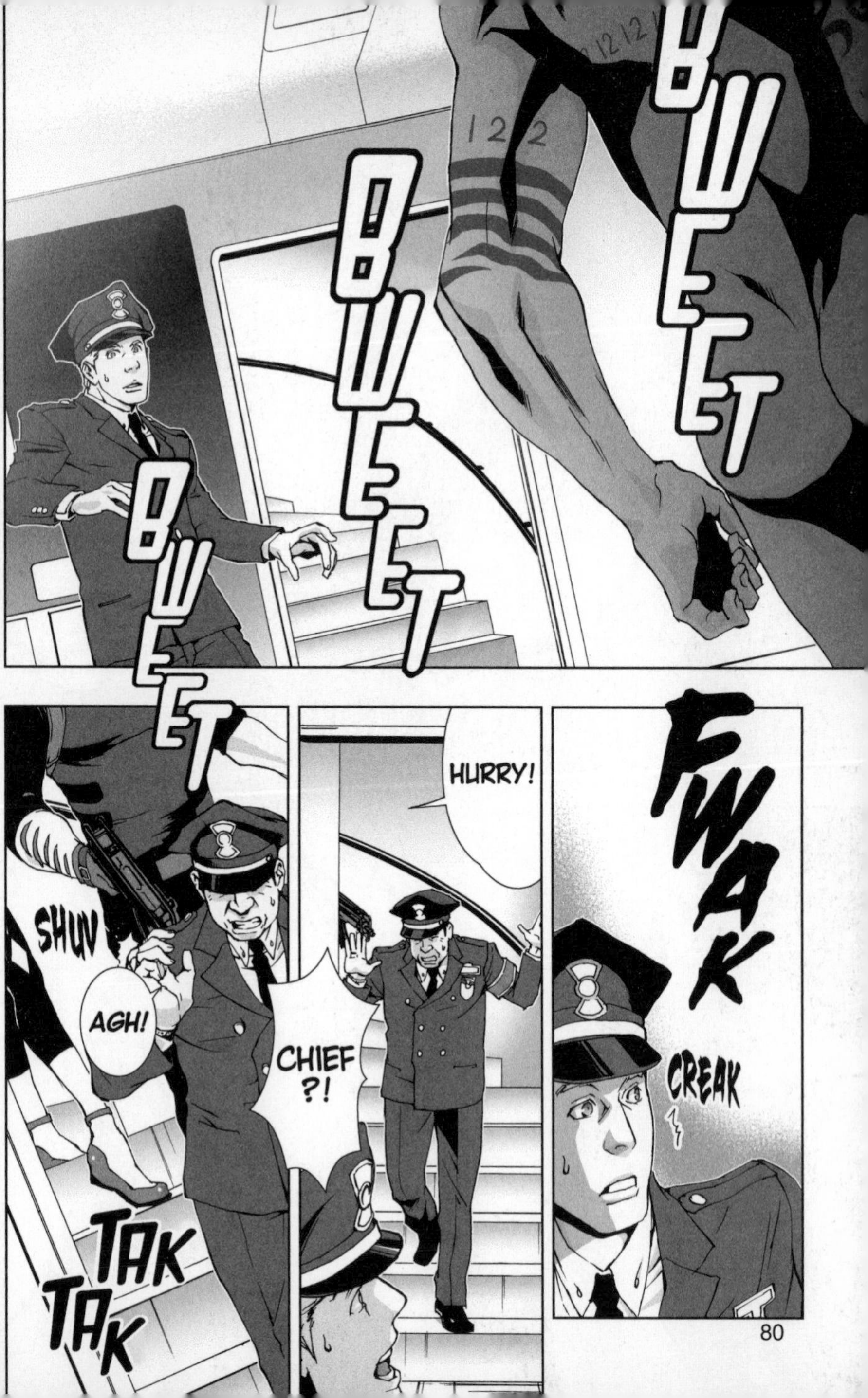
BWEET
BWEET
BWEET
FWAK
CREAK
HURRY!
CHIEF ?!
SHUV
AGH!
TAK TAK

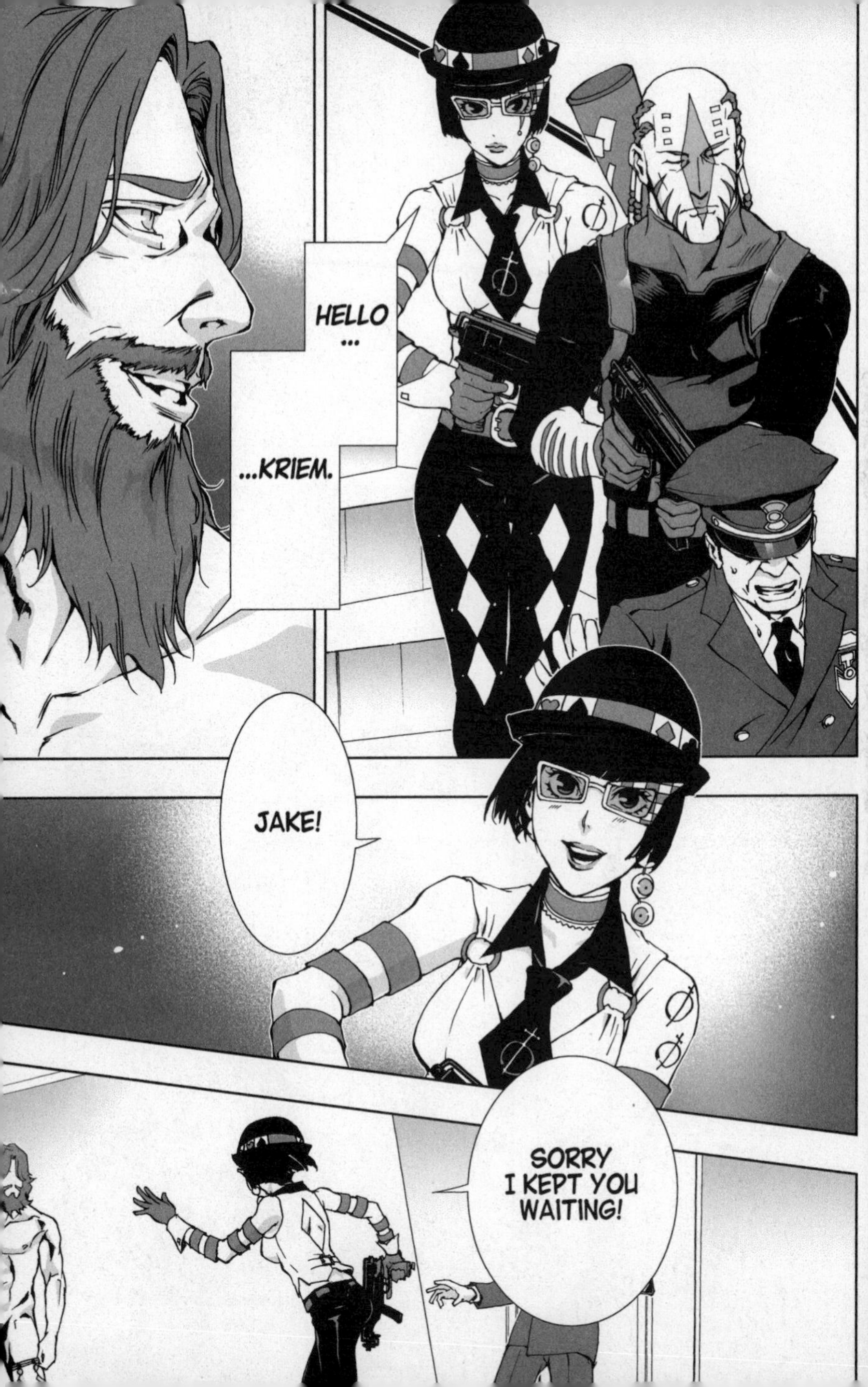
HELLO ...
...KRIEM.
JAKE!
SORRY I KEPT YOU WAITING!

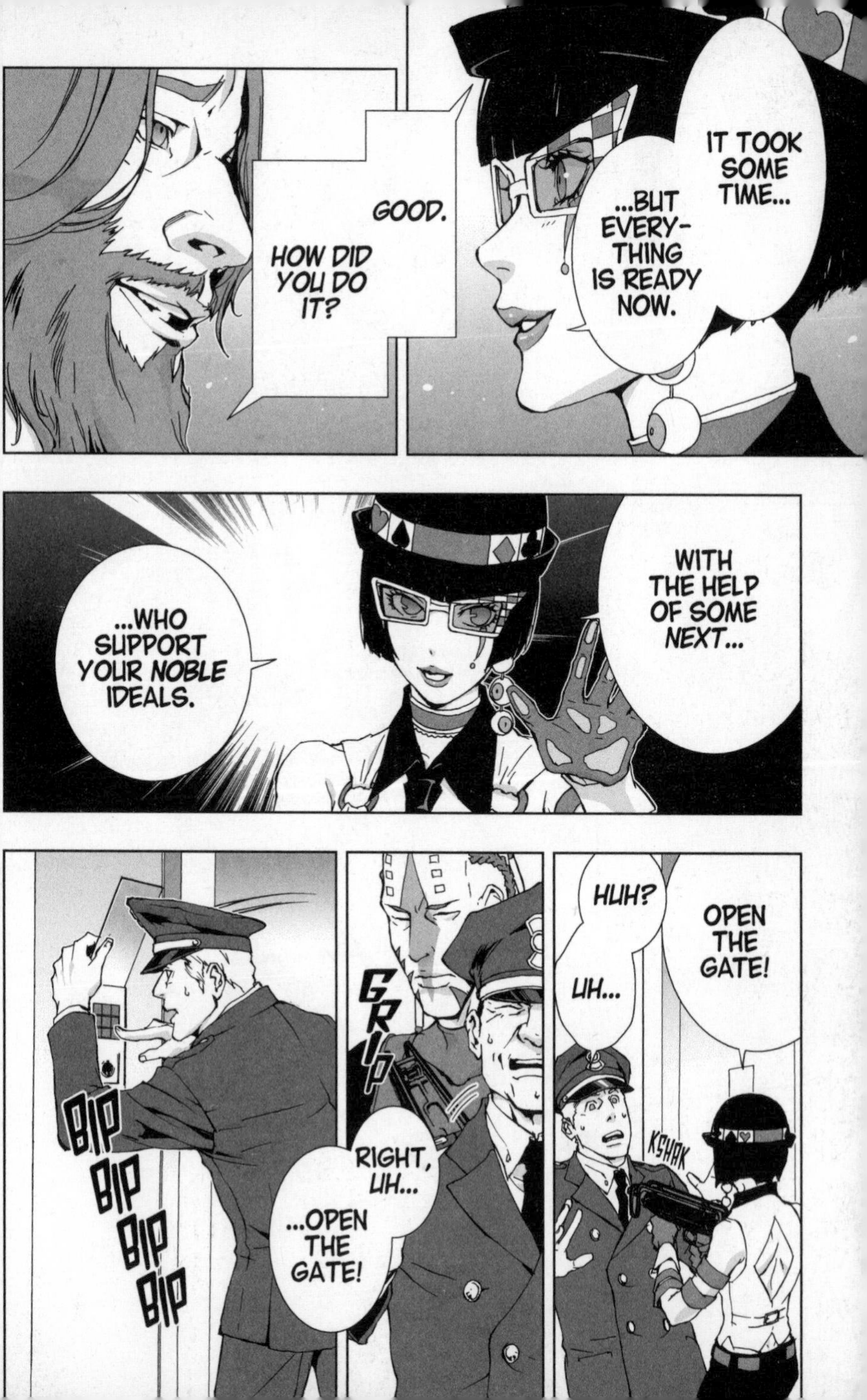
IT TOOK SOME TIME...
...BUT EVERY-THING IS READY NOW.
GOOD.
HOW DID YOU DO IT?
WITH THE HELP OF SOME NEXT...
...WHO SUPPORT YOUR NOBLE IDEALS.
OPEN THE GATE!
HUH?
UH...
KSHAK
GRIP
RIGHT, UH...
...OPEN THE GATE!
BIP BIP BIP BIP

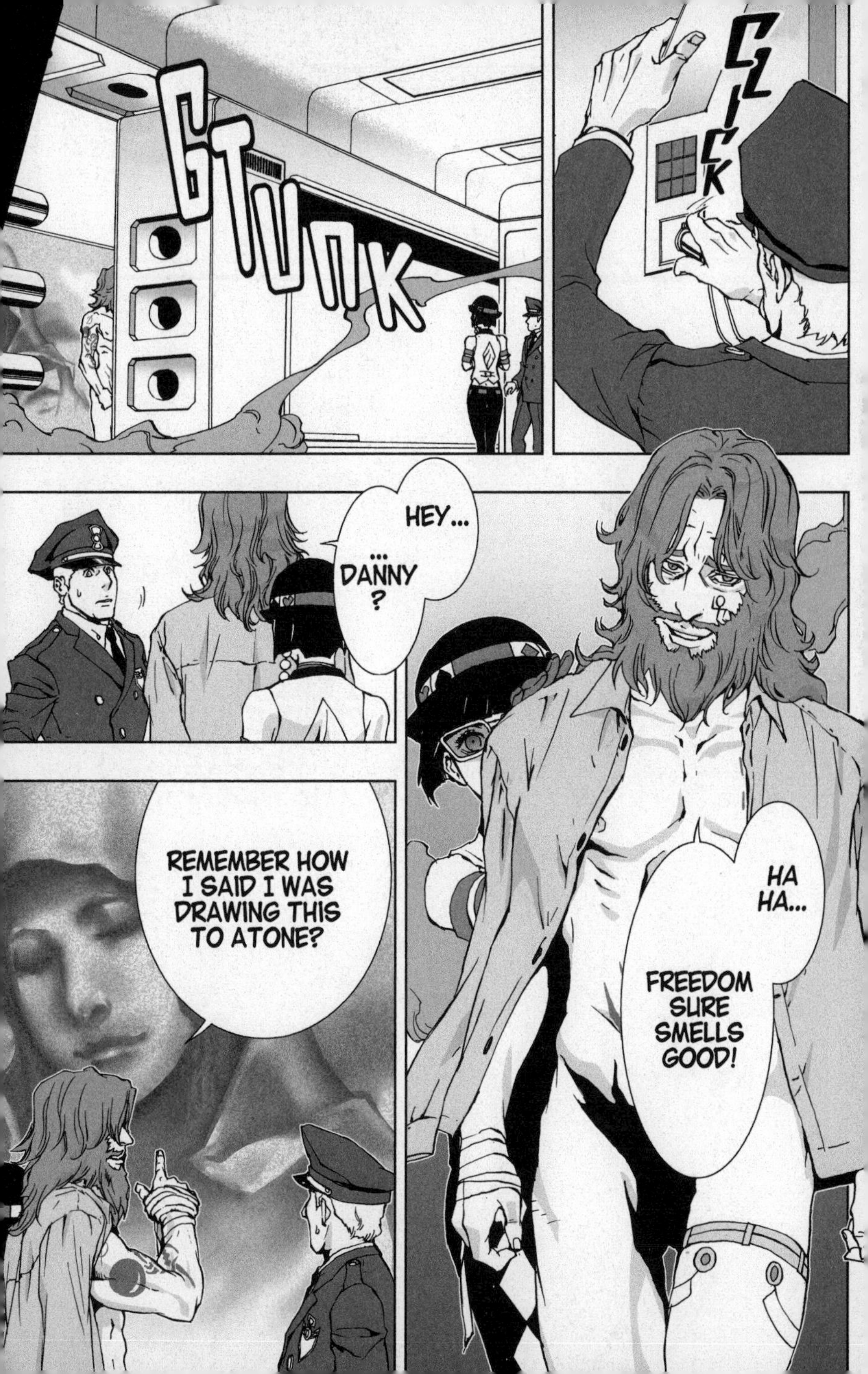
CLICK
GTUNK
HA HA...
FREEDOM SURE SMELLS GOOD!
HEY...
...DANNY?
REMEMBER HOW I SAID I WAS DRAWING THIS TO ATONE?

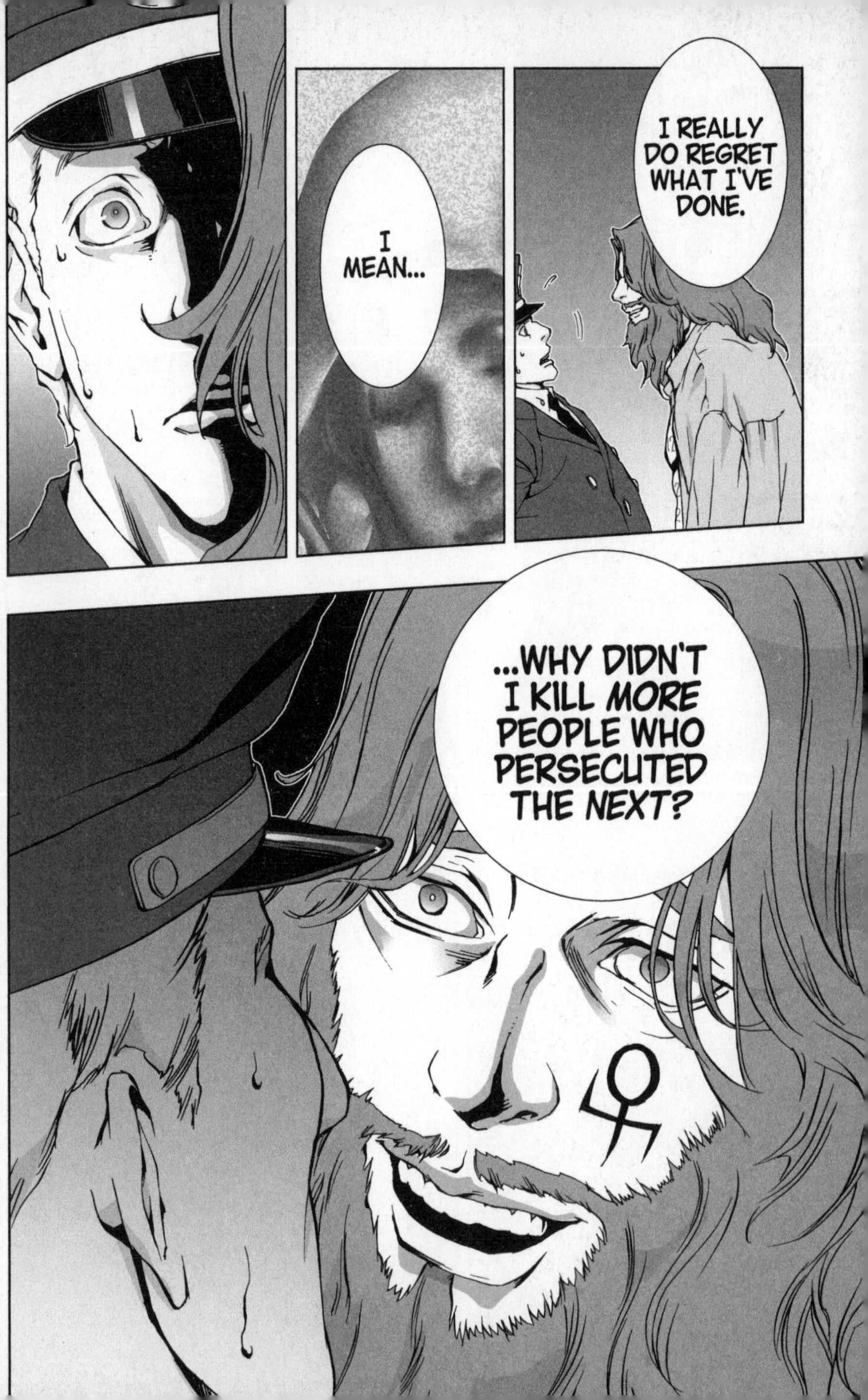
I REALLY DO REGRET WHAT I'VE DONE.
I MEAN...
...WHY DIDN'T I KILL *MORE* PEOPLE WHO PERSECUTED THE *NEXT*?

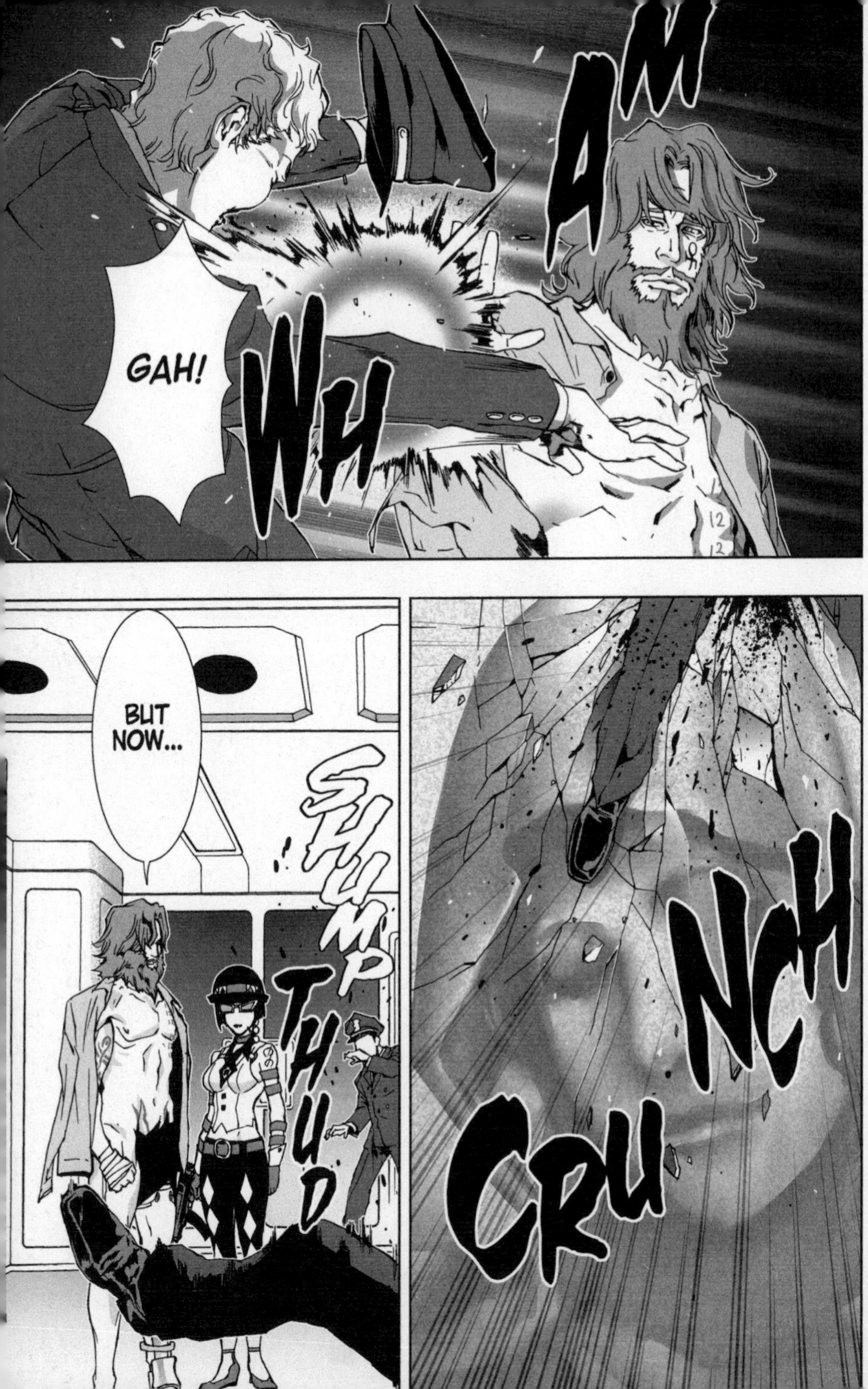
WHAM
GAH!
CRUNCH
BUT NOW...
SHUMP
THUD

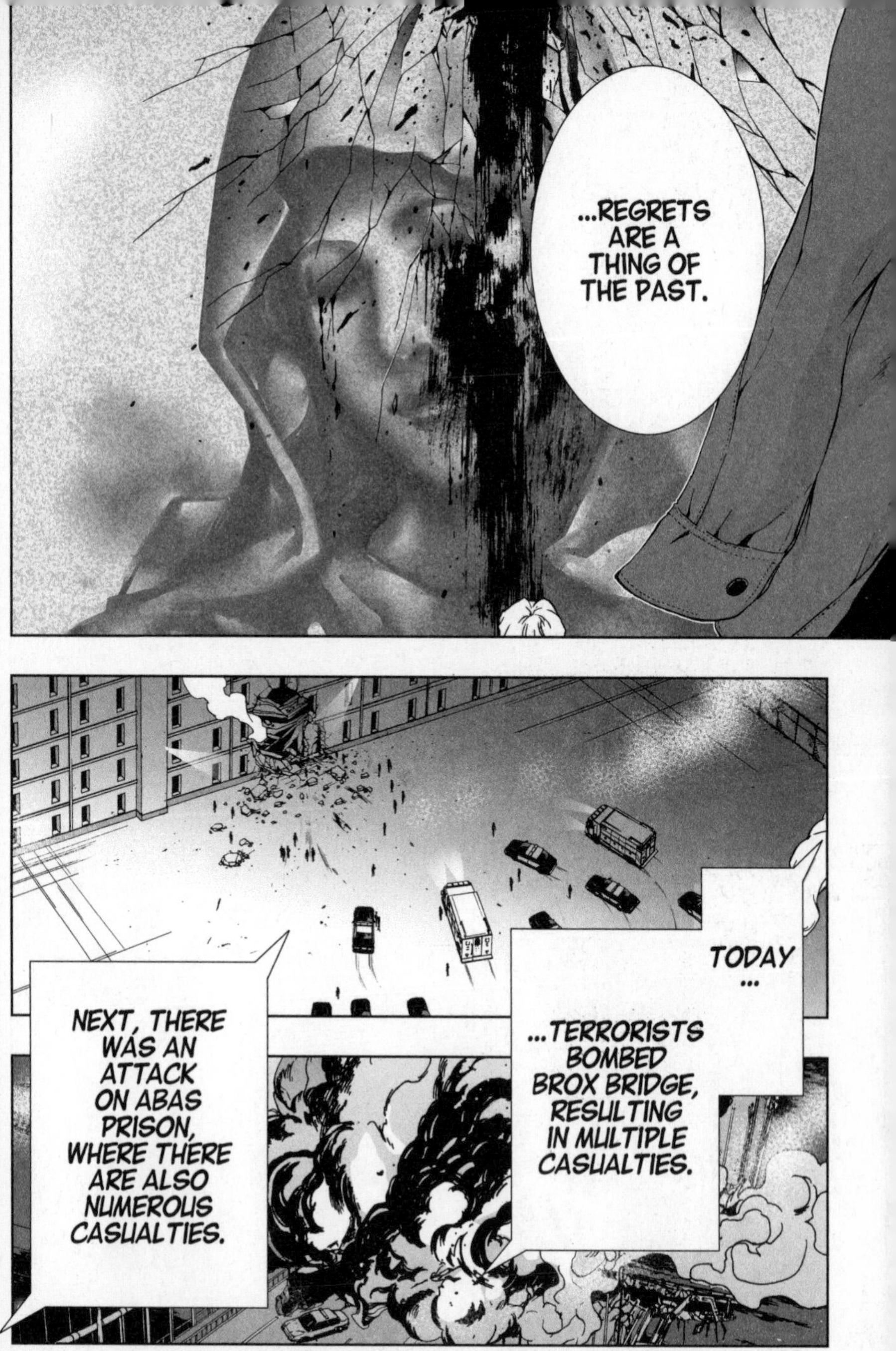
...REGRETS ARE A THING OF THE PAST.
TODAY ...
...TERRORISTS BOMBED BROX BRIDGE, RESULTING IN MULTIPLE CASUALTIES.
NEXT, THERE WAS AN ATTACK ON ABAS PRISON, WHERE THERE ARE ALSO NUMEROUS CASUALTIES.

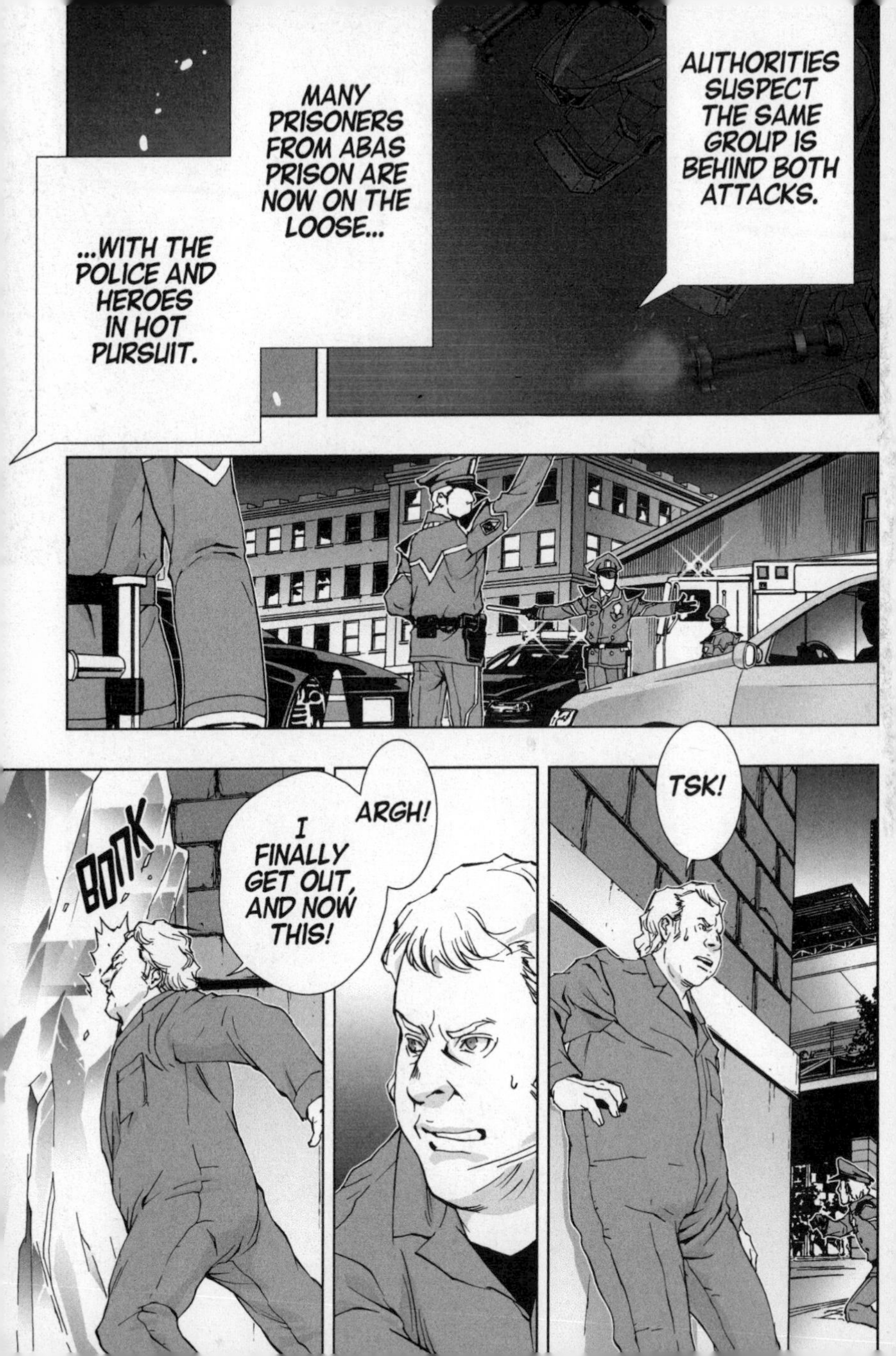
AUTHORITIES SUSPECT THE SAME GROUP IS BEHIND BOTH ATTACKS.
MANY PRISONERS FROM ABAS PRISON ARE NOW ON THE LOOSE...
...WITH THE POLICE AND HEROES IN HOT PURSUIT.
TSK!
ARGH!
I FINALLY GET OUT, AND NOW THIS!
BONK

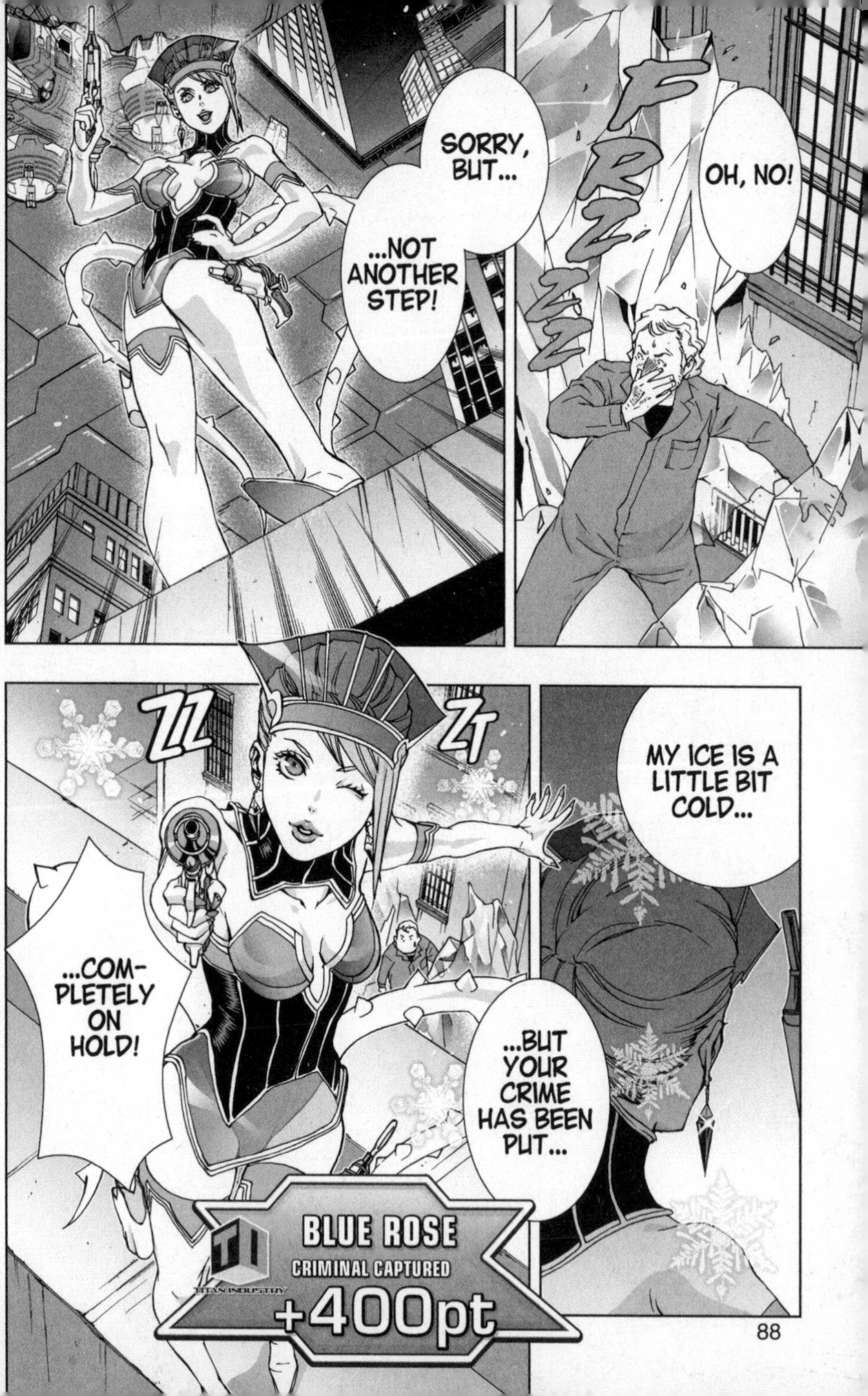
FRZZZ
OH, NO!
SORRY, BUT...
...NOT ANOTHER STEP!
MY ICE IS A LITTLE BIT COLD...
...BUT YOUR CRIME HAS BEEN PUT...
ZZ
ZT
...COM-PLETELY ON HOLD!
BLUE ROSE
CRIMINAL CAPTURED
TITAN INDUSTRY
+400pt

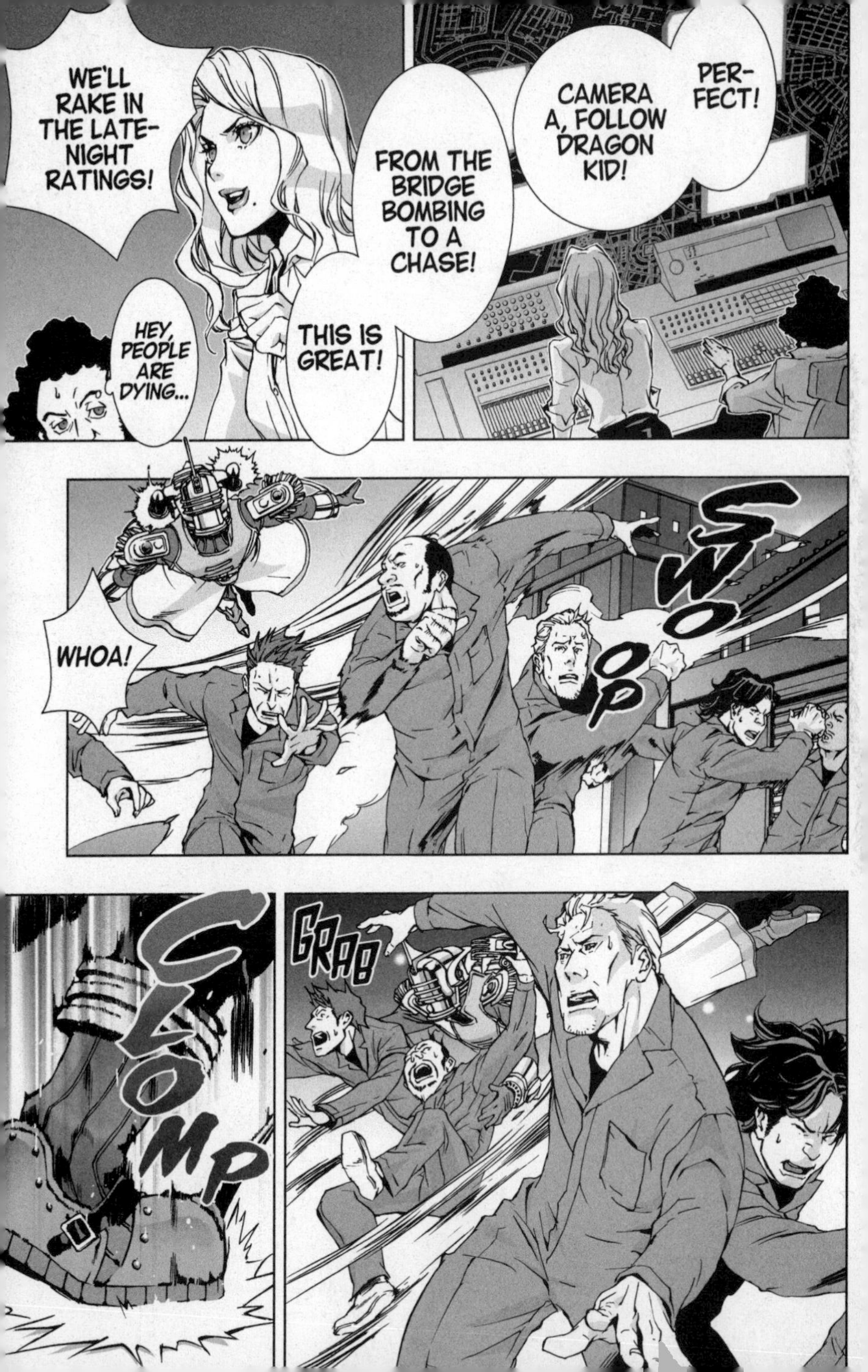
PER-FECT!
CAMERA A, FOLLOW DRAGON KID!
FROM THE BRIDGE BOMBING TO A CHASE!
THIS IS GREAT!
WE'LL RAKE IN THE LATE-NIGHT RATINGS!
HEY, PEOPLE ARE DYING...
SWOOP
WHOA!
GRAB
CLOMP

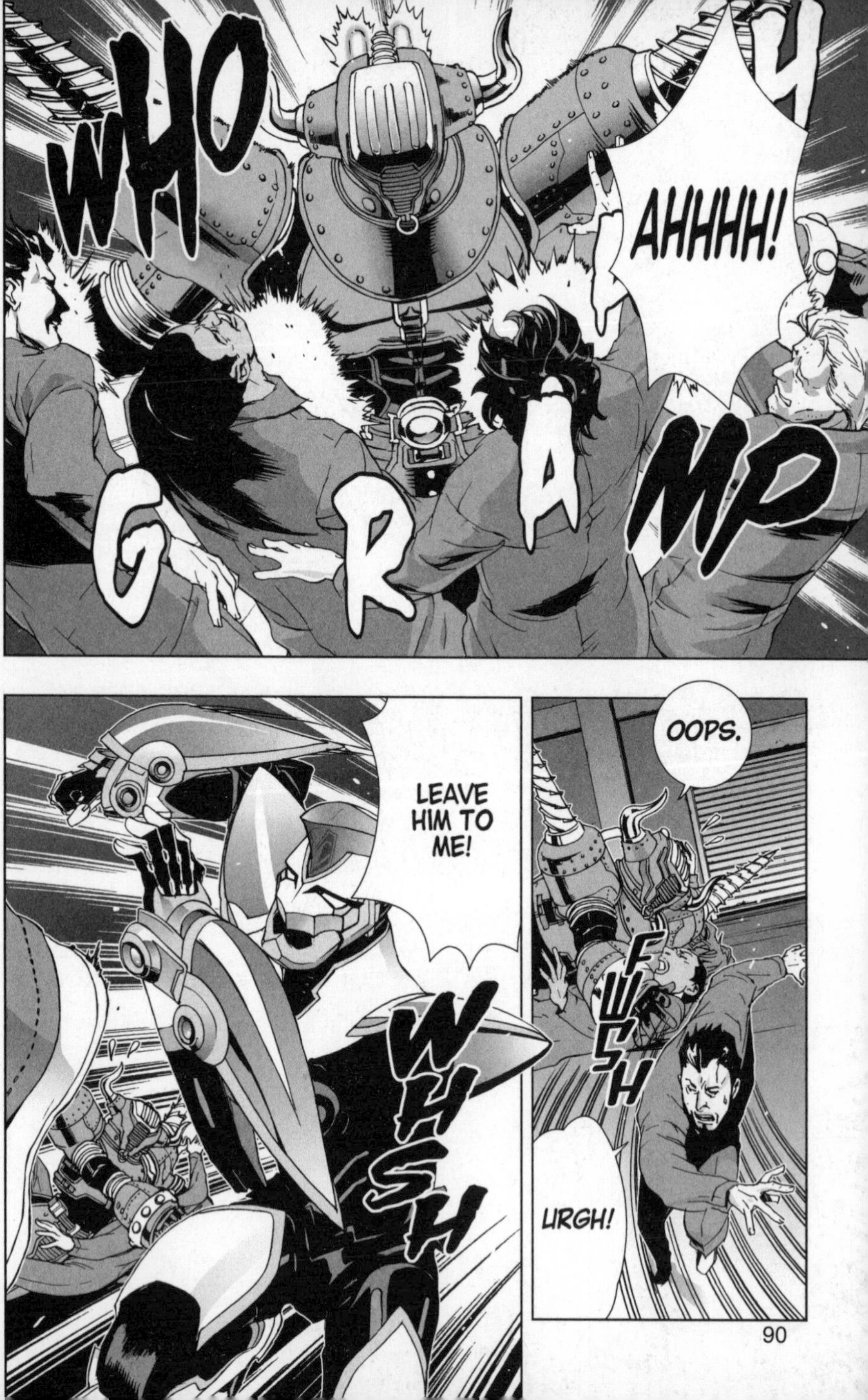
AHHHH!
OOPS.
URGH!
LEAVE HIM TO ME!

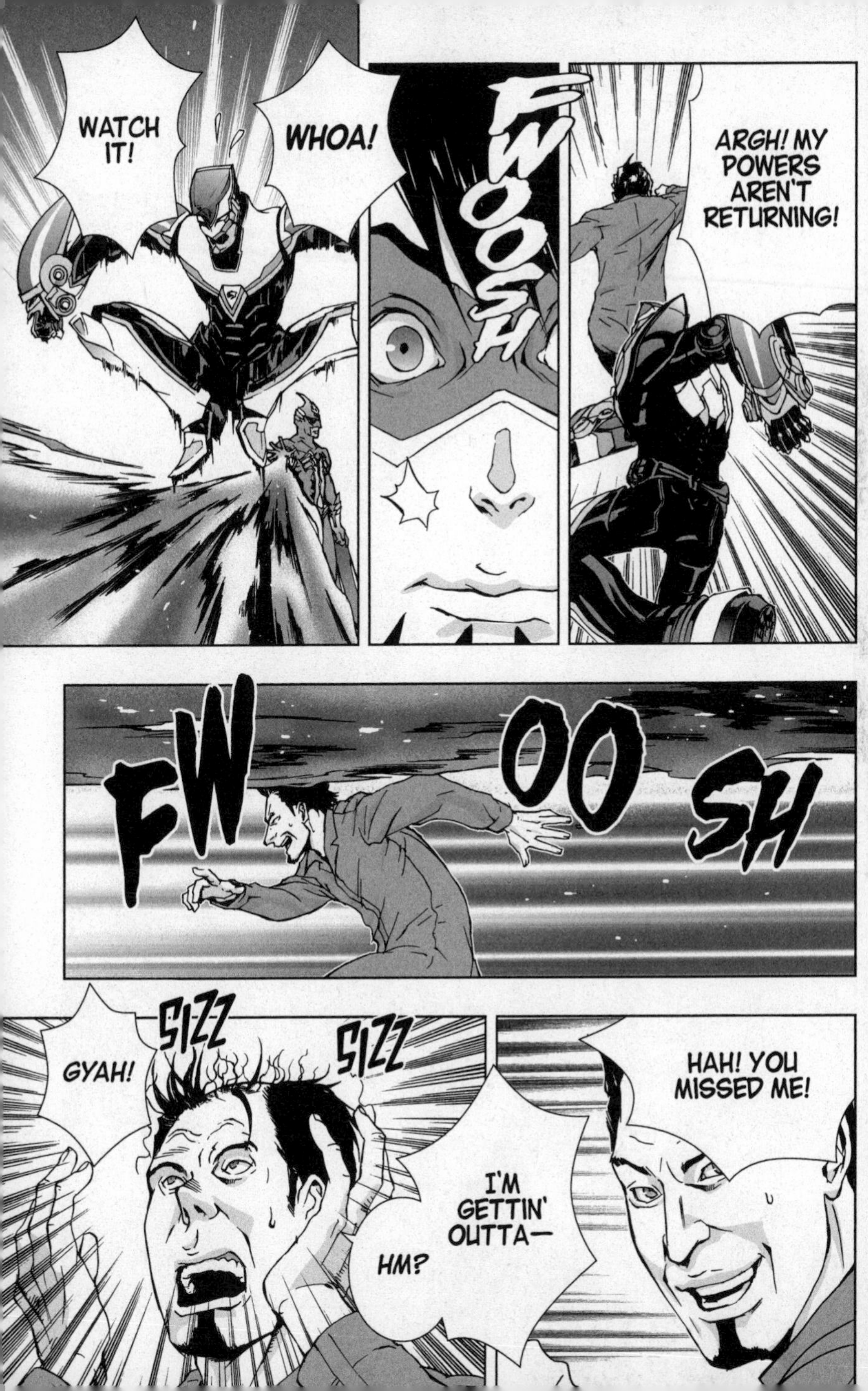
ARGH! MY POWERS AREN'T RETURNING!
FWOOSH
WHOA!
WATCH IT!
FWOOSH
HAH! YOU MISSED ME!
I'M GETTIN' OUTTA—
HM?
SIZZ
SIZZ
GYAH!

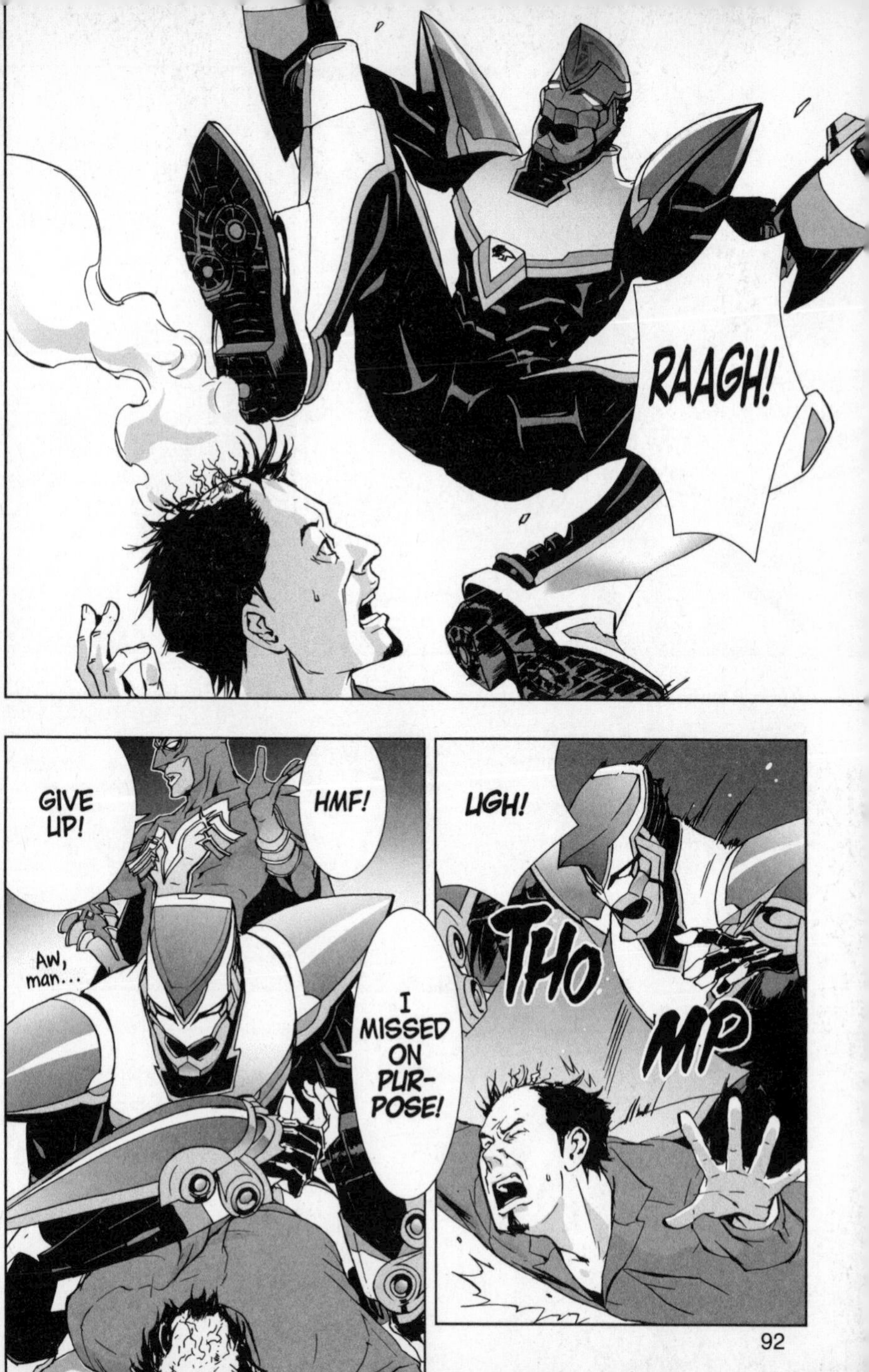
RAAGH!
UGH!
THOMP
HMF!
GIVE UP!
I MISSED ON PUR-POSE!
Aw, man…

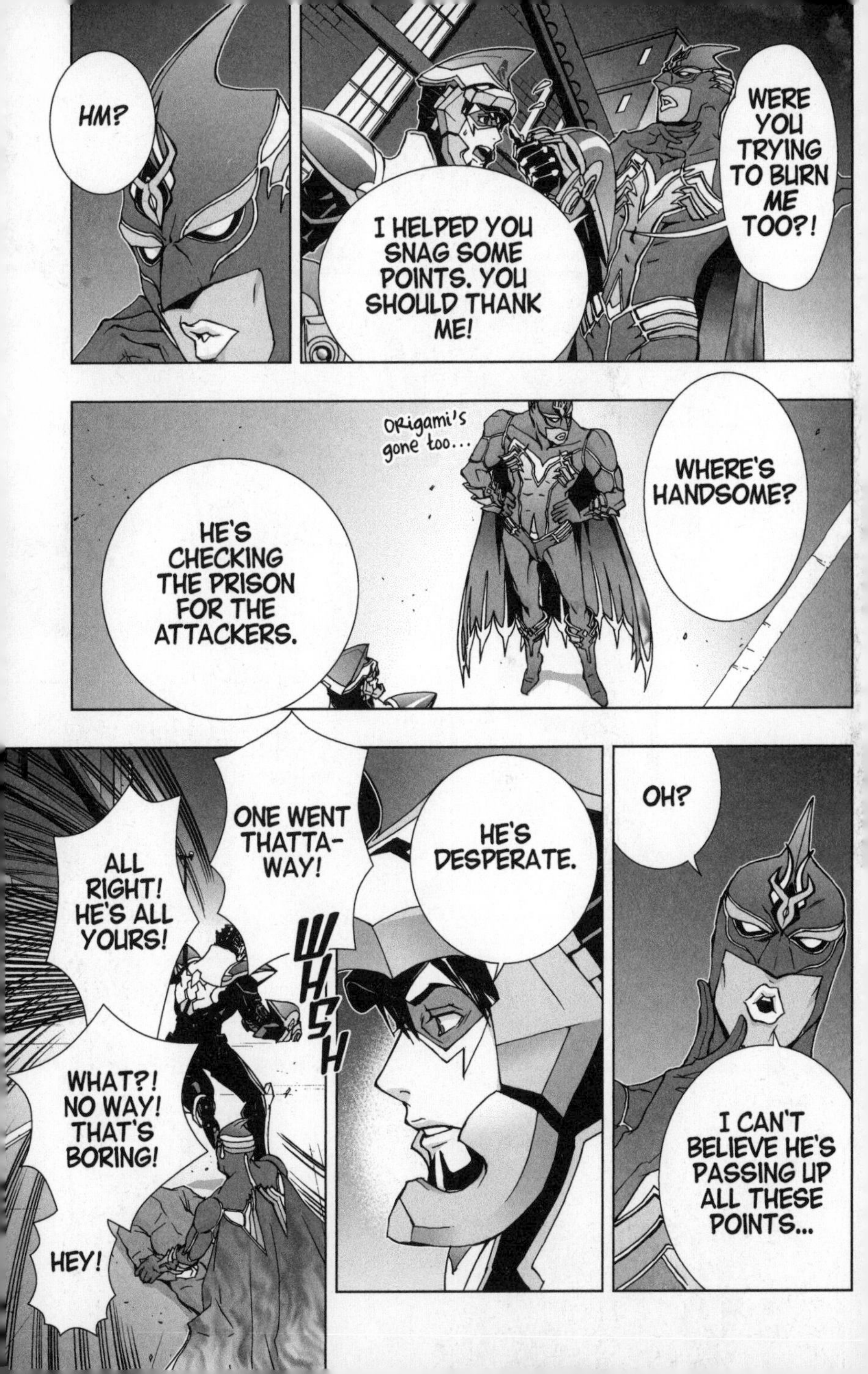
WERE YOU TRYING TO BURN ME TOO?!
I HELPED YOU SNAG SOME POINTS. YOU SHOULD THANK ME!
HM?
WHERE'S HANDSOME?
Origami's gone too...
HE'S CHECKING THE PRISON FOR THE ATTACKERS.
OH?
I CAN'T BELIEVE HE'S PASSING UP ALL THESE POINTS...
HE'S DESPERATE.
WHSH
ONE WENT THATTA-WAY!
ALL RIGHT! HE'S ALL YOURS!
WHAT?! NO WAY! THAT'S BORING!
HEY!

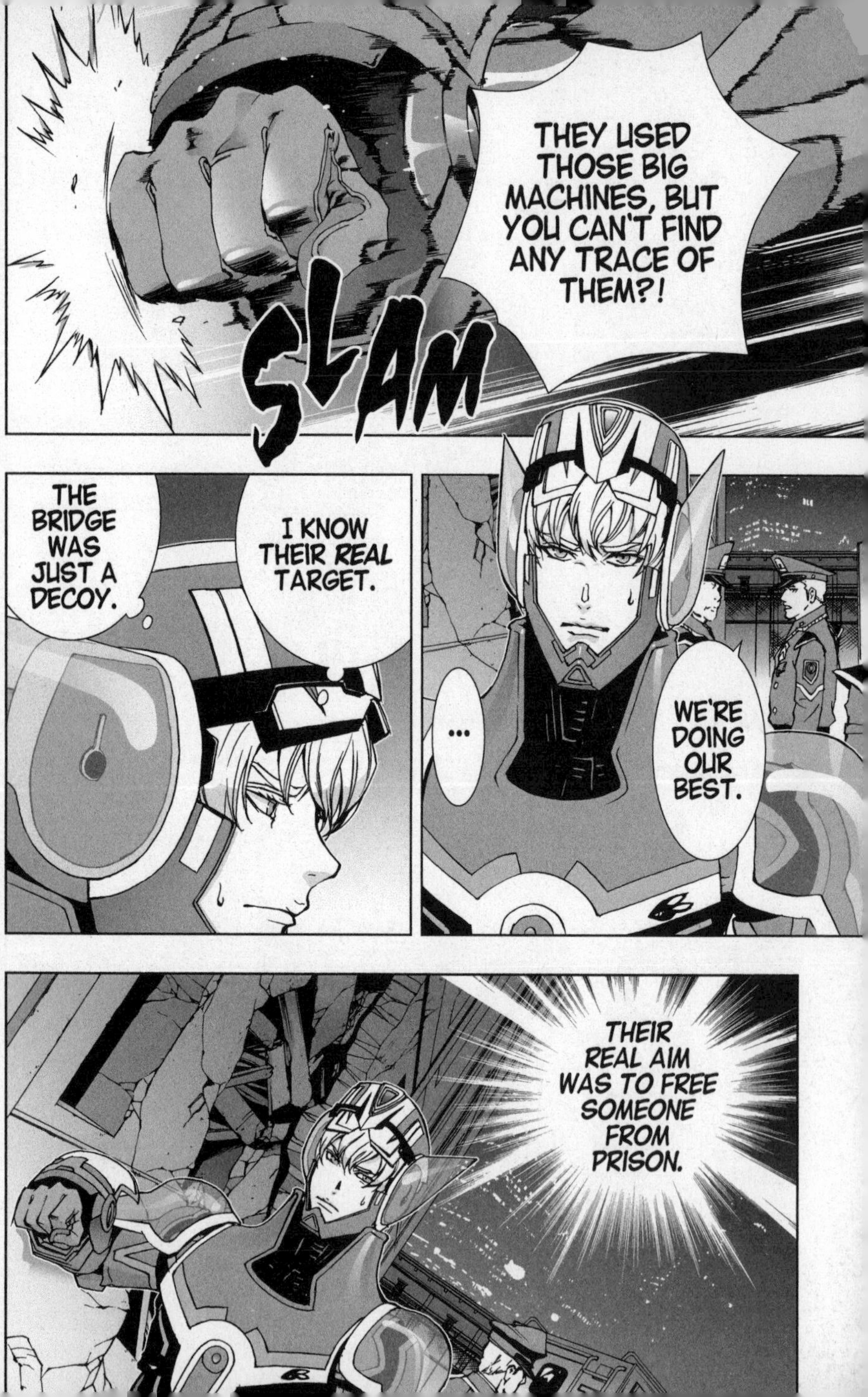
THEY USED THOSE BIG MACHINES, BUT YOU CAN'T FIND ANY TRACE OF THEM?!
SLAM
WE'RE DOING OUR BEST.
...
I KNOW THEIR *REAL* TARGET.
THE BRIDGE WAS JUST A DECOY.
THEIR REAL AIM WAS TO FREE SOMEONE FROM PRISON.

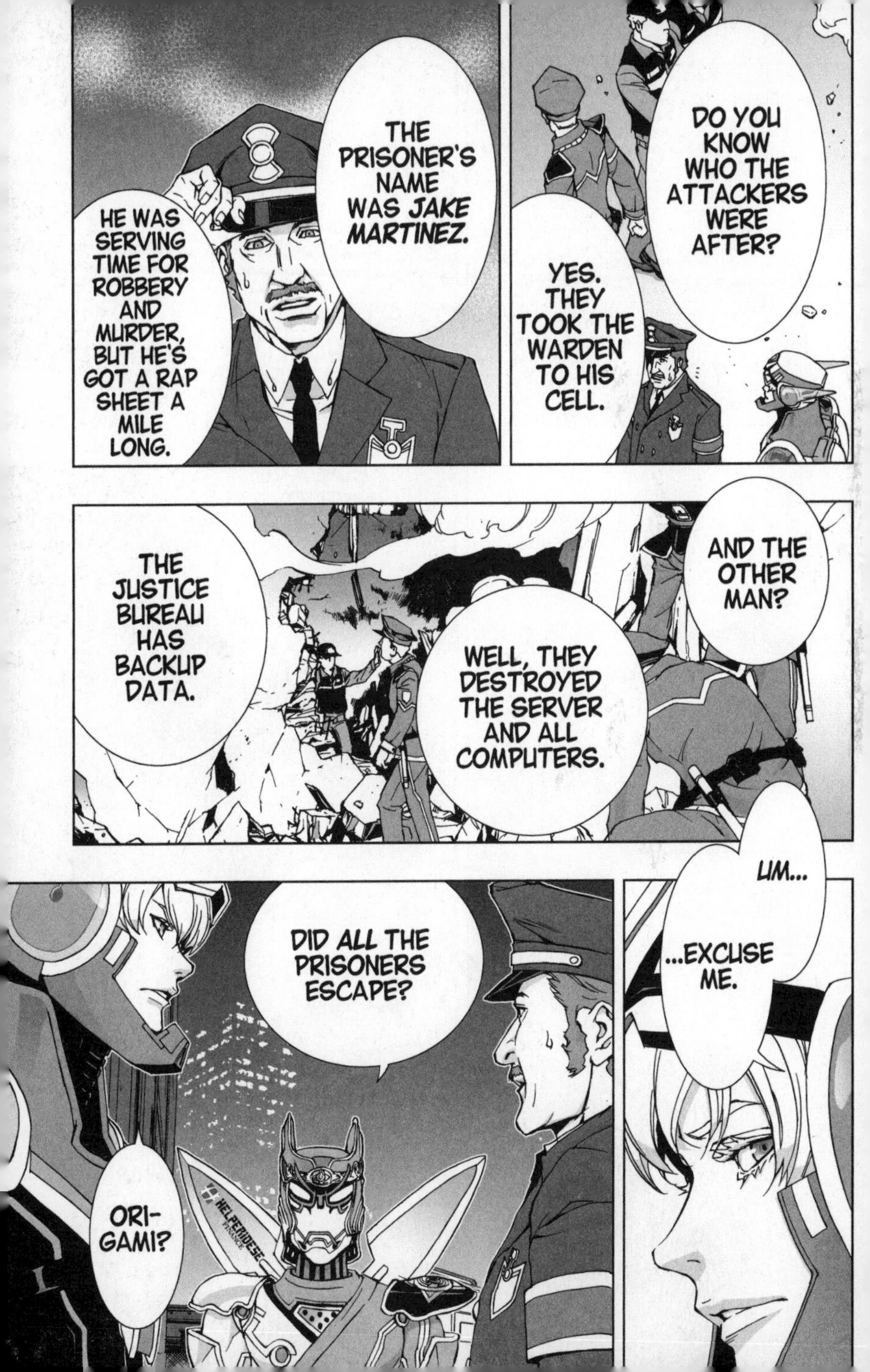
DO YOU KNOW WHO THE ATTACKERS WERE AFTER?
YES. THEY TOOK THE WARDEN TO HIS CELL.
THE PRISONER'S NAME WAS JAKE MARTINEZ.
HE WAS SERVING TIME FOR ROBBERY AND MURDER, BUT HE'S GOT A RAP SHEET A MILE LONG.
AND THE OTHER MAN?
WELL, THEY DESTROYED THE SERVER AND ALL COMPUTERS.
THE JUSTICE BUREAU HAS BACKUP DATA.
UM...
...EXCUSE ME.
DID ALL THE PRISONERS ESCAPE?
ORI-GAMI?

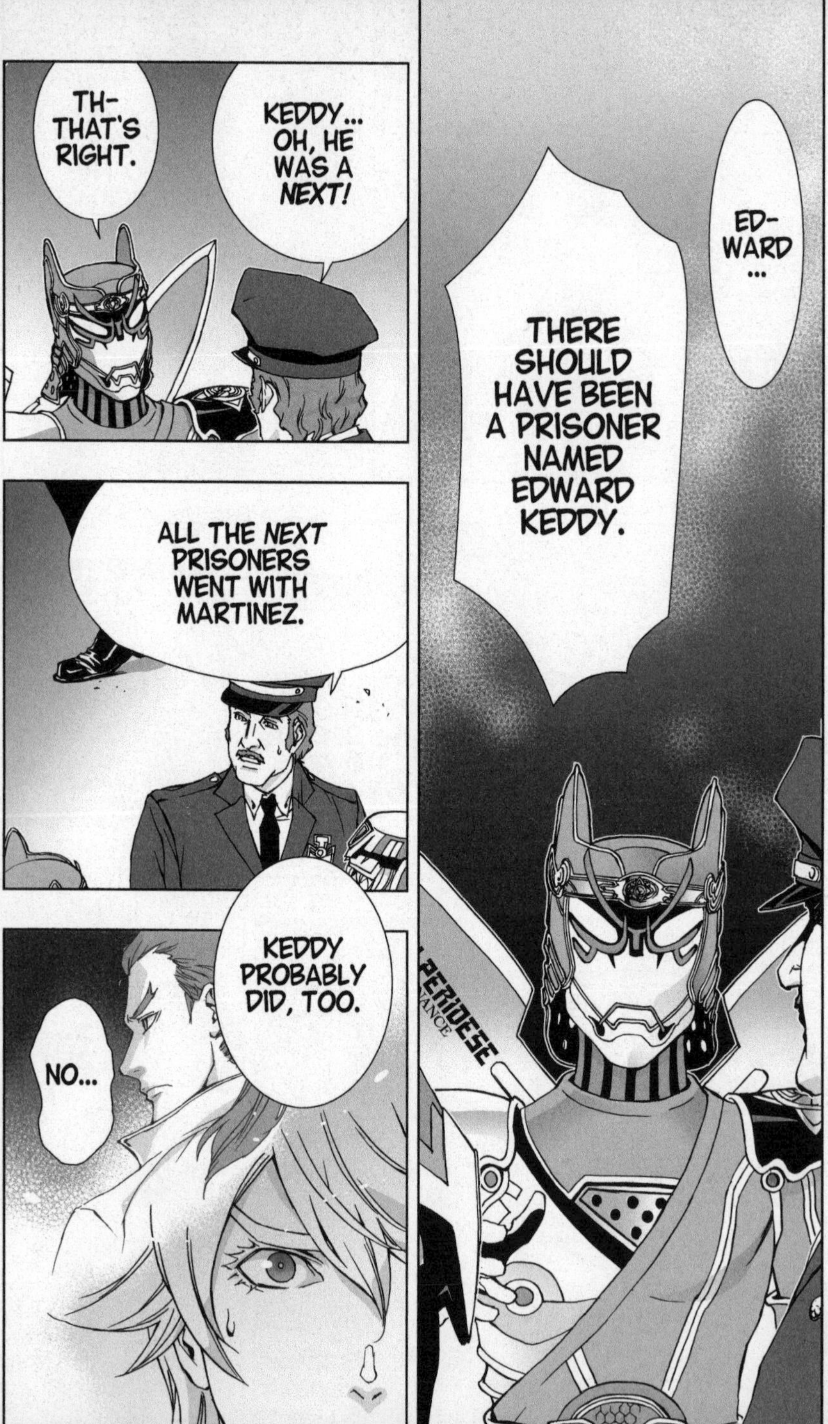
ED-WARD...
THERE SHOULD HAVE BEEN A PRISONER NAMED EDWARD KEDDY.
KEDDY... OH, HE WAS A *NEXT*!
TH-THAT'S RIGHT.
ALL THE *NEXT* PRISONERS WENT WITH MARTINEZ.
KEDDY PROBABLY DID, TOO.
NO...

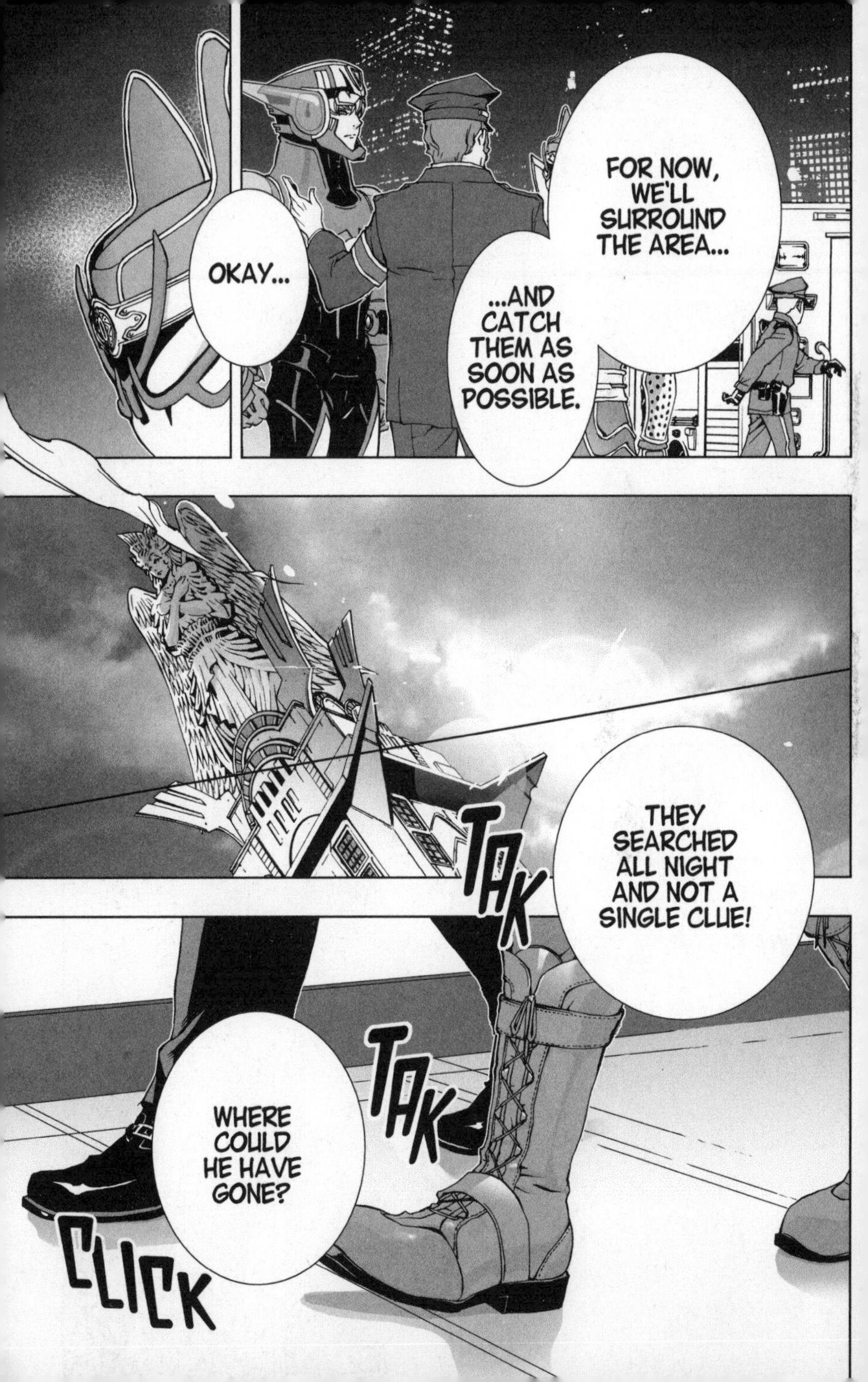
FOR NOW, WE'LL SURROUND THE AREA...
...AND CATCH THEM AS SOON AS POSSIBLE.
OKAY...
THEY SEARCHED ALL NIGHT AND NOT A SINGLE CLUE!
TAK
TAK
WHERE COULD HE HAVE GONE?
CLICK

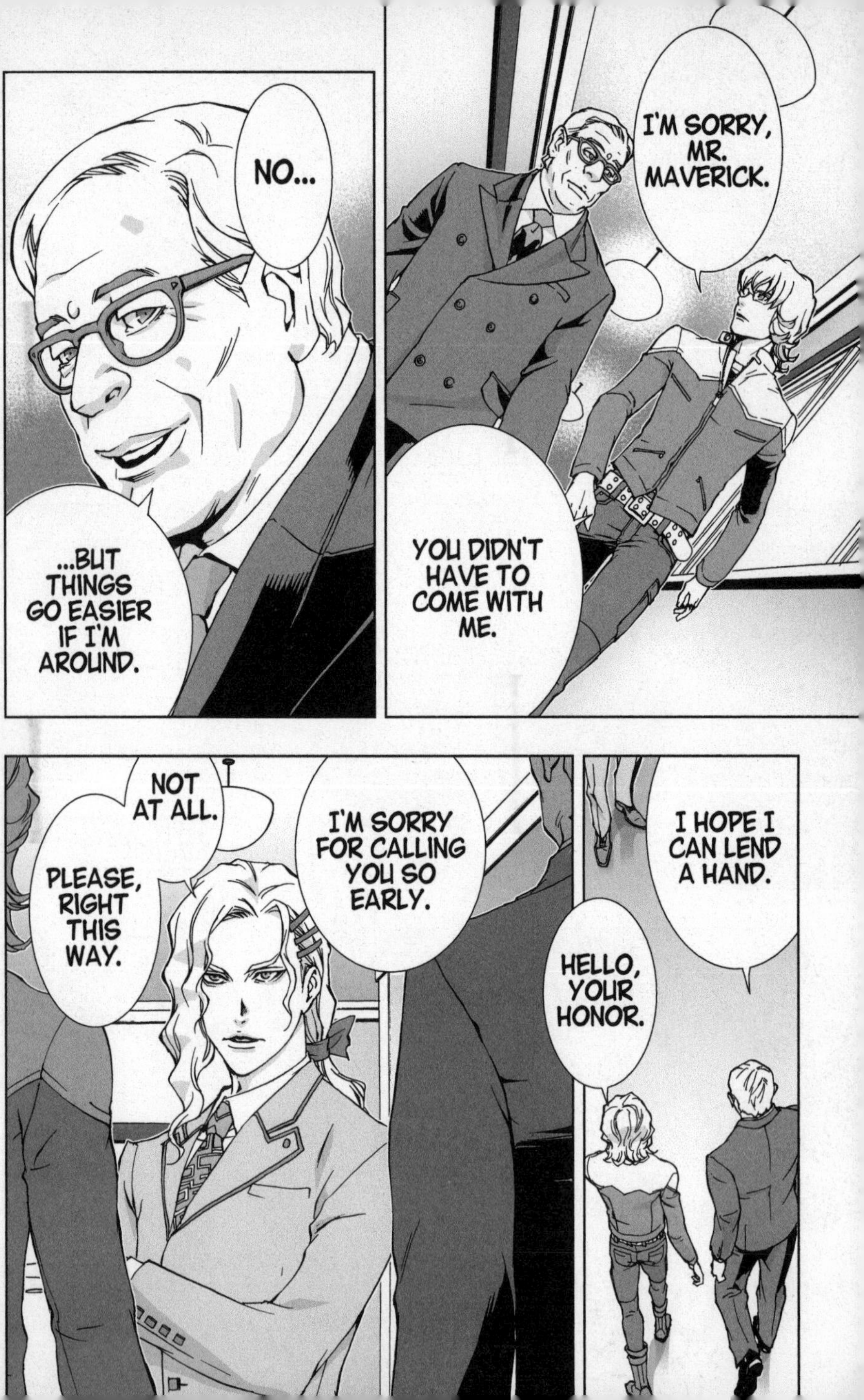
I'M SORRY, MR. MAVERICK.
YOU DIDN'T HAVE TO COME WITH ME.
NO...
...BUT THINGS GO EASIER IF I'M AROUND.
I HOPE I CAN LEND A HAND.
HELLO, YOUR HONOR.
I'M SORRY FOR CALLING YOU SO EARLY.
NOT AT ALL.
PLEASE, RIGHT THIS WAY.

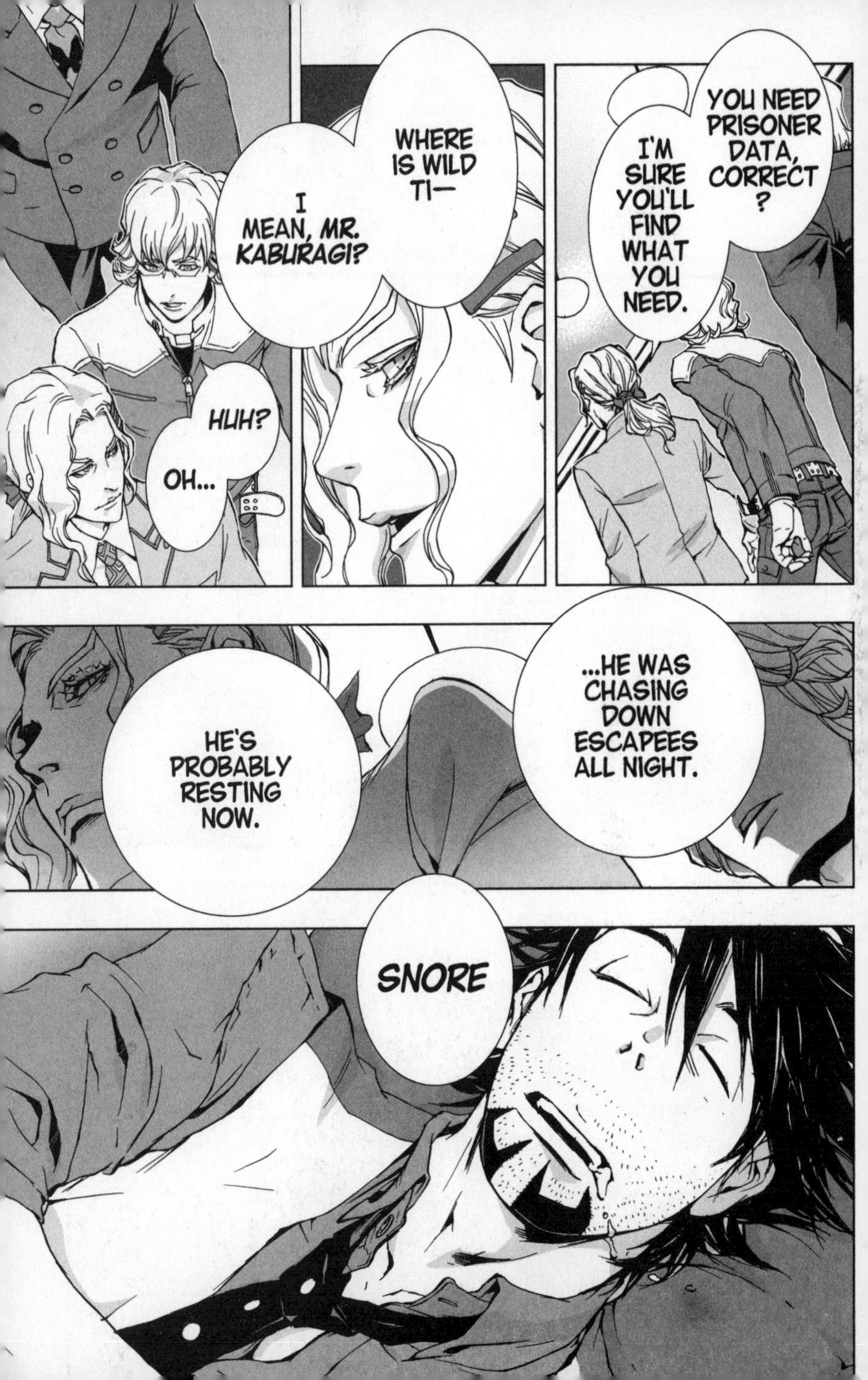
YOU NEED PRISONER DATA, CORRECT?
I'M SURE YOU'LL FIND WHAT YOU NEED.
WHERE IS WILD TI—
I MEAN, MR. KABURAGI?
HUH?
OH...
...HE WAS CHASING DOWN ESCAPEES ALL NIGHT.
HE'S PROBABLY RESTING NOW.
SNORE

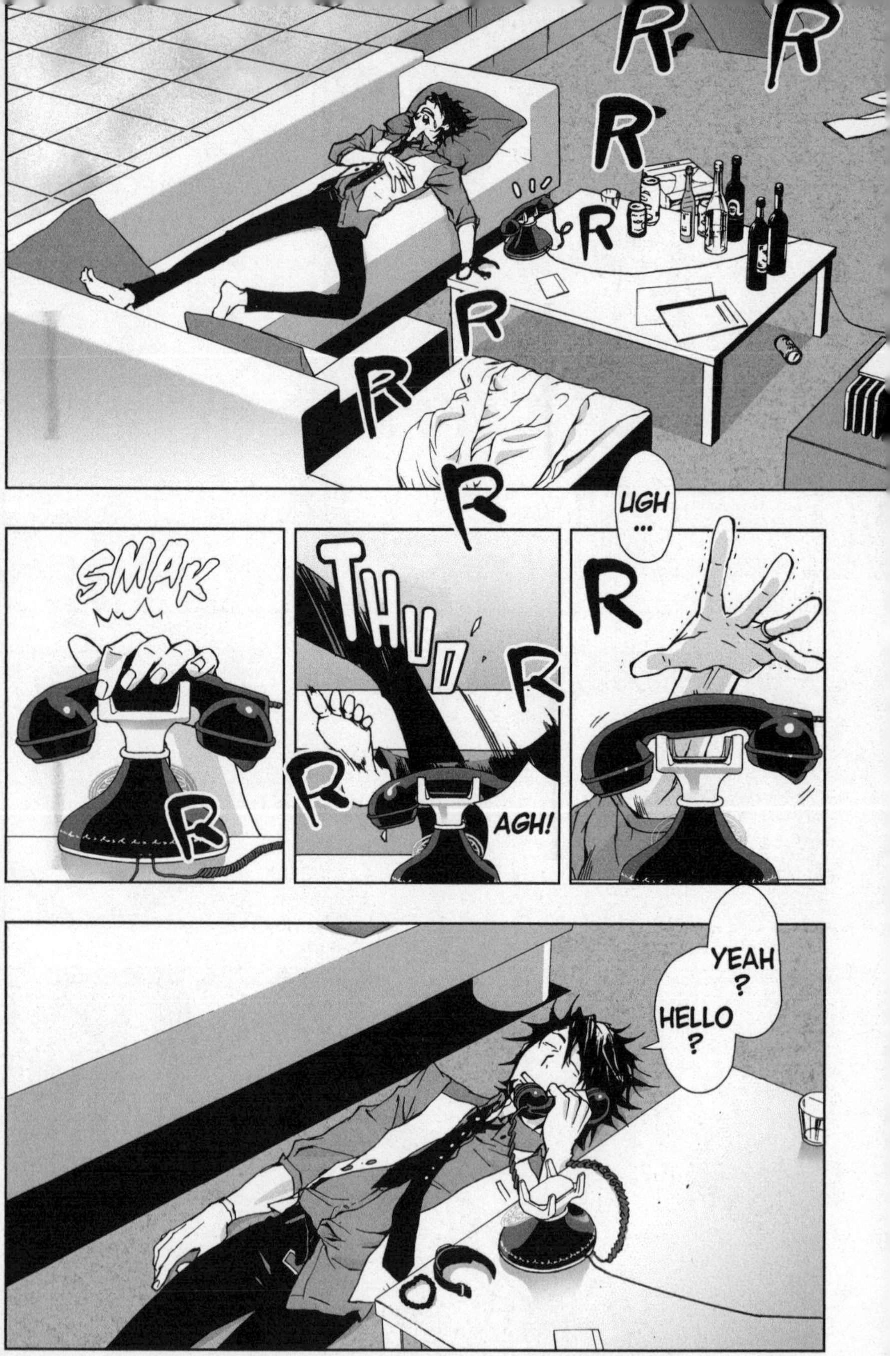
R
R
R
R
R
R
R
UGH...
R
THUD
R
R
AGH!
SMAK
R
YEAH?
HELLO?

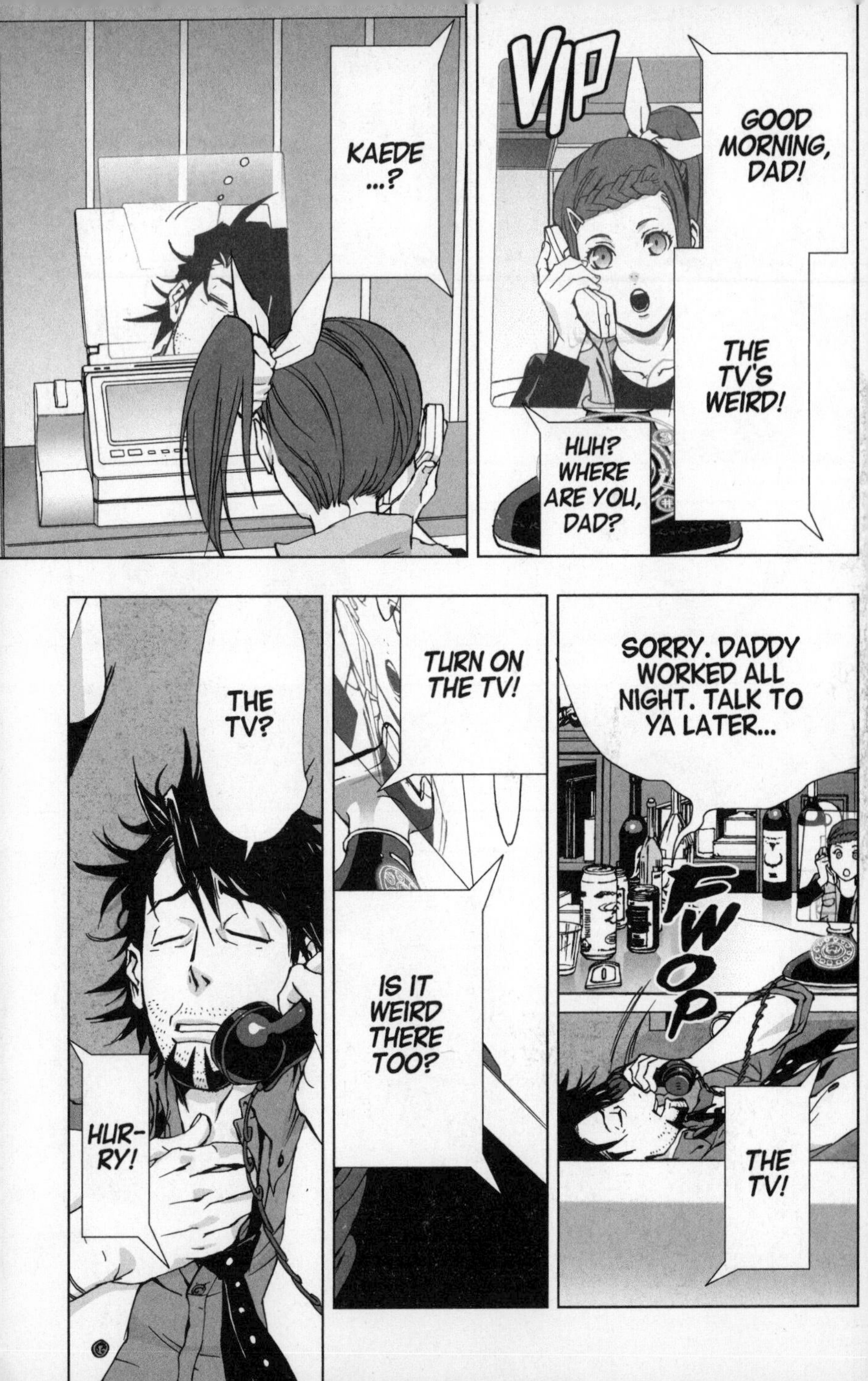
GOOD MORNING, DAD!
VIP
THE TV'S WEIRD!
HUH? WHERE ARE YOU, DAD?
KAEDE ...?
SORRY. DADDY WORKED ALL NIGHT. TALK TO YA LATER...
FWOP
THE TV!
TURN ON THE TV!
IS IT WEIRD THERE TOO?
THE TV?
HUR-RY!

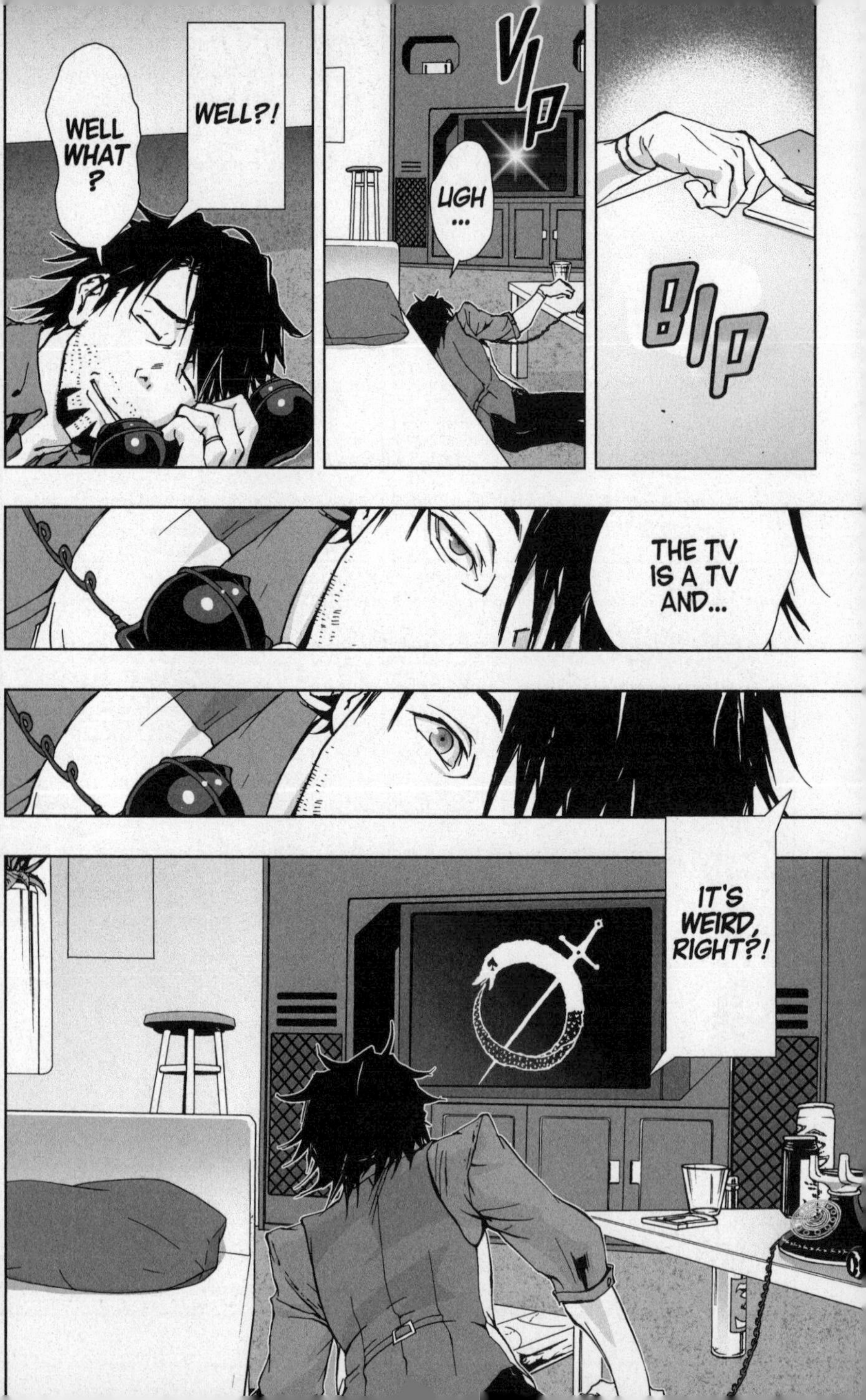
BIP
VIP
UGH...
WELL?!
WELL WHAT?
THE TV IS A TV AND...
IT'S WEIRD, RIGHT?!

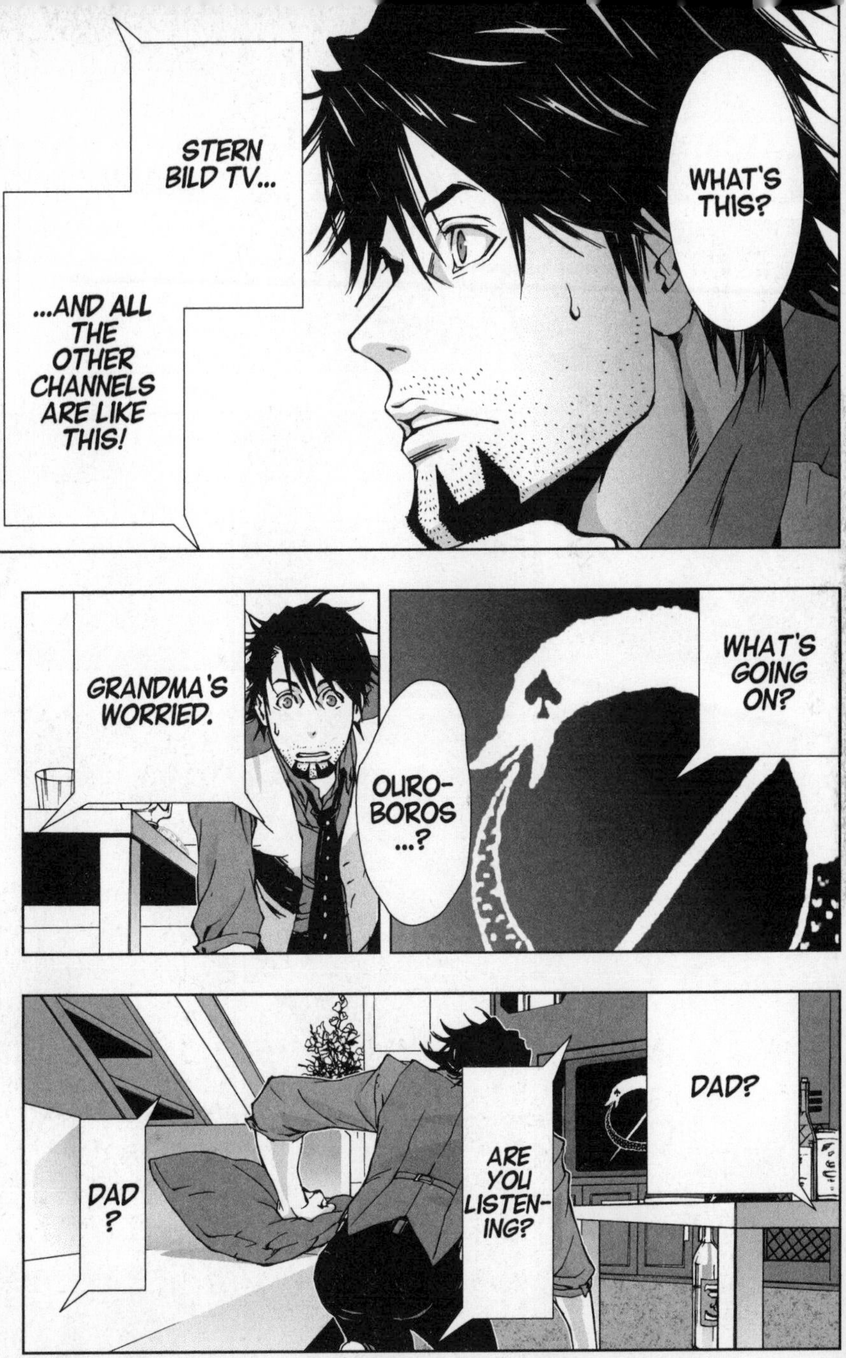
WHAT'S THIS?
STERN BILD TV...
...AND ALL THE OTHER CHANNELS ARE LIKE THIS!
WHAT'S GOING ON?
OURO-BOROS ...?
GRANDMA'S WORRIED.
DAD?
ARE YOU LISTEN-ING?
DAD?

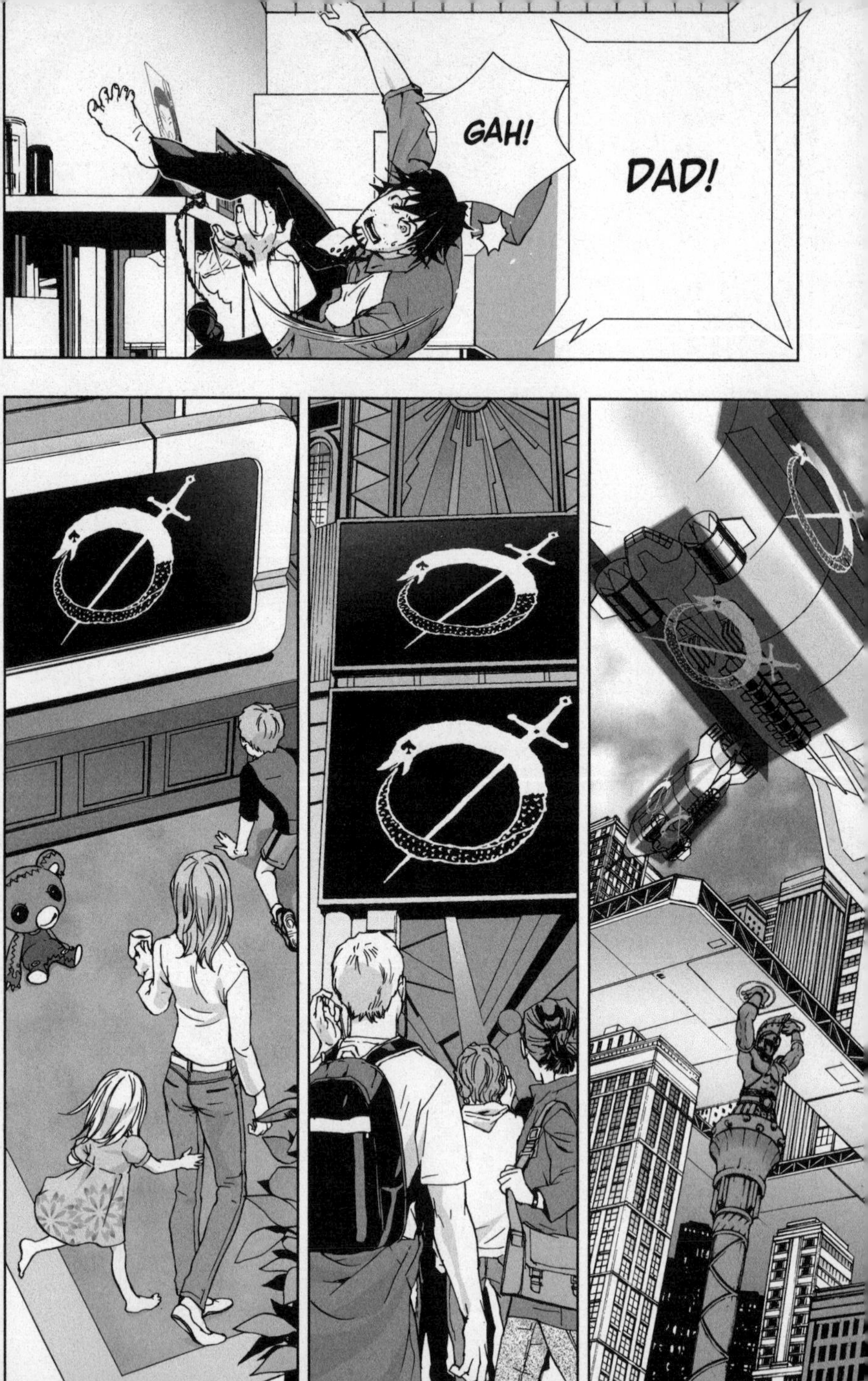
DAD!
GAH!

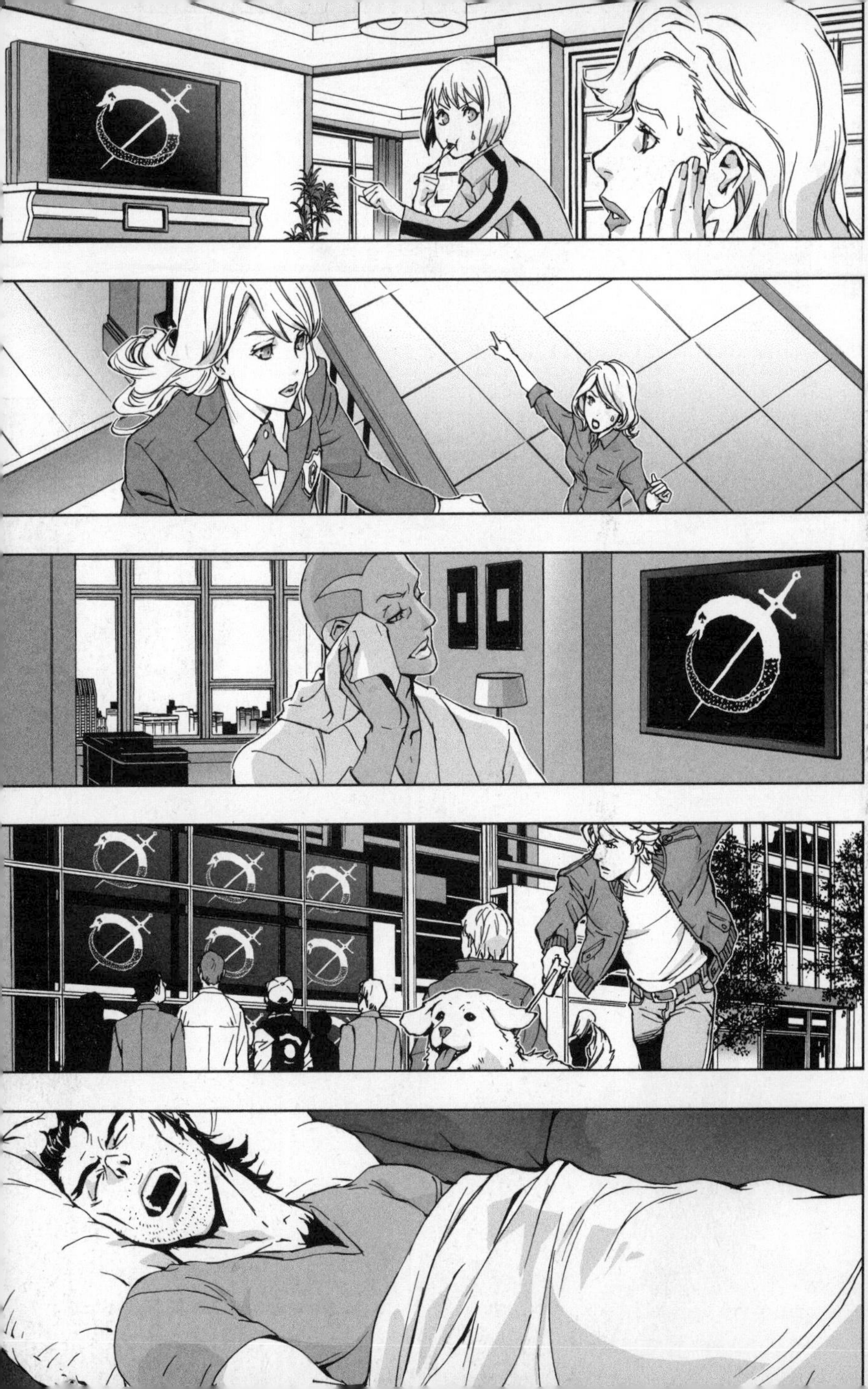

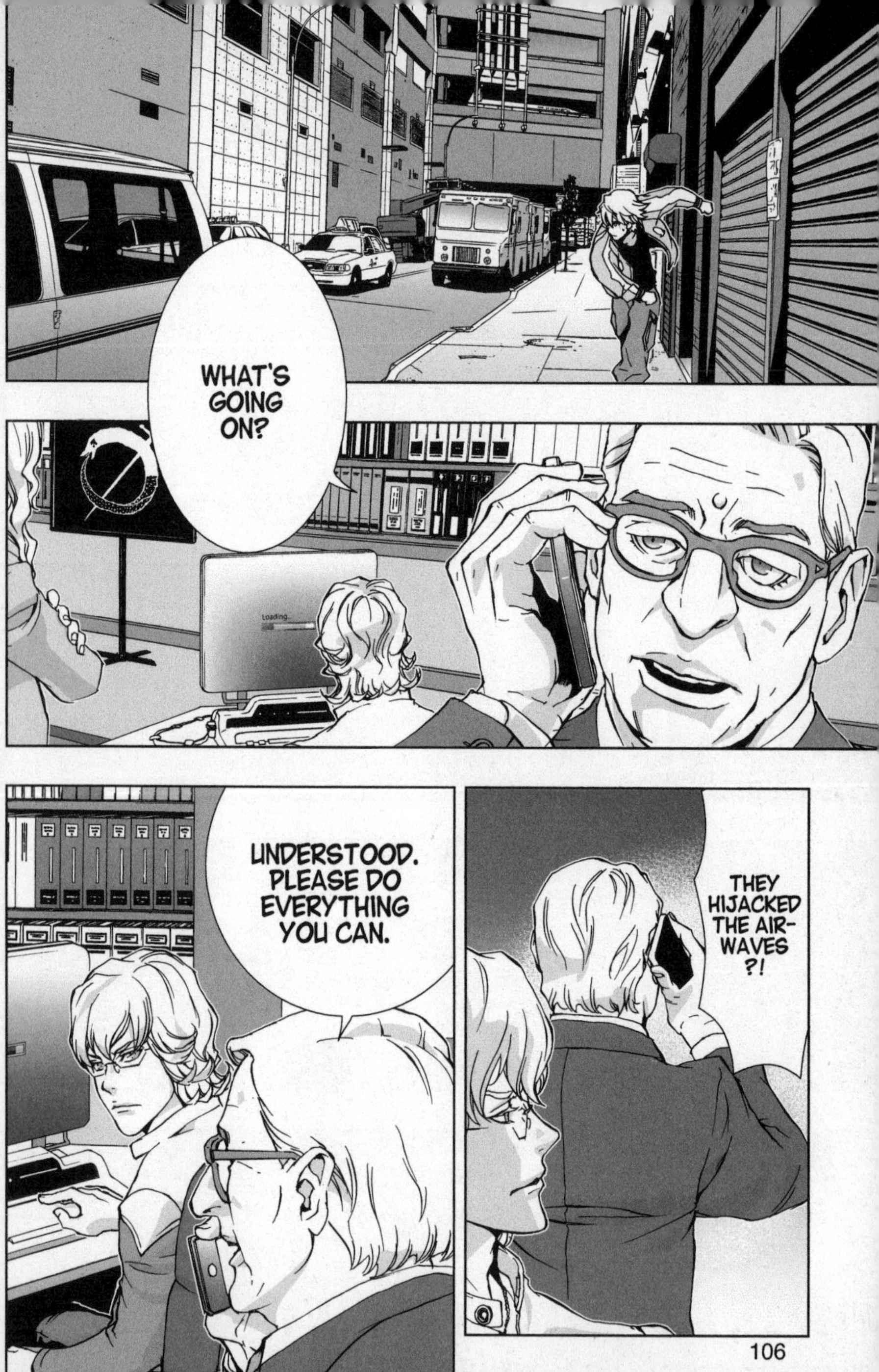
WHAT'S GOING ON?
THEY HIJACKED THE AIR-WAVES ?!
UNDERSTOOD. PLEASE DO EVERYTHING YOU CAN.

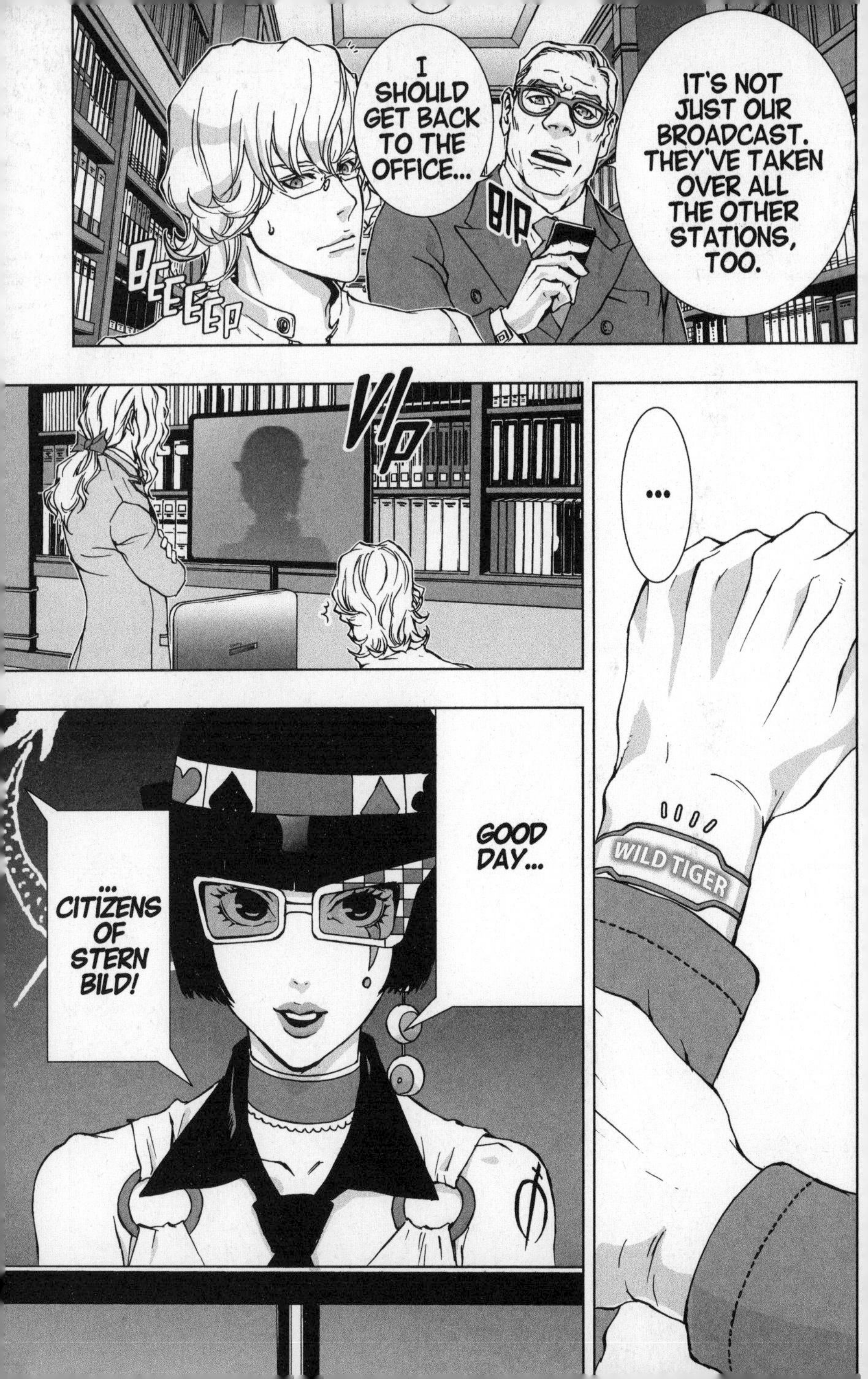
IT'S NOT JUST OUR BROADCAST. THEY'VE TAKEN OVER ALL THE OTHER STATIONS, TOO.
BIP
I SHOULD GET BACK TO THE OFFICE...
BEEEEEP
...
WILD TIGER
GOOD DAY...
... CITIZENS OF STERN BILD!

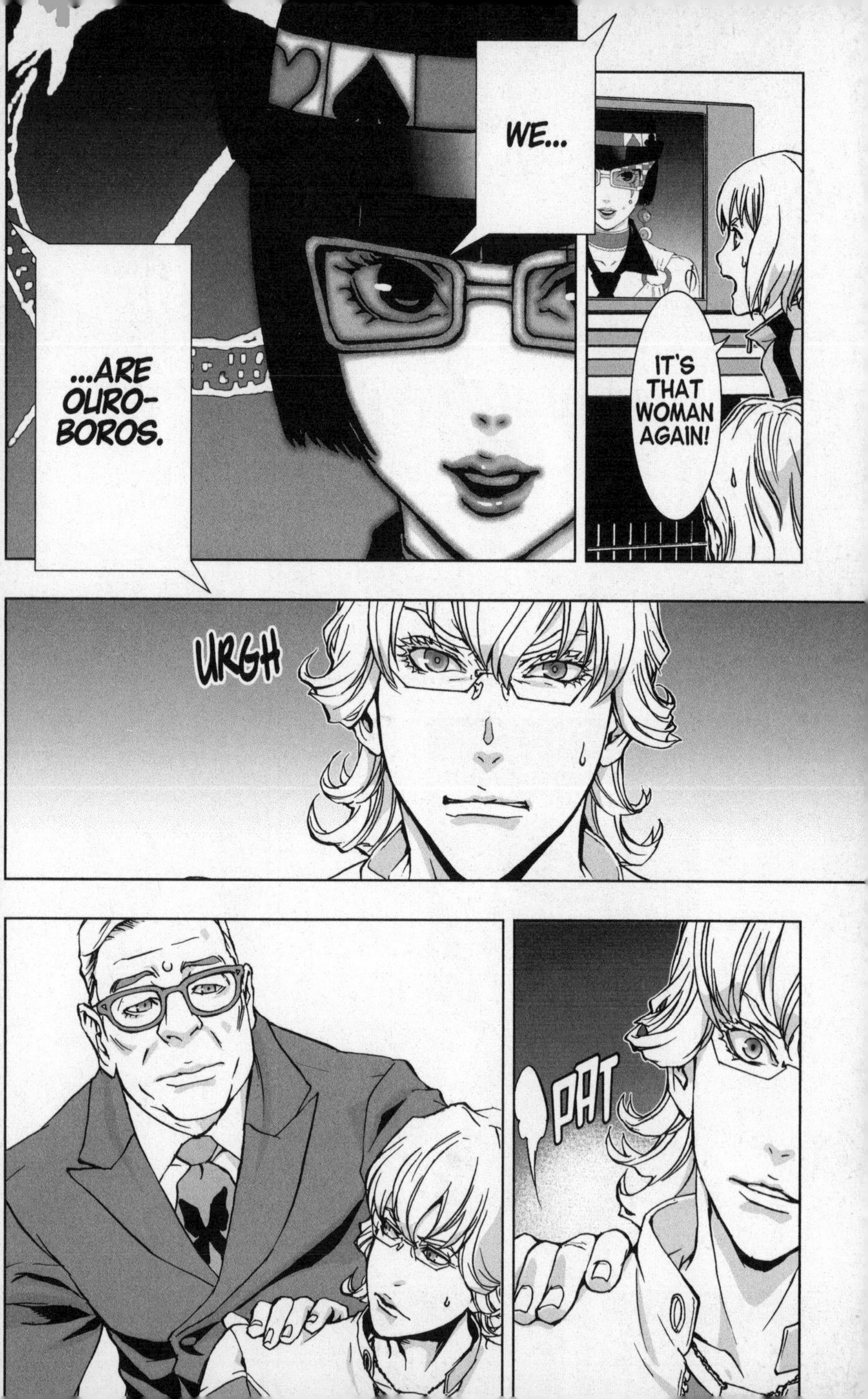
IT'S THAT WOMAN AGAIN!
WE...
...ARE OURO-BOROS.
URGH
PAT

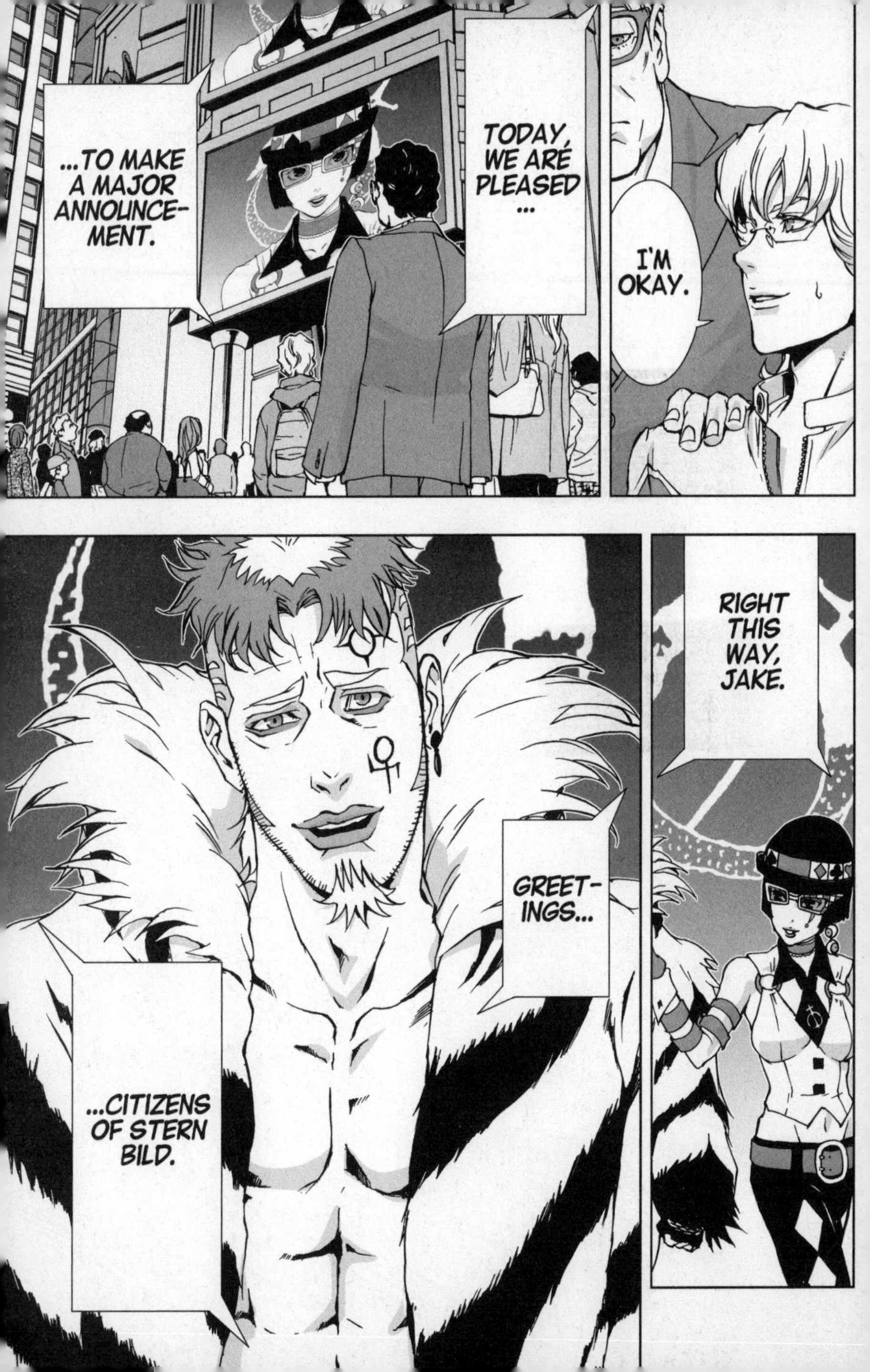
I'M OKAY.
TODAY, WE ARÉ PLEASED ...
...TO MAKE A MAJOR ANNOUNCE-MENT.
RIGHT THIS WAY, JAKE.
GREET-INGS...
...CITIZENS OF STERN BILD.

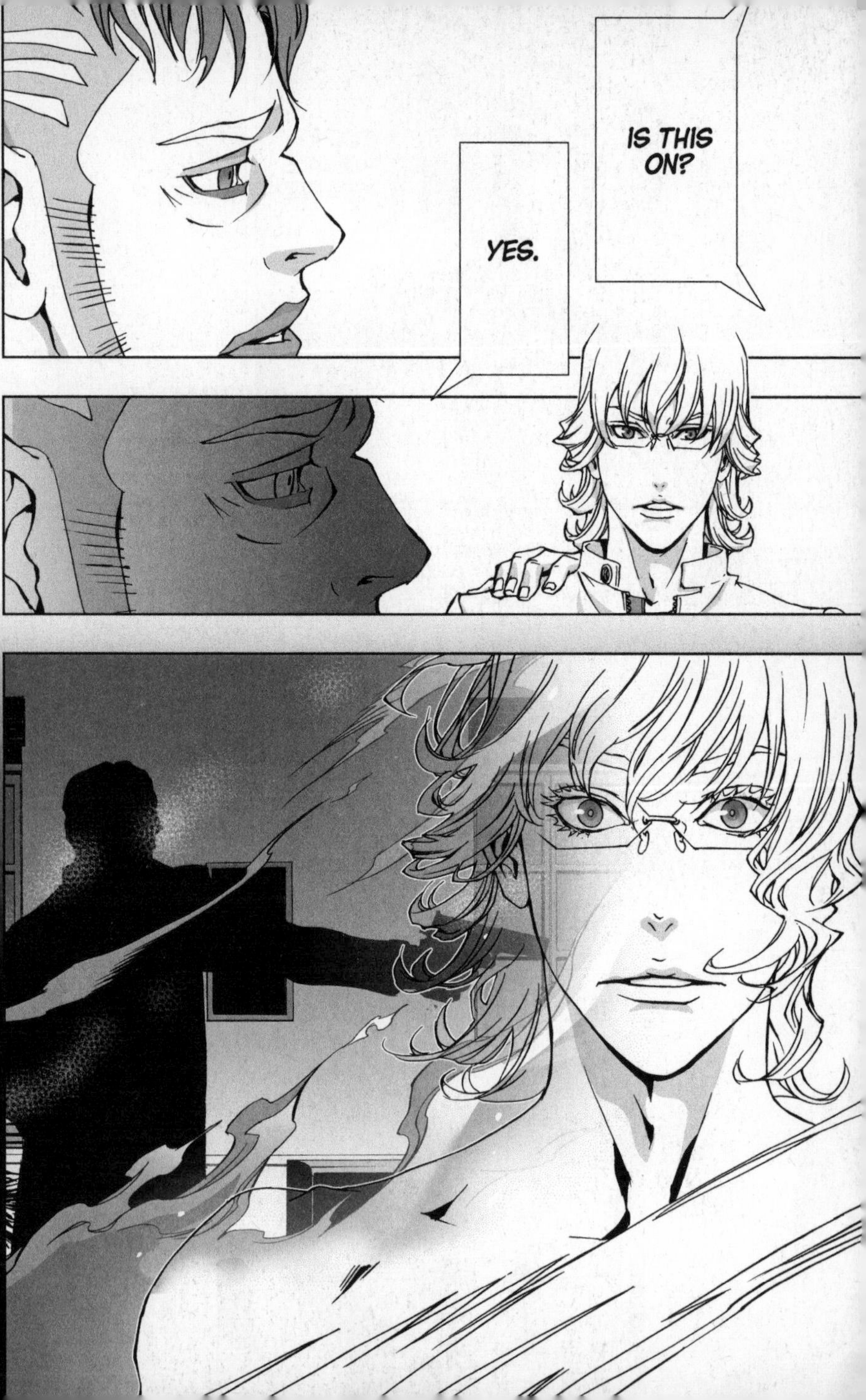
IS THIS ON?
YES.

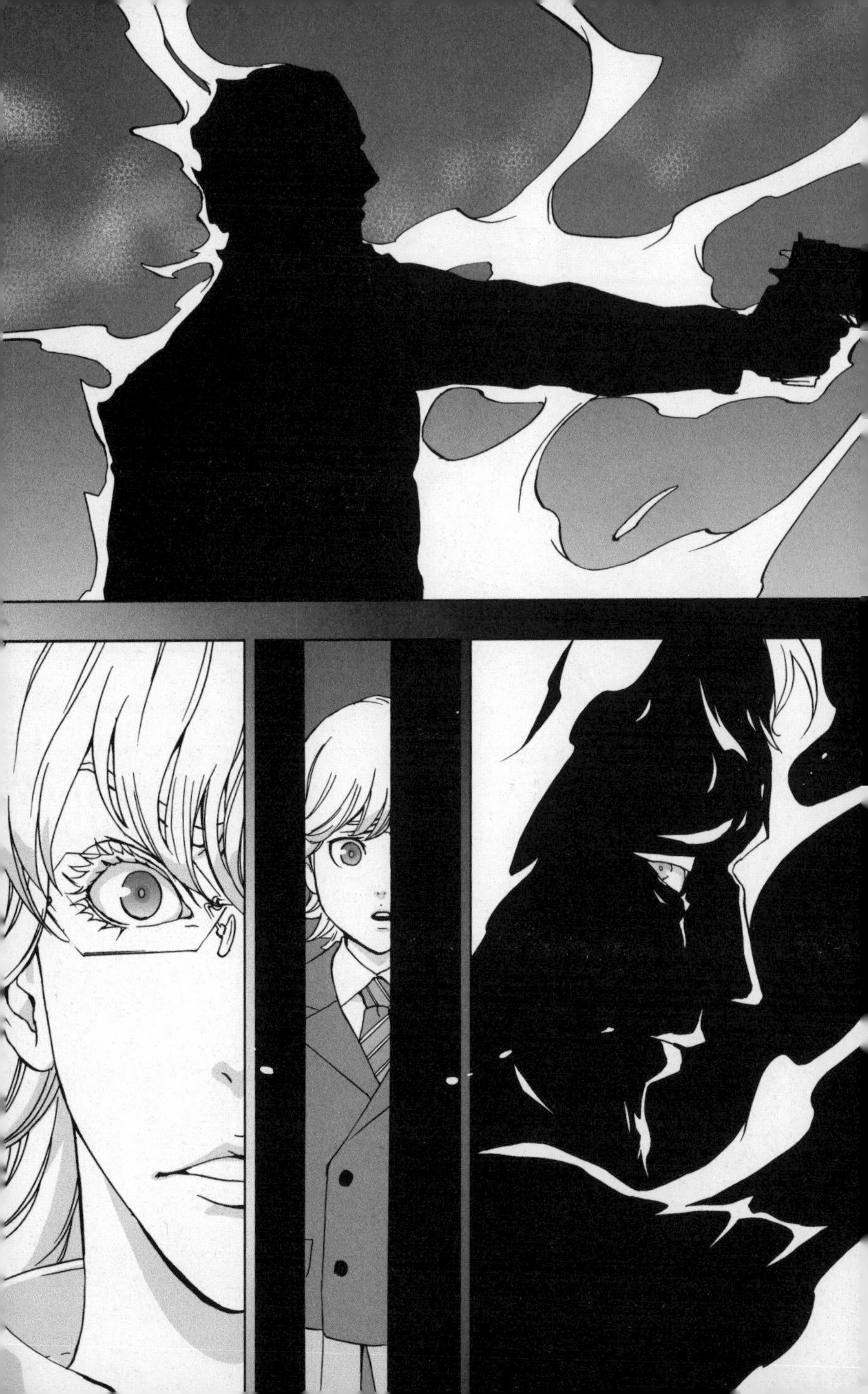

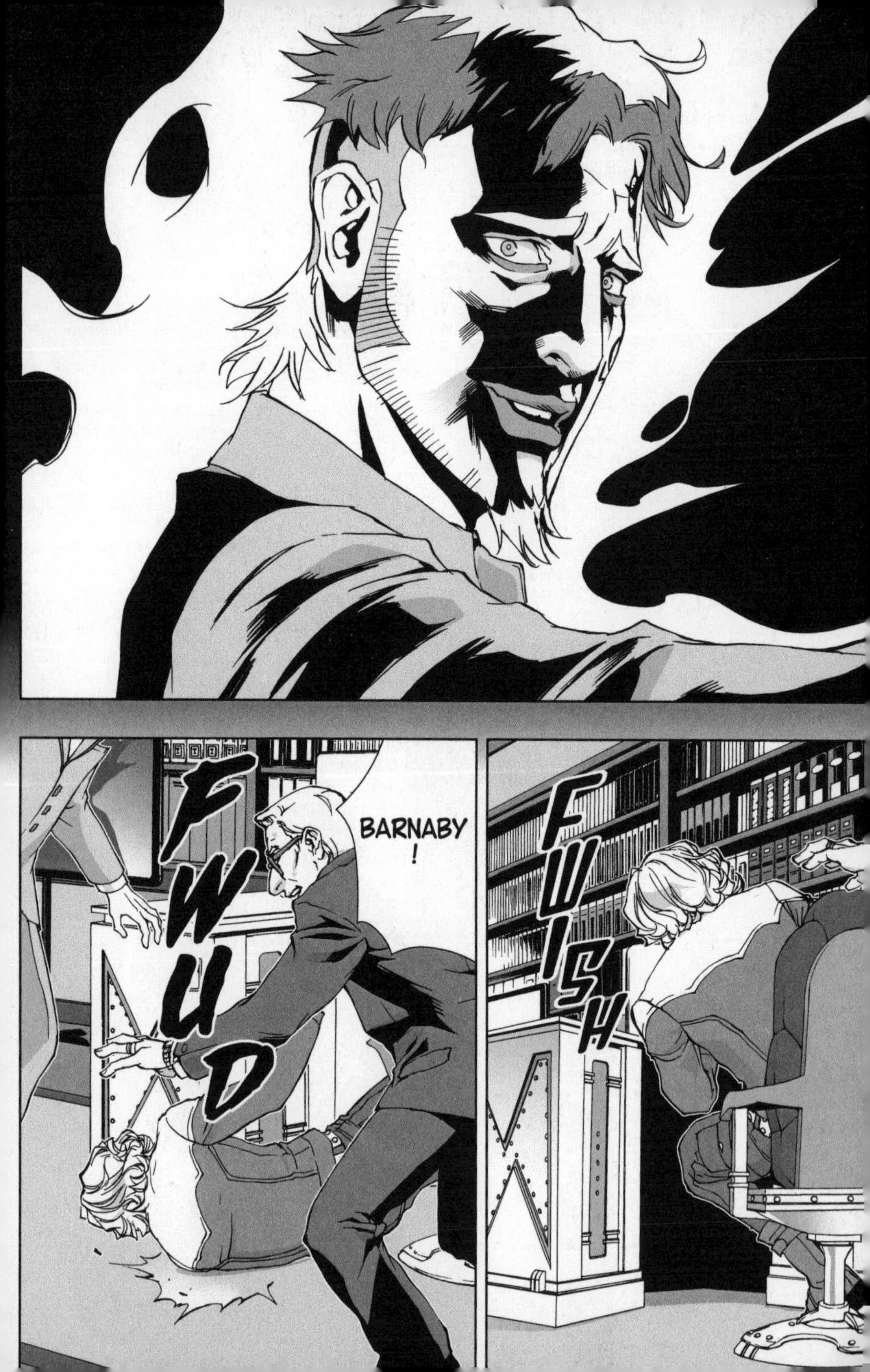
FWISH
BARNABY!
FWUD

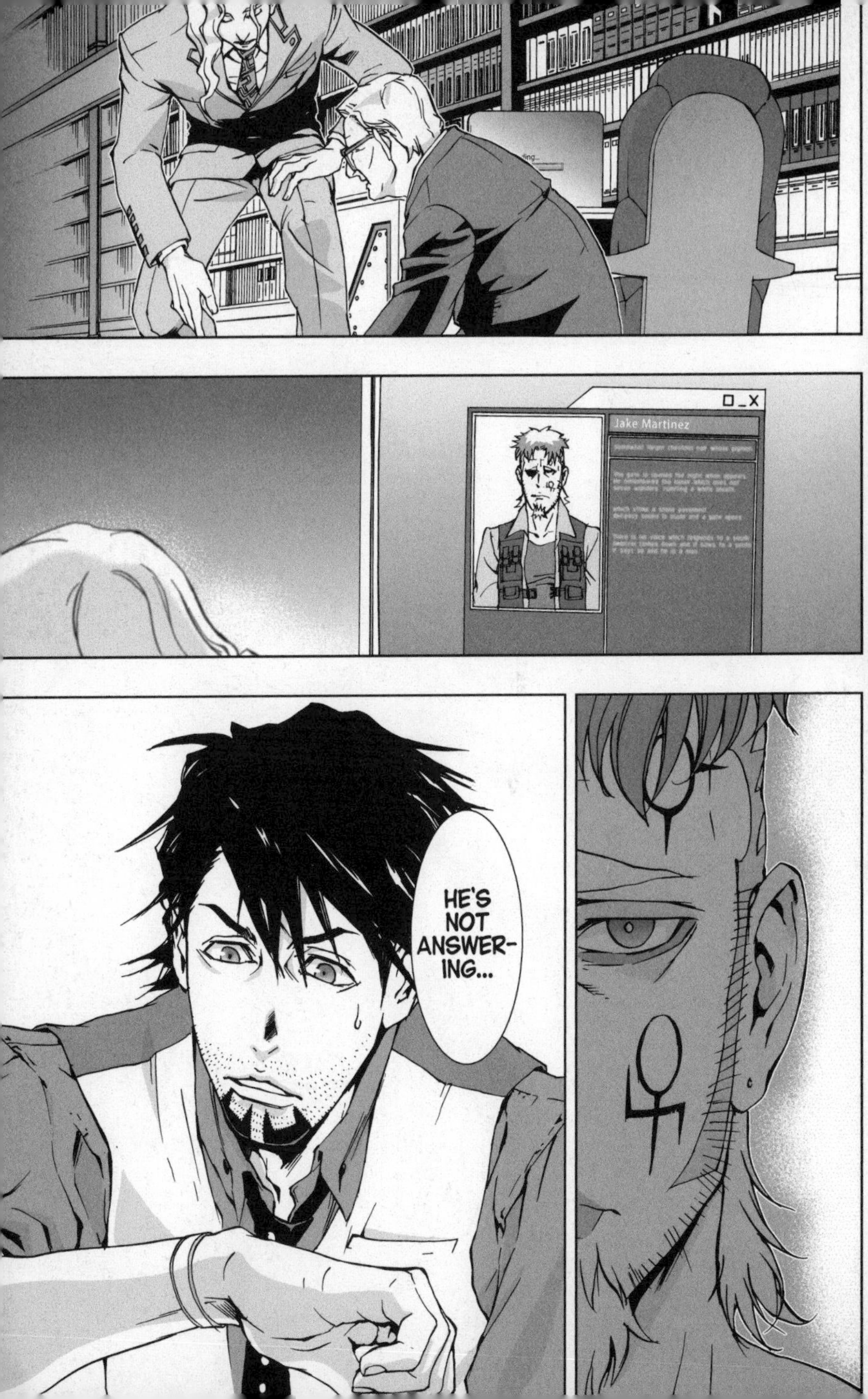
Jake Martinez
HE'S NOT ANSWERING...

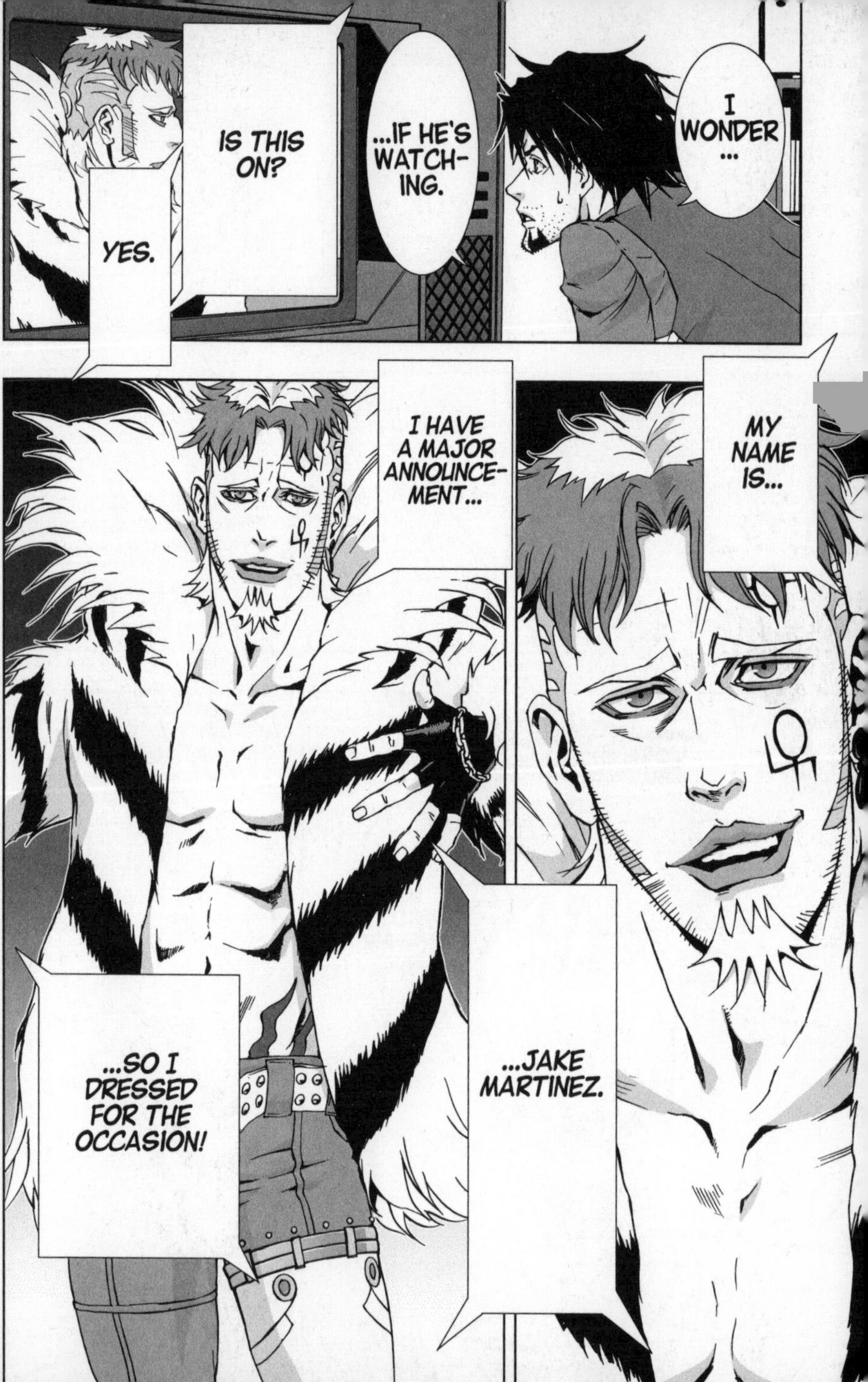
I WONDER...
...IF HE'S WATCHING.
IS THIS ON?
YES.
MY NAME IS...
...JAKE MARTINEZ.
I HAVE A MAJOR ANNOUNCEMENT...
...SO I DRESSED FOR THE OCCASION!

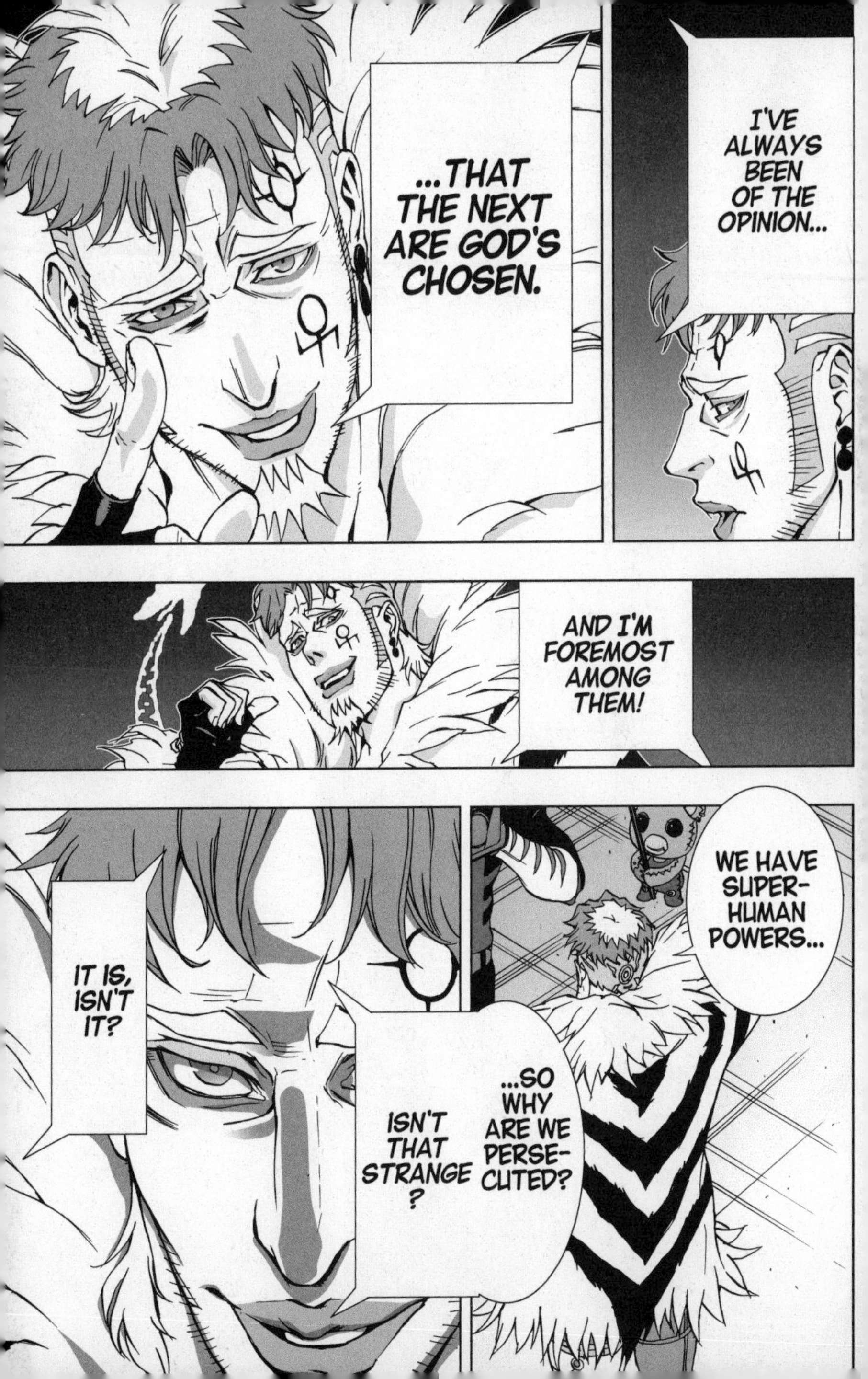
I'VE ALWAYS BEEN OF THE OPINION...
...THAT THE NEXT ARE GOD'S CHOSEN.
AND I'M FOREMOST AMONG THEM!
WE HAVE SUPER-HUMAN POWERS...
...SO WHY ARE WE PERSE-CUTED?
ISN'T THAT STRANGE?
IT IS, ISN'T IT?

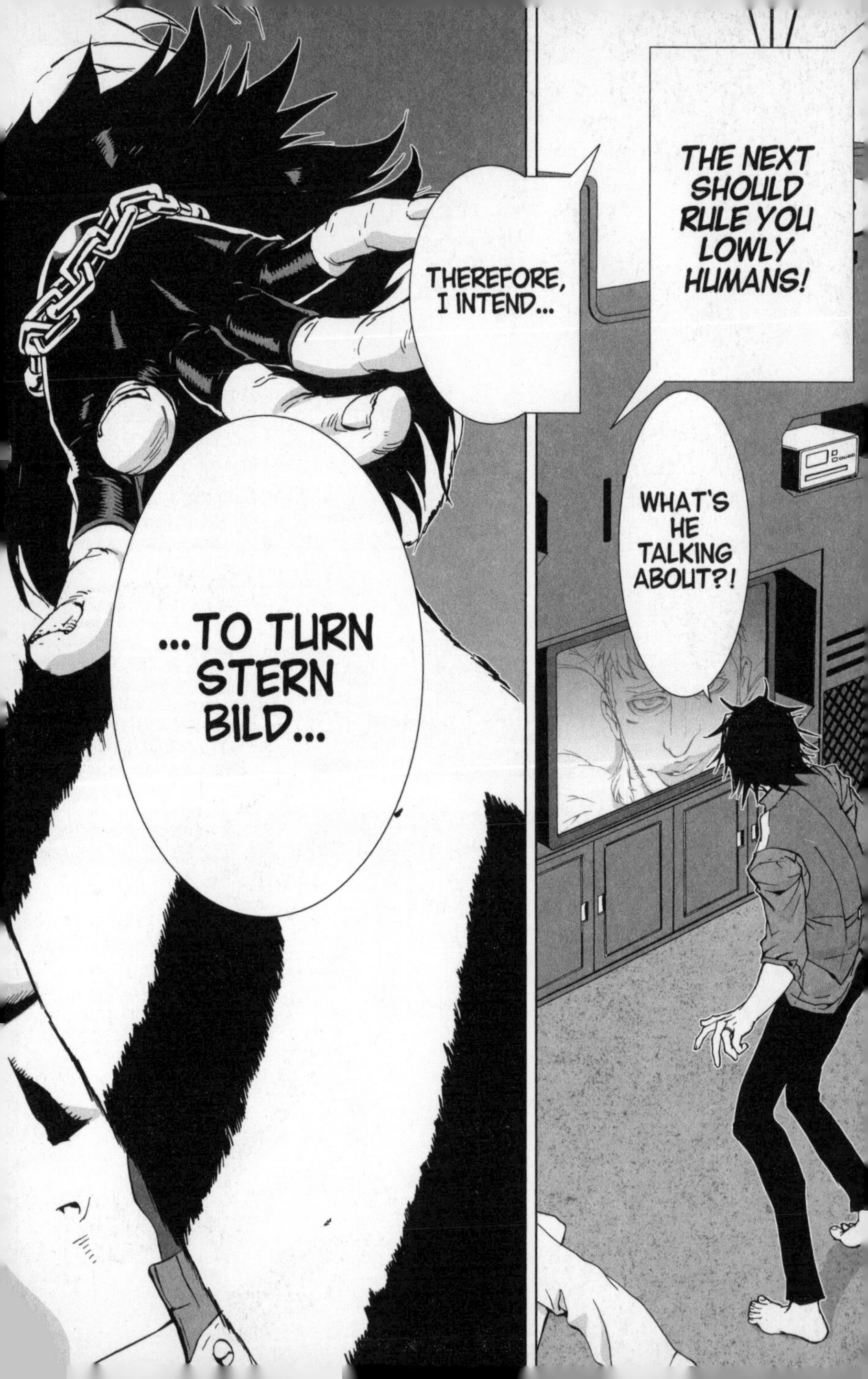
THE NEXT SHOULD RULE YOU LOWLY HUMANS!
WHAT'S HE TALKING ABOUT?!
THEREFORE, I INTEND...
...TO TURN STERN BILD...

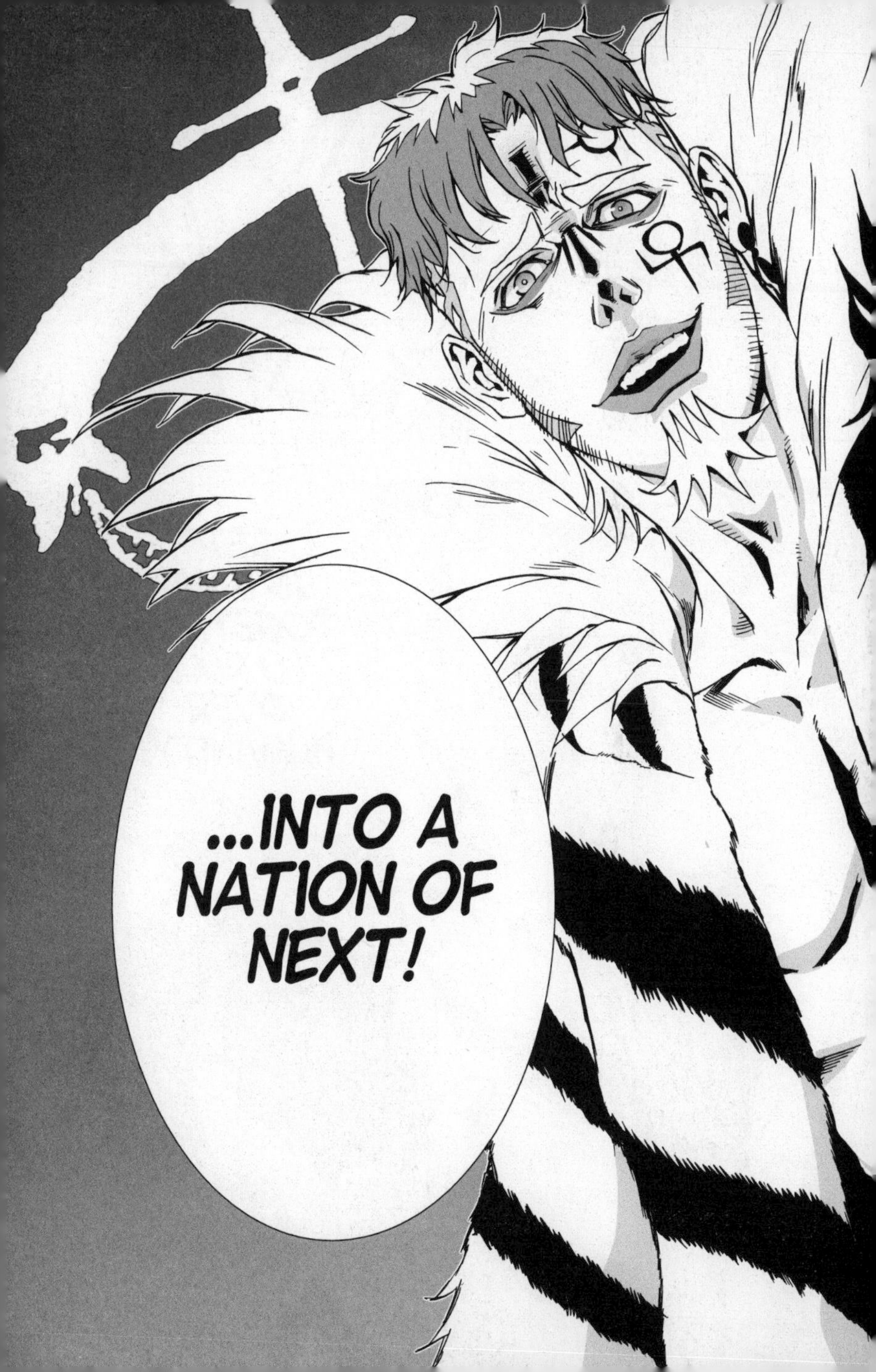
...INTO A NATION OF NEXT!

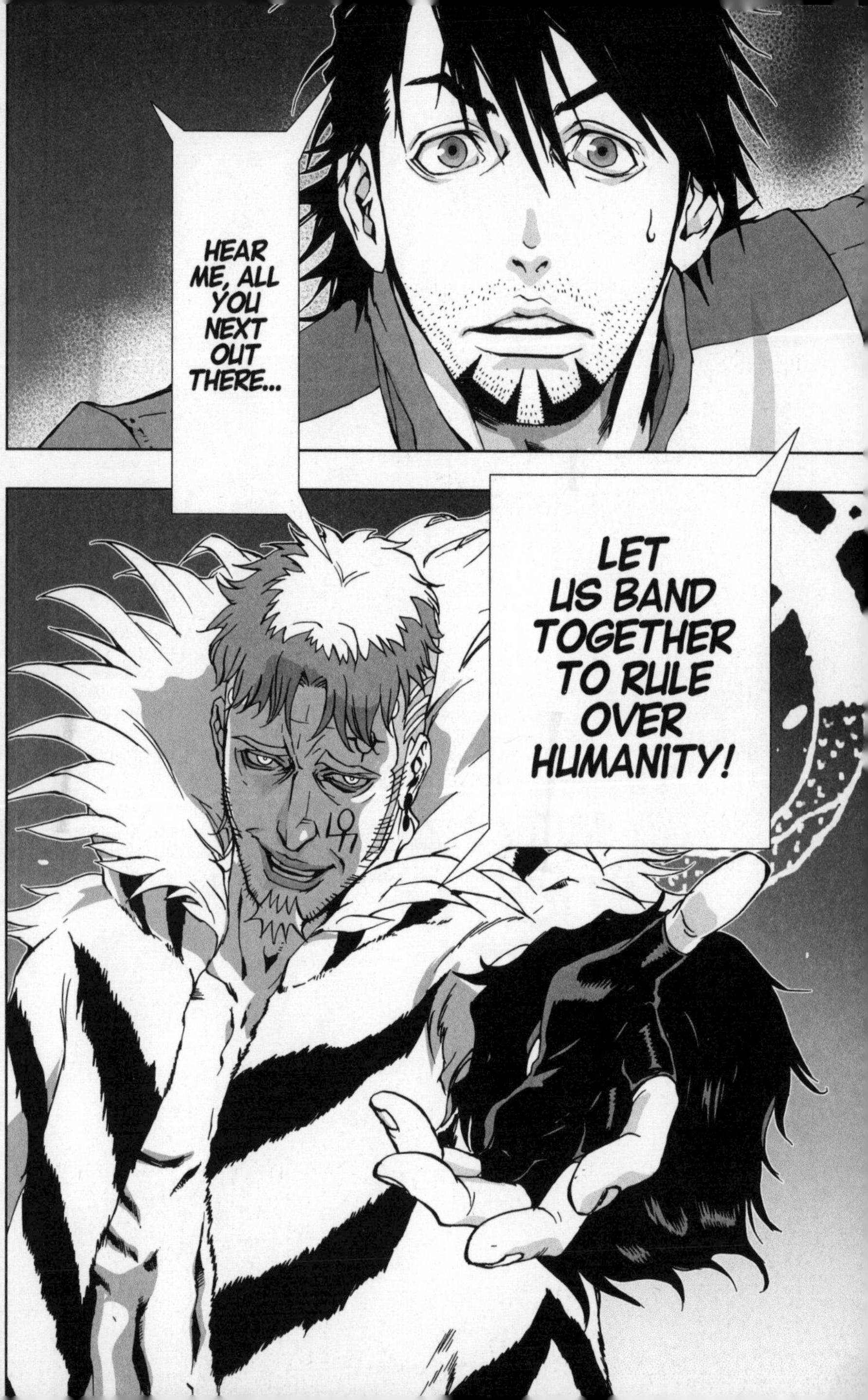
HEAR ME, ALL YOU NEXT OUT THERE...
LET US BAND TOGETHER TO RULE OVER HUMANITY!

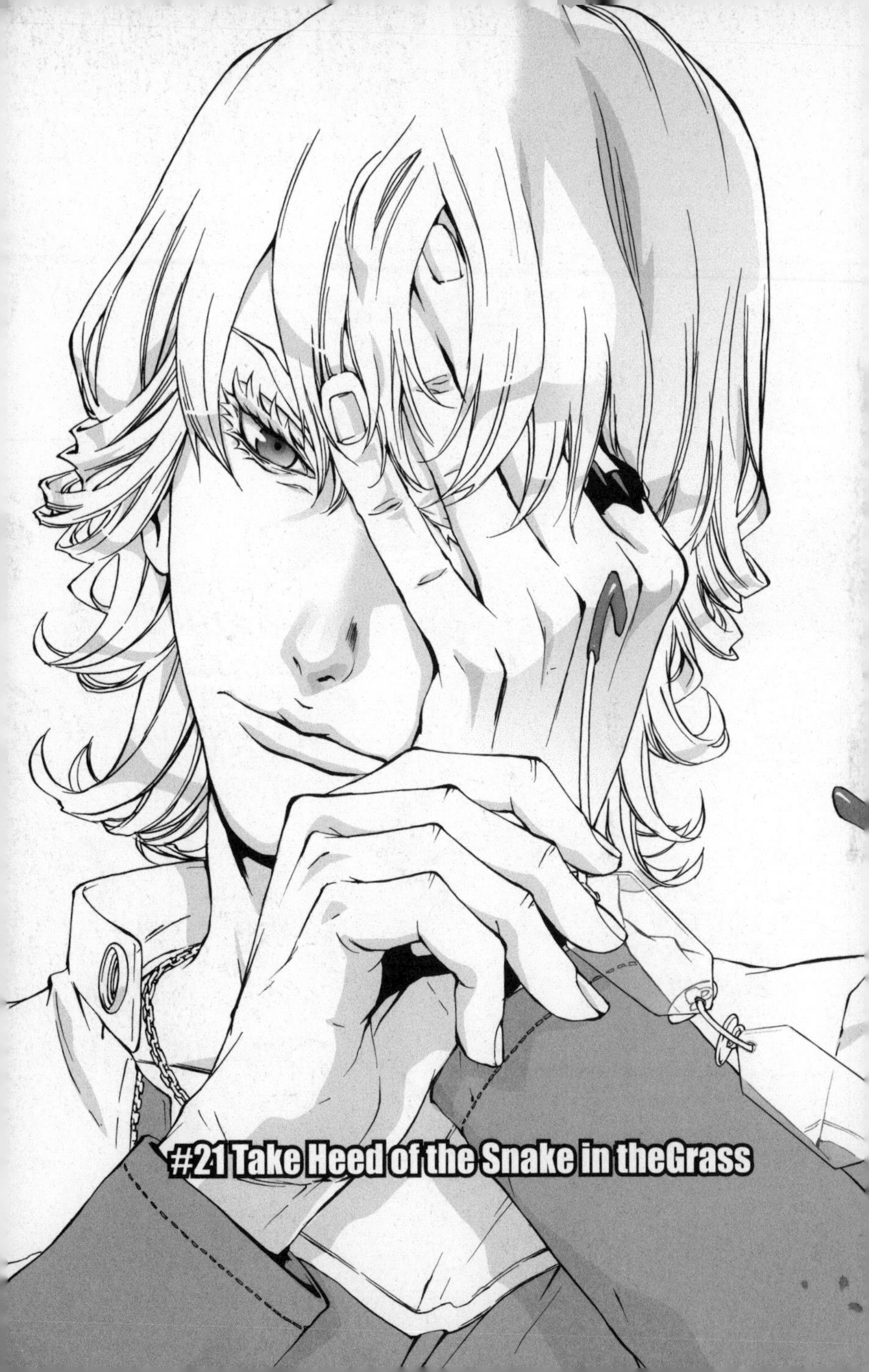
#21 Take Heed of the Snake in theGrass

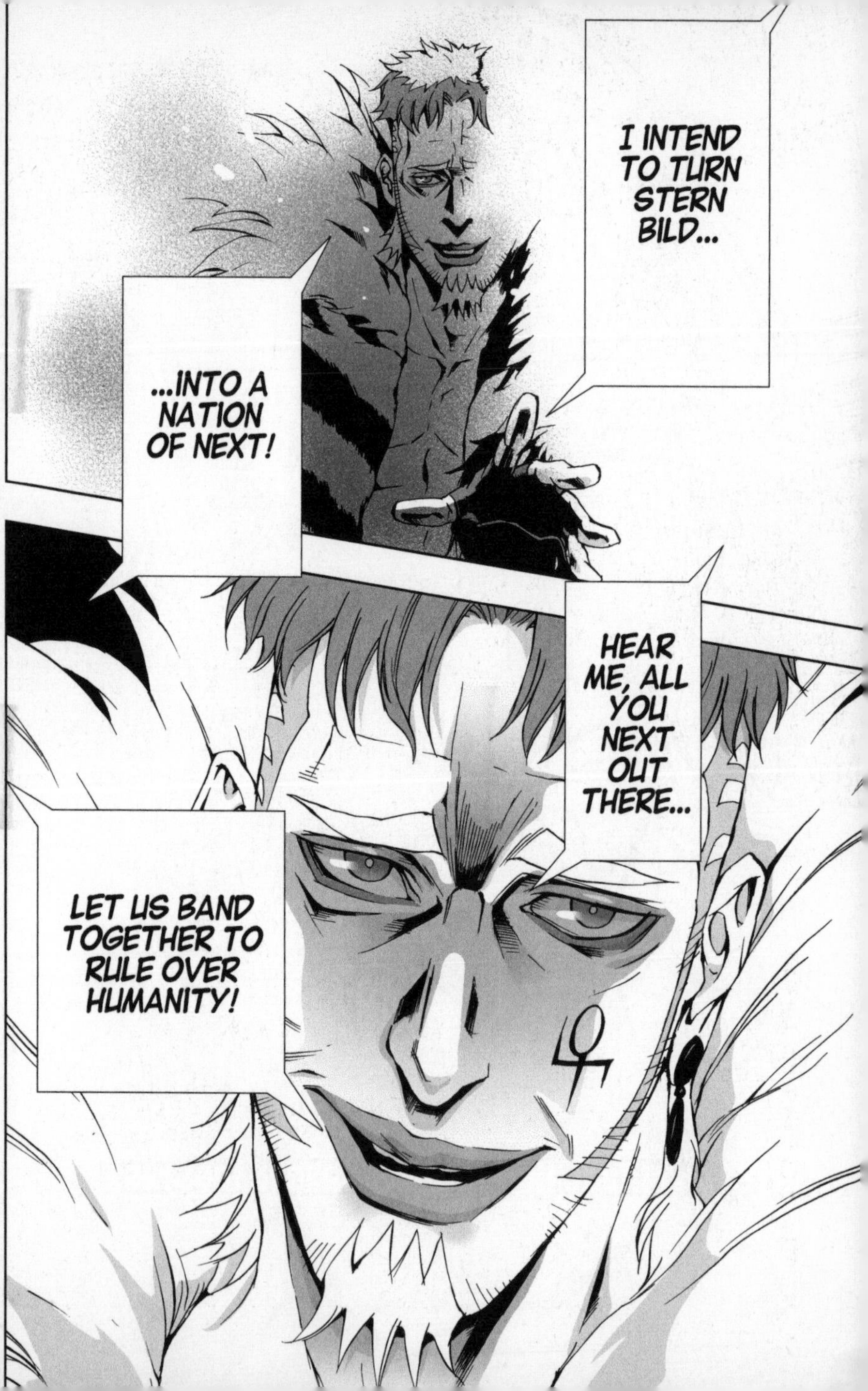
I INTEND TO TURN STERN BILD...
...INTO A NATION OF NEXT!
HEAR ME, ALL YOU NEXT OUT THERE...
LET US BAND TOGETHER TO RULE OVER HUMANITY!

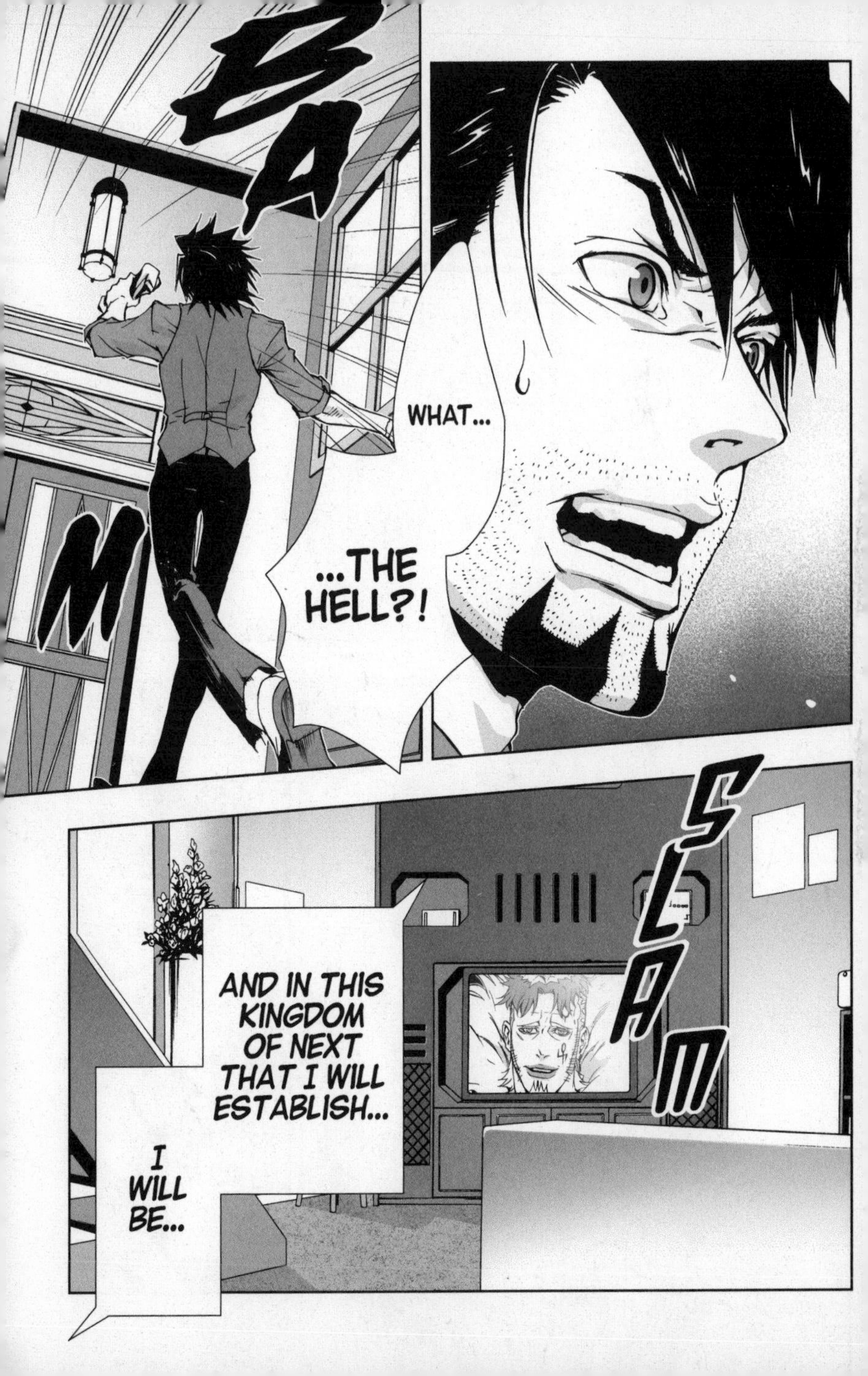
WHAT...
...THE HELL?!
BAM
SLAM
AND IN THIS KINGDOM OF NEXT THAT I WILL ESTABLISH...
I WILL BE...

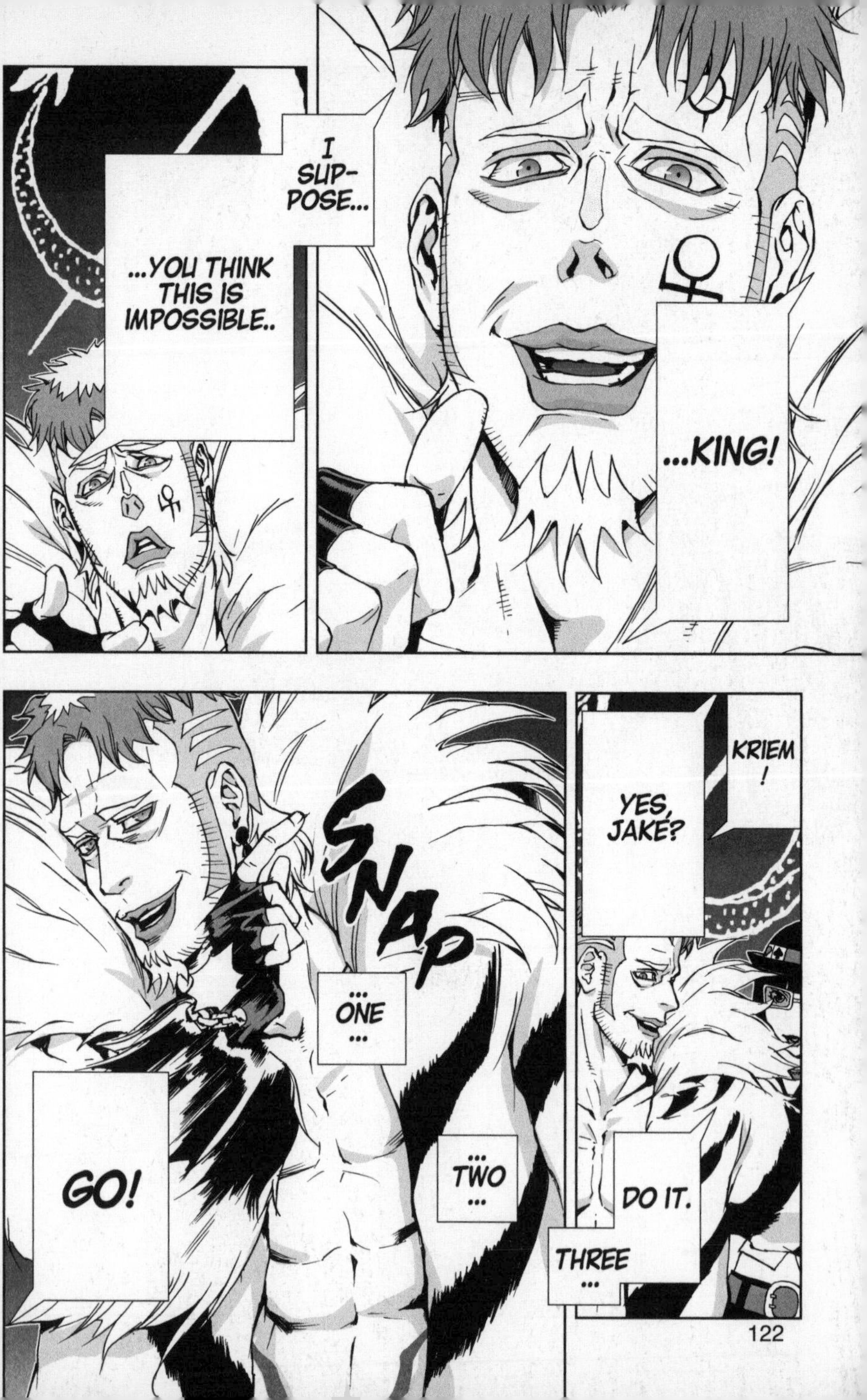
I SUP-POSE...
...YOU THINK THIS IS IMPOSSIBLE..
...KING!
KRIEM!
YES, JAKE?
DO IT.
SNAP
...ONE...
...TWO...
THREE...
GO!

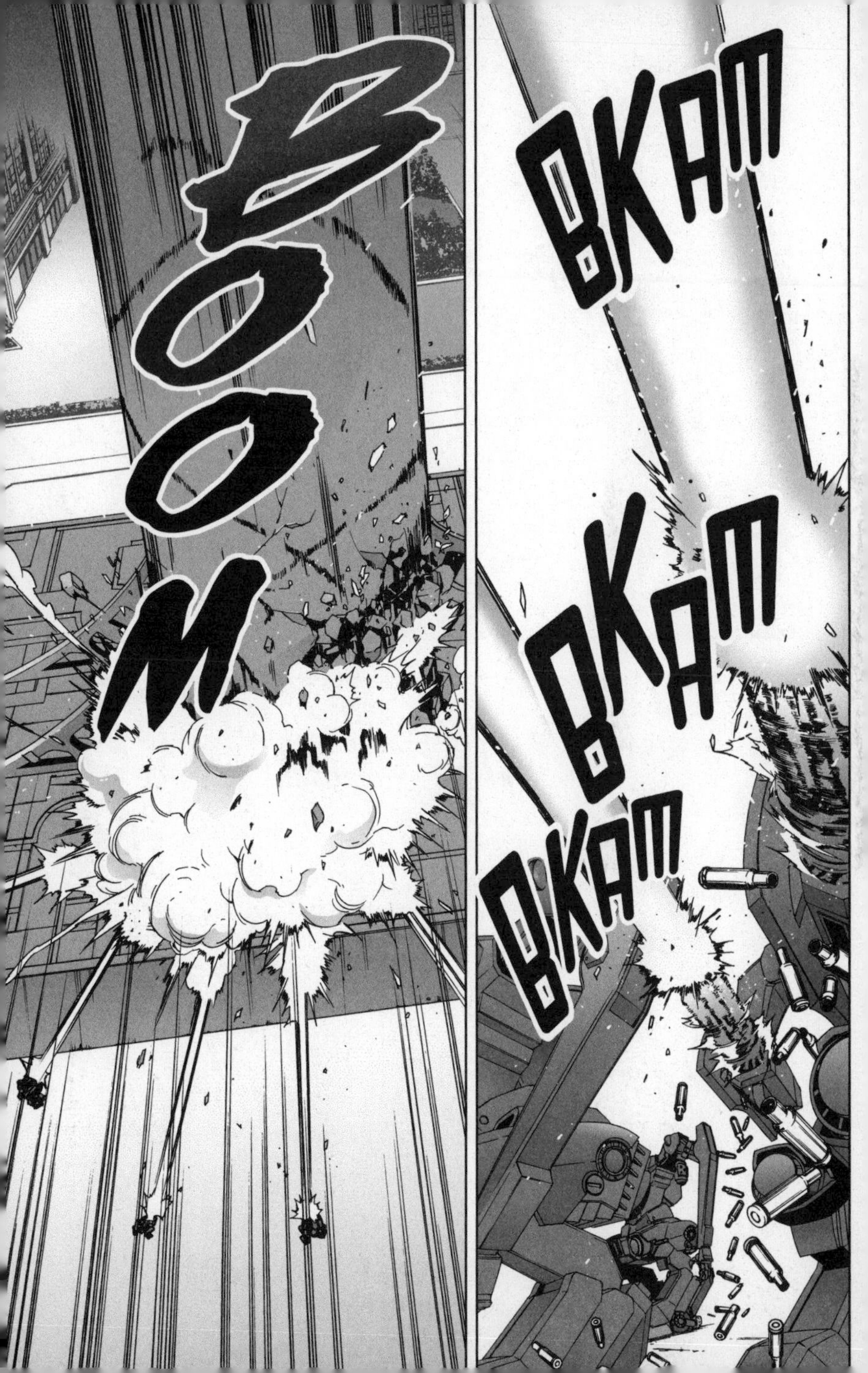
BKAM
BKAM
BKAM
BOOM

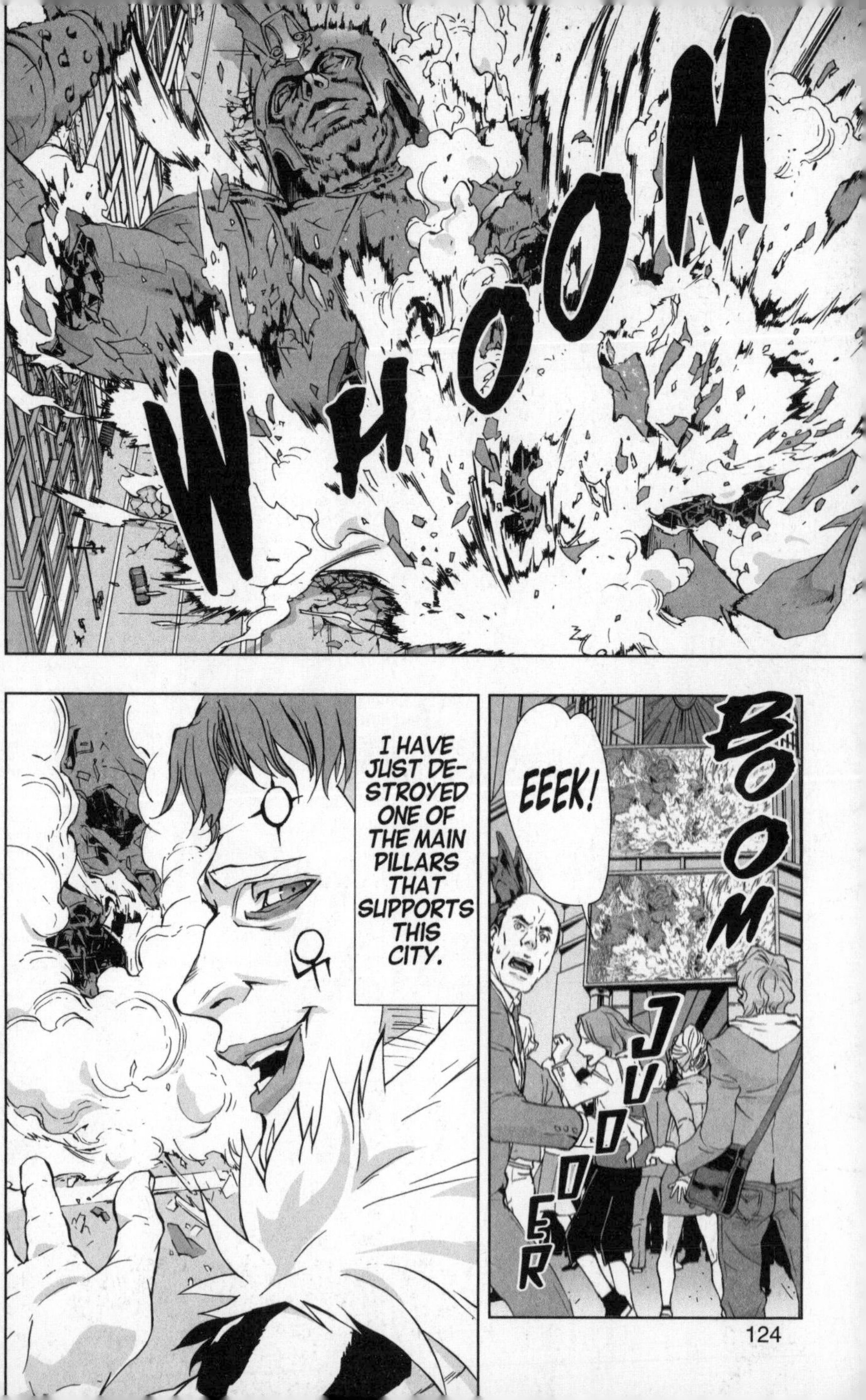
WHOOOM
BOOM
EEEK!
JUDDDER
I HAVE JUST DE-STROYED ONE OF THE MAIN PILLARS THAT SUPPORTS THIS CITY.

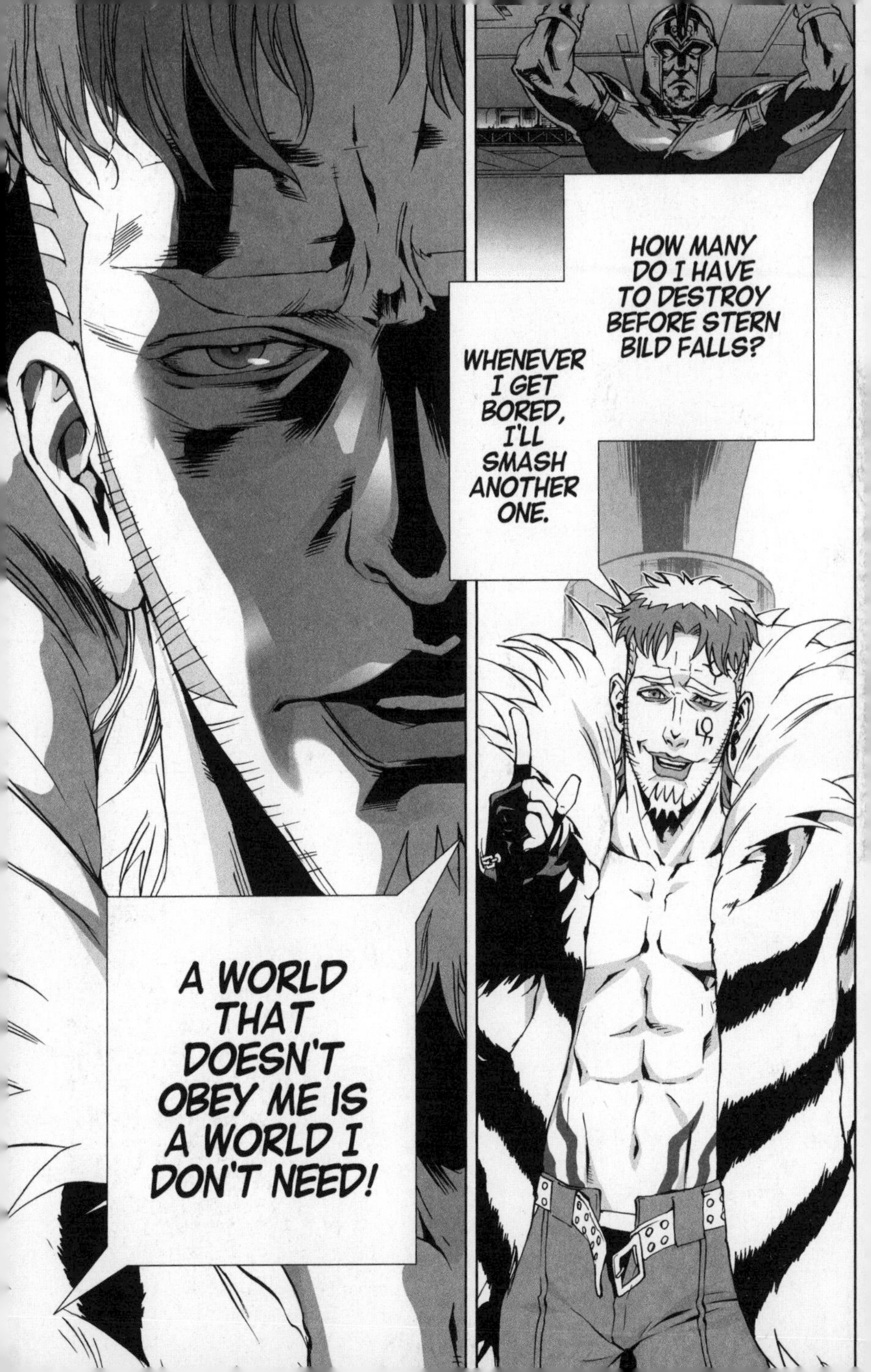
HOW MANY DO I HAVE TO DESTROY BEFORE STERN BILD FALLS?
WHENEVER I GET BORED, I'LL SMASH ANOTHER ONE.
A WORLD THAT DOESN'T OBEY ME IS A WORLD I DON'T NEED!

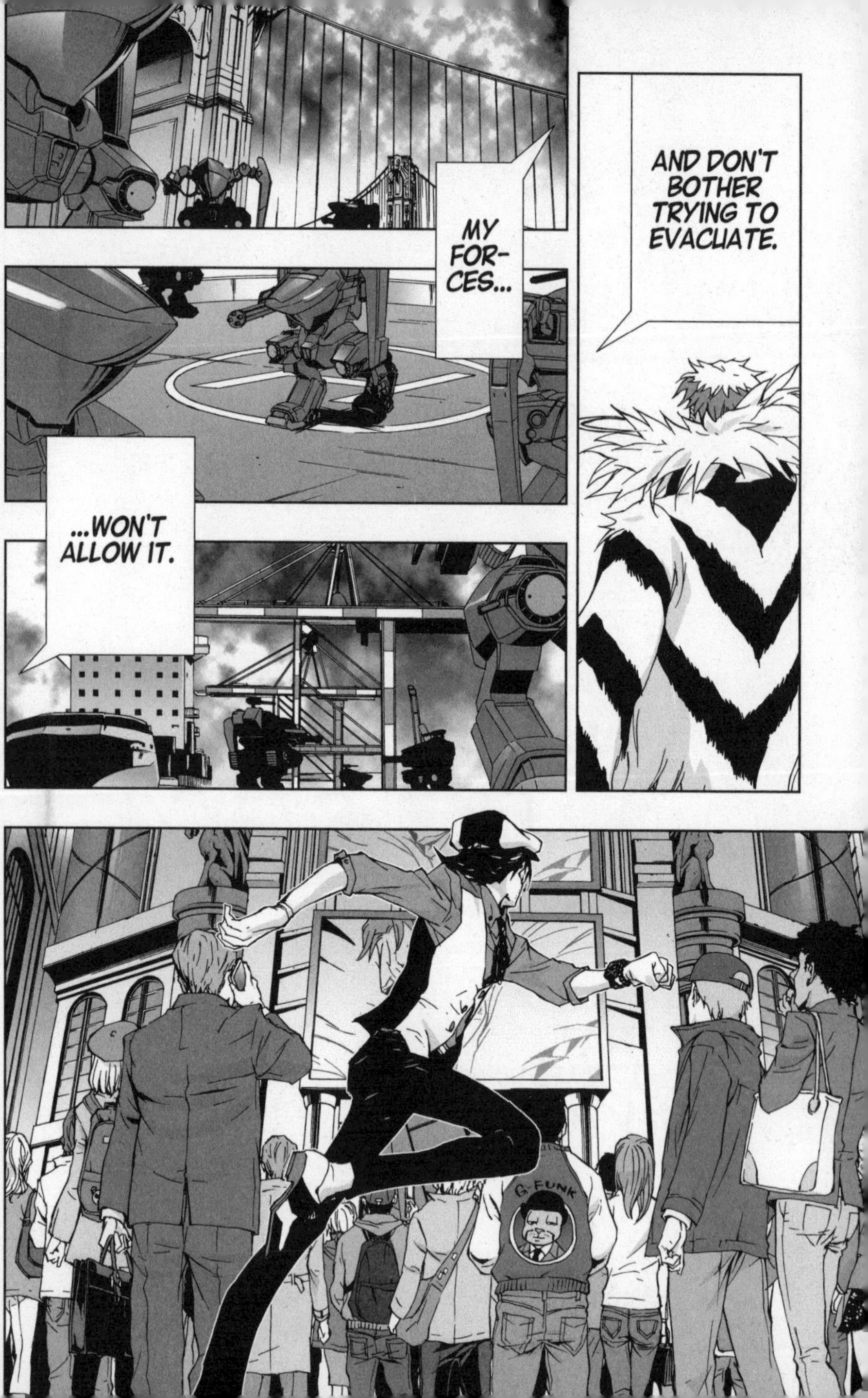
AND DON'T BOTHER TRYING TO EVACUATE.
MY FORCES...
...WON'T ALLOW IT.
G-FUNK

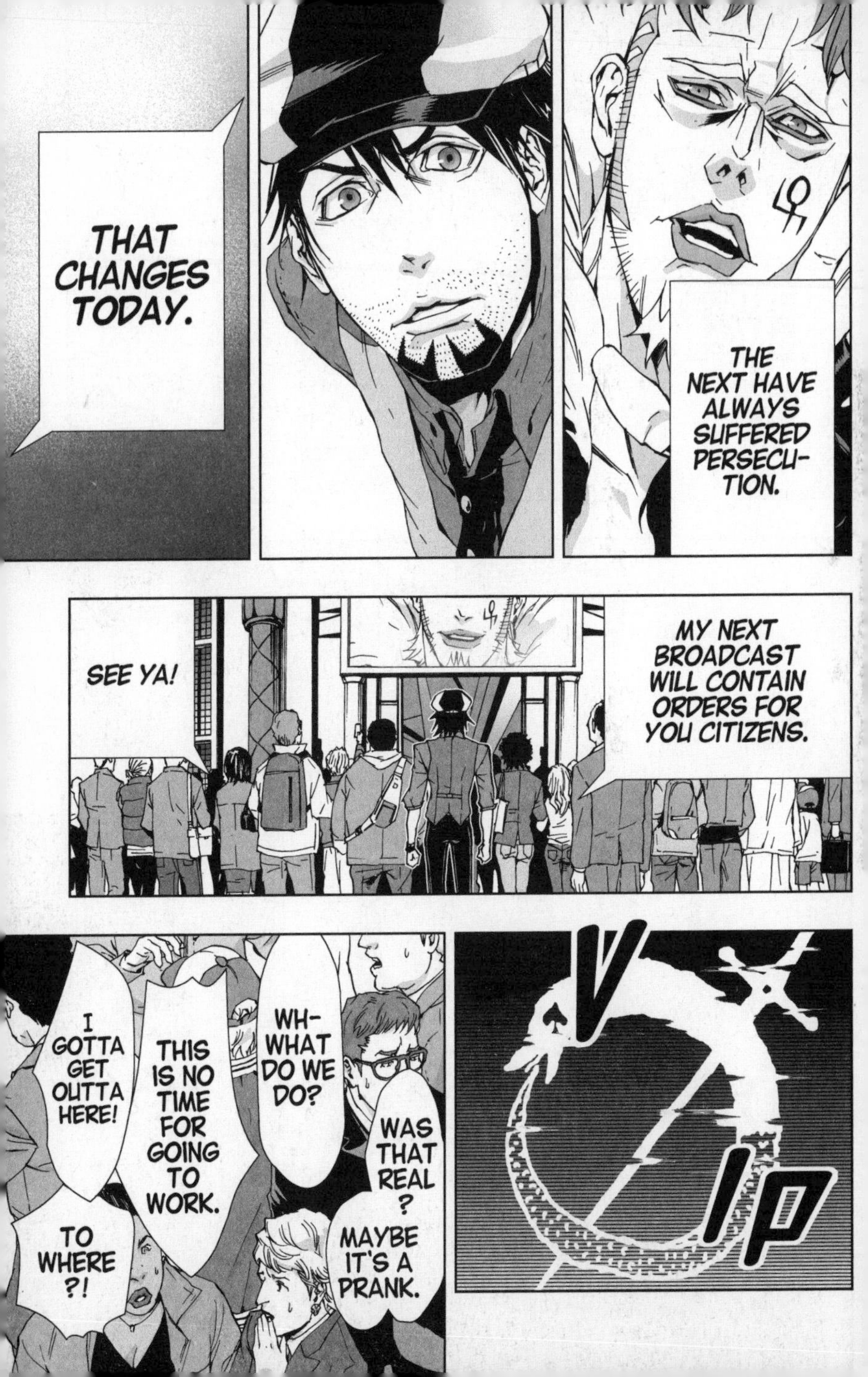
THE NEXT HAVE ALWAYS SUFFERED PERSECUTION.
THAT CHANGES TODAY.
MY NEXT BROADCAST WILL CONTAIN ORDERS FOR YOU CITIZENS.
SEE YA!
VIP
WH-WHAT DO WE DO?
WAS THAT REAL?
MAYBE IT'S A PRANK.
THIS IS NO TIME FOR GOING TO WORK.
I GOTTA GET OUTTA HERE!
TO WHERE?!

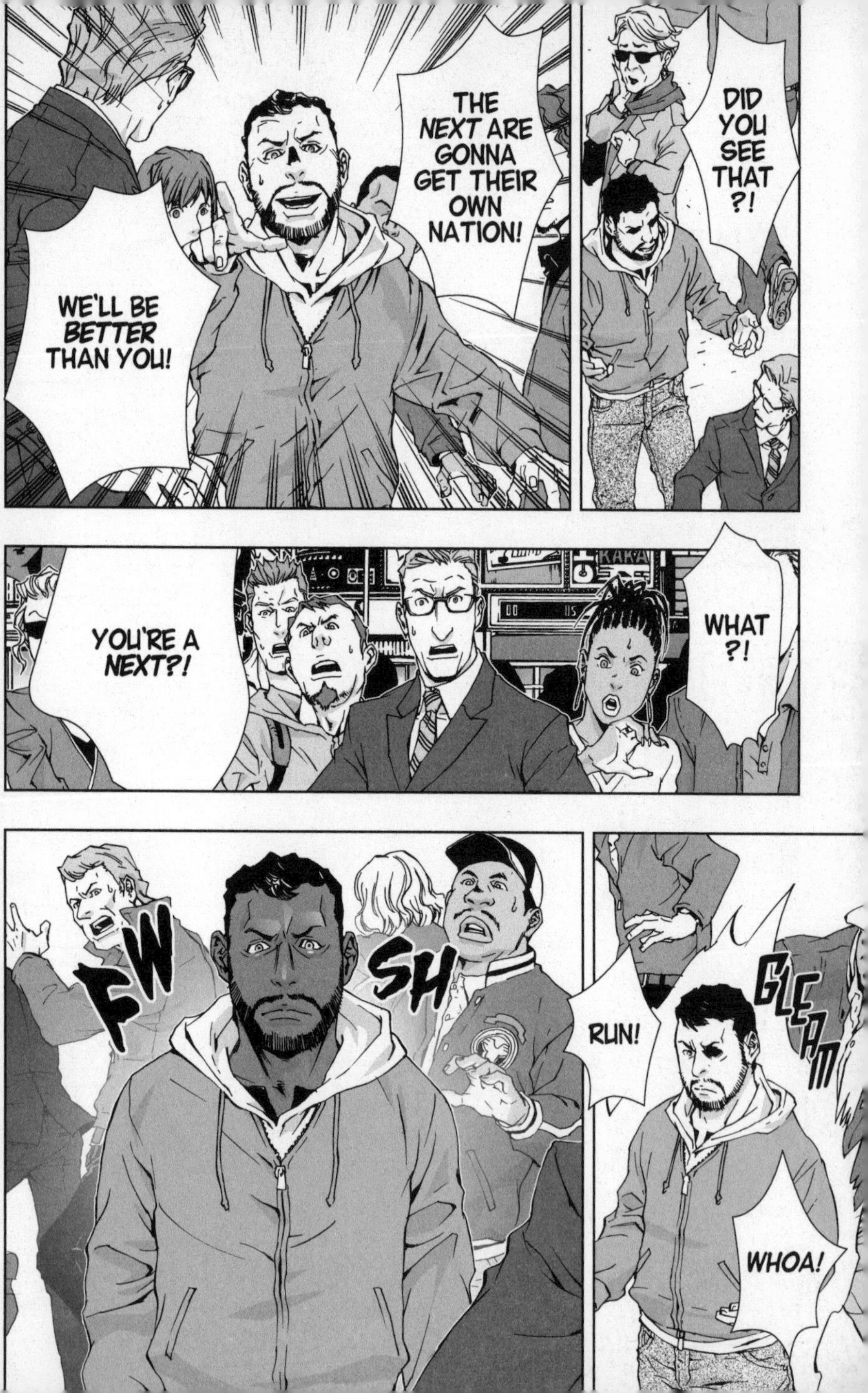
DID YOU SEE THAT?!
THE *NEXT* ARE GONNA GET THEIR OWN NATION!
WE'LL BE *BETTER* THAN YOU!
WHAT?!
YOU'RE A *NEXT*?!
GLEAM
RUN!
WHOA!
FW
SH

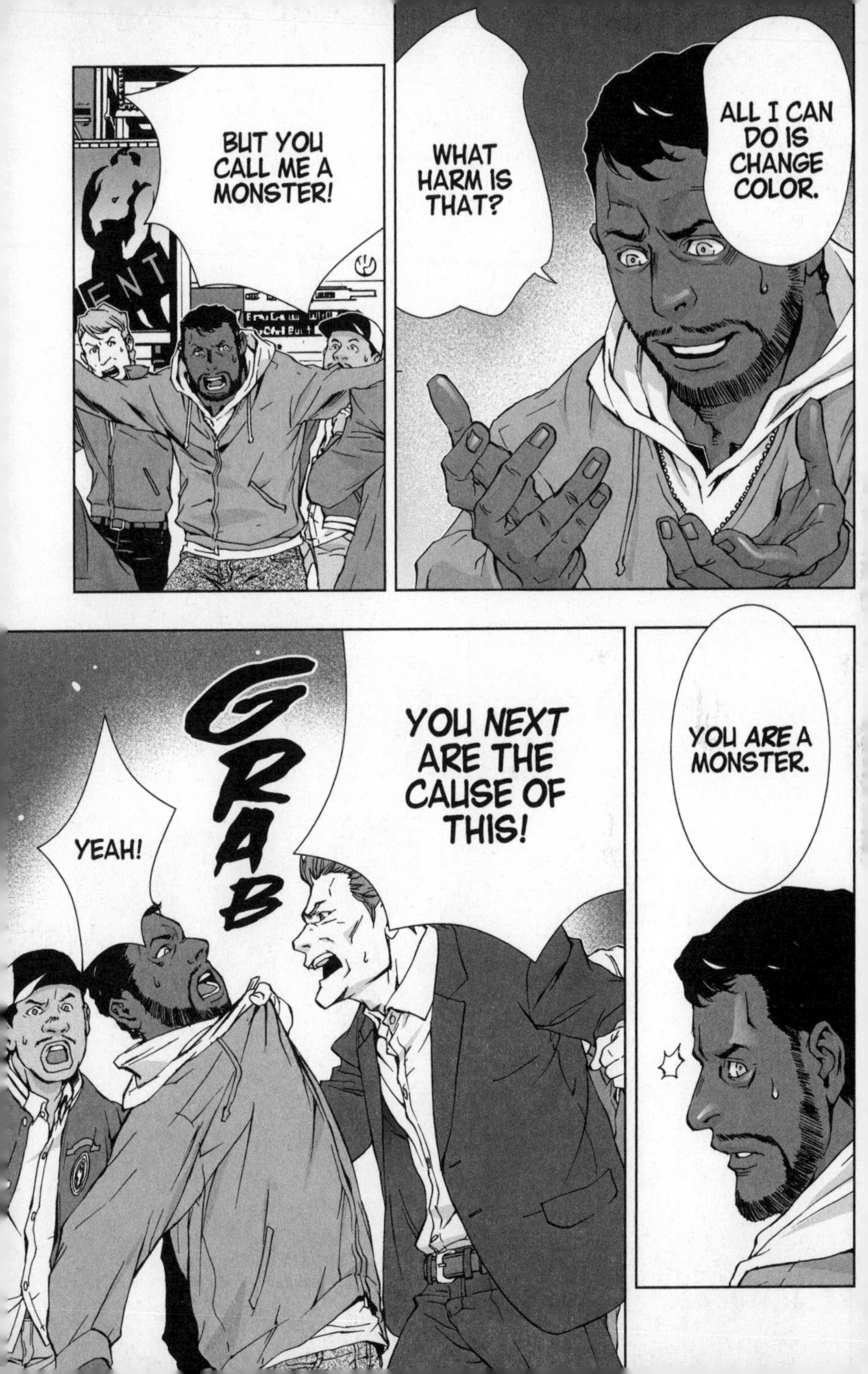
ALL I CAN DO IS CHANGE COLOR.
WHAT HARM IS THAT?
BUT YOU CALL ME A MONSTER!
YOU ARE A MONSTER.
YOU NEXT ARE THE CAUSE OF THIS!
GRAB
YEAH!

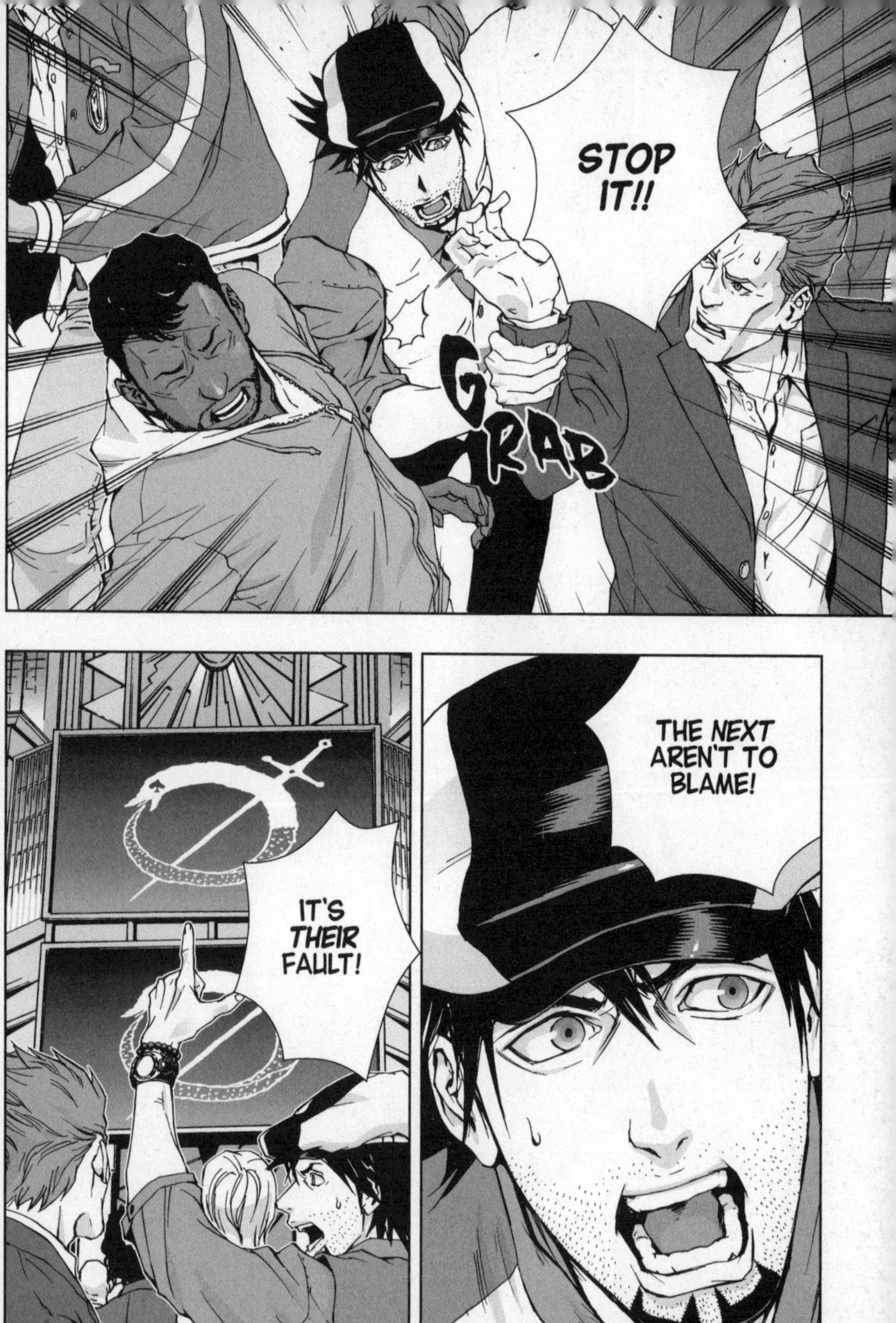
STOP IT!!
GRAB
THE NEXT AREN'T TO BLAME!
IT'S THEIR FAULT!

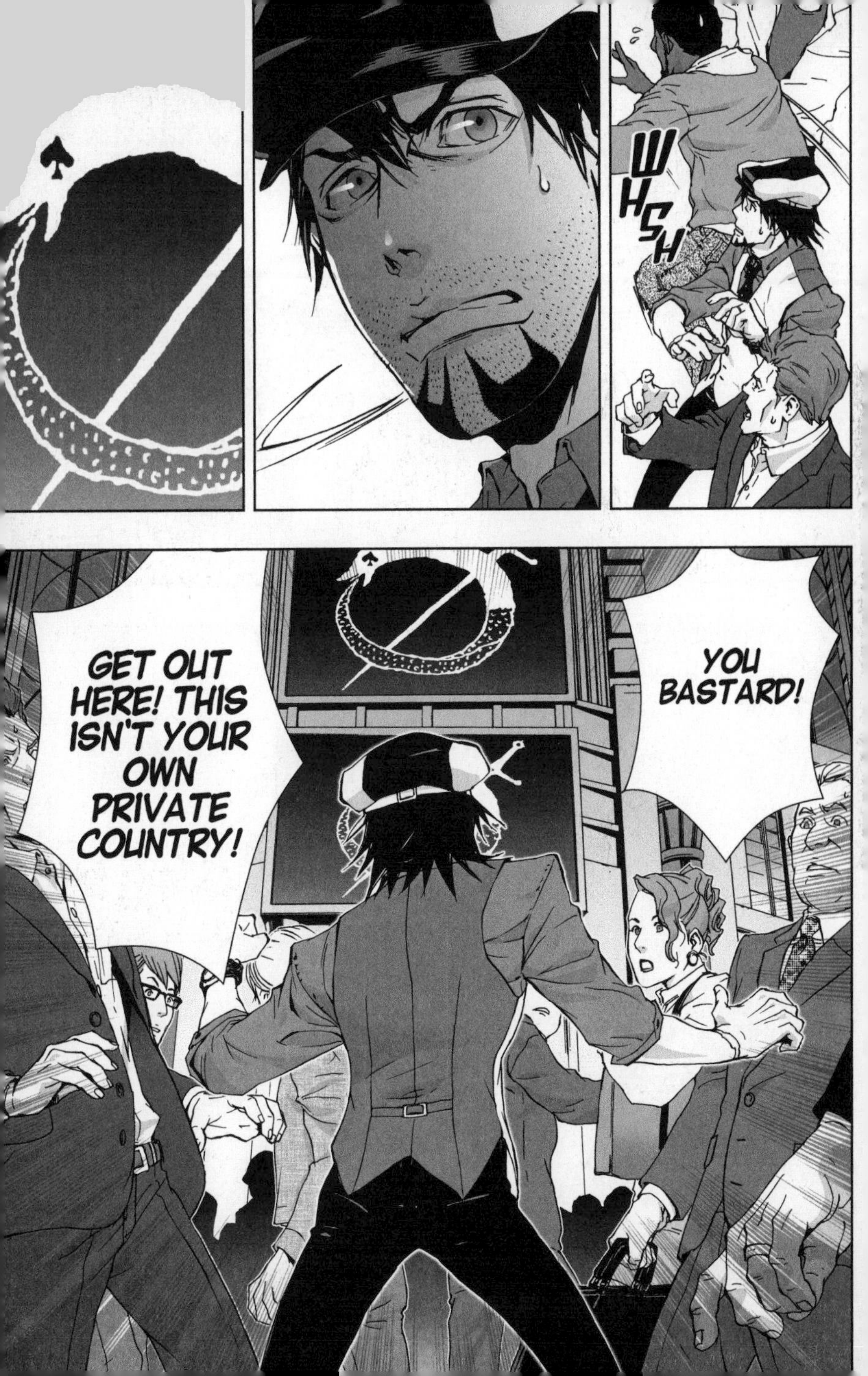
WHSH
YOU BASTARD!
GET OUT HERE! THIS ISN'T YOUR OWN PRIVATE COUNTRY!

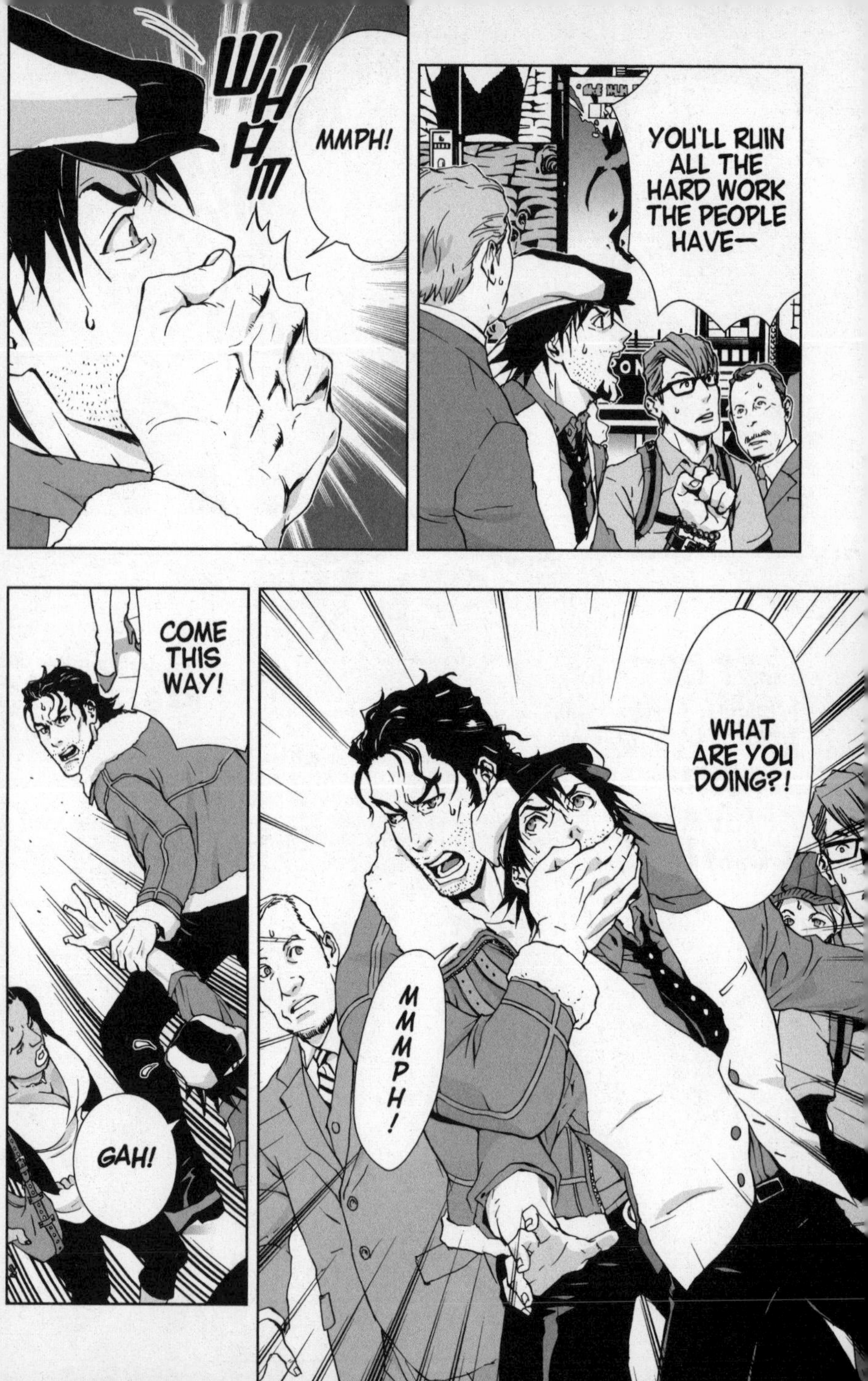
YOU'LL RUIN ALL THE HARD WORK THE PEOPLE HAVE—
WHAM
MMPH!
WHAT ARE YOU DOING?!
MMMPH!
COME THIS WAY!
GAH!

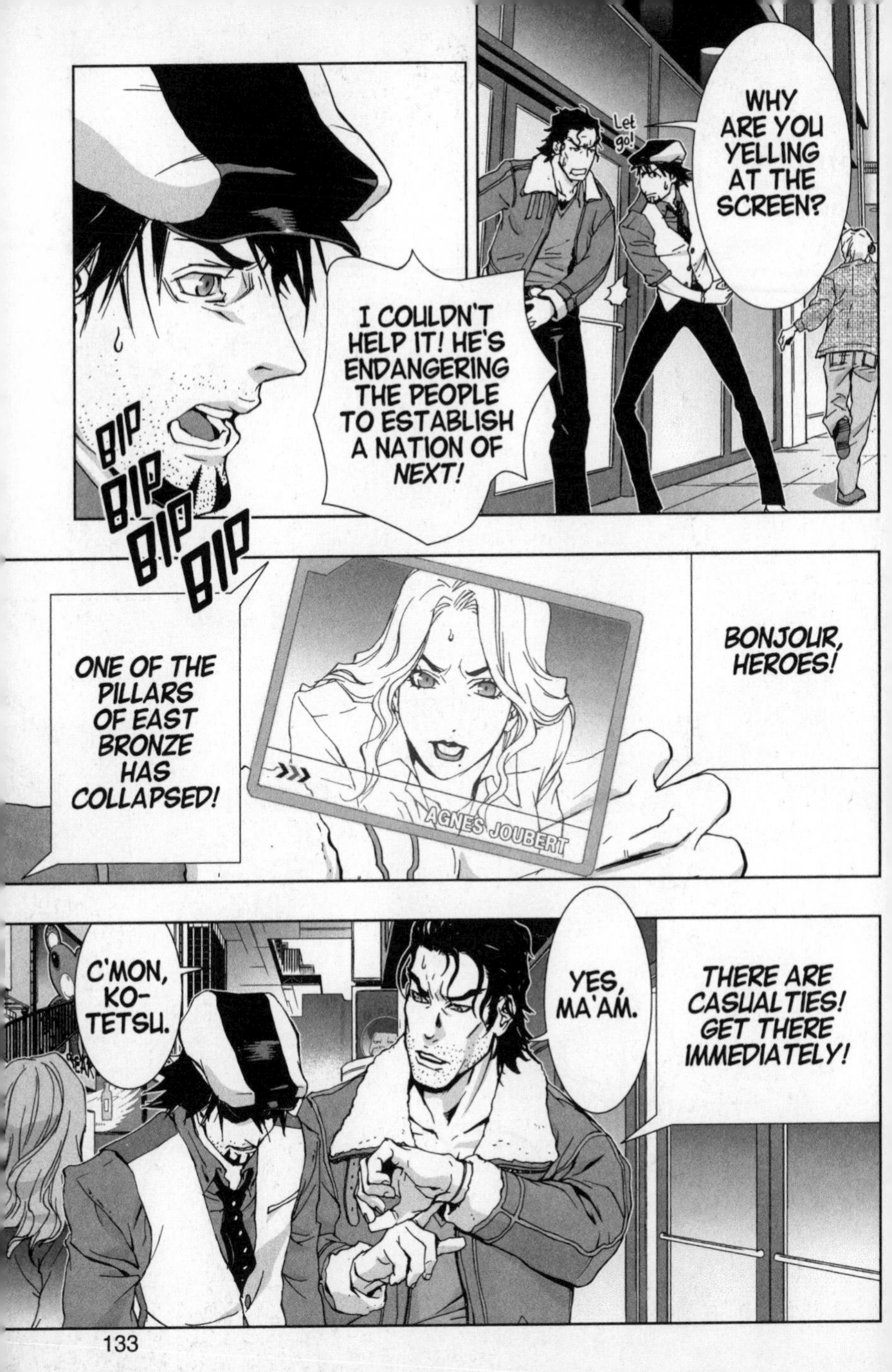
WHY ARE YOU YELLING AT THE SCREEN?
Let go!
I COULDN'T HELP IT! HE'S ENDANGERING THE PEOPLE TO ESTABLISH A NATION OF NEXT!
BIP BIP BIP BIP BIP
BONJOUR, HEROES!
AGNES JOUBERT
ONE OF THE PILLARS OF EAST BRONZE HAS COLLAPSED!
THERE ARE CASUALTIES! GET THERE IMMEDIATELY!
YES, MA'AM.
C'MON, KO-TETSU.

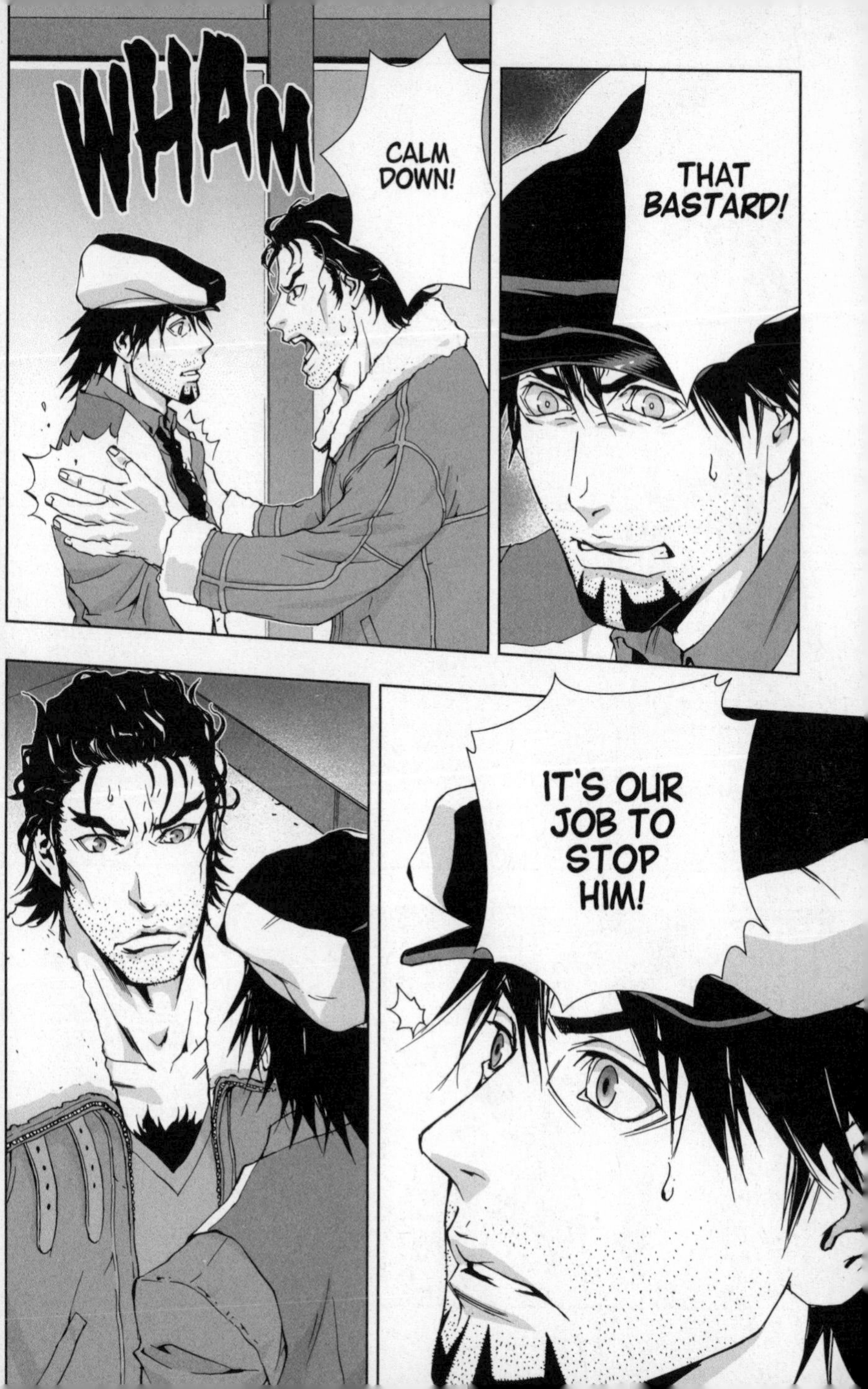
THAT BASTARD!
WHAM
CALM DOWN!
IT'S OUR JOB TO STOP HIM!

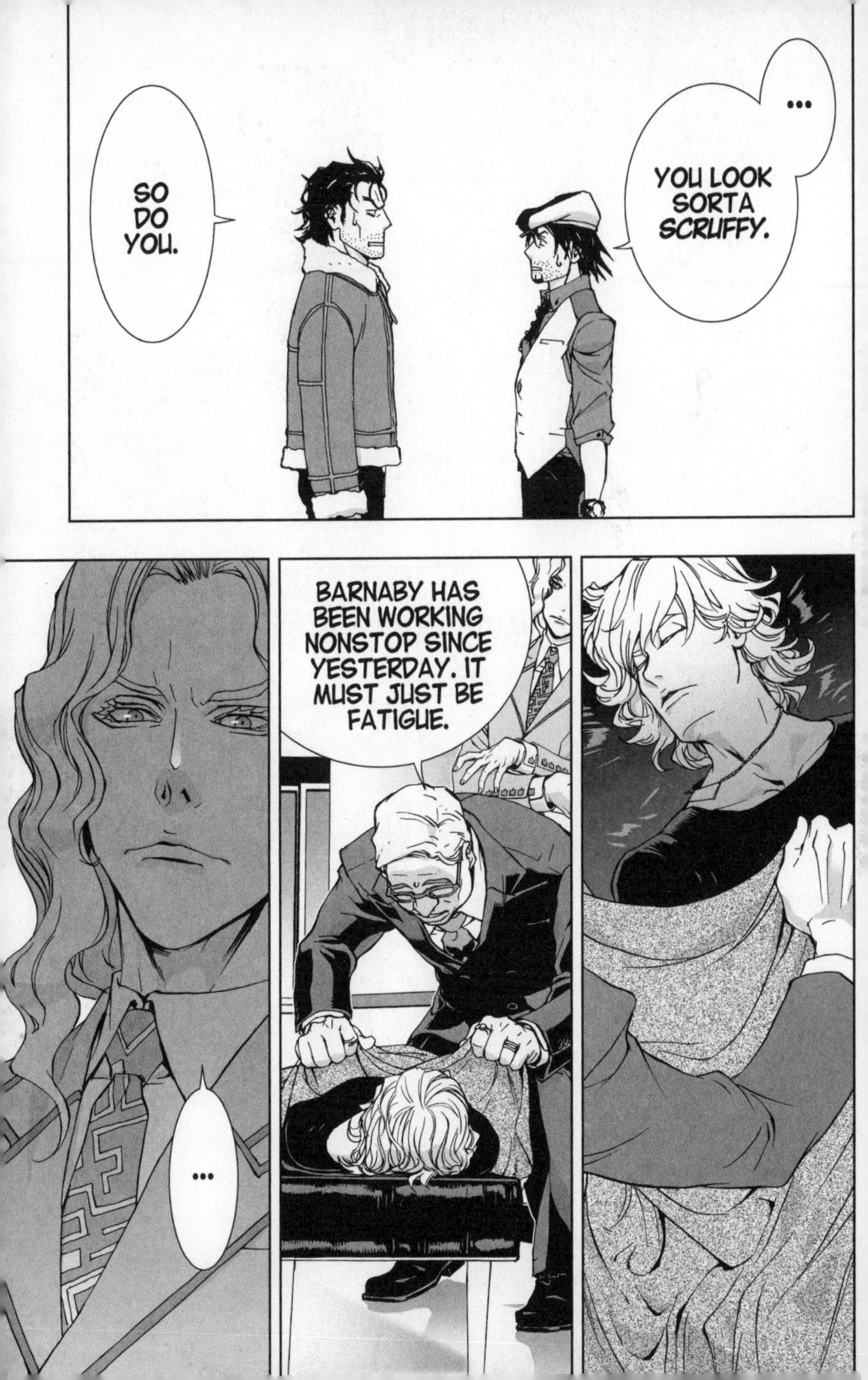
...
YOU LOOK SORTA SCRUFFY.
SO DO YOU.
BARNABY HAS BEEN WORKING NONSTOP SINCE YESTERDAY. IT MUST JUST BE FATIGUE.
...

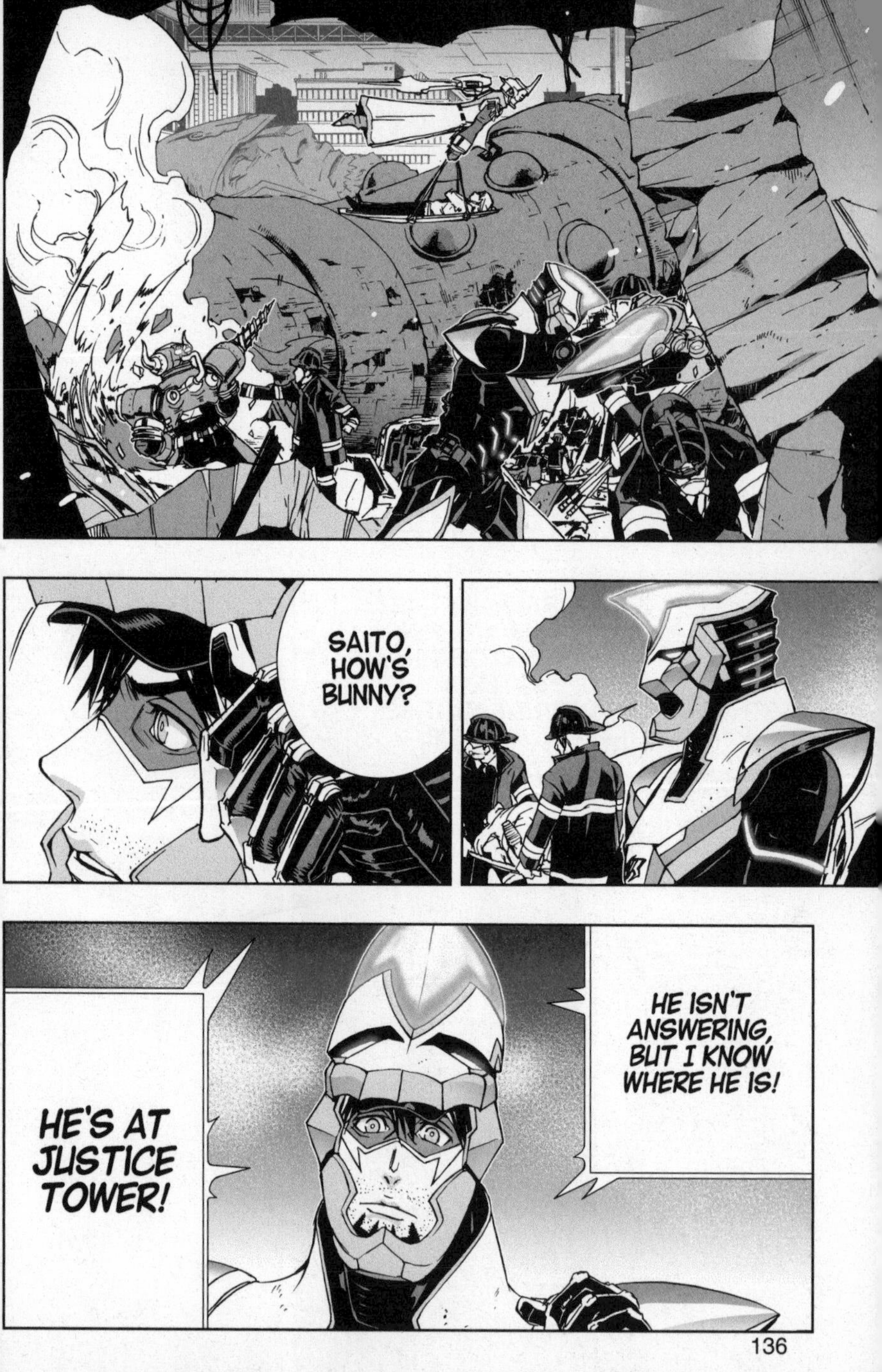
SAITO, HOW'S BUNNY?
HE ISN'T ANSWERING, BUT I KNOW WHERE HE IS!
HE'S AT JUSTICE TOWER!

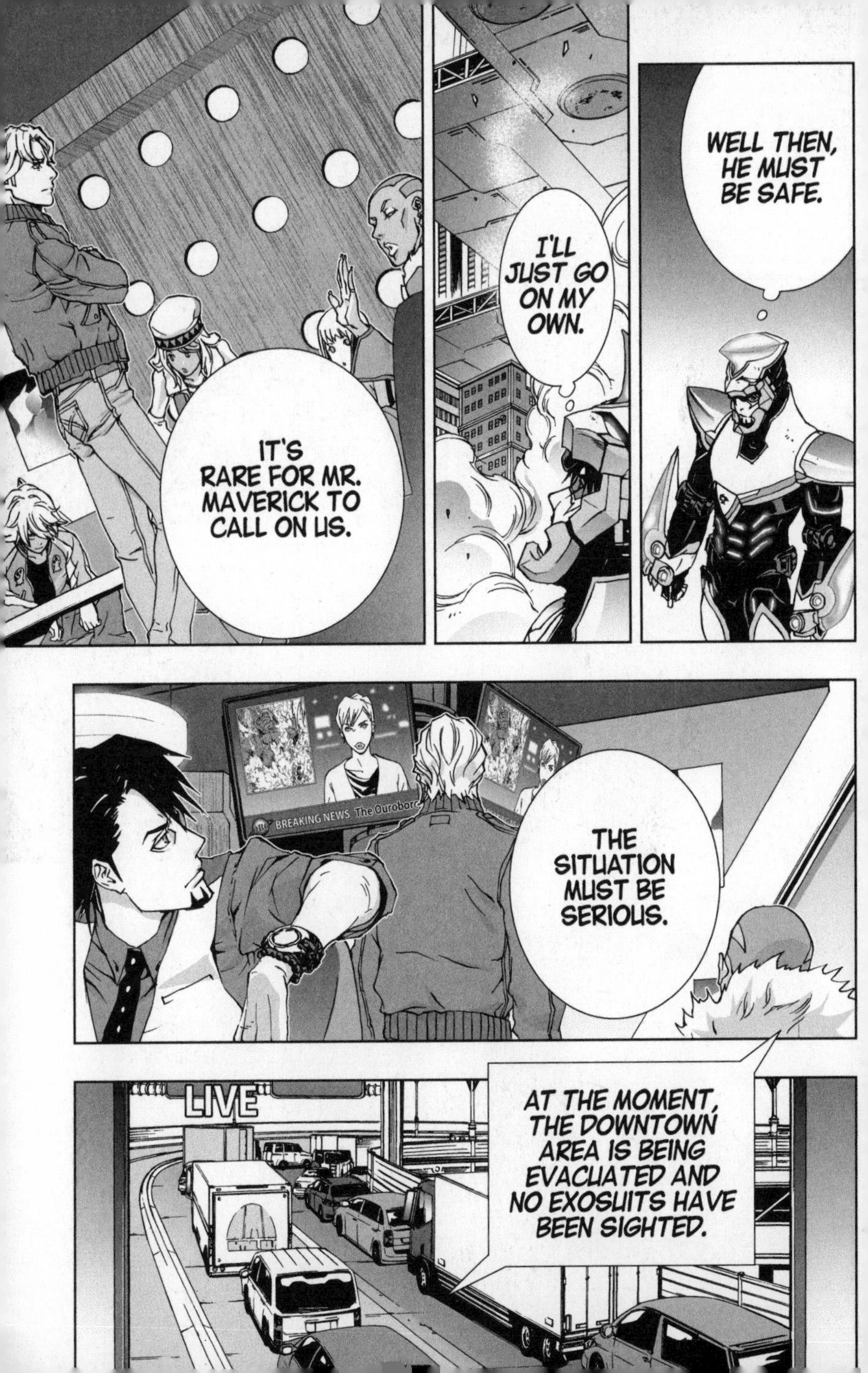
WELL THEN, HE MUST BE SAFE.
I'LL JUST GO ON MY OWN.
IT'S RARE FOR MR. MAVERICK TO CALL ON US.
BREAKING NEWS The Ourobor
THE SITUATION MUST BE SERIOUS.
LIVE
AT THE MOMENT, THE DOWNTOWN AREA IS BEING EVACUATED AND NO EXOSUITS HAVE BEEN SIGHTED.

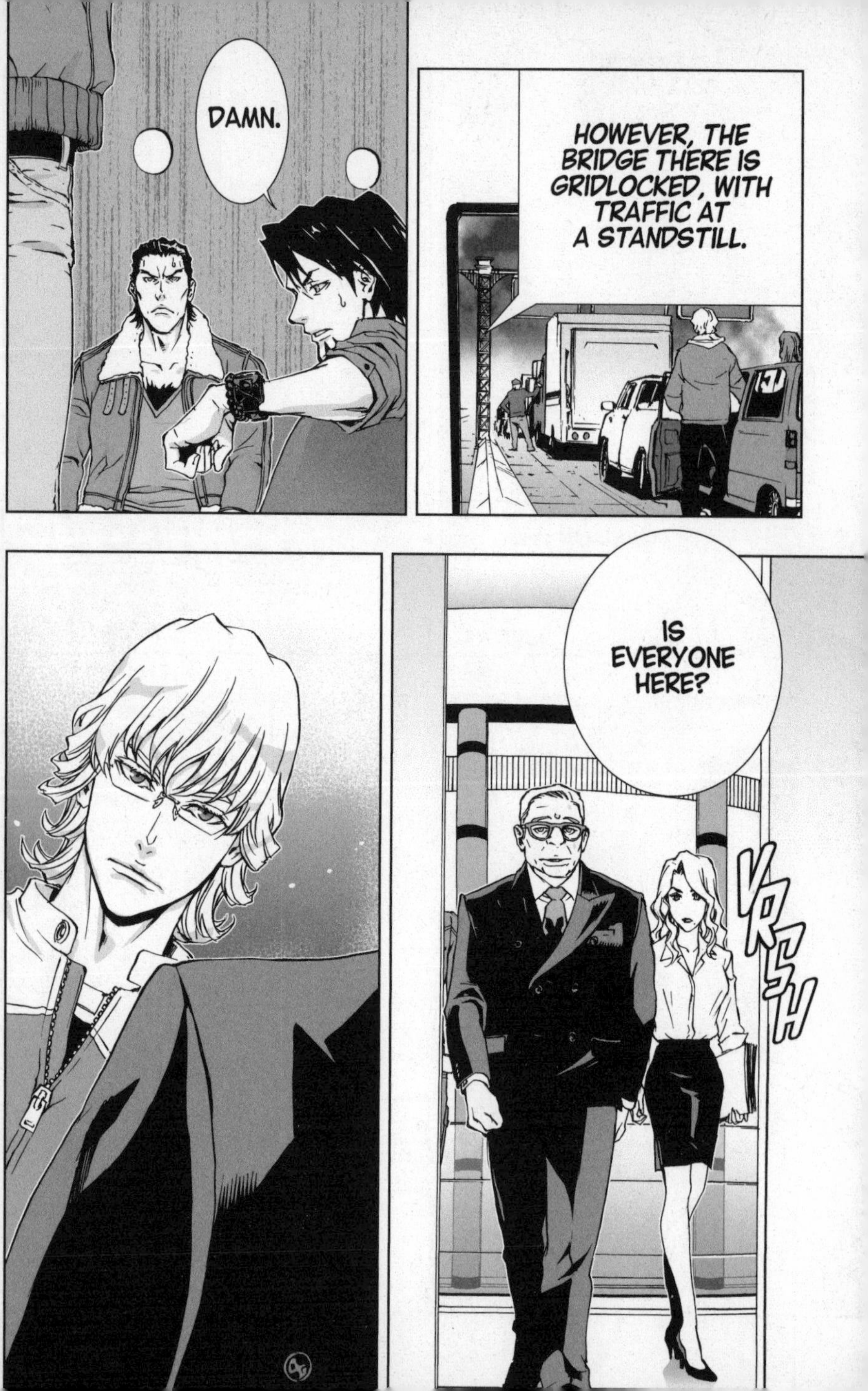
HOWEVER, THE BRIDGE THERE IS GRIDLOCKED, WITH TRAFFIC AT A STANDSTILL.
DAMN.
IS EVERYONE HERE?
VRSH

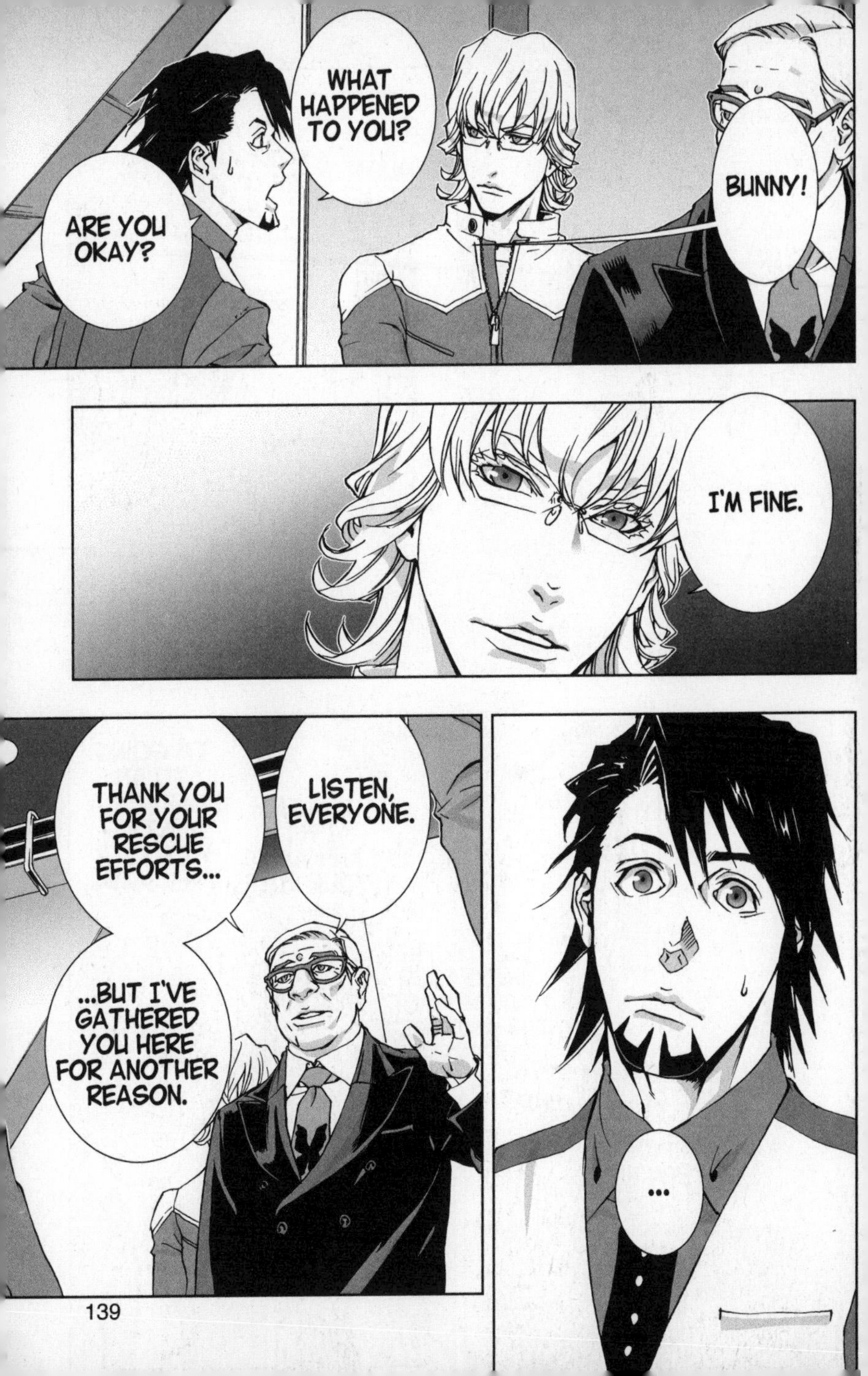
BUNNY!
WHAT HAPPENED TO YOU?
ARE YOU OKAY?
I'M FINE.
...
LISTEN, EVERYONE.
THANK YOU FOR YOUR RESCUE EFFORTS...
...BUT I'VE GATHERED YOU HERE FOR ANOTHER REASON.

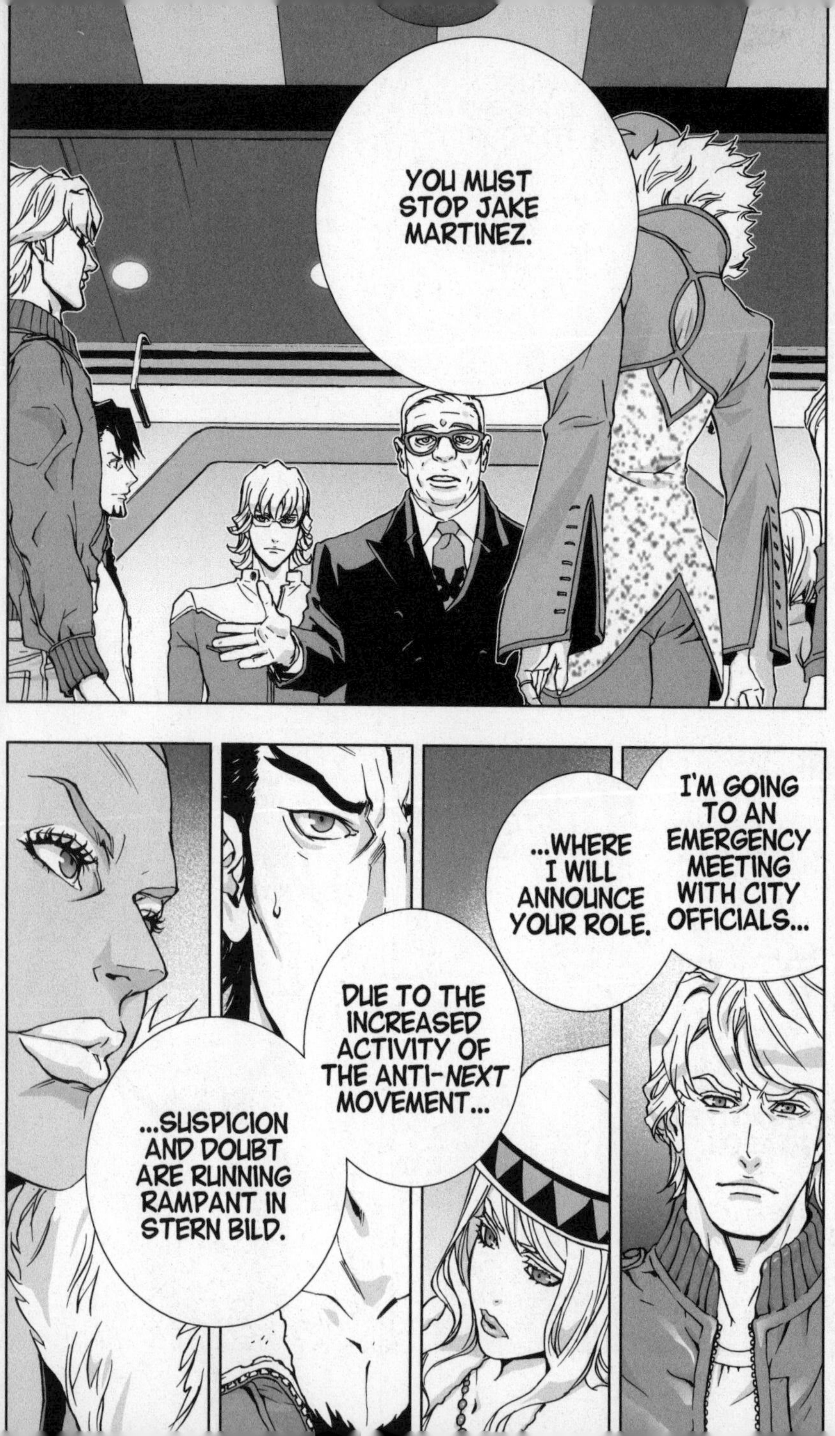
YOU MUST STOP JAKE MARTINEZ.
I'M GOING TO AN EMERGENCY MEETING WITH CITY OFFICIALS...
...WHERE I WILL ANNOUNCE YOUR ROLE.
DUE TO THE INCREASED ACTIVITY OF THE ANTI-NEXT MOVEMENT...
...SUSPICION AND DOUBT ARE RUNNING RAMPANT IN STERN BILD.

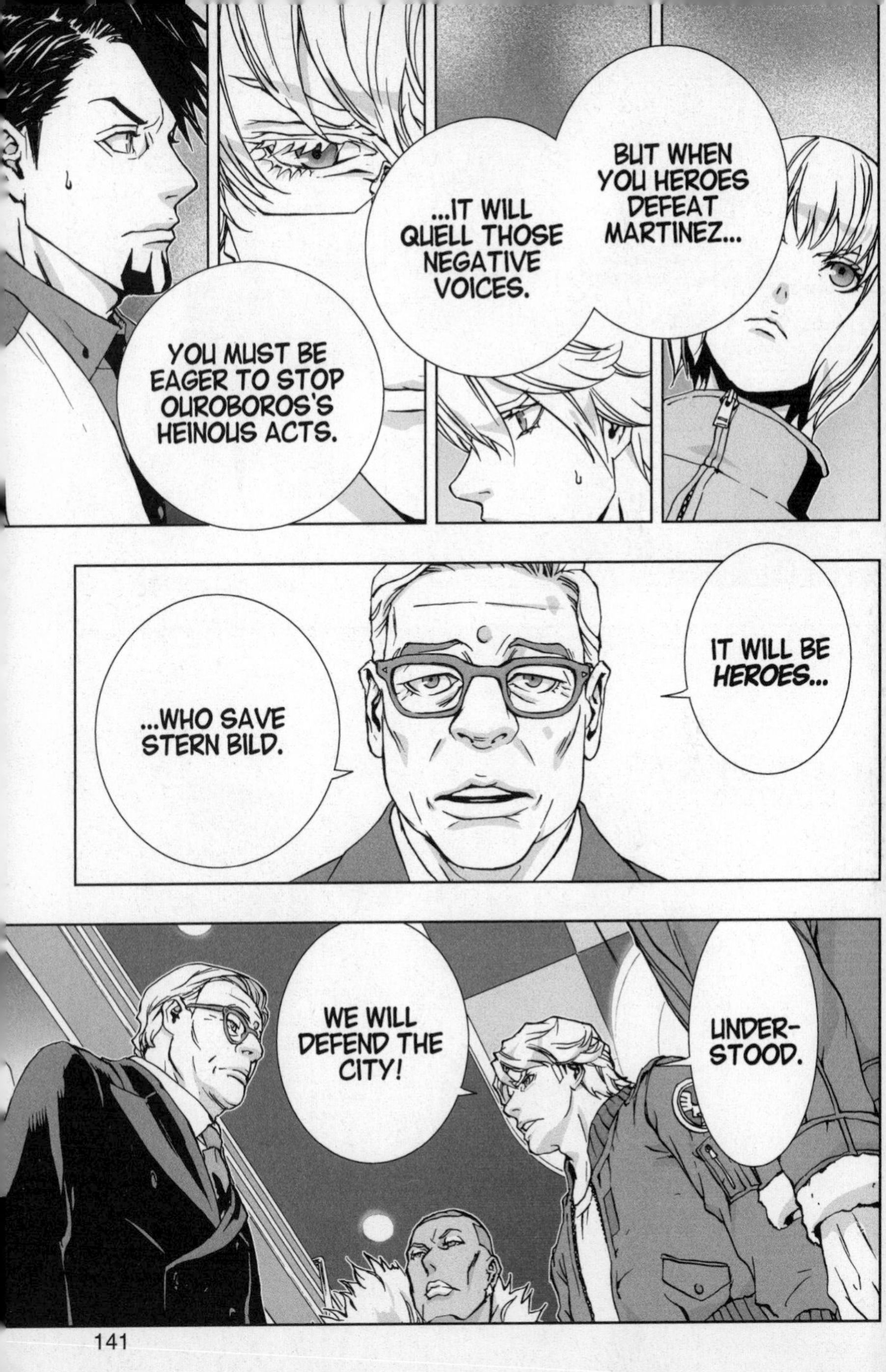
BUT WHEN YOU HEROES DEFEAT MARTINEZ...
...IT WILL QUELL THOSE NEGATIVE VOICES.
YOU MUST BE EAGER TO STOP OUROBOROS'S HEINOUS ACTS.
IT WILL BE HEROES...
...WHO SAVE STERN BILD.
UNDER-STOOD.
WE WILL DEFEND THE CITY!

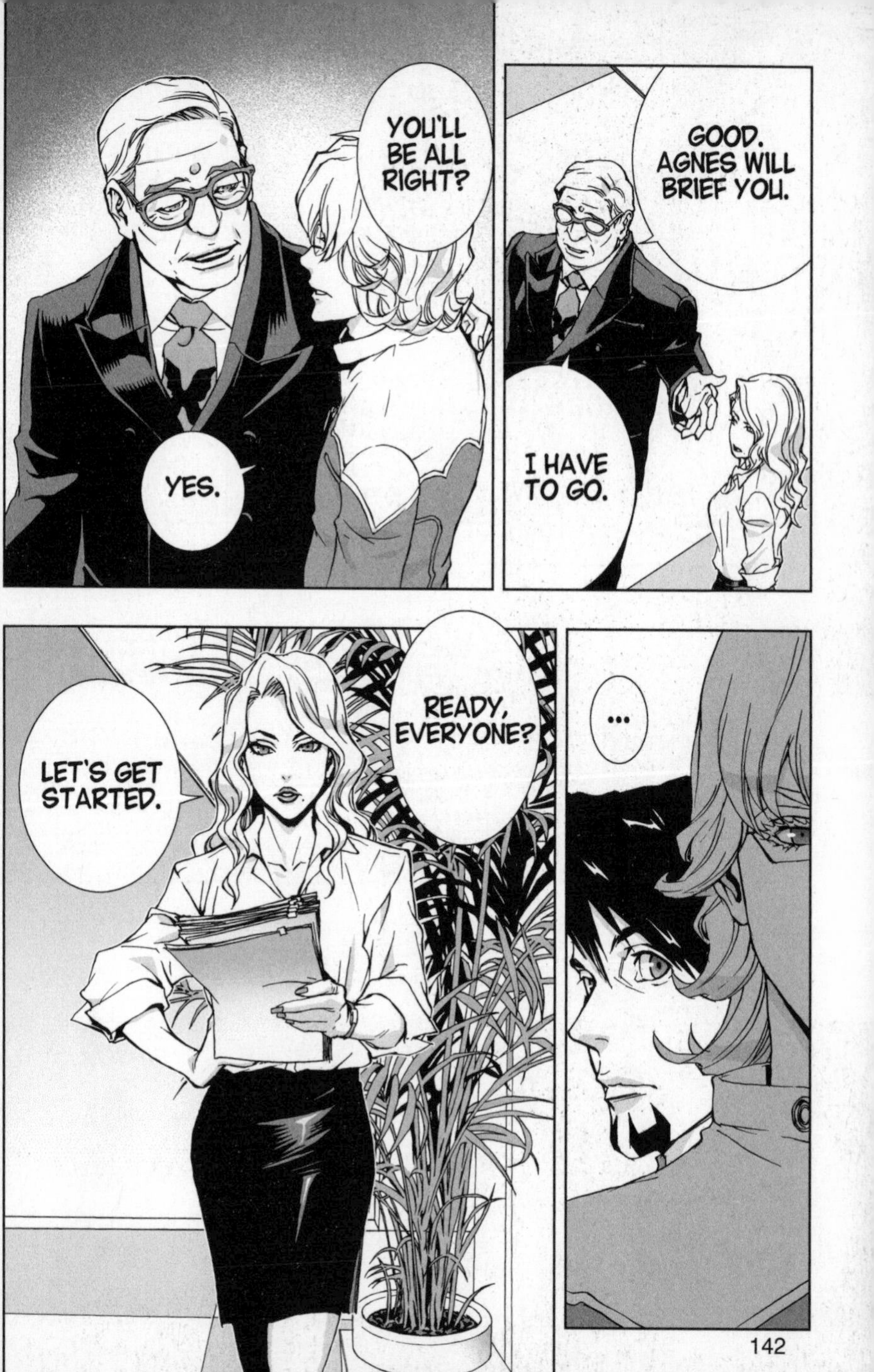
YOU'LL BE ALL RIGHT?
YES.
GOOD. AGNES WILL BRIEF YOU.
I HAVE TO GO.
READY, EVERYONE?
LET'S GET STARTED.
...

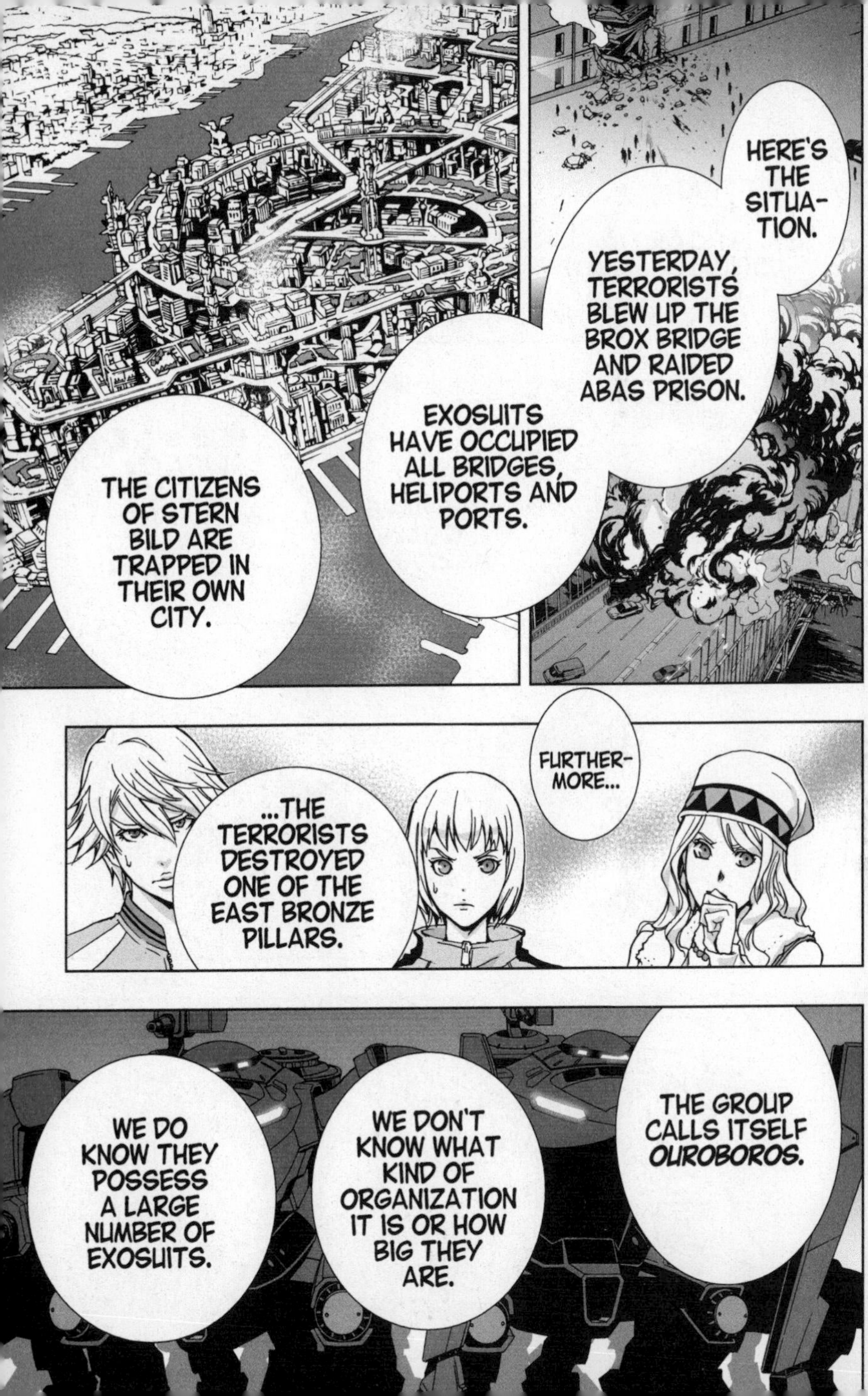
HERE'S THE SITUA-TION.
YESTERDAY, TERRORISTS BLEW UP THE BROX BRIDGE AND RAIDED ABAS PRISON.
EXOSUITS HAVE OCCUPIED ALL BRIDGES, HELIPORTS AND PORTS.
THE CITIZENS OF STERN BILD ARE TRAPPED IN THEIR OWN CITY.
FURTHER-MORE...
...THE TERRORISTS DESTROYED ONE OF THE EAST BRONZE PILLARS.
THE GROUP CALLS ITSELF *OUROBOROS*.
WE DON'T KNOW WHAT KIND OF ORGANIZATION IT IS OR HOW BIG THEY ARE.
WE DO KNOW THEY POSSESS A LARGE NUMBER OF EXOSUITS.

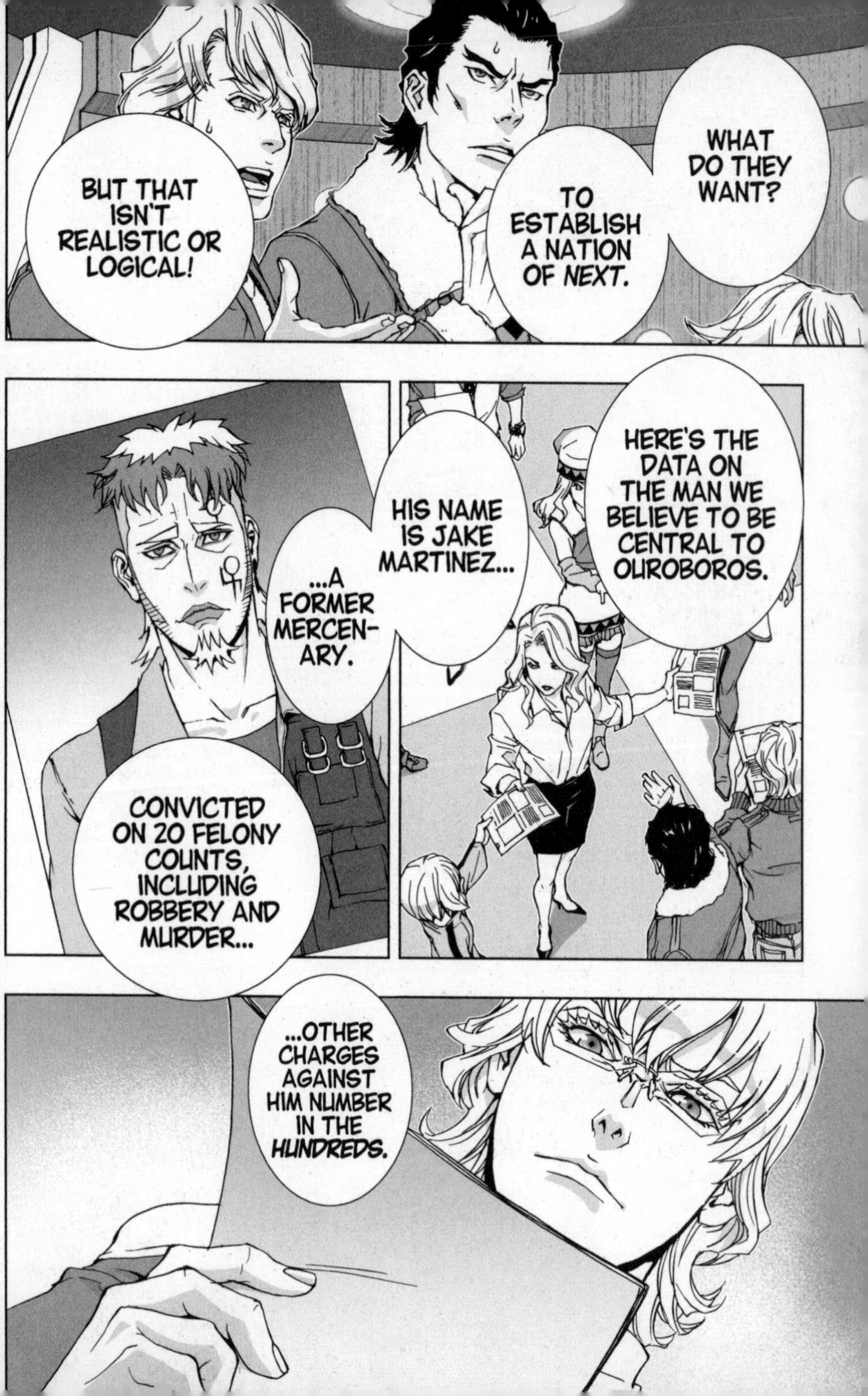
WHAT DO THEY WANT?
TO ESTABLISH A NATION OF *NEXT*.
BUT THAT ISN'T REALISTIC OR LOGICAL!
HERE'S THE DATA ON THE MAN WE BELIEVE TO BE CENTRAL TO OUROBOROS.
HIS NAME IS JAKE MARTINEZ...
...A FORMER MERCEN-ARY.
CONVICTED ON 20 FELONY COUNTS, INCLUDING ROBBERY AND MURDER...
...OTHER CHARGES AGAINST HIM NUMBER IN THE *HUNDREDS*.

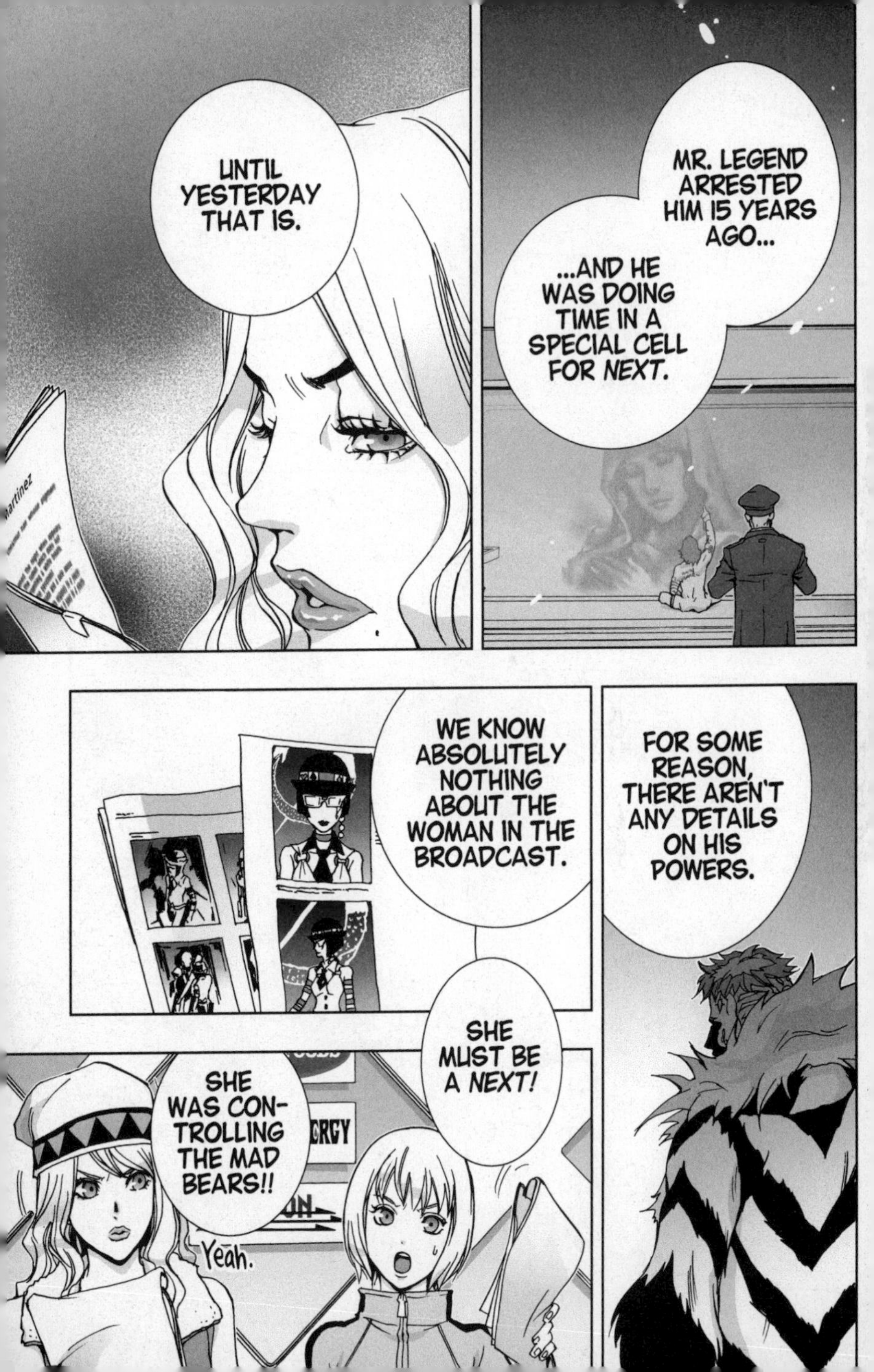
MR. LEGEND ARRESTED HIM 15 YEARS AGO...
...AND HE WAS DOING TIME IN A SPECIAL CELL FOR NEXT.
UNTIL YESTERDAY THAT IS.
Martinez
FOR SOME REASON, THERE AREN'T ANY DETAILS ON HIS POWERS.
WE KNOW ABSOLUTELY NOTHING ABOUT THE WOMAN IN THE BROADCAST.
SHE MUST BE A NEXT!
SHE WAS CON-TROLLING THE MAD BEARS!!
Yeah.

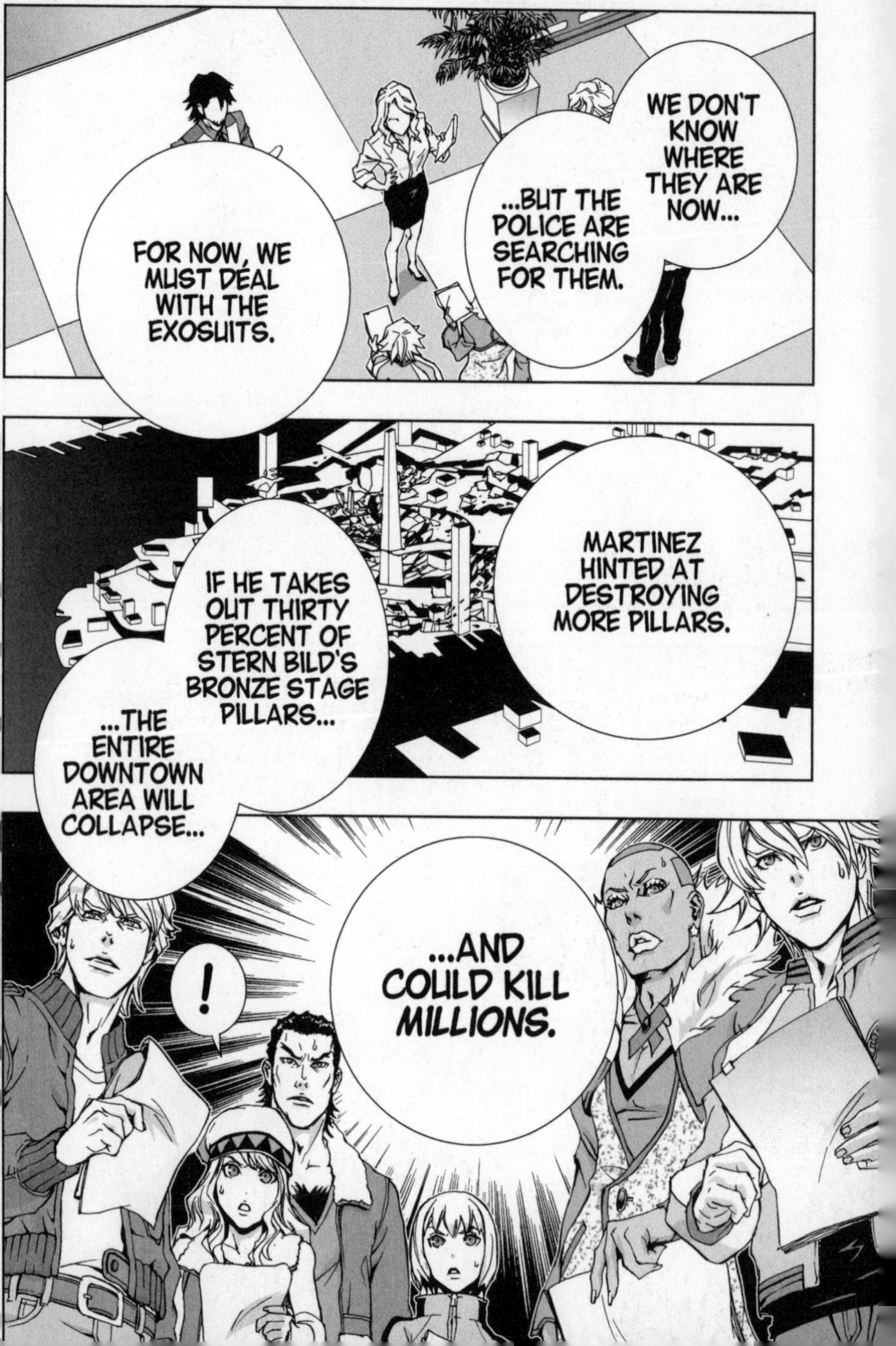
WE DON'T KNOW WHERE THEY ARE NOW...
...BUT THE POLICE ARE SEARCHING FOR THEM.
FOR NOW, WE MUST DEAL WITH THE EXOSUITS.
MARTINEZ HINTED AT DESTROYING MORE PILLARS.
IF HE TAKES OUT THIRTY PERCENT OF STERN BILD'S BRONZE STAGE PILLARS...
...THE ENTIRE DOWNTOWN AREA WILL COLLAPSE...
...AND COULD KILL *MILLIONS.*
!

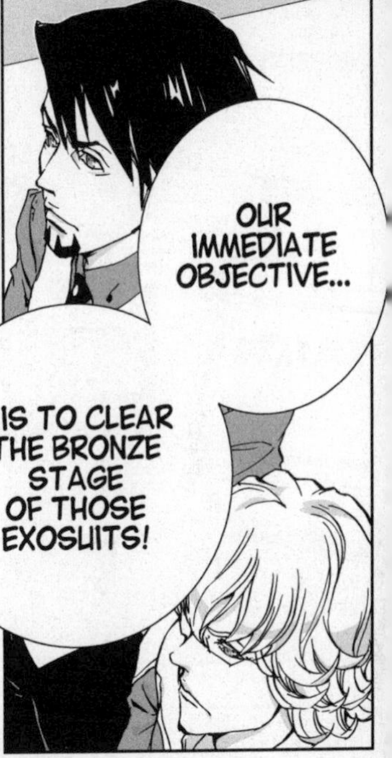
OUR IMMEDIATE OBJECTIVE...
...IS TO CLEAR THE BRONZE STAGE OF THOSE EXOSUITS!

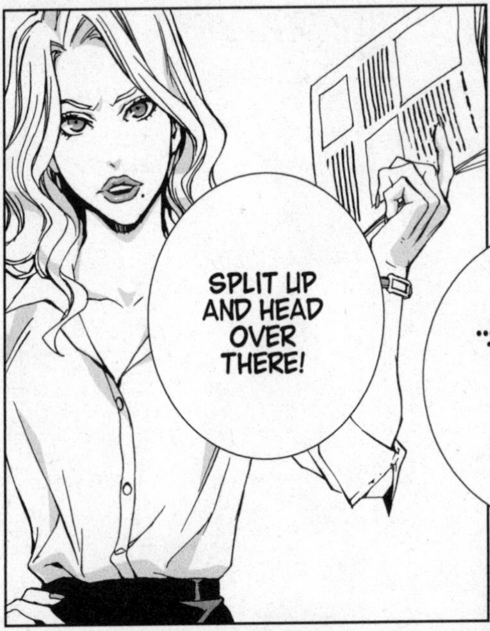
SPLIT UP AND HEAD OVER THERE!

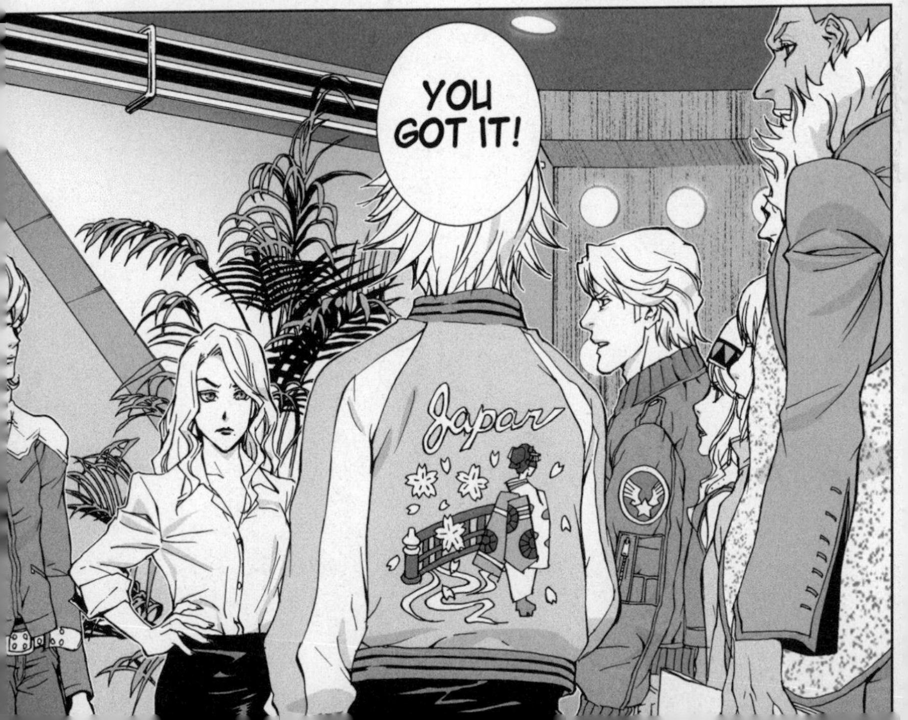
YOU GOT IT!

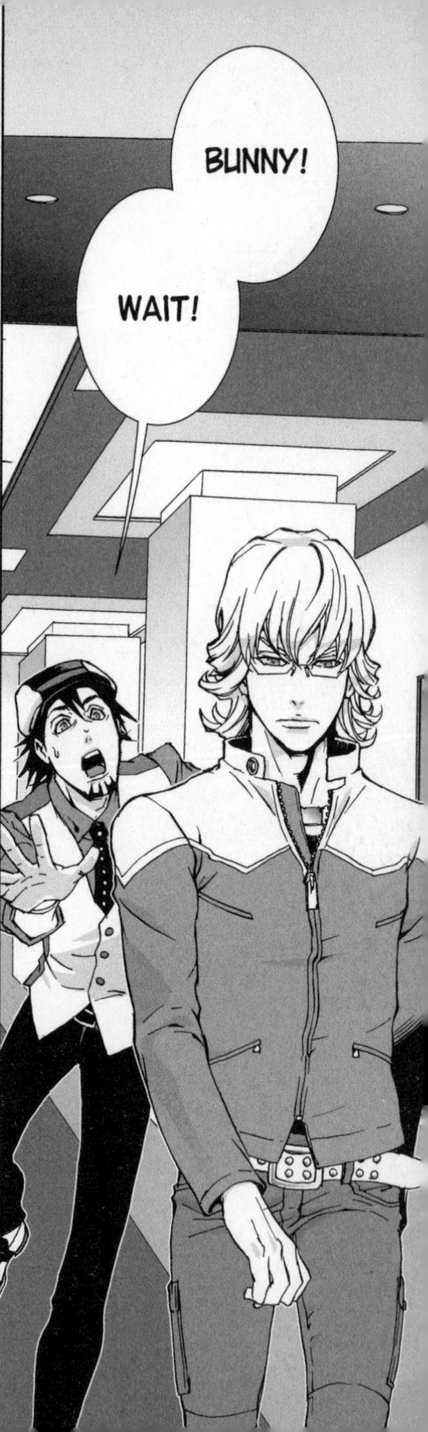
BUNNY!
WAIT!
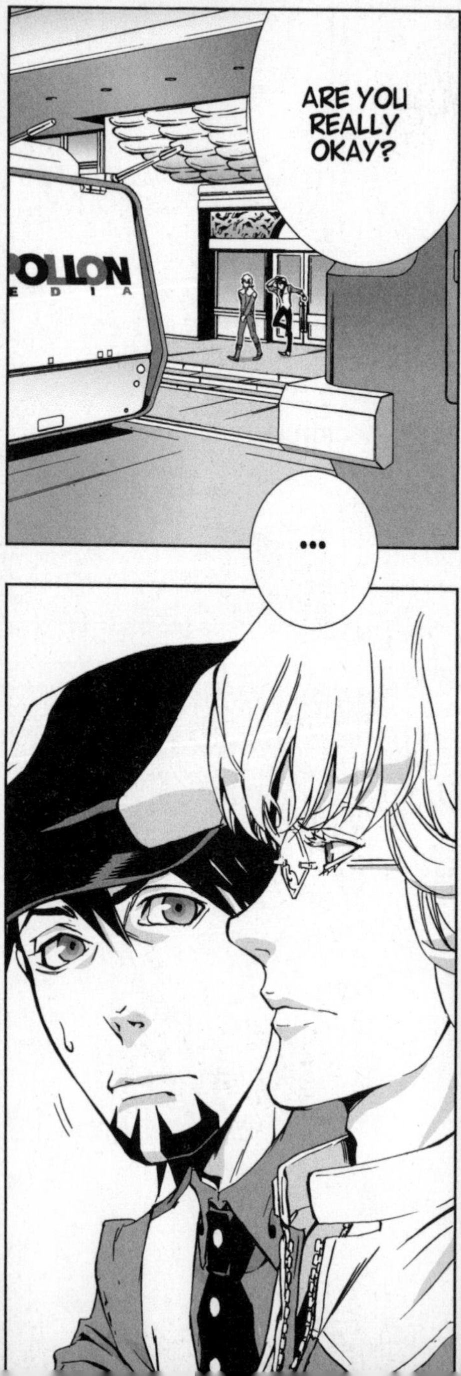
ARE YOU REALLY OKAY?
POLLON
EDIA
...

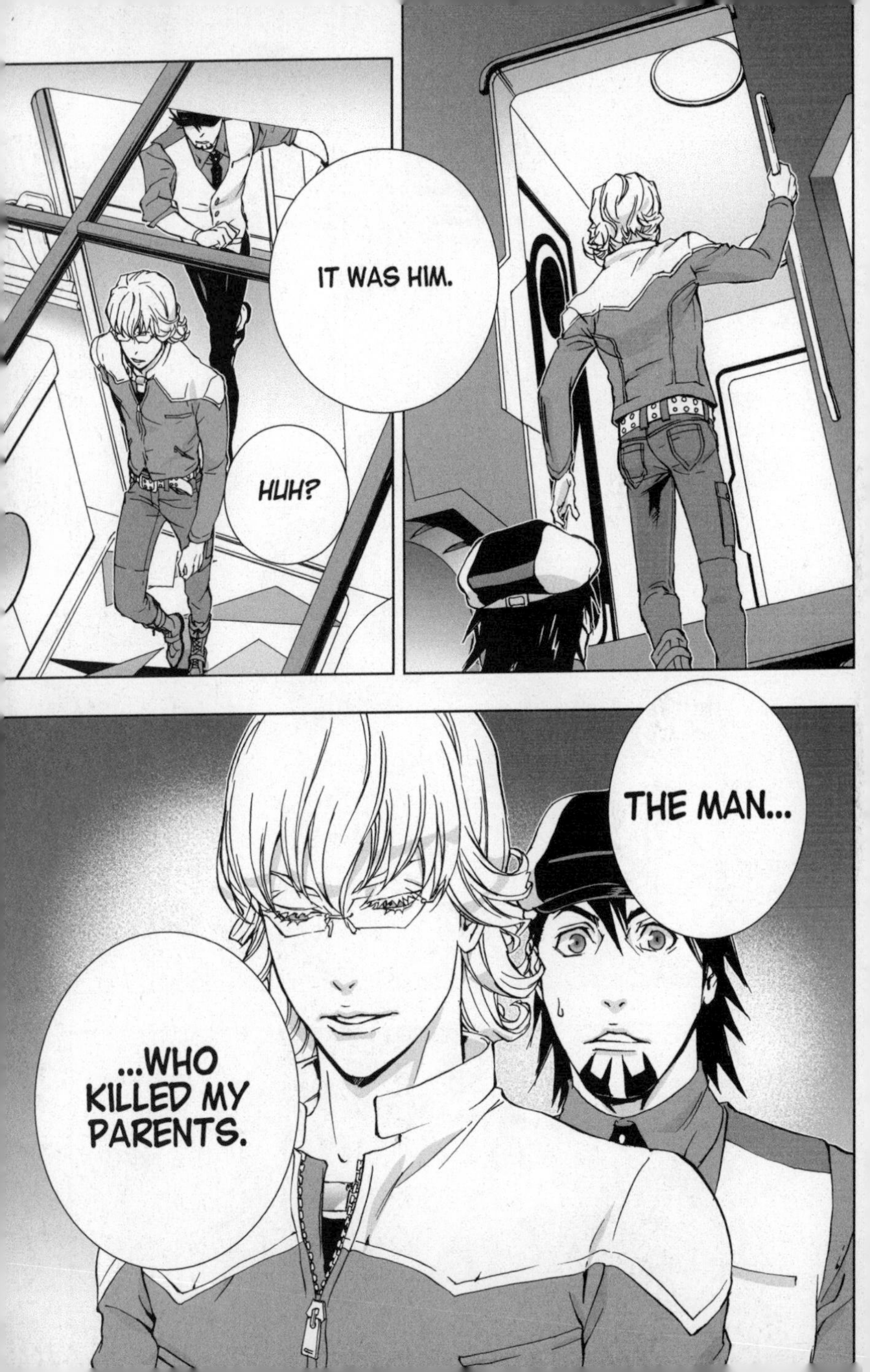
IT WAS HIM.
HUH?
THE MAN...
...WHO KILLED MY PARENTS.

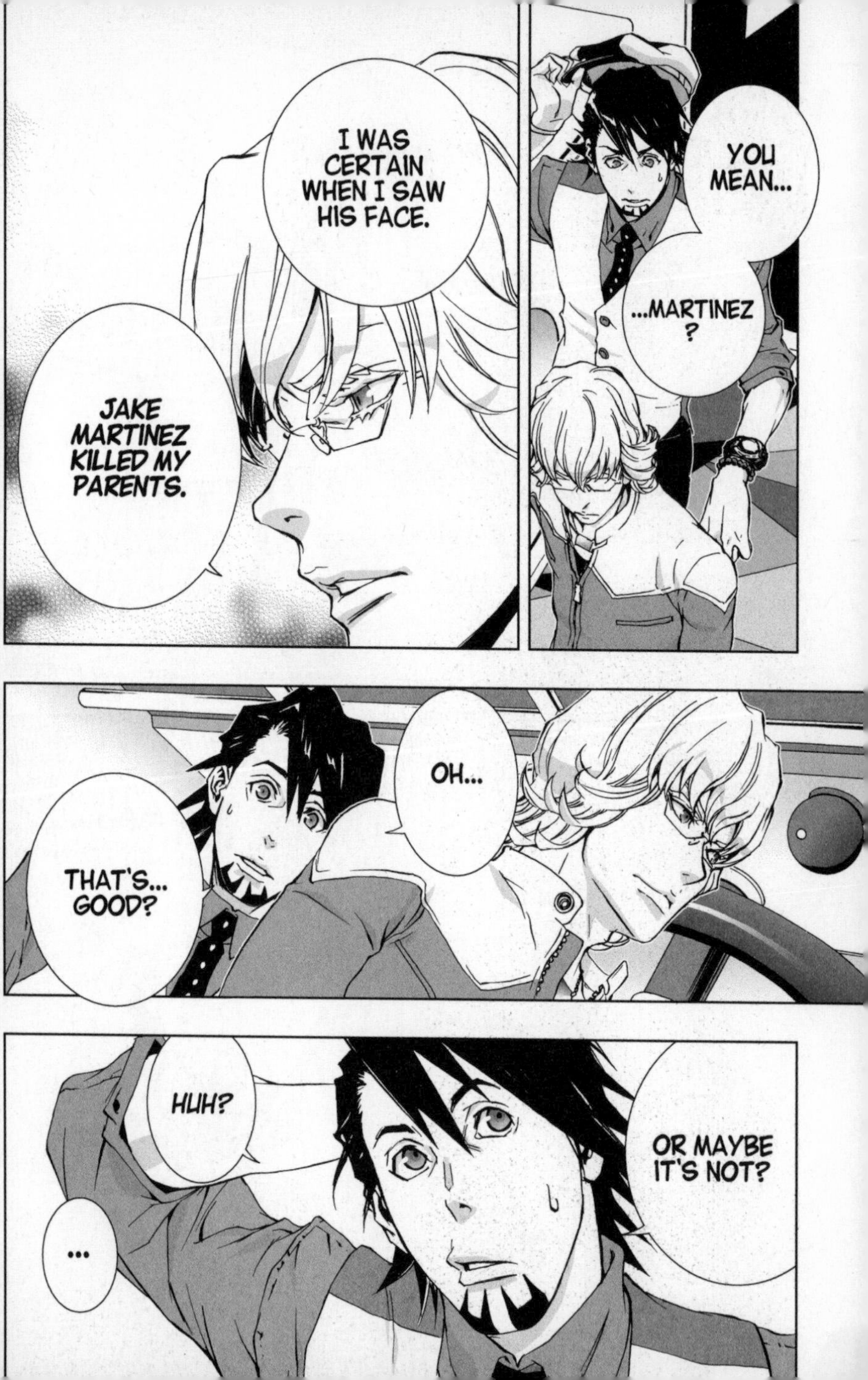
YOU MEAN...
...MARTINEZ?
I WAS CERTAIN WHEN I SAW HIS FACE.
JAKE MARTINEZ KILLED MY PARENTS.
OH...
THAT'S... GOOD?
OR MAYBE IT'S NOT?
HUH?
...

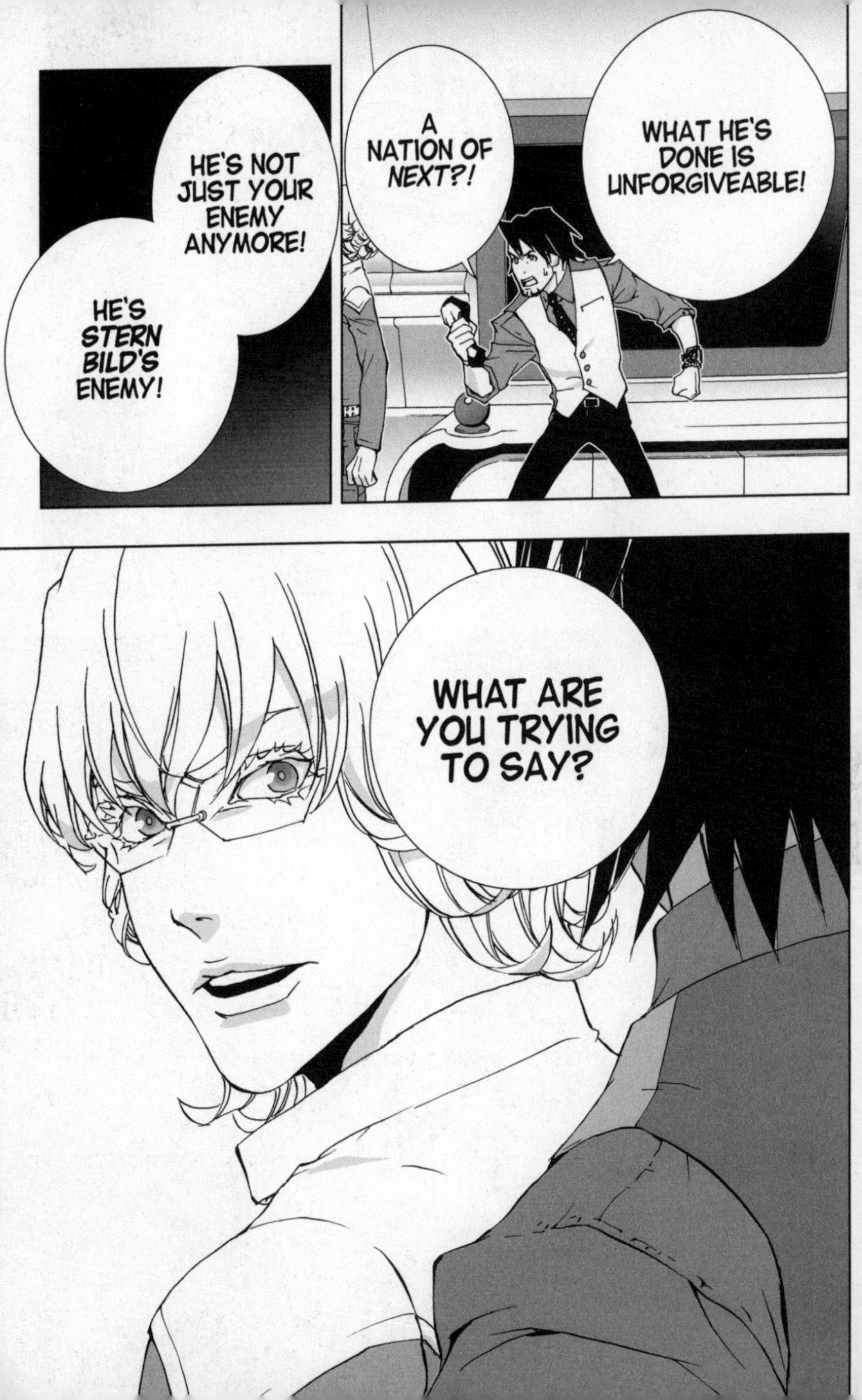
WHAT HE'S DONE IS UNFORGIVEABLE!
A NATION OF NEXT?!
HE'S NOT JUST YOUR ENEMY ANYMORE!
HE'S STERN BILD'S ENEMY!
WHAT ARE YOU TRYING TO SAY?

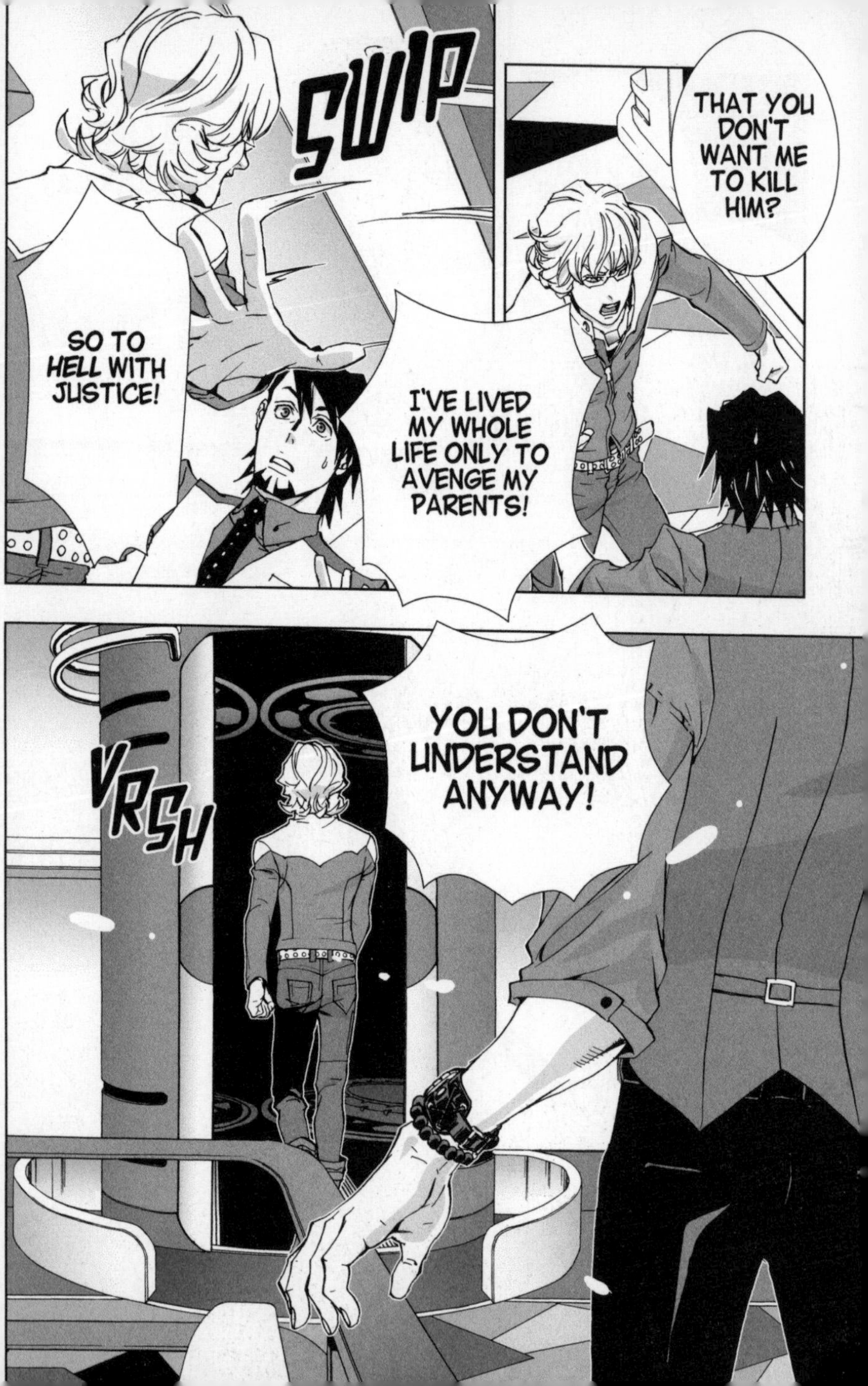
THAT YOU DON'T WANT ME TO KILL HIM?
SWIP
I'VE LIVED MY WHOLE LIFE ONLY TO AVENGE MY PARENTS!
SO TO HELL WITH JUSTICE!
YOU DON'T UNDERSTAND ANYWAY!
VRSH

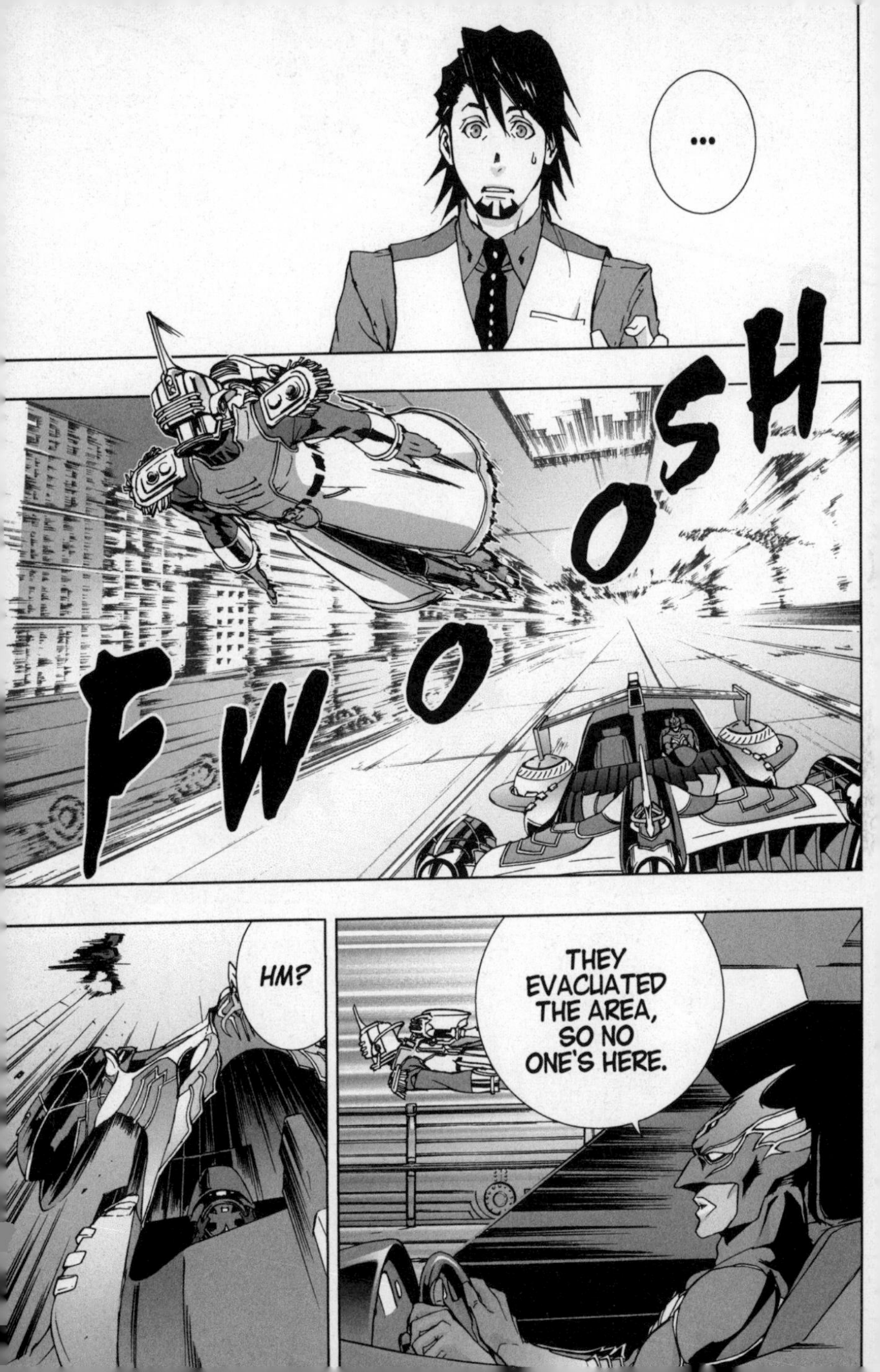
...
FWOOSH
THEY EVACUATED THE AREA, SO NO ONE'S HERE.
HM?

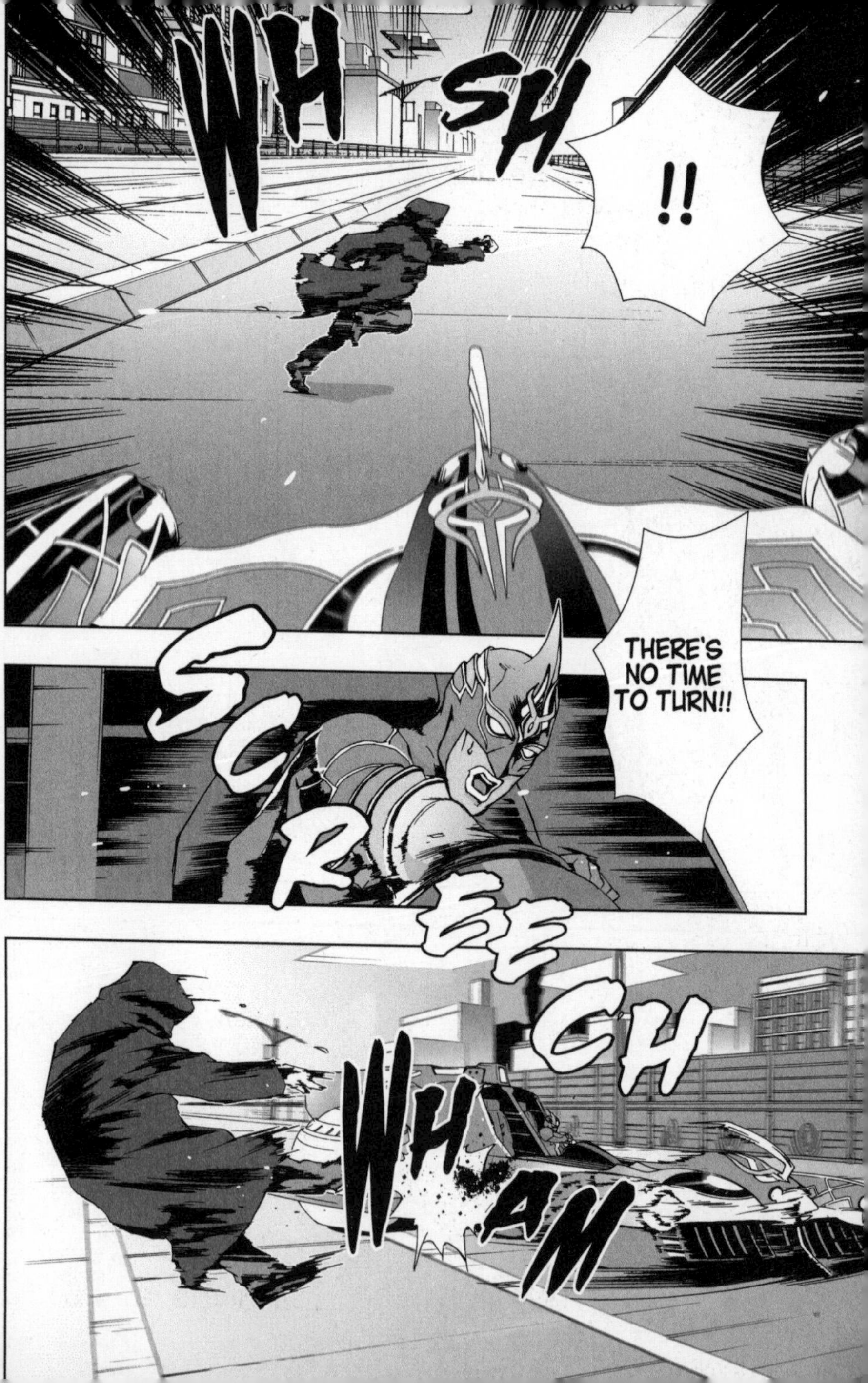
WHSH
!!
THERE'S NO TIME TO TURN!!
SCREECH
WHAM

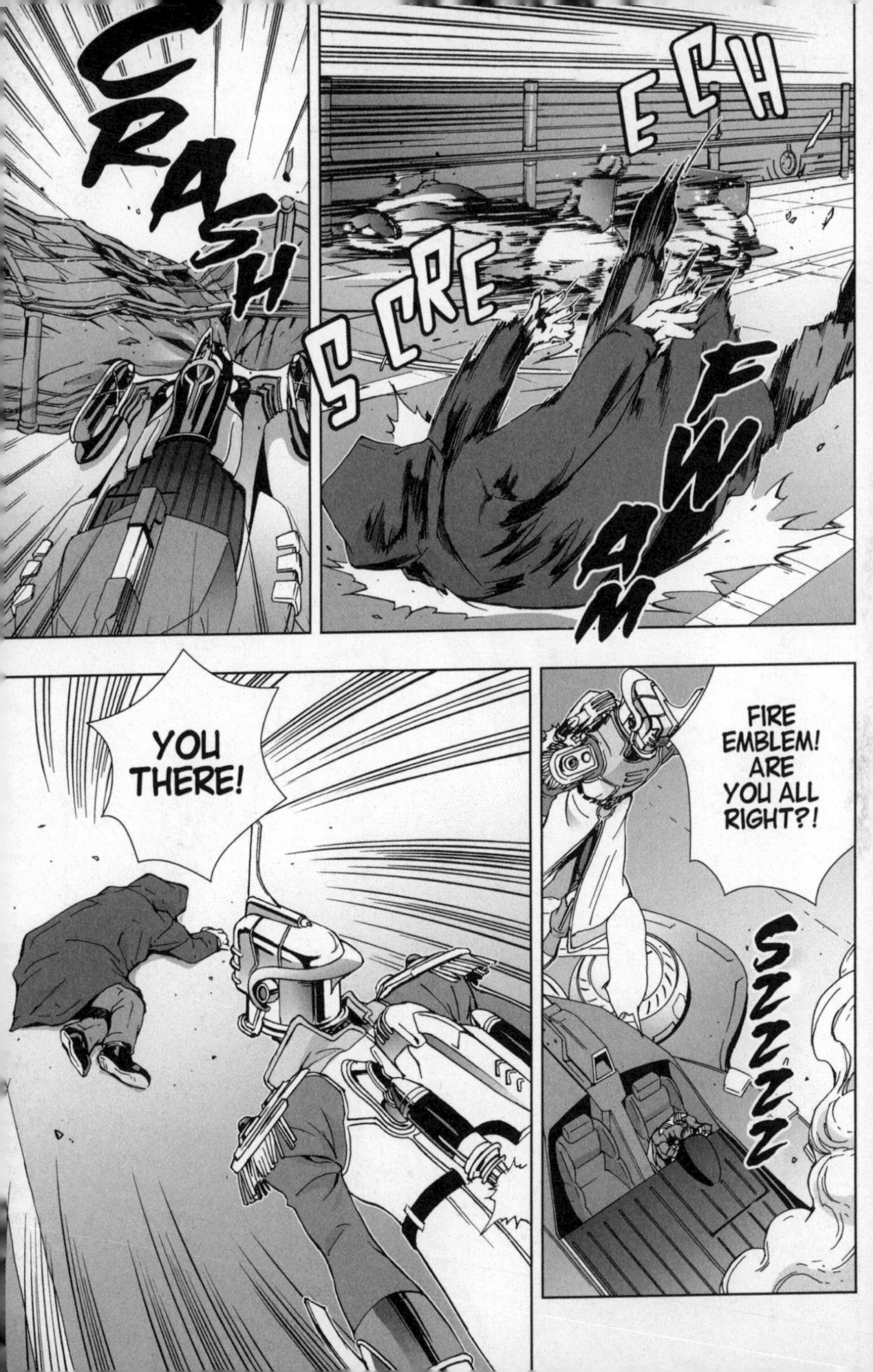
SCREECH
FWAM
CRASH
FIRE EMBLEM! ARE YOU ALL RIGHT?!
SZZZZZ
YOU THERE!

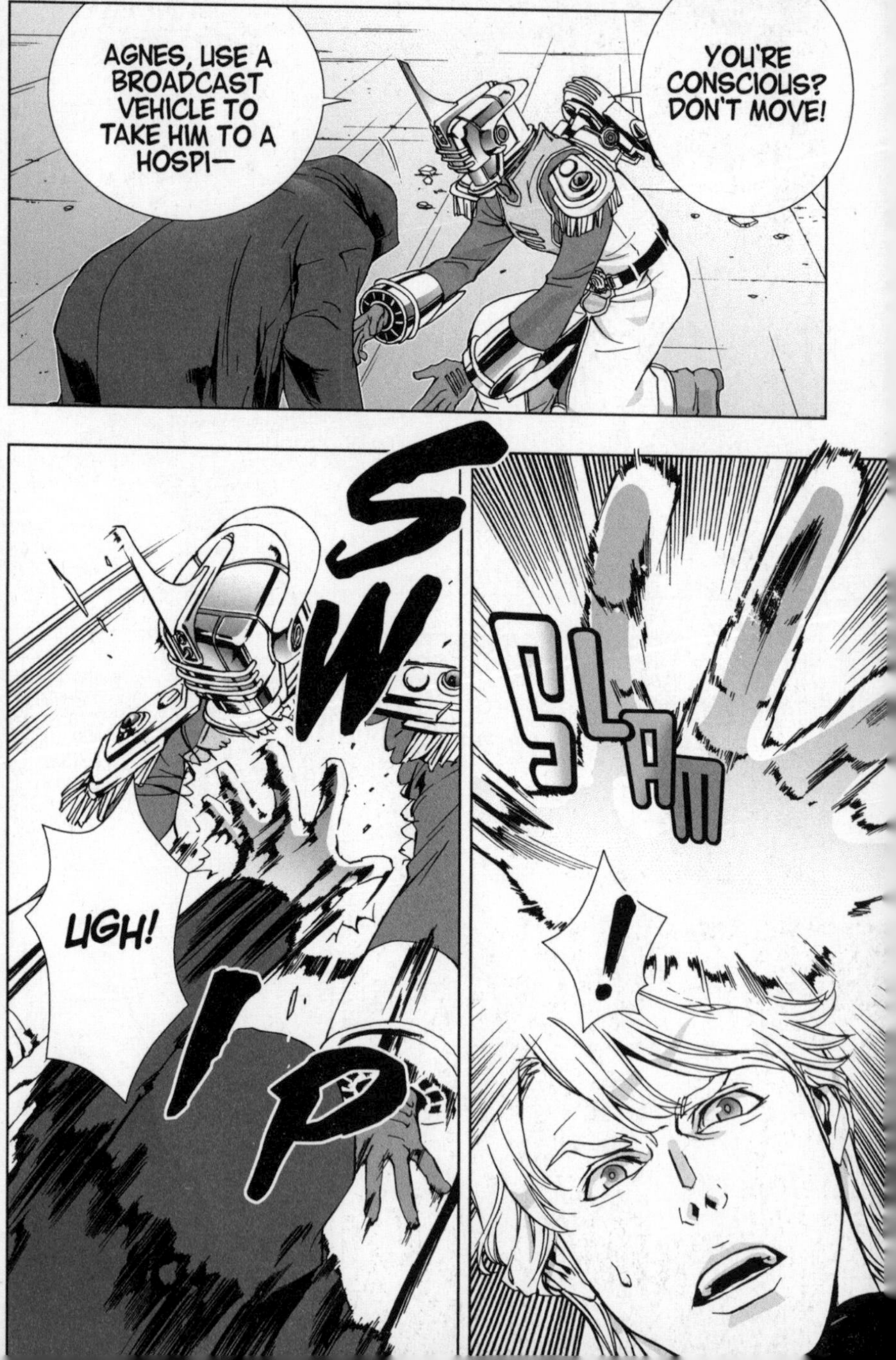
YOU'RE CONSCIOUS? DON'T MOVE!
AGNES, USE A BROADCAST VEHICLE TO TAKE HIM TO A HOSPI—
SLAM
!
SWIP
UGH!

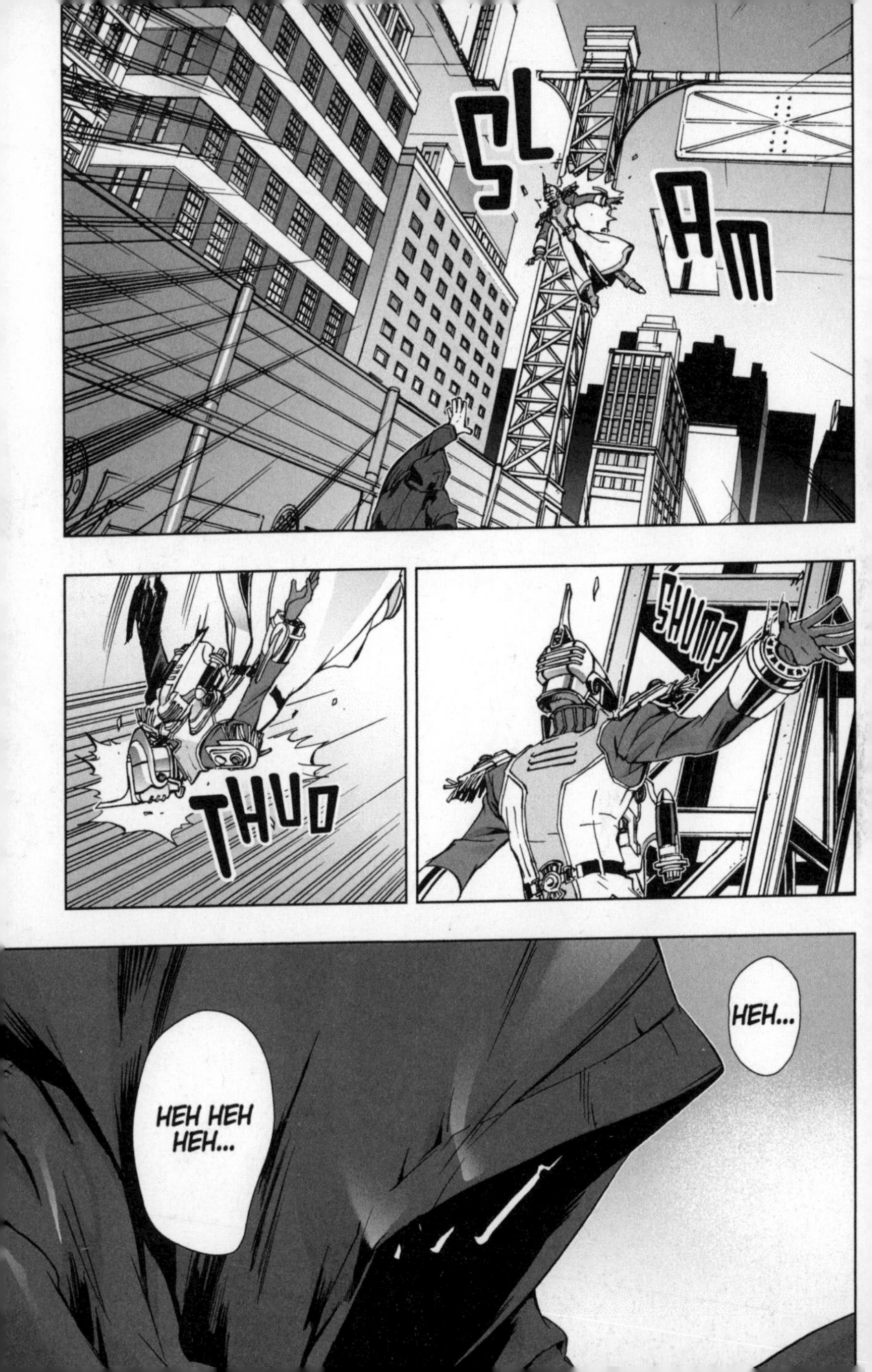
SLAM
SHUMP
THUD
HEH...
HEH HEH HEH...

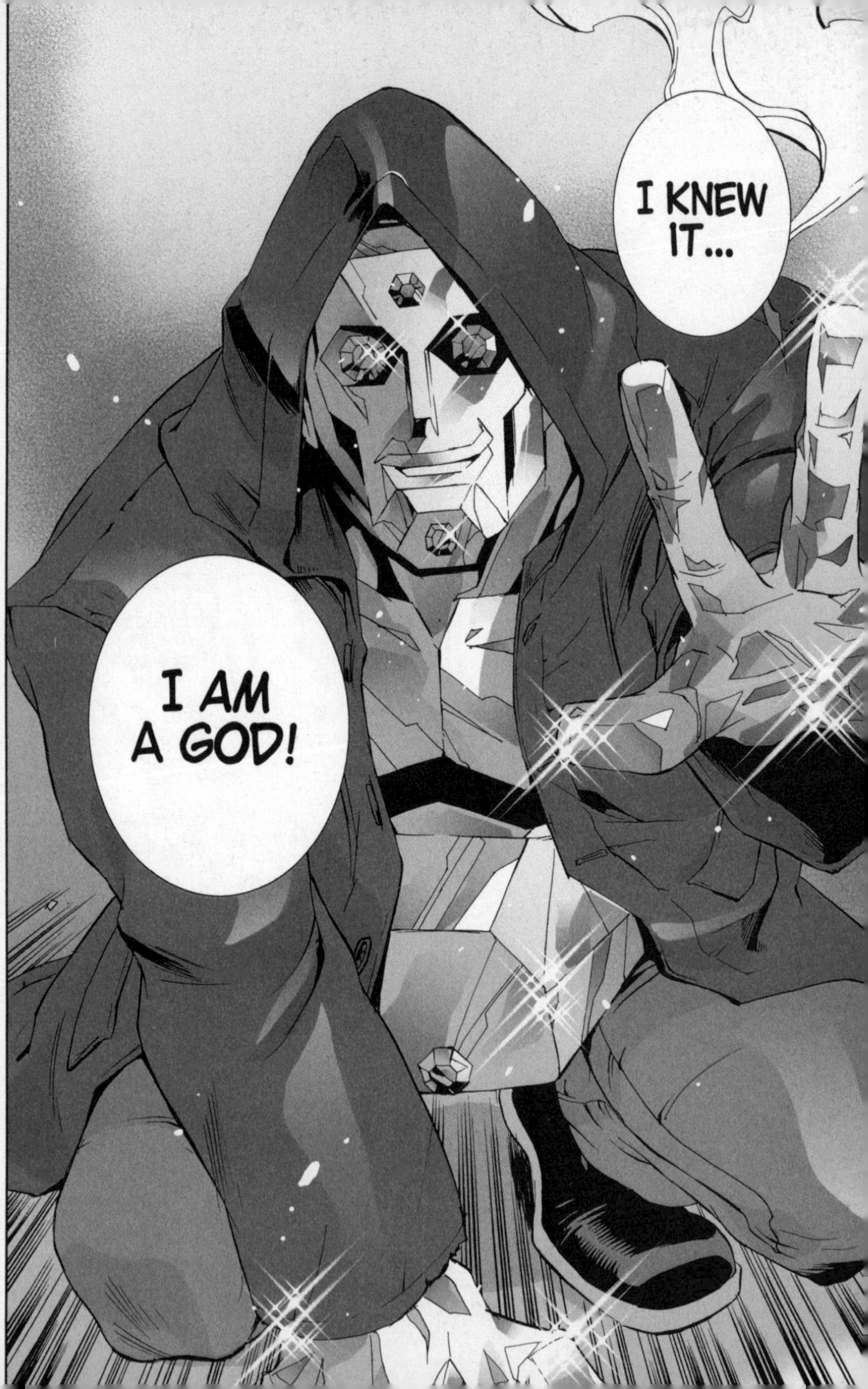
I KNEW IT...
I AM A GOD!

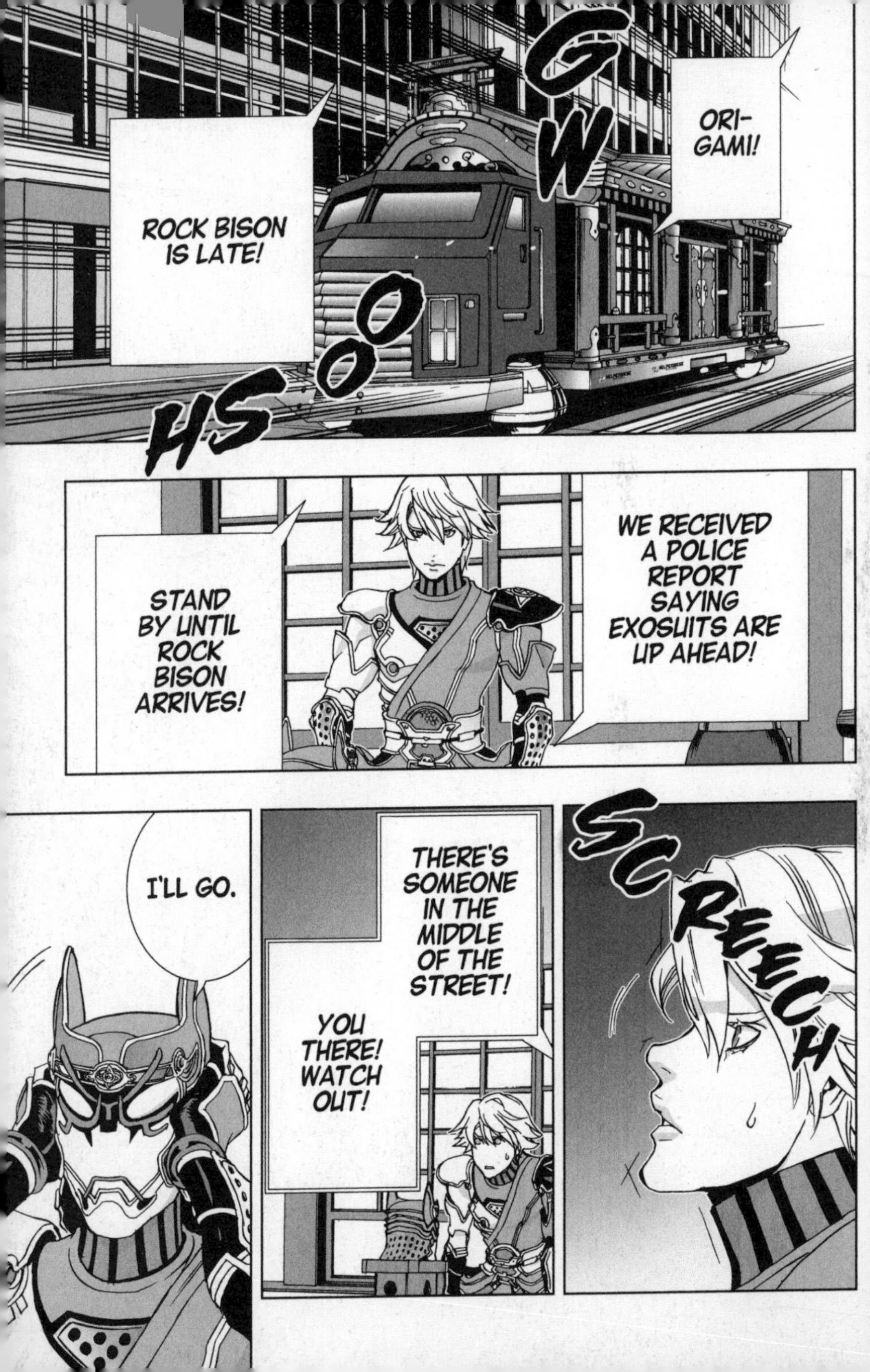
ORI-GAMI!
GWOOSH
ROCK BISON IS LATE!
WE RECEIVED A POLICE REPORT SAYING EXOSUITS ARE UP AHEAD!
STAND BY UNTIL ROCK BISON ARRIVES!
SCREECH
THERE'S SOMEONE IN THE MIDDLE OF THE STREET!
YOU THERE! WATCH OUT!
I'LL GO.

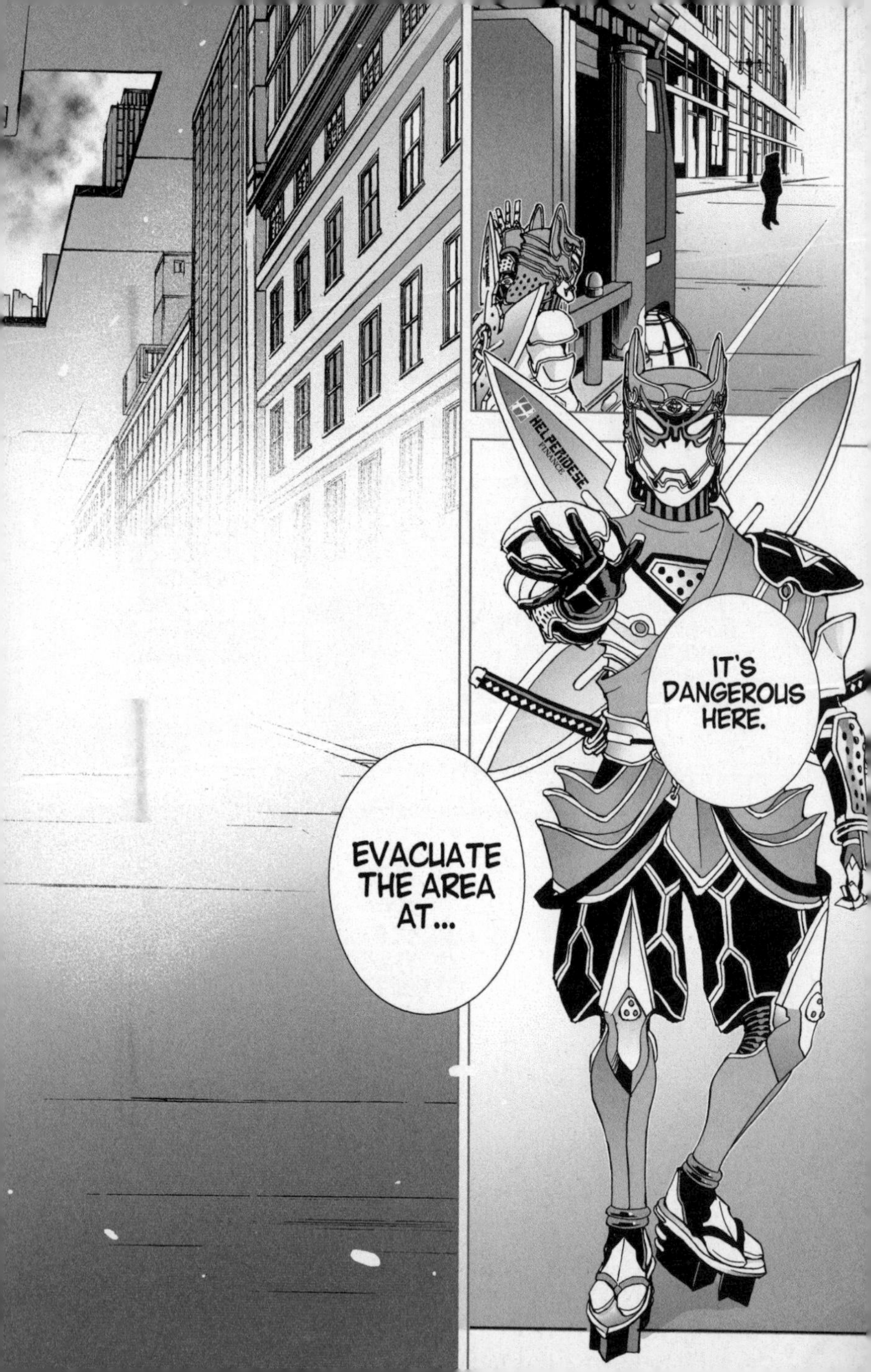
IT'S DANGEROUS HERE.
EVACUATE THE AREA AT...

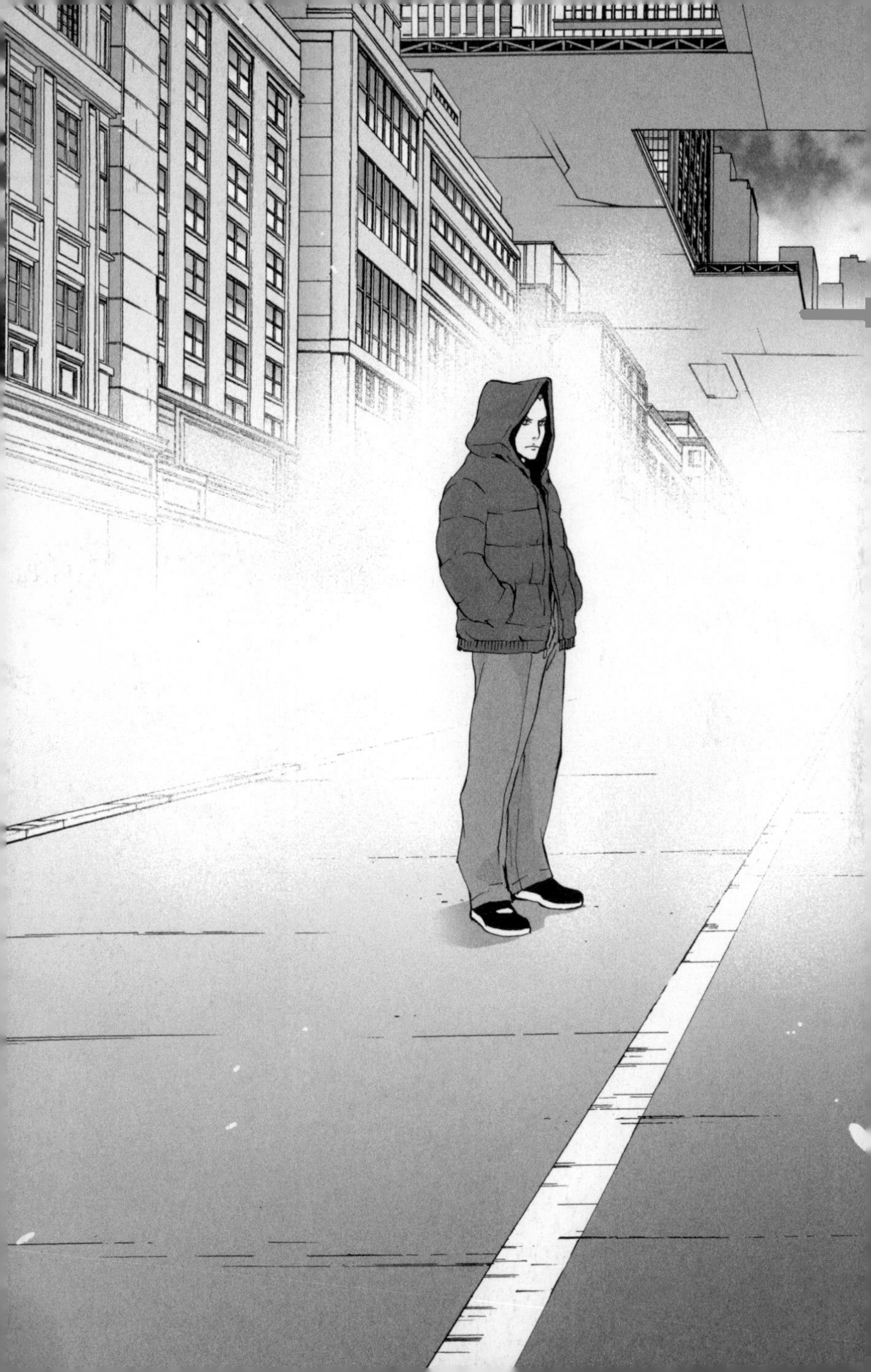

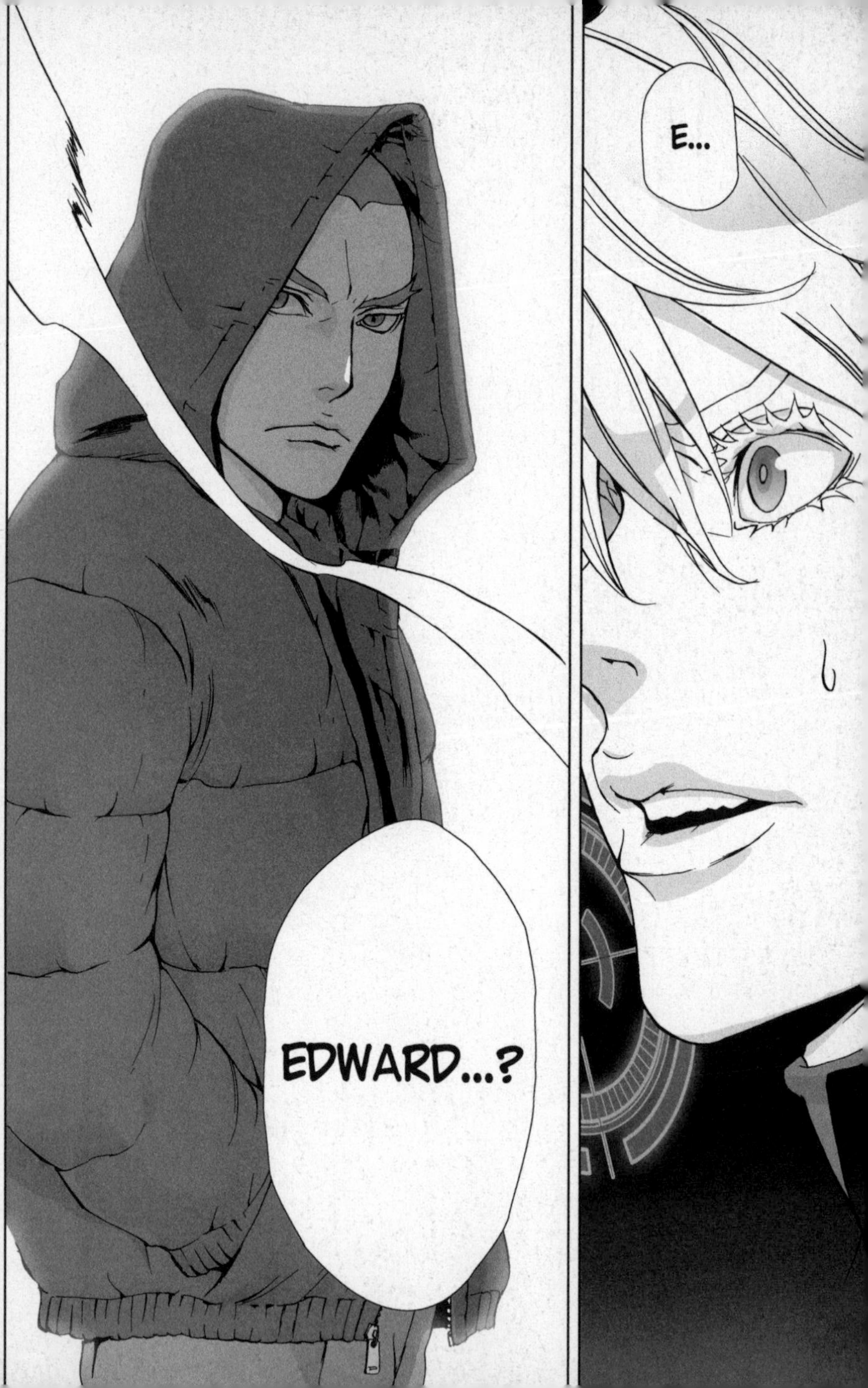
E...
EDWARD...?

TIGER&BUNNY
To Be Continued

Mizuki Sakakibara

Assistants
Ayako Mayuzumi
Beth
Eri Saito
Sachiko Ito
Fuku

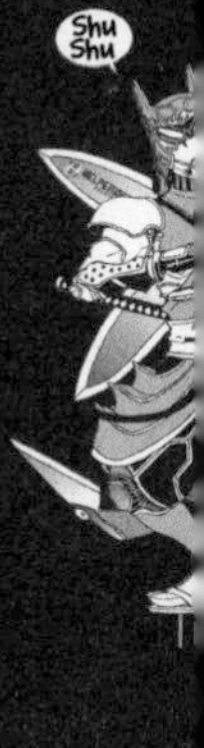
Shu Shu

MIZUKI SAKAKIBARA

Mizuki Sakakibara's American comics debut was Marvel's *Exile* in 2002. Currently, *TIGER & BUNNY* is serialized in *Newtype Ace* magazine by Kadokawa Shoten.

MASAFUMI NISHIDA

Story director. *TIGER & BUNNY* was his first work as a TV animation scriptwriter. He is well known for the movie *Gachi☆Boy* and the Japanese TV dramas *Maoh*, *Kaibutsu-kun*, and *Youkai Ningen Bem*.

MASAKAZU KATSURA

Original character designer. Masakazu Katsura is well known for the manga series *WING MAN*, *Denei Shojo* (*Video Girl Ai*), *I"s*, and *ZETMAN*. Katsura's works have been translated into several languages, including Chinese and French, as well as English.

TIGER&BUNNY 5

VIZ Media Edition

Art **MIZUKI SAKAKIBARA**
Planning / Original Story **SUNRISE**
Original Script **MASAFUMI NISHIDA**
Original Character and Hero Design **MASAKAZU KATSURA**

TIGER & BUNNY Volume 5
© Mizuki SAKAKIBARA 2013
© SUNRISE/T&B PARTNERS, MBS
Edited by KADOKAWA SHOTEN
First published in Japan in 2013 by KADOKAWA CORPORATION, Tokyo.
English translation rights arranged with KADOKAWA CORPORATION, Tokyo.

Translation & English Adaptation **LABAAMEN & JOHN WERRY, HC LANGUAGE SOLUTIONS**
Touch-up Art & Lettering **STEPHEN DUTRO**
Design **FAWN LAU**
Editor **MIKE MONTESA**

Printed in the U.S.A.

Published by VIZ Media, LLC
P.O. Box 77010
San Francisco, CA 94107

10 9 8 7 6 5 4 3 2 1
First printing, June 2014

BLUE ROSE

ⅥⅨⅯ∀ⁿG∀

Read manga anytime, anywhere!

From our newest hit series to the classics you know and love, the best manga in the world is now available digitally. Buy a volume* of digital manga for your:

- iOS device (iPad®, iPhone®, iPod® touch) through the **VIZ Manga app**

- Android-powered device (**phone or tablet**) with a browser by visiting VIZManga.com

- **Mac or PC computer** by visiting VIZManga.com

VIZ Digital has loads to offer:

- 500+ ready-to-read volumes
- New volumes each week
- FREE previews
- Access on multiple devices! Create a log-in through the app so you buy a book once, and read it on your device of choice!*

To learn more, visit www.viz.com/apps

* Some series may not be available for multiple devices.
  Check the app on your device to find out what's available.

DEATH NOTE © 2003 by Tsugumi Ohba, Takeshi Obata/SHUEISHA Inc.
NURARIHYON NO MAGO © 2008 by Hiroshi Shiibashi/SHUEISHA Inc.
ONE PIECE © 1997 by Eiichiro Oda/SHUEISHA Inc.

viz.com/apps

YOU'RE R...
WRO...

Tiger & Bunny reads from right to left, starting in the upper-right corner. Japanese is read from right to left, meaning that action, sound effects, and word-balloon order are completely reversed from English order.

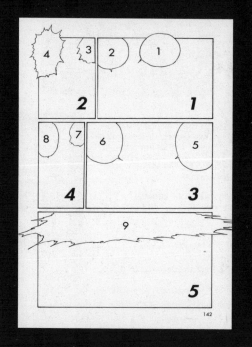

142